BODY OF WORK

40 YEARS OF CREATIVE WRITING AT UEA

BODY OF WORK

40 YEARS OF CREATIVE WRITING AT UEA

EDITED BY

GILES FODEN

ILLUSTRATIONS BY

JEFF FISHER

FULL CIRCLE EDITIONS

Contents

A X J W
Q H V D P
R O Y G
C F N
L M Z B U
E S T K

Introduction

Literature as a living art
by Giles Foden

As if walking along the street and hearing a domestic row from open windows, one now and then becomes aware of arguments taking place in the culture. Lately there have been some about Creative Writing courses and the state of the novel. These are quarrels in which Malcolm Bradbury might have taken a hand, were he still alive, borrowing Seamus Heaney's hurling stick to land sequential blows on the journalists and other public intellectuals who have voiced disquiet about such courses.

Writers themselves voice that disquiet less frequently these days, now that so many of us work in universities. One of the darker pleasures of working in the School of Literature, Drama and Creative Writing at the University of East Anglia (there are also many lighter pleasures) is opening job applications from authors who were formerly antagonistic. We have a little list, but the task of filling up the blanks I'd rather leave to you.

I begin with an intention to discuss Creative Writing at UEA from the late 1960s to the present, in order to introduce this book. There will be appropriate focus on Bradbury himself, but also on many other inter-relations. I am already conscious that this intention will involve a digest of the earlier history and continuing practice of Creative Writing within universities here and in the United States. I am aware, too, that it may further involve some review of the types of writing that are the so-called 'output' of Creative Writing courses.

These I shall largely limit to the field of the novel, as that is the form most often charged with having been corrupted by the growth of Creative Writing as an academic discipline. Usually the charge is either that Creative Writing induces realism (as a genre) or that it induces lack of realism (in terms of student expectations).

The novel is also my own form: I am not a professional literary critic. I am accordingly aware that a lurking volition towards creative writing is embedded in my critical writing. This should not necessarily be construed as a revolt against academic scholarship. There is a tradition of non-academic critical writing that has its own establishment, and this may be appealed to without right of admittance. The reason I mention Heaney above is because he has set the bar in recent decades for this type of writing, a form of critical discourse that is not just acutely alert to creative practice, but also actively constitutes it.

It is usually those without such distinction who make blanket objections to Creative Writing courses. Having failed by middle age to produce any substantial literary work themselves, they are like those people who, arriving late and breathless at a bus stop, shake their fists at the departing bus.

There is often an unhealthy moral tone to the objections. In fact, they are so often couched in terms of sinfulness (as Adam Mars-Jones's piece in this volume recognises) that I cannot help but think of the saint that Ian McEwan recalls in the memoir-essay collected here: 'I had composed one of the worst radio plays ever written, about a saint who is so good he stinks, and everyone who comes across him, what with the world being so corrupt, is compelled to vomit.' Yes, there are some bad apples, some Creative Writing courses which deserve opprobrium, but there are defective courses in law and chemistry, too. Creative Writing, at least, is not a threat to public safety; it may even be a boon to it, as I try to show in my conclusion.

During the late 1960s Malcolm Bradbury faced some of these issues when trying to push through UEA's MA in Creative Writing as a course proposal, prior to the degree's founding in 1970-71. As he put it, writing of himself and co-founder Angus Wilson in the introduction to *Class Work*, a 1995 anthology of fiction by UEA graduates:

> What neither of us entirely recognised was the degree of suspicion in which Creative Writing had come to be held in Britain. It was generally regarded as a dangerous American invention, like the vacuum cleaner and the hula hoop – and certainly not one that had a place in the literature department of a British university.

The arguments advanced by critics of Creative Writing in the academy – that writing can't be taught, that all writers need to do in the way of training is read, that writing courses only serve 'deadheads who want to be taught naturalism'[1] are not new. Nor is the jostling effect writers can cause at a university. When Nabokov was proposed for a chair in literature at Harvard in 1957, the language theorist Roman Jakobson is said to have objected, saying 'Gentlemen, even if one allows that he is an important writer, are we next to invite an elephant to be Professor of Zoology?'

There are actually several versions of this remark and one Nabokov biographer has it being made eleven years earlier. At any rate, it was part of a longer-running narrative of friction between the pair, conflict emblematic not just of rivalry between exiled Russian geniuses but also of the role of the writer in the academy.

Unless one counts Sir Arthur Quiller-Couch, Bradbury and Wilson were the original English elephants. Now is a good time to consider their legacy, as 2011 is the fortieth anniversary of the founding of the UEA MA. The pieces in this collection of essays, memoirs and poems reflect the multiple experience of tutors, students and visiting fellows associated not just with the Creative Writing MA in Prose Fiction but also with its sister MAs in Poetry, Scriptwriting and Life Writing.

Some of the contents of this volume have been published elsewhere, or given as lectures. In some cases these pieces have been updated. Where necessary, prefatory notes explain the previous occasion of publication. Other pieces have been newly commissioned. The publishing history of each piece is explained in the acknowledgements.

Most of the contents of *Body of Work* document the lived experience of being a writer, on the UEA course and at other times. A number of essays elucidate ongoing issues in Creative Writing pedagogy, in particular the dynamic between Creative Writing and formal academic literary criticism that has now been established at all levels of English studies at UEA. This actualises institutionally the 'two bodies' inhabited by Malcolm Bradbury himself and by later novelist-critics on the staff such as Amit Chaudhuri and Rebecca Stott, who are both represented here. There is a 'third body', too, which is the creative writer who is also a regular contributor to the national press and literary journals, and he/she is another typical figure in this volume.

Another cross-fertilisation comes from UEA's strength in translation (it is home to the British Centre for Literary Translation and a well-regarded MA in Translation Studies), which builds on the work of Clive Scott, W.G. Sebald and others. The poem by George Szirtes in this volume speaks to that, as does 'Losing My Voice' by Andrew Cowan, a former student on the MA course and now Director of Creative Writing at UEA. All of these elements – the creative, the formal-critical and the journalistic-critical, and the international/interdisciplinary – are part of a composite, evolving vision for the practice and study of writing. This vision was fostered principally by Jon Cook, a long-term member of the UEA English staff and now Professor Emeritus, and by his colleague in American Studies, Chris Bigsby. It is now being continued by Cook's successor as Dean of Humanities, David Peters Corbett, who himself studied at the university in the 1970s.

This organic process would probably not have happened if Bradbury had not joined the staff of UEA in 1965. To Bradbury as a person, like the Slakan hero Valdopin in his novel *Rates of Exchange*, 'a great many stories attach; who is to know whether they are true or false?'. He would, a reading of his novels and critical writings suggests, enjoy that legacy, with its slight scent of intrigue. After all, much of his work, both critical and creative, probes the reliability of human narrative, even of subjectivity itself.

As a teacher, he was mostly regarded fondly. Norwich-based writer Paul Willetts (biographer of Julian Maclaren-Ross and Paul Raymond), who studied under Bradbury in the 1980s, recalls 'a friendly figure in a grey jacket whose nickname, because of his pallor, was "Talcy Malcy", i.e., as if he had been dusted with talcum powder'. Probably students were not aware that Bradbury had had a major heart operation in 1958 and was not expected to live beyond middle age.

As a writer working at UEA now, one is very much aware of Bradbury's presence. His spirit seems to haunt the corridors. And no wonder: along with Wilson, Bradbury was formative in making the teaching of writing at UEA what it is today. He is the source of the emphasis on reading (the works of others, in the workshop and across literary history) and rewriting (one's own work), which remains the fundamental basis of Creative Writing teaching at the university.

It is invariably said, to me or my colleagues, and not quite correctly, 'Oh, you do Malcolm Bradbury's old job.' Not quite correctly because universities and the ways in which they engage with writers have changed a great deal since the period in which he was here (1965–95). Not quite correctly because the Maid's Head on Tombland, which was Malcolm's haunt, has been replaced as a preferred site of discourse by the Alexandra Tavern on Stafford Street. But there are still many echoes. Now that the MA in Creative Writing has existed for so long, there is a strong historical sense of the many writers who have taught or are teaching on the course – who include Angus Wilson, Angela Carter, Rose Tremain, Andrew Motion, W.G. Sebald, Patricia Duncker, Michèle Roberts, Andrew Cowan, George Szirtes, Lavinia Greenlaw, Amit Chaudhuri, Rebecca Stott and Trezza Azzopardi – being wound together in an armature.

Lorna Sage, who co-founded Life Writing at UEA with Janet Todd and whose fiction classes many Creative Writing students took, is another part of the story. The Life Writing course was then developed by Richard Holmes, as he describes in these pages. Relaunching it from scratch, he made it a vibrant and popular part of UEA's writing programme, which is now being taught by Kathryn Hughes, William Fiennes and Helen Smith. In 1995, Andrew Motion became Professor of Creative Writing at UEA, and the following year he launched a poetry strand within the Creative Writing MA. Now directed by Lavinia Greenlaw and George Szirtes, it has produced many prizewinning poets, such as Sam Rivière, Meirion Jordan and Tom Warner.

One should not forget the fleeting but foundational figure (as Kathryn Holeywell has shown in a journal article)[2] of Ian Watt, author of *The Rise of the Novel* (1957). Watt established the English department at UEA in 1963 and brought Angus Wilson on to the staff, before swiftly returning to the United States. Why did Watt himself only stay one year? 'There was some story about the Watts' pet boa constrictor feeling the cold,' as Sage coyly put it, in an obituary of the critic Nicholas Brooke, who took over from Watt as Dean of English. Some remarks of Brooke's in a letter to Angus Wilson that Holeywell quotes will ring true to any creative writer at a university: 'The very object of having you here is defeated if our demands conflict with your own writing.'

Let's not pretend that the writers in this university, perhaps any university, can be corralled together other than through the institution. Even today, the writers on the staff at UEA do not cohere stylistically or philosophically. But there are, nonetheless, commonalities. That common armature is involved with an undeceived belief in the value of literary intentions. A still developing clarity – like mist rolling back over a grassy floodplain on the Norfolk coast – about what can be objectified in the teaching of writing and what can't, that's involved in it, too. It is, moreover, involved with being honest about the failings of writing, and establishing whether or not they can be corrected (can it be done without losing the essential identity of the piece or should we eschew such old-fashioned notions?). It is involved, above all, with that recognition of the importance of reading: with taking best historical practice as a guide, descriptive rather than prescriptive, to artistic strategies. All that we really do is point students to an atlas of the past.

Already many UEA students have themselves become part of the atlas. Writers such as Ian McEwan, Kazuo Ishiguro, Anne Enright, Andrew Miller and Tracy Chevalier determine the literary landscape. Many more recent UEA graduates seem likely to do the same, figures such as Joe Dunthorne, Tash Aw, Owen Sheers, Adam Foulds, John Boyne, Mohamed Hanif, David Flusfeder, Clare Wigfall, Naomi Alderman, Phil Whitaker, Paul Murray, James Scudamore, Jane Harris and Anjali Joseph. The writing of some of these authors is included in this book; the full 'body of work' by former UEA students is represented by a bibliography, compiled by Andrew Cowan.

This range and depth of talent cannot be claimed *only* as the product of a single set of MA programmes at one university. That would be ridiculous. In particular, the legend of Ian McEwan as 'the first Creative Writing student at UEA' needs adjustment. McEwan's own account in these pages does that job. But the list does show the wrong-headedness of those who make a general claim that Creative Writing courses are stultifying.

One possible reason for the criticisms is the rapid rise during the past decade of the number of Creative Writing courses offered, not just by universities but also by organisations such as the Faber Academy, the Royal Society of Literature, and the *Guardian*. Ninety-four British universities now offer a range of postgraduate degrees in Creative Writing and in any one year there are usually more than 10,000 short-term Creative Writing courses or classes on offer in the UK.

It has been said that the popularity of such courses is because of a crisis in so-called traditional Eng Lit. I don't think that's quite true, though it is entertaining to watch how the professors react when the subject is broached – viz. John Sutherland, retired Lord Northcliffe Professor of Modern English at University College London, comparing creative writers at universities to 'pandas at Chinese zoos'.

The elephants and the pandas – if that is what we must be – have been around a long time now. The debate about Creative Writing can be situated historically.

As DW Fenza has shown in an article in *The Writer's Chronicle* (March 2000), the term 'creative writing' was probably first employed in the sense we now understand it by Ralph Waldo Emerson on 31 August 1837 in 'The American Scholar', an address to the Phi Beta Kappa Society at Harvard. Emerson proposed 'creative writing' and 'creative reading' as antidotes to 'the restorers of readings, the emendators, the bibliomaniacs of all degrees', in other words the prevailing character in literary studies, which was seen as backward-looking and not appropriate for the developing American sensibility. The first writing classes in this new spirit were given by Barrett Wendell at Harvard in the 1880s.

In 1884 Henry James published his classic essay 'The Art of Fiction' in *Longman's* magazine, arguing against fixed prescriptions as to novelistic method and choice of subject matter. He was responding to a lecture given in the same year by the English critic and novelist Walter Besant, which attempted to lay down 'the laws of fiction'. While Besant's lecture has sunk into relative obscurity, it is still well worth reading, though the game has changed somewhat, as the following remarks suggest:

How can that be an Art, they might ask, which has no lecturers or teachers, no school or college or Academy, no recognised rules, no textbooks, and is not taught in any University? Even the German Universities, which teach everything else, do not have Professors of Fiction…

The field of 'perfect freedom' called for by James could perhaps only have developed in America: 1930 saw the founding of what would become the Iowa Writer's Workshop, still the most well-known Creative Writing course in the United States.

Over the same period in Britain, writers were beginning to identify the creative element in critical writing (Matthew Arnold's 1865 essay 'The Function of Criticism at the Present Time' insists upon this) and the critical element in creative writing. T. S. Eliot's 1932 essay 'The Function of Criticism' contains a much-quoted passage: 'the larger part of the labour of an author in composing his work is critical labour; the labour of sifting, combining, constructing, expunging, correcting, testing; this frightful toil is as much critical as creative.' In other countries, too, the critical aspect of writing was being recognised. In his *Talks with Tolstoy* (1922) A. B. Goldenveizer records the great Russian novelist as saying in June 1905: 'In a writer there must always be two people – the writer and the critic. And, if one works at night, with a cigarette in one's mouth, although the work of creation goes on briskly, the critic is for the most part in abeyance, and this is very dangerous…'

The danger comes when what scriptwriter Keith Tutt charmingly refers to in his essay in this collection as 'the vomit draft' is not cleaned up and corrected. At this point the crutch of the cigarette must be put aside and the eye must scan the page in the cold light of morning. Nonetheless, there remains a fair amount of smoking in this book, from Bradbury himself ('Pipe-smoker of the Year', as Clive Sinclair's piece has it), through Ian McEwan's invitation to a cannabis smoke-in, to Glenn Patterson's being simply unable to hear analysis of his work without a cigarette in his hand.

Analysis and creativity, formal academic criticism and generative artistic work, have always coxed and boxed in universities. In Britain, there has long been overlap between the context of what we now know as Creative Writing and its presence within what I call for shorthand 'traditional English studies'. This history needs some unpacking as it goes some way to explaining the still sometimes scratchy context of Creative Writing as an academic discipline in Britain today.

In 1912 the poet and novelist Sir Arthur Quiller-Couch was appointed Professor of English Literature at Cambridge. Perhaps he, actually, was the original British elephant in the lecture hall. His Cambridge inaugural lecture series, published as *On the Art of Writing* (1916), is the source of the writers' axiom 'murder your darlings':

To begin with, let me plead that you have been told of one or two things which Style is *not*; which have little or nothing to do with Style, though sometimes vulgarly mistaken for it. Style, for example, is not – can never be – extraneous Ornament.

You remember, may be, the Persian lover whom I quoted to you out of Newman: how to convey his passion he sought a professional letter-writer and purchased a vocabulary charged with ornament, wherewith to attract the fair one as with a basket of jewels. Well, in this extraneous, professional, purchased ornamentation, you have something which Style *is not*: and if you here require a practical rule of me, I will present you with this: 'Whenever you feel an impulse to perpetrate a piece of exceptionally fine writing, obey it – wholeheartedly – and delete it before sending your manuscript to press. *Murder your darlings.*'

But let me plead further that you have not been left altogether without clue to the secret of what Style *is*. That you must master the secret for yourselves lay implicit in our bargain, and you were never promised that a writer's training would be easy. Yet a clue was certainly put in your hands when, having insisted that Literature is a living art, I added that therefore it must be personal and of its essence personal...

The fractious founding of the Cambridge English faculty, which 'Q' oversaw, was from the outset embroiled in a creative-critical dynamic. The conditions in which Quiller-Couch took up his position would soon be overshadowed by the outbreak of the First World War. This meant that the Germanic philological tradition, which along with classical studies was one of the parents of serious literary enquiry at British universities, had to be expelled or at least camouflaged. Its replacement by Quiller-Couch's dreamy English folklorism, which is related to the work of the Georgian poets, was never going to be comfortable. Q remained at Cambridge until his death in 1944, but at least a decade earlier his attempt to create an English creative-critical tradition was blasted to pieces by the twin forces of Modernism and the rise of his former pupil F. R. Leavis at Cambridge. The Q effect was, for creative writers at British universities, disastrous, as Quiller-Couch came to represent everything against which professional academic literary critics in this country defined themselves.

There may be elements of Q's legacy that one wishes to rescue, and some that did persist. It is possible to argue that his insistence on literature as *personal* developed into one of the strains of thinking which resisted the incursion of Continental thinking during the Great Structuralism Row at Cambridge in the early 1980s, but there were many resistances to that (ironically, these were as much personal as ideological).

Despite the increasing professionalism of literary studies at Cambridge and other British institutions since the days of Q, creative writing survived in the shape of greater provision for visiting writer posts. Often the visitors would have contact with students that amounted to Creative Writing teaching. One such at Cambridge was the Judith E. Wilson Fellowship. Paul Muldoon held this in 1986–7, tutoring me and the scriptwriter Lee Hall (writer of *Billy Eliot*), before immediately coming to take his writer's fellowship at UEA (1987–8), which experience is rendered in the poem 'Saffron' in this volume. He was followed at Cambridge by Adam Mars-Jones (1987–8), who had held the UEA fellowship previously (1983–4).

There were similar informal arrangements for Creative Writing teaching at other universities, such as the writer's workshop known as the Group, established at Queen's University Belfast in 1963 by Philip Hobsbawm, which was attended by Seamus Heaney, Ciaran Carson, Muldoon and others. But besides UEA, the only other formal Creative Writing course in the UK before the 1990s was at Lancaster University: in an article in *Critical Quarterly* in 1984 David Craig revealed that Lancaster had been offering, intermittently, some element of undergraduate Creative Writing tuition since 1969, and finally introduced an MA course in 1983.

These examples of the cross-currents between informal Creative Writing tuition in traditional academic settings in Britain and the evolution of formal Creative Writing teaching at places like UEA show that, as a discipline, it need not be considered oppositional. Besides, there have long been Eng Lit scholars at universities all over the country well able to balance academic rigour with a deep sense of 'literature as a living art'. They have not become 'dry' in other words, wearing the carpet with their shoes like the scholars in Yeats's poem, and the enthusiasm for literature that they have conveyed to their pupils has been just as important in literary developments over the past half-century as the rise of Creative Writing.

In America, as usual, things had moved much more swiftly. The evolving history of Creative Writing courses there is well described by D. G. Myers in *The Elephants Teach: Creative Writing Since 1880* (1995). More combatively, Mark McGurl's *The Programme Era: Postwar Fiction and the Rise of Creative Writing* (2009) examines the substantial influence on modern American literature of MFAs and similar courses. The current situation worldwide is surveyed in Paul Dawson's *Creative Writing and the New Humanities* (2005).

Creative Writing as an academic discipline depends, as does any university subject, on the calibre and motivation of the staff and the talent and enthusiasm of the students. It is also informed by the institution in which the teaching takes place: its traditions, its intellectual currents, its 'culture'.

But in the end, the writer always must come back to his or her personal creative heartland, and to the small lamp glowing in a window and the white paper within, waiting to be filled. No amount of learning can take away the exigencies of that challenge. And that is something we teach at UEA, albeit nearer the end than the beginning of the course: now you're on your own, mate, it's your skin in the game.

Yet amid that blankness and loneliness lies the possibility of communion – through language – with other readers and other writers. An awareness that human beings are not discrete units is at the heart of this. Many of the pieces in this book speak to both the loneliness and the communion.

But the title, *Body of Work*, does not just refer to that cohesion. It is also intended to convey the sense of literary work having once been produced by an author's hands and fingers, then handled by those of readers. How writing is voiced in the mind of both author and reader seems to me intimately connected with this. It is something the workshop process deployed at UEA and elsewhere is designed to illuminate, though of course it can only illuminate it in a very partial way. (I don't see that reading on screen alters the case categorically; it's simply a different type of handling.)

This doubly incarnate dynamic between writer and reader is part of what is entailed by my own conception of Quiller-Couch's phrase 'literature as a living art'. Our words come out of flesh and what they are trying to flesh out is not just a fixed fictional scenario within the pages of a novel or poem. The whole business is so much more oscillatory, so much more transitional, so much more *alive* than that. For the words are also going to flesh; the expressivity goes both ways. What goes between writer and reader is not so much a text as an experience, maintained in phase space between the historico-physio-psychological circumstances of a book's production and those in which its meanings are absorbed and transformed, in the reader's mind, body and environment.

In this way author and reader are briefly correlate. We are all history men and history women, joined in a ghostly turn through variant systems and domains within systems. Our writing and reading is like a mist-like diffusion through these adjacent membranes or surfaces. It's something that travels, a textual nomad, through different narrative environments. Something that changes its nature with each writing and reading, but mysteriously remains within the grip of the original words.

How strong that grip is, how long it lasts, comes down to the power of the writing, the responsiveness of readers, and the social conditions in which reading takes place. Critically, it is concerned with the tricky issue of intentionality: the relationship between what an author sets out to do and how the resulting work is interpreted. Since the New Critics Wimsatt and Beardsley, since Barthes and Foucault, the topic has not been adequately theorised to take account of the fact of Creative Writing within universities. Creative Writing courses depend on a more resilient sense of intention and a more personalised view of what Foucault called 'the author function' than much modern criticism allows. Bradbury himself put the issue pithily: 'Since Angus and I were both novelists as well as teachers of literature, and took our profession seriously, it seemed somewhat strange for us to be announcing the Death of the Author in the classroom, then going straight back home to be one.' (*Class Work*).

Oh the author, 'that anachronistic personage, the bearer of messages, the giver of lectures to cultural bodies', as Italo Calvino has it, what is to be done about him, what is to be done about her? T. S. Eliot offers one answer when he writes (I forget where) that the writer is only a writer when he is actually in the process of writing; so perhaps we need to make a distinction between author and writer. Lorna Sage, as usual, gets to the core issues in her superb essay 'Living on Writing' (collected in *Grub Street and the Ivory Tower*, edited by Jeremy Treglown and Bridget Bennett, 1998):

[But] the death of the Author has been foundational for the Ivory Tower of literary studies. Almost every major critical 'school' or 'ism', from Russian Formalism to

Richards's experiments with anonymised passages for analysis in Practical Criticism, to New Criticism, Structuralism and since, has insisted that serious criticism must address itself to the text, even though that has been defined very variously, sometimes consisting of the individual poem or novel or play, sometimes of a whole genre, sometimes of a great tradition, sometimes of a whole literature. The main shift here, over the post-war period, has been that instead of insisting, as modernists and their critical commentators had done, on the integrity, richness, autonomy and self-reference of the text, postmodernists and deconstructionists have opened it up, emphasising the continuity of literary and non-literary discourses, the ragged edges of textuality and its inner indeterminacy. The death of the Author Barthes and Foucault were calling for at the end of the 1960s meant this: the death (as Foucault said) of the *author-function*, which had outlived assaults on the Intentional Fallacy, and on romantic notions of creative genius. This function survived in modernist and avant-garde thinking as a transcendental anonymity, and it was this last refuge of the (God-like) point of origin that was under attack. This function worked to guarantee the authority and wholeness of the canonised Work. Remove it and you remove the imaginative and conceptual separateness, the ontological priority, of literary texts. This is the move that brings about the contemporary divorce of critic and reader, and renders old-fashioned 'close reading' redundant.

Sage goes on to outline the emerging research culture around Creative Writing that has emerged as a consequence of that divorce. That culture has grown a little in the decade or so since she was writing, but not very rapidly, despite the growth in the number of courses:

So who in the Ivory Tower 'represents' the contemporary writers of fiction (poetry, drama)? True to the times I think increasingly the answer is: they themselves. Not novelists who also practise literary criticism like Brook-Rose, but those who teach Creative Writing. I have been describing the Ivory Tower as if it were inhabited fairly exclusively by poststructuralists, but it's not, though they have set the tone over the last twenty years or so. Even the recent national Research Assessment, which set out to judge the productivity of academics in the UK, acknowledged this fact by including Creative Writing as a *form* of research into English Literature. Increasingly, and not only in the United States, where Creative Writing is usually a separate department, the business of analysing the workings of words on the page is in the hands of writing teachers. And many of them would say that what they really teach is reading, and that they have become (thanks to theory's domination in criticism) the main custodians of the canon, too. But they don't write this down, they do it orally, in classes. And because this is an activity that doesn't generally advertise itself in books and journals it's easy to underestimate its importance.

One route out of this impasse would be the development of a genuine Creative Writing pedagogy, 'written down' but remaining open minded in the spirit called for by James, a theory for teaching writing which reconciles pragmatism with idealism, and which modulates positivism (based on stylistics, workshops and other methodologies) with a proper respect for the slipperiness of language and the diversity of the individual imagination. As a first step, my colleague Andrew Cowan has accordingly developed a useful idea around 'Blind Spots: What Creative Writing Doesn't Know' in a journal article.[3] This ongoing work is part of an exciting moment in which both writers and critics at UEA are involved. Through the *via negativa* it opens up the possibility of a deconstructive, experimental approach to Creative Writing, which could provide a much needed counter-balance to the predominantly generative methods and realist aesthetic delivered by most Creative Writing courses, including our own. It allows for two forking paths – we could call them the path of McEwan and the path of Sebald, but that would be to oversimplify – to find a way back together, a place to meet in the woods.

I think that, when he died, Bradbury himself was getting close to developing such a philosophy, 'the options and the possibilities' being the linking clue:

> After twenty-five years, I am still not totally convinced myself that writing can be taught – if by that is meant that writers of small talent can be transformed, by the touch of a hand or the aid of a handbook, into significant authors…But what certainly can be created is a significant climate around writing, in which talented and promising authors are taken through the problems, general and specific, universal and personal, of their form and ambitions, shown the options and the possibilities, challenged, edited, pressured, hastened, treated as members of a serious profession. (*Class Work*)

People can dispute the value of that 'significant climate', but after forty years in Britain, and far longer in America, its actual existence cannot be denied. It's time for the many writers who teach on Creative Writing courses to stand up and make a case for what they do, and that means meeting head-on the criticisms, whether they come from within or without the academy. Some of the contributors to this volume do that by producing the analogy (as Besant did in his lecture all those years ago) of training in the arts of music or painting.

Focusing myopically on limits to teaching, antagonists of Creative Writing fail to realise that taking a good Creative Writing course is, in itself, a process of idealisation. Its instrumental, pragmatic efforts are directed towards ideal texts. That is, not a single ideal text to which all teaching aspires, but the ideal form of each text to which a particular student is aspiring. That is why this question of intention is very important; but trying to help students discover and realise their aims does not mean ignoring the real liability (and theoretical certainty) that those aims will be misinterpreted once on the page. The workshop system, which Bradbury was the first to bring to the UK from America, and involves about twelve students reading and notating each other's work, is predicated on eliminating as many as possible of those misinterpretations.

In prose forms in which story is often (but by no means always) the primary factor, the grounds for these misinterpretations often relate to the sequencing of transitions in time and space, to glitches of register, to implausibilities of plot or character, or to errors in handling of perspective. Of course, the instability of language in general, its fallen nature, means that 'mistakes' will continue to occur. The author will not engineer in the reader's head all the effects he or she was hoping to achieve. But that does not mean one should not, in the space of the workshop, that *tenemos* in which trust is paramount, make a collective approach to improvement.

Frequently, too, the workshop process is an aid to organisation, the paramount factor in novels of this type. By this I don't mean clearing a path to one's desk, though that is important, or using diagrams (as Nabokov did): I mean that in helping students become more detached and judicious about their writing, the good Creative Writing course allows the novel to become the self-organising entity which, at its best, it is. The ideal that was sought in the first place becomes scaffolding that can be kicked away, to allow the unpredictable trajectory of the self-organisation to deliver something new.

It's when the totality of that evolving creative experience – in which every word set down carries a story forward with ever-accelerating intensity (Flaubert's *progression d'effet*) – is conveyed to the reader, as a kind of call, that the language which the author has encoded can live again in the reader's head. The author's intentions and the ideal to which they were directed, then become ghostly presages of another individual experience. This foundational call and response is akin in some respects to Leavis's idea of literature as a collaborative act of reconstitution between human minds.

With some student writers, the initial map that they are trying to follow is much harder for the tutor to decipher. The ideals of these writers are often not conceived in story terms but as something much harder to describe: a voice, a consciousness, some kind of awareness. Often it is described in relief, as explicitly anti-realist. As a teacher in these cases, one must inculcate an authentic openness to the possibilities of language. One encourages the students to go out into the world with a cocked ear. At the same time, one shows them to the work of other novelists. It's in these two places that they can best listen for the elusive mental artefact which they are trying to discover while engaged in composition.

While there is certainly a celebratory tone to some of the contents of this book, that is not always the case. Many of the writers collected here remember the painful difficulty of composition as students, and many still appreciate that difficulty. Different literary projects present different literary problems, and self-doubt lurks in every writer's heart. Fame for past glories counts for little when facing what effectively becomes an existential struggle, book by book, page by page. No one understood this better than Joseph Conrad. As he recounts in his autobiographical memoir *A Personal Record* (1912):

Here they are. 'Failure' – 'Astonishing': take your choice; or perhaps both, or neither – a mere rustle and flutter of pieces of paper settling down in the night, and indistinguishable, like the snowflakes of a great drift destined to melt away in the sunshine.

So perhaps we should reschedule our definition of the Creative Writing course: not a process of idealisation, but a process of defeated idealisation – defeated, transformed, above all experienced. And that, actually, is what is involved in the production of 'the living novel': the novel which, to quote from V. S. Pritchett's book of that title, conveys 'a direct apprehension of life', an appreciation above all of its dynamism and complexity and how that interrelates with the dynamism and complexity of the mind and body. It's what Shelley called 'the poetry of life', in the context I show below; and for other genres equivalent authorities might come to our aid. We *know* this thing in our own consciousness as we live it, even though it is very difficult to characterise the intimate strain of how it comes into being again, in altered form, in the limbo world of the text.

For reader as well as writer, that dream world of creative activity is involved with the ever-unfolding realisation that there is always another way to arrange a number of distinct objects in a dimensional relation. That open-endedness is part of the challenge of arranging the time series and spatial configurations of a piece of writing; it is also the door through which readers' minds are able to move in and out of the world of the text, processing the information that it contains in their own way, perhaps inferring other worlds than those the author intended.

Many university critics seem to have forgotten these experiential aspects of literary culture, and that is one reason for the growth in what John Mullan calls 'popular forms of literary discussion' (*How Novels Work*, 2006): reading groups, blog discussions, Q&As with authors at literary festival. This is the cultural movement of the present decade, while the movement of the previous two decades involved an elevation (perhaps precursory of the popular movement) of the status of literary journalism, as Sage recognised:

> Our current interest in literary journalism – not just in doing it, but in writing about it – is an admission that many academics have been missing the personalities of writing, writing's character, the stories of how books are structured, received, sold, understood or not, *made*. ('Living on Writing')

I overstate the case, probably. There are certainly some critics who have bridged the gulfs. A technical understanding of the reciprocal experience of the novel or poem, the play of voices calling and responding that is involved in literature as a living art, isn't so far away from some recent theorisations of the 'event' of reading, or what Derek Attridge calls 'the singularity of literature'. And it is a mistake, if I have been giving that impression, to match 'critical' with 'objective and disinterested'. The rise of theory has included a number of serious challenges to that idea, hence the more creative, or artful, nature of certain strains of theoretical writing, which overtly acknowledge the experiential.

Bradbury's close friend and fellow writer David Lodge is the person who has come closest to articulating fully the complexities and paradoxes of the actual experiences of writing and reading, as in this passage in his seminal paper 'The Novel Now' (1988):

> Is the implied author of a novel – the creative mind to whom we attribute its existence, and whom we praise or blame for its successes and failures – the 'same' as the actual historical individual who sat at his desk and wrote it, and who has his own life before and after that activity, or an identity who exists only at the moment of composition? Can a novel be 'true to life' or does it merely create a 'reality effect'? Is reality itself such an effect? Is the absence of the writer from his own text that which spurs him to refine and polish his language so that his meaning will be effectively communicated without the supplementary aids of voice, gesture, physical presence, etc., which assist communication in ordinary speech? Or is the association of meaning with presence a fallacy which writing, through its inherent ambiguity and openness to a variety of interpretations, helps to expose?
>
> Structuralists and poststructuralists will give one set of answers to these questions and humanist or expressive realist critics another set. Most writers, I suspect – certainly I myself – would be inclined to say in each case, 'Yes and no,' or 'Both alternatives are true.' But the expressive realist theses (that novels arise out of their authors' experience and observation of life, that they are works of verbal mimesis, and so on) are based on common sense, the grounds for believing them are self-evident. The grounds for believing the antithetical propositions are not self-evident, and the value of contemporary literary theory may be that by articulating them it prevents – or would prevent if it were more accessible – the total dominance of our literary culture by expressive realism.

Like Lodge, Bradbury made an accommodation between the two propositions in his life and work, recognising that the elements of fiction (plot, character and so on) are not reducible to easy précis and educational transmission any more than are those elements of fact which constitute aspects of the nature of reality. In the revised introduction to his essay collection *The Novel Today: Contemporary Writers on Modern Fiction* (1977, 2nd edn 1990), reprinted here, Bradbury proposes two critical histories of fiction: the first emphasising the novel's propensity towards generic realism, interrelation with historical events and faithful documentation of the world; the second emphasising its propensity towards formal experimentation, reflexive self-examination and scepticism about the very possibility of 'faithful documentation':

> That change, that oscillation, has left us with two different codes for talking about the novel. One, coming from the aesthetics of realism, emphasises plot and character, setting and theme, denouement and discovery. The other comes from the new

symbolist aesthetics of what came to be called the Modern Movement, and it emphasised other terms: myth, symbol, abstraction, angle of vision, point of view, stream of consciousness.

Ten years before the end of the last century, in the second edition of *The Novel Today*, Bradbury could write 'today many novelists seem impatient with the inherited codes both of realism and modernism'. Some fairly recent critical writing by Zadie Smith in the *New York Review of Books* ('Two Paths for the Novel', 20 November 2008) suggests that the two codes still prevail and that writers have not achieved the ideal synthesis that Bradbury – the critical fox pursuing the white flash of the creative rabbit-tail – chases in his introduction. Yet the picture may be more complex than Smith allows. It may be that as novelists now we are already, in fact, writing an evolved combination of those two traditions.

Reviewing two novels, Joseph O'Neill's *Netherland* and Tom McCarthy's *Remainder*, Smith sketches out two contending futures for the novel in remarkably similar terms to those employed both by Bradbury in *The Novel Today* in 1977/1990 (the two introductions themselves bear comparison) and Lodge in 'The Novel Now' in 1988:

> These aren't particularly healthy times. A breed of lyrical Realism has had the freedom of the highway for some time now, with most other exits blocked. For *Netherland*, our receptive pathways are so solidly established that to read this novel is to feel a powerful, somewhat dispiriting sense of recognition. It seems perfectly done – in a sense that's the problem. It's so precisely the image of what we have been taught to value in fiction that it throws that image into a kind of existential crisis, as the photograph gifts a nervous breakdown to the painted portrait.

Smith's analysis is persuasive, but it doesn't quite accommodate a feeling that within O'Neill's beautifully achieved vision there is much symbolic material that does, actually, constitute reflexive self-examination of his own biography and personality, the 'fictionality' of his own being. It may be a critical solecism to say so, but *Netherland* is really about *him*, it's the masked textual residue of Joe O'Neill's psychodrama. I think there are a lot of contemporary novels that are like this, i.e., which seem to be in the dominant mode of expressive realism but which are actually raking a lexical surface of realism over something riskier, more experimental, more *personal*.

For writers themselves one answer to Smith's forking path (which maps on to the fork of McEwan/Sebald) is greater mindfulness of the novel's midway reality between materiality and immateriality. Tom McCarthy's *C*, which made the Man Booker shortlist in 2010, is a highly significant contemporary novel which has something of that. But so, with their smuggled-in cargo, are a number of notionally realist novels published during the same period, including *Netherland*. I think this applies to Ian McEwan's novels, too: as with any writer, his books are a displacement of turbulent emotional and mental processes. They take symbolic shape from that displacement, at the same time as being the product of technical control. When people react against that control, saying he is 'cold' (as my students sometimes say), they misunderstand that his feelings must have gone through a complex process of reification to produce the notionally realist text. As readers, we maybe need to look harder for the symbolic potential in the work of McEwan and other neo-realists.

The difference between the two paths is a question of tone and emphasis not of type. The distinctions revolve around how much the workings are exposed, along with the balance between narrative prose and other discourses. Go too far in any one direction and the textual entity starts to lose its novelistic identity.

The spirited discussion around Gabriel Josipovici's *What Ever Happened to Modernism?* (2010) is relevant here. But all this is not just about Modernism, it's also about the longer historical tradition of those forms of Romanticism which put the uncertainties and other feelings of the authorial persona at the centre of the literary work, as opposed to another tradition which seeks to remove or abstract the author's personality, or at least subordinate it to the story of a novel or the form of a poem.

The fact is, the text which makes a settlement between the astringencies and richness of experimentalism, the gifts and beguilements of introspection, and the dangerous satisfactions of a story or a shape has long been a Holy Grail. The search for it long predates the establishment of Creative Writing in Britain. The challenge now at UEA and in the wider continuum of literary experience is to find new ways of thinking and talking about novels and other genres that clear a free discursive space above ground, rather than disappearing down the narrow rabbit holes of one 'code' or another.

Related challenges include the risks and opportunities around the dissemination of writing on multimedia platforms, structural issues in the agenting, publishing and selling of books, and the convergence of national literatures attendant on globalisation and the Internet. These uncertainties are a small part of a much larger pattern of early twenty-first-century shocks and crises which literature, with its uncanny ability to scope emergent behaviour, will predict as well as reflect.

The role of the creative writer may turn out to be highly significant in the digital age, as human beings begin to confront the problem that 'our ideas are underdetermined by our observations', as thinkers such as Henri Atlan and Sander van der Leeuw have recognised. There are scales and dimensions on which things are not being measured and it is in these domains that future shocks are being stored up, waiting to happen, who knows when. As a society we just cannot measure all these scales and dimensions, or keep the data from all those that we do measure in our heads at the same time. This means that there is an intrinsic limit to the possibility of control in physical and social systems, as continuing financial and environmental crises demonstrate. Yet the global data set is growing exponentially, and we make decisions based on its inadequate rendering of reality every day, effectively seeding the future with further error: this relates to the problems around subject/object relations that Coleridge had in mind when he wrote that 'existence is its own predicate'. Further exploration of his thinking on these matters is one route by which we might get to new ways of seeing which reconcile both the polarities of novelistic traditions and those of creative and discursive writing.'[4]

There is a growing need to use narrative and metaphor and the other tools of creative writing to concentrate the flux of information. That is one of its uses as both an academic discipline and an artistic practice. Underlying that may be a requirement for writers to use the creative imagination to intuit future scenarios and inculcate flexibility about a range of possible outcomes, in order to build better social resilience. (A requirement but not an obligation: certainly we would be wise to be wary as well as stirred by the call to commitment, as John Spurling's piece in this volume demonstrates.)

This intuition of future scenarios may relate to a coming proleptic turn in fiction that critics have identified.[5] At any rate, some words which Shelley wrote in his *A Defence of Poetry* have never been more relevant, both out in the world and (as I consider my original intentions) in my own head right now; that is to say, in the two realities with which all writers wrestle and find themselves wanting:

We have more moral, political, and historical wisdom than we know how to reduce into practice; we have more scientific and economical knowledge than can be accommodated to the just distribution of the produce which it multiplies…We want the creative faculty to imagine that which we know; we want the generous impulse to act that which we imagine; we want the poetry of life; our calculations have outrun conception; we have eaten more than we can digest.

1   Will Self's introduction to *Riddley Walker* (2002) by Russell Hoban. 'This book breaks the alleged rules of literary composition. Of course, there aren't really any rules, or if there are, they're there for deadheads who want to be taught naturalism by some berk in the Fens.' Not being in the Fens – not quite – UEA was pleased to welcome Self in 2008 to give his lecture 'Reverse Engineering the Synoptic I, Towards an Understanding of W. G. Sebald's Methodology'.

2   'The Origins of a Creative Writing Programme at the University of East Anglia, 1963–1966', *New Writing*, vol. 6, Issue 1 (2009).

3   *TEXT*, vol. 15, No. 1 (April 2011).

4   See Elaine Hock's article 'Dialectic and the "Two Forces of One Power": Reading Coleridge, Polanyi, and Bakhtin in a New Key' in *The Polanyi Society Periodical* 23.3 (1996-97): 4-16 (http://tinyurl.com/3jezqsf).

5   See Mark Currie's article 'The Novel and the Moving Now' in *Novel: A Forum on Fiction*, vol. 42, No. 2 (Summer 2009), pp. 318–26, (http://tinyurl.com/6x2ah5j)

Giles Foden (*b.* 1967) was appointed Professor of Creative Writing at UEA in 2007. His novels include *The Last King of Scotland* (1998) and *Turbulence* (2009). He was formerly an editor at the *Times Literary Supplement* and the *Guardian*, and AHRC Fellow in Creative and Performing Arts at Royal Holloway, University of London.

Beginnings

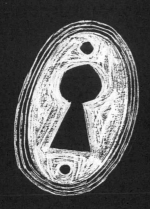

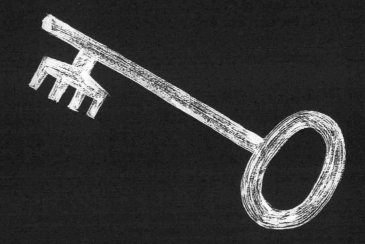

Toe

Tom Warner

It makes sense to start with the toe and work up.
I pull off my sock to check my own dumb digit,
get a sense of proportion, follow cables and joints
to the nub that's furthest from my head and mouth.
It's best not to think too much, just get something down:
a big toe from which to build the foot, the shin, the head.
I warm a pound or so of clay between my clammy hands
and roll out the capital letter of his body's first line.

When he's complete, I'll prop a ladder against his chest
to scratch a title into the bluish slab of forehead,
then wait for him to move a toe or suck up breath.
Tonight I'll lead him, broad-backed, into your city,
leave him to sleep in oily lock-ups and walk the streets
with nothing but this poem rolled beneath his tongue.

Tom Warner (*b.* 1979) received his MA in Creative Writing from UEA in 2001. That year he won an Eric Gregory Award for his poems, which later featured in *Faber New Poets 8* (2010). In 2009–10 he was Poet in Residence at Newark, Nottinghamshire, as part of the Poetry-on-Trent Project, supported by the National Lottery through Arts Council England. In preparation for this, he paddled 170 miles down the length of the River Trent in an open canoe. He won an Arts Council Escalator Prize in 2011.

Thank You, Brother Martin

Mick Jackson

For most of the 1980s I was a singer in a band, which I still maintain is just about the coolest way to spend your twenties, as long as you don't mind being perpetually broke. It never seemed to bother me. Then again, I lived in a state of absolute conviction that within days the world would finally succumb to our charms and buy our records in such numbers that the royalty cheques would choke my letterbox.

This conviction remained more or less unshaken until I was within touching distance of my thirtieth birthday. Our record label was dragging its feet about recording another album and, frankly, who could blame them? Our earlier releases had barely turned a profit, and over the previous twelve months we'd only managed to cobble together three or four new compositions, each one weirder than the one before. The final nail in the coffin came when our keyboard player – one of the few real musicians among us – announced that she was leaving the band to strike out on her own. It took about five seconds for me to appreciate that this meant the end of my musical career.

A couple of months earlier I'd happened to read an article about the Creative Writing course at the University of East Anglia, which had made a name for itself by producing writers such as Ian McEwan, Kazuo Ishiguro and Rose Tremain. The photographs accompanying the article showed a group of intensely pensive people reclining in luxuriously upholstered armchairs. Presumably they were contemplating the complexities of contemporary literature. It looked kind of fun. I already had a handful of ideas for short stories – ideas which had proved too unwieldy for the lyrics of a song, but it was several days after the bombshell about the band's imminent break-up before I remembered that article. Suddenly the clouds parted and my future was revealed to me. I would trade the ripped jeans and sweaty T-shirt of the alternative music scene for the more dignified tweeds of the world of publishing.

I decided that I should put a little time aside in which to develop those first short stories – a decision which still seems entirely sensible. But for some reason, rather than just sit at a desk at the local library, I determined that the most appropriate place to commence work on my writing was in a Benedictine monastery in Devon.

I'd gone to college just down the road from Buckfast Abbey, so was vaguely familiar with the place, and I must have heard somewhere how most abbeys welcome guests – even non-believers – who might benefit from a few days of quiet contemplation. In my defence I would point out that I was still young enough to consider doing a thing for no better reason than because it seemed potentially interesting. When I wasn't performing or rehearsing I was a life model for a professional painter...I regularly stayed up past midnight…I liked to cha-cha-cha. And if Jack Kerouac spent his summers perched on a mountaintop in the North Cascades awaiting enlightenment, then I would withdraw to the cloisters of a West Country monastery and await my own. Ten days later, I was driving my battered Triumph Toledo down the A38, heading for Buckfastleigh.

I was welcomed by Brother Martin, one of the younger monks. He signed me in, then led me upstairs to the residential quarters and opened the door to my room. Is it conceivable that I was just the tiniest bit disappointed? Was I secretly hoping for a windswept cell with nothing but a stone slab on which to sleep? Quite possibly. The room before me was modestly furnished – a single bed, a chest of drawers, a wash basin, a desk and chair – but was twice the size of my bedroom back in Hackney. And a good deal warmer. Perhaps monastic life wasn't quite as austere as I'd been led to believe.

I unpacked my clothes, the notebooks that contained my ideas and the blank sheets of A4 on to which I hoped they would magically transpose themselves. I also took along *La Terre* by Émile Zola (in translation, not the original French) and the collected poems of Philip Larkin.

Brother Martin had informed me that the front door would be locked at 9 p.m. and, sure enough, on the hour I heard a great clunk echo through the building. Hmm. I began to feel a little incarcerated. What if there was a fire? What if I suddenly decided that I didn't want to hang out with the monks any more? I opened the leaded window. If I jumped, I might only break the one leg.

Within a couple of minutes I'd managed to plot a way down the network of drainpipes. That seemed to calm me down. I read a little Zola and a little Larkin, changed into my pyjamas and went to bed.

It was still pitch-black when I heard a tapping at my door. Someone popped their head in. 'Are you with us, Michael?' he whispered into the dark.

I assured him that I was. He pulled the door to behind him. Where on earth was I? And why were people knocking on my bedroom door in the middle of the night?

I washed, dressed and crept down the corridors to the refectory in the basement. One or two monks were buttering toast and pouring milk over their cornflakes. I nodded in their direction, made myself a cup of tea and took a seat at one of the long tables. After a couple of minutes I thought I might as well have a boiled egg. But over the days that followed I discovered that I could have as leisurely a breakfast as I wanted – I would still find myself back in my room well before seven o'clock, which left a great many hours of the day stretching off into the distance. Which, of course, was why I'd arranged to come down here in the first place.

Quite a few of those hours I spent sitting at my desk, thinking. Some of them I spent staring out of the window. There was even the odd one when I managed to put pen to paper. A couple of times a day I would leave my room and go down to the abbey, especially when there was some choral music to be heard, and when the weather was fine I'd go out to the gardens, where I'd sit and think some more.

Even taking into consideration the occasional catnap, the days still seemed impossibly long and would, I'm sure, have been quite overwhelming if they hadn't been broken up into more manageable pieces by the mealtimes. Breakfast was self-service, whereas lunch and dinner were brought to the table by the brothers. It must have been mid-February when I visited, because I remember heart-shaped cupcakes being handed out on what I later realised was Valentine's Day.

Talking wasn't allowed at the table, so requesting the salt and pepper from one's neighbour necessitated a certain amount of pointing. While we ate, one of the brothers would sit at a lectern and read aloud. I couldn't quite identify the text. Not the Bible, but certainly something religious. Each day a different brother took it in turn to read, and I convinced myself that at this rate I, too, would be called upon to sit at the lectern and deliver my own mealtime commentary. I'd have to pop back up to my room and grab my Larkin. Weirdly, I suspected he'd go down quite well.

But the lack of conversation certainly was a bit of a shock to the system. I'm a natural-born chatter and chewer of the cud. Unfortunately, since I tended to encounter very few brothers in the daytime and talking was verboten while we ate, it became apparent that the only exchange I was likely to have was when Brother Martin tapped on my door at the start of the day.

One morning I happened to wake as he made his way along the landing. He knocked and popped his head into the room.

'Are you with us, Michael?' he whispered.

'I am, yes. Thank you, Brother Martin,' I told him.

That was about the longest conversation I had all week. It wasn't just the spoken word from which I was abstaining. I hadn't had a drop to drink since the previous Saturday. And when I went to bed at night I lay on my back and kept my hands firmly by my sides. At this rate, by the time I climbed back into my car I'd be practically immaculate.

At first I'd found it almost impossible to tell one monk from another. Some were older/balder. Some wore spectacles, some did not. It was two or three days into my little retreat before I worked out another means of telling them apart. As I passed them, I would catch the occasional glimpse of footwear among the folds of their robes. Most of the brothers favoured the traditional brogue or desert boot or sandal. But once or twice I caught a glimpse of a New Balance or Nike trainer on the feet of the younger monks. This probably had as much to do with comfort and insulation against the cold stone floors as fashion. But it did remind me that some of these men were the same age as me.

By the end of the week I'd managed to finish my Zola, had worked my way through my collected Larkin and completed a decent first draft of half a dozen short stories, which would form the supporting material of my application to UEA. I packed my bag, wrote out a cheque to the monastery (fortunately payment was on a pay-what-you-can-afford basis), said goodbye to Brother Martin and headed back out into the world. Later that day I was onstage at Bristol University, shouting into a microphone.

Within a few months the band had split up and I'd moved to Cambridge, where I got a part-time job as a care assistant, which left me plenty of time to work on my short stories. As things transpired, my application to UEA was rejected. After a protracted period of sulking, I would finally re-apply and was offered a place the following year.

It was only recently that I saw how going on retreat wasn't simply a way of forcing myself to work on my writing, but also a way of immersing myself, albeit briefly, in what I imagined a writer's life to be – namely, absolute solitude. On that score, I'm happy to admit I was mistaken. Writing might benefit from peace and quiet, but treating it as a state requiring conditions of quarantine makes it akin to a sickness, and I don't buy into that.

What I do believe in is a need for ritual, or to put it more mundanely, routine – and that if there isn't time and space set aside in which to do it, then one shouldn't be surprised if nothing ends up on the page. There might be the odd moment of transcendence and even enlightenment, but they are few and far between.

Mick Jackson (*b.* 1960) received an MA in Creative Writing from UEA in 1992. His first novel *The Underground Man* (1997) was shortlisted for the Man Booker Prize and for the Whitbread Award for best first novel. His most recent book is *The Widow's Tale* (2010), which was East Anglian Book Awards Book of the Year.

Discovering Books

Mohammed Hanif

Once upon a time, when I was eighteen, I found myself locked up in the Pakistan Air Force Academy's cell, along with my friend and partner-in-crime Khalid Saifullah. We had been caught trying to help another classmate pass his chemistry exam, something he had failed to do twice previously and this was his last chance to save himself from being expelled. The logistics of our rescue effort involved a wireless set improvised in the Sunday hobbies club, a microphone concealed in a crêpe bandage around the left elbow of our friend, and a Sanyo FM radio receiver. We were caught whispering a reversible chemical equation into the transistor.

We were in breach of every standard operating procedure in the academy rule book, and faced certain expulsion. For two days, while we waited to discover our fate, we planned our future. Khalid, always the worldly-wise one in this outfit, decided that he would join the merchant navy and travel the world. I came from a farming family in which even the most adventurous members of our clan had only managed to branch out into planting sugar cane instead of potatoes. Education, jobs, careers were alien concepts. The academy was supposed to be my escape from a lifetime that revolved around wildly fluctuating potato-crop cycles. And here I was, already a prisoner of sorts, facing a journey back to a life I thought I had left behind.

In the end they looked at our relatively clean records and let us off the hook. As a punishment, we were barred from entering the academy's television room – and walking. For forty-one days we had to stay in uniform from dawn until dusk, and whenever we were required to go from point A to B we had to run. Khalid went on to become a marathon runner (before, years later, dying in an air crash, while trying to pull a spectacular but impossible manoeuvre in a Mirage fighter plane). I discovered the academy's library.

I had barely noticed that the college had a very well-stocked library. The librarian, an eagle-nosed old civilian, walked around with a large bunch of jangling keys, although his wares were not in any danger of being stolen. I spent some afternoons staring at the books from behind the glass doors, as my classmates watched videos in the television room (including the fellow who had scraped through his chemistry exam and survived, but would die years later in our then president General Pervez Musharraf's moronic military adventure in Kargil on the India-Pakistan border).

How do you ask for a book when you are eighteen and have been brought up in a household where the only book is the Koran and the only reading material an occasional old newspaper left behind by a visitor?

'I want that book,' I told the librarian, pointing tentatively towards a cupboard which contained a thick volume of something called *The Great Escape*.

The librarian, relieved at having found a customer, took out his bunch of keys, removed one of them and asked me to go and get it myself. So grateful was I for getting that book that I brought him a samosa and a cup of tea. That turned out to be a good investment, because the next day the librarian handed me the bunch of keys as soon as I entered. I browsed randomly, recklessly, read first paragraphs, authors' bios and made naive judgements. Oddly, *The Cross of Iron* wasn't a religious thriller but a war novel. *Crime and Punishment* had very little crime in it. Was Salman Rushdie related to the famous pop singer Ahmed Rushdie? Mario Puzo and Mario Vargas Llosa sounded like cousins, but their books were completely different. Someone called Borges had written *Doctor Brodie's Report*, which had a skeleton on the front but nothing very scary between its covers. You could open any of Mr Harold Robbins's books and find a steamy sex scene between pages 13 and 17.

There was a whole shelf devoted to Gabriel García Márquez. I wondered why they always described his writing as 'magical realism' when it was quite obvious that he had stolen all his ideas from my grandmother's stories and just changed the names of the characters. An abridged version of *War and Peace* was found, but the librarian friend hinted that abridged books were for sissies, so a complete version was offered and read. I was convinced it was all true. Who could make up all those names? I was quite relieved to find out that almost everyone thought George Eliot was a man. *As I Lay Dying* was a nice title, so I read it. So was *Valley of the Dolls*. The authorities got really concerned when I was caught in my navigation class reading *Notes from the Underground*, hidden under a map that I was supposed to be studying. My reaction was to start missing classes and spend more time in the library.

There was a cupboard full of our dead military dictator Field Marshal Ayub Khan's masterpiece *Friends Not Masters*, a passionate explanation of his relationship with America. I wondered if our then military dictator General Zia knew that a character in Salman Rushdie's *Shame* was modelled on him. Discovering books was like stumbling on a second adolescence. I discovered new sensations in my body. It was even better. It was guilt-free and I could show off.

Not that anyone cared. And then one day, in an attempt to improve my knowledge of geography, I picked up a book called *Tropic of Cancer*. Now this was a library where Reader's Digest arrived with all adverts featuring female models torn out, where chapters dealing with reproduction in the biology books were stapled together, and if Raquel Welch sneaked into a film advert, the censors made sure that her legs were covered with black ink. No wonder that *Tropic* went on to become the most borrowed book in the academy that year.

Mohammed Hanif (*b.* 1964) graduated from the Pakistan Air Force Academy as a pilot officer, but subsequently left to pursue a career in journalism and literature. He received an MA in Creative Writing from UEA in 2005. His first novel *A Case of Exploding Mangoes* (2008) was Commonwealth Writers' Prize Best First Book winner (2009) and was longlisted for the Man Booker Prize. His most recent novel is *Our Lady of Alice Bhatti* (2011).

Interlude: Beginning Writing

Amit Chaudhuri

In 1984 my parents moved to a small, appealing flat in St Cyril Road, Bandra. My father had retired from his corporate position, as the head of a company, the previous year: the year I'd gone to England as an undergraduate. At the time of his retirement, we moved out of the 4,000 square-feet, four-bedroom flat on the twenty-fifth storey of Maker Towers 'B' on Cuffe Parade, and briefly occupied the company guest flat at 'Brighton' in Nepean Sea Road, overlooking the sea (I had lived, from when I was about nine years old, in buildings that had an unobstructed view of the sea). From there we moved to the first flat my father actually owned in Bombay, a two bedroom apartment in a building in Worli called 'Sea Glimpse', whose lift had a sign saying "Use Lift At Your Own Risk". The sea, from here, was a blur. But buildings in Bombay have their own biographies and destinies, and are named, at birth, with presumably the same mixture of wishful thinking and superstition as our children are.

My father had bought this flat from the company years ago, for a sum he could afford. It took us by surprise; it was the sort of building we had seldom visited, let alone lived in. The ramshackle lift, with its dark shaft like the inside of a toilet in a small town, and the message on the top of the door, made my mother and me smile resignedly at the sort of life that was in store for us after my father's retirement. But, property prices in Bombay being what they are, even this flat, with its view of the dirty blur of the sea, the back of the Aarey Milk Colony, and the distant figures, at twilight, of a line of defecating squatters by the promenade on the sea face – even this flat was not worth little. The blur which constituted the sea – like a smear on the glass which a duster had failed to wipe away – would itself have raised its price by a few hundred thousand. Almost as soon as we occupied this flat, we decided to sell it. The difference from those company flats, where all those parties used to be thrown so unthinkingly every one or two weeks, was too much to contemplate for too long. People – prospective buyers, of whom there is a rich supply in Bombay – came in to survey the flat; our faithful maidservant Bai distracted their attention away from the rats who had come to inspect the kitchen from the neighbouring flat, towards the drawing room and the verandah.

From this view of the sea, separated from me by glass, and with the flat yet unsold, I left for England; the untrustworthy lift, one last time, took me and my bags downstairs. In England, in the anonymity of my life in London, I kept hearing of my parents' attempts to locate a suitable new flat, and to find buyers for their own. Their search took them to Bandra, a part of the city we used to once take outings to, two or three times a month, but which was now proliferating with 'developments' and new buildings that would be more affordable than anything in the southern parts of the city. St Cyril Road was one of the lanes off Turner Road where I remembered seeing a building coming up, still incomplete, on one of our tours around that, and other, areas before I went to England. I had recalled liking it then, though it was still an unfinished series of rooms, with labourers moving in and out of them; liking it for the lane it was situated in and into whose life it was sketchily emerging. But my memory of it is as fragmentary, as ridden with gaps, as the structure itself. Besides, we had been told then by an estate agent that its rate per square foot made the flats slightly beyond our reach.

Suddenly, one day, I heard the flat in Worli had been sold and the one in St Cyril Road purchased, the exchange of money and the simultaneous relinquishing and exchange of properties taking place almost overnight. The Worli flat had been sold to a family called Ambo for thirteen lakhs; the new flat in the Eden of St Cyril Road had been bought for fifteen. The difference had been made up with my mother going to Calcutta to sell some of her gold jewellery. The remaining one lakh my father had borrowed from the HDFC. The jewellery had been sold for two reasons; although my father had been a Finance Director, then a Managing Director, of a multinational company, his income had had a huge tax imposed upon it – 75 per cent – and a stringent ceiling – it could rise no higher than 10,000 rupees – under Indira Gandhi, and the ceiling and the tax would substantially remain unchanged until a long time later, when the country entered (too late for my father) the era of 'liberalisation'. The other reason, of course, was that my parents came from East Bengal; they had no ancestral property, no hinterland, no inheritance, to fall back on; they had started their lives from scratch after 1947.

'Yes, it's happened,' said my mother on the phone to me, recounting how Mr Ambo, in the end, had paid my father 10,000 less than thirteen lakhs, how he'd been distressed because his own father was unwell, and pleaded that my father accept the twelve lakh 90,000, which he did. I have never seen Mr Ambo and never will, but his name is enough for me to feel the proximity of his presence; I see him, and his family, enter the new flat, with the blurred view of the sea from the balcony, close the door behind them, and then I don't have to think about them again. There had been a moment of panic, my mother told me – it was all interesting in hindsight – when my parents realised they had given Mr Ambo the key to the flat before they had taken the money from him. She was now speaking to me from the flat in Bandra, where she would be ensconced for a few years to come.

I arrived at the flat, I think, in the summer of '84. It was after midnight; most flights from London to Bombay landed in the small hours of the morning. The door was opened by a man I didn't recognise; a corridor led to the phone at the end, and on the left were three rooms – the sitting room, my room, and my parents'. The kitchen and the guest room, which had been converted into the dining room, were on my right. At 2 a.m., awake with what felt like a heightened caffeine-induced awareness, but which was the deceitful alertness of jet lag, I couldn't have taken in these details. I sat in my parents' room, excited, surrounded by bags and silence, and talked in a way it is possible to at such moments, when the rest of the world is asleep. Later, I went to my room to lie down, like an interloper who's been put in his place.

I should have slept the next morning till ten, but was woken up by half-past six or seven. There was an eerie chorus about me, disorienting and frightening, urgent enough not to be confused with the final moments of a nightmare; it was birdsong. For more than fifteen years I'd lived in tall buildings; I had forgotten how violent this sound could be, how it could drown out everything else.

It's hard to let go of your old life. But that is what I did when I moved here. Gone, those four-bedroom apartments and that sea view, the perspective of the Marine Drive – those precipitous visions, first from the twelfth storey on Malabar Hill, then the twenty-fifth storey on Cuffe Parade. But those flats were on lease; they were company flats, they did not belong to my father. And yet the years there, and the memories I inherited from them, did belong to me.

Now I was here. While this lane was called St Cyril Road, all the lanes that ran parallel to it were also named after saints, most of them as obscure as St Cyril. Mentioned together, those names became a fading, if absurd, hallelujah to a way of life.

A balcony joined my room to my parents'; opposite, there was a three-storeyed house and, on eye-level, a flat in which an ageing Parsi couple lived. This couple absorbed me at certain moments; the way they sat face to face with each other, at either end of the verandah, the old man never actually looking at his wife, but at something else, while the wife regarded him sullenly through her spectacles. She had a loud voice, and reprimanded him with it; I could hear her angry Gujarati words. He never answered back, but kept staring at that mysterious object.

This couple became part of my new life, my new sensibility; for them I exchanged the view of the Arabian Sea, of Bombay's mercantile and civic power – the land that inexorably advances upon the sea, so that there are apartment and office buildings, even auditoriums and theatres, today, where there had been only water yesterday; the thirty-five storey Oberoi Towers and the Air India building, with its logo shining at the top; the pale dome of the old Taj in the midst of other buildings.

I must have been lonely in that old life; sometimes I was conscious of that loneliness, and sometimes I mistook it for a sort of unease. But I can find no other explanation for my welcoming of St Cyril Road into my life. It wasn't that the flat was the first one my father properly owned in Bombay. It was the discovery of a community – made up, predominantly, of Goan Christians – and of the lanes and by-lanes in which that community existed. What I had missed in my childhood, without knowing it, was community; we had camped – our nuclear family; my father, my mother and myself – in company apartments; I had surveyed, from windows and balconies, the expanse of the city, and, through binoculars, the windows and balconies of other multi-storeyed buildings. I had not suspected the need, in myself, for physical contact, the need to be close to ground level, within earshot of my surroundings, to be taken out of myself, randomly, into the lives of others.

Like a shadow moving first in one direction, then another, itinerants came and went. The lane changed with the seasons; there was a gulmohur tree facing our verandah, which shed its blossoms during the monsoons and, by summer, was again orange with flowers. I found these little changes marvellous.

The birds that had woken me the first morning after my arrival became a part of our daytime lives, as we did theirs; their excrement hardened into green scabs, every day, on the balcony's banister. In the mornings, they fought upon the air conditioners, and I could hear their claws scraping against metal. Each morning, their twenty-minute bout started afresh. Opening the bathroom window, I could see the air conditioner protruding outward; occasionally, a pigeon or crow set up home on it, and would fight off intruders. If I saw a pigeon alighting on the verandah with a twig in its beak, I knew a home was in the making somewhere, either on the branches of the jackfruit tree that stood next to our balcony with a kind of awareness, or on one of the air conditioners, our compulsory accomplices in middle-class comfort.

Our building itself stood in the place of a cottage that had once belonged to a Christian family. I had heard the family lived in the ground-floor apartment, but I had never seen them. Perhaps they rented the flat out or had paying guests; because employees of Air India came and went from it at odd times of the day, including a beautiful girl, infrequently glimpsed from my verandah, who was supposed to be an air hostess. And there were other cottages and houses in the lane, I'd noticed, that seemed to be going in the direction that the house that had once stood here had gone, towards disappearance and non-existence.

This was the place I returned to in the summer, and for the short break in the winter. The rest of the year I lived in England. It was my ambition to be a poet; the ambition had taken me to England.

I was doing nothing much in London; I hardly had any friends. I hardly attended lectures at University College. But I was writing poems; these poems were like little closed rooms, like the rooms I lived in in England; they were closed to everything but literary influence. No door or window was left open to let in the real world, or to admit the self that lived in that world; in the closed room of the poem, I tried on yet another literary voice or a style I had recently found interesting. I speak of this in architectural terms because that is what would strike me most when I returned to Bombay, to St Cyril Road, for my holidays: the continual proximity of the outside world; a window left open; the way the outside – manifested as noise, as light – both withheld itself and became a part of the interior life.

I wrote a poem in 1985, while living in the studio apartment on Warren Street. It was called 'St Cyril Road, Bombay,' and I must have written it between avoiding lectures, looking despondently out of the window, and eating lunch at half-past three. From where, at the time, St Cyril Road came back to me, I don't know; here, though, is the poem.

Every city has its minority, with its ironical, tiny village
fortressed against the barbarians, the giant ransacks and the pillage
of the larger faith. In England, for instance, the 'Asians' cling to their ways
as they never do in their own land. On the other hand, the Englishman strays
from his time-worn English beliefs. Go to an 'Asian' street
in London, and you will find a ritual of life that refuses to compete
with the unschooled world outside. In Bombay, it's the Christian minority that clings
like ivy to its own branches of faith. The Christian boy with the guitar sings
more sincerely than the Hindu boy. And in St Cyril Road, you're familiar
with cottages hung with flora, and fainting, drooping bougainvillaea,
where the noon is a charged battery, and evening's a visionary gloom
in which insects make secret noises, and men inside their single rooms
sing quaint Portuguese love songs – here, you forget, at last, to remember
that the rest of Bombay has drifted away, truant, and dismembered
from the old Bombay. There, rootless, garish and widely cosmopolitan,
where every executive is an executive, and every other man a Caliban
in two-toned shoes, and each building a brooding tyrant that towers
over streets ogling with fat lights…Give me the bougainvillaea flowers
and a room where I can hear birds arguing. I won't live in a pillar of stone,
as ants and spiders live in the cracks of walls, searching for food alone
in the sun-forgotten darkness. That's why I've come to St Cyril Road
to lose myself among the Christians, and feel Bombay like a huge load
off my long-suffering chest. Woken up at six o' clock in the morning
by half-wit birds who are excited in the knowledge that day is dawning
on the sleeping lane – that's what I want. The new day enters my head
like a new fragrance. I rise, dignified, like Lazarus from the dead.

'I like the parody of Yeats,' said a friend after reading it. 'Yeats?' I said disbelievingly; I hadn't been thinking of Yeats. 'Yes, silly,' she said, smiling, and pointed out my own lines to me: 'where the noon is a charged battery, and evening's a visionary gloom / in which insects make secret noises, and men inside their single rooms / sing quaint Portuguese love songs…' I saw now that, unknowingly, I'd tried to transform St Cyril Road into Innisfree; to trace a similar journey of desire. 'There midnight's all a glimmer, and noon a purple glow / And evening full of the linnet's wings,' Yeats had said. I replaced the linnet's wings with the nocturnal sound of crickets I'd heard each day after sunset.

The view from the room I lived in on Warren Street was very different from St Cyril Road. There was a restaurant opposite, Tandoor Mahal; it was one of three or four Indian restaurants, all of which seemed fairly successful, English people hunched inside them mornings and afternoons, except this one. It looked like the family of the man who owned it – a balding Sylheti Muslim in a suit with a round face and compassionate eyes – were in and out of the restaurant all day, but almost no one else. I can remember seeing the two daughters, who would have been in their early teens, and the energetic little boy, their younger brother, many, many times, but never a single customer.

I was not quite sure if this was England, or somewhere else; I was never sure how to characterise or categorise this place. It certainly did not approximate any idea of England I previously might have had. Next to the restaurant was another three-storeyed house, like the one I lived in, in whose attic lived a tall Englishman who I presumed was a painter. I thought this because he often went about carrying large canvases. A friend came to see him frequently; a shorter, stockier man who had moustaches, whom I used to call 'Lal', because he resembled a man of the same name who used to be a director in the company my father had retired from. There was a graceful bonhomie in their meetings, which mainly took place on the pavement before the black door to the house, near a parking meter, and it was always interesting to note, in passing, the angularity of the taller man juxtaposed with, and almost reaching toward, the settled centre of gravity of the stockier companion. The tall man seemed in danger of being blown away by a wind. Lal, the stocky man, sometimes had a dog with him. There was a strange loneliness, or aloneness, about them; they seemed impervious to the passers-by making their way towards the Warren Street tube on the right.

What was I doing here? It was a question I often asked myself. I had come to England to become, eventually, a famous poet. The ambition left me lonely. I hardly went to college or attended lectures. Instead, I sleepwalked through that area around Fitzroy Square, Grafton Street and Tottenham Court Road, stepping in and out of newsagents', surreptitiously visiting grocers' and corner shops, while I waited to become famous. Knowing my attachment to Larkin, my mother bought me his new book of selected prose, *Required Writing*, for my twenty-second birthday. There were two interviews in it. Larkin was a reluctant interviewee; he was always politely admonishing the interviewer for his stupidity. When asked by Robert Phillips of the *Paris Review*, 'Was it your intention, then, to be a novelist only?' because of Larkin's two early novels, Larkin said, in his unfriendly but interesting way, 'I wanted to "be a novelist" in a way I never wanted to "be a poet", yes,' as if 'wanting to be' was a necessary but misleading part of a writer's life. As for myself, I wanted to 'be' a poet; I had never thought of 'being' a novelist. It was towards this end that I'd come to England; and sent out my poems to the National Poetry Competition, as advertised in the *Poetry Review*, a pound the entry fee for each poem submitted.

Those first years of living in London made me acutely aware of light and space and weather, and how they influence ways of life. And it was partly this, I suppose, that made me see St Cyril Road in a new way, that made me, in Warren Street, write the poem, and allowed, for the first time, a 'real' place, a real locality, to enter my writing. At that time I didn't know anything unusual had happened. I was pleased enough with the poem; but I was pleased with almost every poem I wrote. Later, that poem would become my first publication in England; it would appear in the *London Review of Books*, its long lines clustered at the bottom of a page, in 1987.

By the time the poem was published, we were already thinking of leaving of St Cyril Road. The flat that had been bought with such excitement three years ago – the small three-bedroom flat with its perspective of the lane – was up for sale. On long walks down St Cyril and St Leo roads my parents had discussed the matter with me, and we had come to the same conclusion. For a variety of reasons, my father was under financial pressure; and the debt of one lakh rupees from HDFC had still not been quite resolved. We would move to Calcutta; my father had bought a flat there in a government-erected block in 1975. My father, at that point in time, could not afford, we decided, the luxury of two flats in two cities; and his plan, anyway, had always been to retire to Calcutta.

I didn't mind the idea of moving to Calcutta; I encouraged it. All my life, I'd been vociferous about my dislike of, my impatience with, Bombay, and the fact that Calcutta was my spiritual home. And the money, once the flat was sold, would be a comfortable investment for my father. In the meanwhile, I continued to explore the area, and the explorations continued to result in poems. In 1986, when I took a year's break between graduating from University College, London, and leaving for Oxford, I wrote 'The Bandra Medical Store':

When I first moved here, I had no idea whatsoever
where the Bandra Medical Store really was. But someone

in the house was ill. So I ventured out, let my legs
meander to a chosen path, articulate their own distances.

I guess my going out for medicine, even the illness, were just
excuses for me to make that uninsisting journey

to a place I hadn't seen. Two roads followed each other
like long absences. The air smelled of something not there. Branches

purled and knitted shadows. There was a field, with a little landslide
of rubble, and a little craggy outline of stone.

I drifted past heliotropic rubbish heaps, elderly
white houses. An aircraft hummed overhead. And did

the houses look like rows of slender barley from the pilot's
window, row pursuing row, held in a milieu of

whiteness, unswayed by a clean, flowing wind?
Then the 'plane donned a thick cloud. All it left was a cargo

of loaded silence. I supposed that I must be lost.
It grew evening. Trees fluttered in the dusk-sough

like winged, palaeolithic moths eddying towards
the closing eye of the sun. I asked someone, 'Do you know

where the Bandra Medical Store is?' The directions
he gave me were motionless gestures scrawled on

a darkening fresco. I stepped forward, intentionally
trampled a crisp leaf, which then made the only

intelligible comment of the evening. But I took care
not to squash a warrior-ant that scuttled before me.

He was so dignified, so black. Had I been smaller, I'd have
ridden him back home, or off into the sunset.

I sent this and four other poems to Alan Ross, and he wrote back to me in two weeks, a note with a few scribbled comments on the poems, saying he would keep it and another one for publication. The poems would appear in the *London Magazine* during my first term in Oxford, in October 1987. But the lane itself was changing; the cottages were being torn down; six- or seven-storeyed buildings, like the one we lived in, were coming up in their place.

At around this time, when I was writing these poems, I also began to write a novel. I went to one of the small Gujarati-run shops on Turner Road and bought a lined notebook, such as shopkeepers and accountants use; its hardboard cover bore the legend *Jagruti Register*. I wrote a few lines every day; and, on certain days, I wrote nothing at all. I wrote without anxiety, and tried to allow the petit-bourgeois life of my uncle's family in Calcutta into the excitement of the written word. I tried to solve, as I wrote, the paradox of why this life, so different from the world I'd grown up in on Malabar Hill and in Cuffe Parade, had been a joy to me; the same paradox that made the location of my father's post-retirement life a joy.

Film stars came to see the flat (who but film stars, businessmen and companies can afford Bombay real-estate prices?). I was told that Naseeruddin Shah was looking to move from his two-bedroom flat to a three-bedroom one; and, one morning, I saw him in our sitting room with his mother-in-law Dina Pathak, who, right away, seemed to know her own mind, and his. I struggled not to look too hard at him, because he had recently won a prize at an international festival. He was shy, if stocky and muscular after his workouts for *Jalwa*, and sent a momentary smile in my direction. Then he went about peeping into our rooms.

A property takes time to sell in Bombay, for the same reason it takes time to buy one. And so the final transaction – and my parents' departure to Calcutta, and the flat itself – remained in abeyance. 'White' money was scarce; my father wanted payment in 'white'. Helen came to see the flat; Helen, who had danced for us so many times, settled into matrimony and middle age, wearing a salwar kameez. She was an utterly charming woman; she had deliberately exchanged her sensual aura for an air of ordinariness; and yet she had a style of interaction that was seductive in its openness and warmth. She loved the flat and the lane; she had the thrilled air of a convert that I'd had when I first moved here. 'I *must* have the flat, Mr Chaudhuri,' she said to my father irresistibly, and I could almost visualise her living in it.

By the time I returned home from Oxford in the summer of 1988, I had a first draft. An extract – chapter seven in the finished book – had appeared in a national periodical; publishers had written to me, enquiring after the novel. As potential buyers wandered through the flat, I found, going through the pages of the notebook, that, to my alarm, I would have to excise the first two or three chapters, for which, now, there seemed no need, and rewrite the beginning and several other chapters. As I began to cut out and jettison what I had once thought were necessary links and co-ordinates, I noticed a form taking shape, a form that absorbed and pleased me. And then I fell ill, probably with the strain: my condition was diagnosed as hepatitis. I couldn't fathom how I had got it; I never drank anything but boiled water.

Nine days in the Special Wing of Nanavati Hospital, on the drip; then back to the flat in St Cyril Road. I missed Michaelmas term in the new academic year in Oxford. 'Oh, hepatitis!' said the hushed voice of the accommodation officer at Holywell Manor, wondering if she might catch it from a long-distance call. 'Yes, *do* take your time.'

That Christmas, as in my poem, the young men came to the lane, guitar in hand, singing carols. I had finished revising the novel, after a horrible, protracted period, and then typed it on my father's Olympia typewriter. The typescript, after my excisions, came to eighty-seven pages. I sent this to the agent who'd been in touch with me after the publication of the extract. At first, she was worried by the size of the manuscript; later, she said she'd send it to William Heinemann. Recovered from hepatitis, back to health and normalcy and the routine disappointments they bring, I returned to England in January 1989, after it had lately snowed around London. I got a phone call which informed me that William Heinemann were 'excited' about the manuscript. I was still to become familiar with the language publishers use.

The flat was sold – not to Helen, but to a Punjabi businessman called Chandok. He could pay the entire amount in 'white'. Eight years ago, when I went to Bombay, I walked into the building on St Cyril Road and saw that Chandok's name was still there on the nameplate. I have no idea what this small investigation was meant to confirm.

My agent, after a considerable silence, called me one evening to say, 'Amit, I have two pieces of bad news for you. The first is that Heinemann have turned down your book.'

'What's the other one?' I asked.

'I've stopped being an agent.' She was getting married.

I then went to another agent, Imogen Parker, who, too, had expressed enthusiasm for my work. She was one of the most determined and plain-speaking and intelligent people I met in the business; like Helen, she was a survivor, and had an odd, sparkling beauty. 'Don't worry,' she told me (she would herself marry and leave the agency in a couple of years), 'your book will be published.'

Amit Chaudhuri (*b.* 1962) is Professor of Contemporary Literature at UEA. His novels include *Afternoon Raag* (1993) and *Freedom Song* (1998). Among the prizes he has won are the Commonwealth Writers Prize, the Betty Trask Award, the Encore Prize, and the *Los Angeles Times* Book Prize. He is a Fellow of the Royal Society of Literature. He has also published a number of books of literary criticism and is an acclaimed practitioner of Indo-Western experimental music. His most recent novel is *The Immortals* (2009).

Choosing English

Patricia Duncker

When I was at secondary school in Jamaica fifty years ago I was taught Creative Writing in English by a teacher called Mrs Davies. We didn't actually describe this activity as creative writing. We were not encouraged to be creative. Creativity was subversive and intellectually suspect. People who were creative were either sodomites or had affairs with other men's wives. So we weren't creative. In any case, we were all girls. Poetry counted more than prose, so we left out prose, and only men wrote poetry. This contradictory problem was never addressed. We called our poetry sessions English Composition and were told that anything we wrote or better still copied out into our exercise books had to be properly spelt, punctuated with elegance, and grammatically correct. For English Composition we were required to compose a poem in a recognised form or learn one by a Great English Author, then stand up in class beside our desks and speak the lines aloud. Mrs Davies had read everything already and knew it all by heart. Therefore, if we were not word-perfect, she noticed. If any one dared to write a poem of her own, she would be wise to rhyme. If Mrs Davies didn't like what you were reciting, whether copied or original, after about the first line, she pulled no punches whatsoever. She simply shouted 'Next!' And you were rarely allowed to complete a poem without interruption.

'Straighten your back. Breathe. Louder, girl. Head up! Don't mutter. None of us can hear you. Next!'

A wave of nationalist poetry, celebrating all things Jamaican, swept the island. Mrs Davies didn't think much of this phenomenon. One such unfortunate poem, written by Hugh Doston Carberry, known as Dossie, became quite popular and sticks in my memory. The title, 'Nature', led the unsuspecting to think that it might compete with Wordsworth, and this is how it begins.

> We have neither summer nor winter,
> Neither autumn nor spring.
> We have instead the days
> When the gold sun
> Shines on the lush green canefields –
> Magnificently.
>
> The days when the rain beats like bullets on the roofs
> And there is no sound but the swish of water in the gullies
> And trees struggling in the high Jamaica winds.

One member of my class, which was thirty-five strong, no one daring to whisper or fidget, stood up to recite H. D. Carberry's effusion, and took a false turning.

'We have instead the days / When the lush green canefields…'

'Shine on the gold sun, I suppose!' yelled Mrs Davies contemptuously, 'Next!'

The next girl began, 'The moon like a yellow banana on a blue enamel plate…'

She got no further. 'Next!' shouted Mrs Davies. I can still hear her, shouting 'Next!'

Mrs Davies used to teach English Literature in exactly the same way – we learned massive chunks of poetry by heart, stood up in class and recited line after line after line. I scored quite a coup with 'I wandered lonely as a cloud', simply because I was word-perfect and the poem was gratifyingly short.

'Very good, girl. Now describe a daffodil in your own words.' Mrs Davies knew all our names, but never used them unless she intended to pounce. There was a momentary diversion. 'Leslie Lewis, take that gum out of your mouth! Spit it out now! Into your handkerchief. At once! Go on girl, go on. Daffodils. What are you waiting for?'

None of us had ever seen a daffodil, because we were children of the tropics. Great English Authors didn't write poems about bougainvillaea or hibiscus. So when Wordsworth described daffodils we all just looked blank. And I had no words other than his to praise the miraculous dancing host. I stood there, hesitating, my recent triumph fading away. Mrs Davies went home and came back with a calendar called *Flowers of Britain*. She turned to March, held it up for us and said, 'This is a daffodil.' We all looked at it, and I remember Leslie Lewis whispering to me, 'Oh, it isn't golden, it's yellow.' And there was only one daffodil, its great powdered trumpet leering towards us.

The thing that now strikes me about the daffodil incident is this. If you have never seen the earth die, if you have never seen it go grey, brown, blue, all colour disappearing into a mound of damp mulch, if you have never smelt frost on dead leaves, then you have no idea what daffodils mean, for they are the first real sign of spring. They are the first sign of colour that comes back. But for us the resonance of the seasons had no meaning. We saw a single yellow daffodil. And we had, indeed, never seen either summer or winter, neither autumn nor spring. Those northern time-markers were empty words.

I was the only white-skinned child in that class. Some of the other teachers were white, but not Mrs Davies. She was a middle-class Jamaican, educated in Jamaica, who had never, I believe, visited 'the mother country', any more than I ever had. I can remember everything Mrs Davies taught me. Contrary to all appearances and conventional expectations, she was a very effective teacher. I can still see her straight back, powerful brown arms, thickly powdered face and flowered dresses, the dark purple of her lipstick and the matching varnish on her nails and toes. She never sweated or looked hot. She carried a shiny black handbag. We dreamed that she marched the concrete walkways of our school, dangerous, armed. Her powerful perfume eddied through the still air when she turned to write on the blackboard. Studying Great White Male English Authors in the tropics had a very peculiar effect on my brain.

Mrs Davies told us that we must always do our best and write well in English, because the greatest writing in the world is written in English. Here is the gist of what she told me during the years I sat in her class, concentrating, anxious. Many other languages have been poured into English: Greek, Latin, French, Anglo-Saxon, Norse, and all those Celtic languages. English is a magpie language; she has stolen and absorbed all other tongues. She has grown rich and fat through appropriation and theft. It's a very supple language, because it will reach out towards Caribbean languages and embrace unintelligible dialects. Dig and you will find English words hidden there. English has archaeological levels of history and time left buried in the language, like a fossil record. These levels are astonishingly beautiful, subtle and multi-coloured. English is one of the richest languages in the whole world. English has a vocabulary like Ali Baba's cave. This is because of the Empire. The English have left their language lurking in Africa and Asia, India, Australia and the Americas. But English has taken as much as she has given, absorbed other words, – jodhpurs, tiffin, camouflage, déjà vu, – into her capacious skirts. She has a hierarchy of registers, formal English, biblical English, judicial English, casual English, in which you can greet your neighbours and chat. You must never use obscene English. Young ladies do not swear. But you must understand it when Shakespeare does. You must choose English. And you must respect your language. You will never be disappointed when you dig down into that language. You will be astonished at what you will find.

Mrs Davies taught me to love the way this language can produce gorgeousness, without necessarily producing meaning. The grandeur of English, she explained, lies in its capacity for excess. You must never be excessive, but English can be. Shakespeare is, of course, the master of excess. The greatest English writer is Shakespeare. I believed her. Here, once again, are the daffodils, from *The Winter's Tale*, where Perdita praises the flowers of spring,

Daffodils,
That come before the swallow dares, and take
The winds of March with beauty.

I remember reciting that speech and memorising a great parade of flowers that I could not imagine and had never seen. Thus Shakespeare became a sacred text, flooded with secret meanings. The other passage, which I recited, standing to attention in that cool classroom haunted by sea winds, is from *Timon of Athens*, when he says,

Come not to me again; but say to Athens
Timon hath made his everlasting mansion
Upon the beachèd verge of the salt flood,
Who once a day with his embossed froth
The turbulent surge shall cover.

This is Timon's epitaph, spoken with great authority and dignity. He is transformed into a mollusc, and in the house of many mansions he has chosen the seashore, where he will spend eternity. I was born on an island; I heard the sea throughout my childhood; I smelled its presence. I knew where to find Timon, for I, too, had walked the beachèd verge of the salt flood.

Shakespeare is never on a man's list of the writers who have influenced him. He was, however, on Iris Murdoch's list as the 'patron saint of novelists', and for me he remains a big, big love, possibly because he is so intensely imagined by other writers, re-written, re-interpreted. Virginia Woolf said, 'This is not "writing" at all. Indeed, I could say that Shakespeare surpasses literature altogether, if I knew what I meant.' I know what she means. He's like a glossary with which we can interpret everything else. The poetry of the plays hollows out an empty space for other writers to occupy. There is an emptiness at the core of Shakespeare's work, where the author is not. That space is taken up by the Renaissance tradition of arguing both sides of the case with equal conviction. Shakespeare unites the two things I value enormously in writing: poetry and plot. He gives us the big scenes. His plays are like grand operas with the poetry as the music. And he always gives us the huge, dramatic confrontations – I am thinking of the temptation scene in *Measure for Measure*, where Lord Angelo confronts the novice nun Isabella, and indeed himself, for the first time. 'What's this, what's this?…What dost thou, or what art thou, Angelo? Dost thou desire her foully for those things / That make her good?' Big scenes don't come better than that one.

Which plays haunt me most insistently? Sometimes I brood about individual characters. I am very attached to his villains – Iago and Edmund, in particular, for their intelligence, ingenuity and inventiveness. Shakespeare's villains are usually in charge of the plot, and as a writer to whom the plot, any plot, whatever the plot, remains crucial, these characters represent a rich field of admiration and inquiry. Villainy in Shakespeare's plays is always excessive. But sometimes there are plays without real villains; especially modern in its cynicism and daring is *Troilus and Cressida*. The character that beguiles me most in that play is the dog-fox, Ulysses, for his sceptical reason. But Troilus, the ardent and passionate lover, is his opposite, and in the debate concerning Helen – should they keep her or give the mad bitch back and save their young men's lives? – Troilus declares 'What's aught, but as 'tis valued?' Indeed! All writers reveal what they value – in their languages, silences, praise-songs, class structures, their choice of work, for their characters and for themselves. I listen hard to other writers, to their fictions, their poetry, their secrets. What do you value? What do you really desire: wealth, fame, the eyes of the world, or this man's art and that man's scope? Those are the usual things. Shakespeare, however, keeps his cards close to his chest. I don't know what he valued.

Even his sexuality proved a bit of a mystery. Bring on the sonnets for bi-sexual rage, especially 'Th' expense of spirit in a waste of shame / Is lust in action…' Give me *King Lear* for the savagery of the politics imagined therein: 'So distribution should undo excess,

/ And each man have enough.' *The Tempest* for intellectual cussedness, *As You Like It* and *A Midsummer Night's Dream* for the laughs and for making the upper classes look pompous, ignorant and silly.

I once gave a rare interview where my questioner had done her research and read my books, all of them, carefully. She pointed out, taking me by surprise:

'You have written: "As a woman writer I am in the business of luring the Furies back out of their hutch and into the field." What did you mean?'

To answer this question I have to address the issues that never were raised, defended or disputed in Mrs Davies's classroom, but simply assumed. Prose does not count and women cannot write. I would never have dared to argue with Mrs Davies then, and in some ways I don't wish to quarrel now. She gave me daffodils and Shakespeare. But I would have loved to learn by heart the poetry I have learned since, the poetry written by women: Elizabeth Barrett Browning's *Sonnets from the Portuguese*; Emily Brontë's 'No coward soul is mine'; Christina Rossetti's 'Goblin Market', and anything, anything at all, by Emily Dickinson. I possessed no knowledge of that long-submerged stream of women's writing, which raged, invisible, beside and beneath the wonders of Palgrave's *Golden Treasury*, and the various poetry anthologies ransacked by Mrs Davies. And I would have liked to get started somewhat earlier on the great novelists, women and men, banned from our narrow colonial curriculum.

And yet, and yet. I may have been cheated of other women's writing when I was a child, but I was not silenced. Mrs Davies gave us to understand that women do not write and then taught us how to do so. She celebrated complex literary English. But it was up to us what we did with it. She abhorred facile, clichéd, easy writing. I cannot imagine her ever reading a romantic novel. But I can easily see her reading Oscar Wilde and Swinburne. We would never be able to write as well as Shakespeare, but then nor would anybody else, whatever sex they were. She taught me to love poetry and to speak out in public. No audience would ever be as fearsome as Mrs Davies. She expected, and demanded, perfection. But never, for the rest of my life, will I ever accept the pernicious gospel that was fed to me by every institution I encountered, that women are necessarily second-class, second-rate, second-best, just because we are women.

Be good sweet maid and let who will be clever. Women are still often the recipients of these insidious double messages. I was praised for being clever, then, obscurely, punished for refusing to think or act as women are supposed to do. It takes time, courage and the solidarity of other women to acquire the virtues of insolence, which cannot, in my opinion, be overestimated. A woman who says no and means no, as our mythic ancestor Lilith once did, leaves chaos in her wake. In my early world, order and injustice held hands. The creation of chaos (and this lies within the grasp of every angry woman who desires to act) blooms like a subversive blessing.

What do I value? The freedom I have to think for myself.

Who were the Furies? They are the instruments of women's vengeance. The Furies, who appear to Orestes in Aeschylus' *Oresteia*, are avenging the death of a woman, the woman he murdered, his mother Clytemnestra, who murdered her husband Agamemnon, to avenge the murder of her daughter Iphigenia. This chain of familial deaths in the House of Atreus appears endless. The Furies are the manifestation of a woman's anger. Anger is the least acceptable emotion in a woman and the one that is most necessary. Women are supposed to be very calm, docile, peacemakers, life-givers. We are supposed to be charming, conciliating, helpful, kind. Listen to that list. Is that supposed to be a row of virtues? What do we do with the dissenters, the women who resist? How on earth do we read ambitious, difficult writing that regards this list as a recipe for creating super-serviceable slaves? I wanted to make writing that resists. Anger gives you clarity, information, energy and fearlessness. I think it's very healthy to be a savagely angry person.

Anger affects the plots of fictions. Especially the endings. Many readers expect and look for resolutions that involve compromise, reconciliation and forgiveness. Even the *Oresteia*, beautiful and suggestive as it is, ends in a law court with justice handed out to mortals by the gods. The Furies are bought off with a shrine and obligatory honours paid to them by all the people of Athens, including those who might have been toying with the idea of murdering their loved ones.

This is where Shakespeare becomes very interesting. Some things cannot be repaired, healed or made good. And he knows it. There is always a loose end in his plays, a question mark. Sometimes it's a spare character – like Antonio at the end of *The Merchant of Venice*, who can't be married off, because the man he loves is going to marry Portia. Think of Malvolio or Kent or Jacques – the characters who refuse to be part of the happy endings, who gather themselves up, make excuses or stalk off the stage. But sometimes it's an odd final twist to the plot that remains unresolved, unexplained; as in *A Midsummer Night's Dream*, when the fairies invade the palace, chanting their threats and blessings; or the strange and terrible end to *The Tempest*, when Prospero doesn't speak as an actor, but in character, drawing attention to his own exhausted powerlessness. I like uneasy endings. I treasure the loose ends. I think it's a good idea never to be assimilated into the collective happy ending and, like Jacques, to remain unashamedly enraged.

So I choose Shakespeare and I choose English. In many ways it was a literary language I had to learn. So much within its walls and histories seemed mysterious, meaningless. English is the language of diplomats, negotiators and liars. And it's the ideal language for writers, for that's the same thing as being a liar, because you can say one thing and mean forty different, other things. If you are any good as a writer you have made it all up, even the truthful parts, all the bits that really happened. And, above all, the ironies and ambiguities you can produce in English, give the language its edge. And yes, of course, it's a reader's language. When I finally went up to university, nine years after leaving Mrs Davies's classroom, reading a subject simply meant reading books, and the books had to be the best. Poetry still came first. The languages of poetry were more intense, elusive and metaphorical than anything else I read. Poetry appeared closer to philosophy, to a real literature of ideas. But I discovered torrents of prose, as intense and poetic as the modernist writing that seduced me entirely, and at last, Jane Austen, Charlotte Brontë, George Eliot, Charles Dickens, Joseph Conrad, Henry James. I have spent my writing life trying to reconcile those two recalcitrant sisters: poetry and plot.

English will reward you as a reader, but you have to be a very active reader, concentrated, anxious and engaged. Or you will miss something rich and vital. I hear Mrs Davies: 'Wake up, girl. Don't doze off. Next!'

Patricia Duncker (*b.* 1951) is a former Professor of Creative Writing at UEA (2002–6). She is the author of five novels, including *Hallucinating Foucault* (1996), winner of the McKitterick Prize and the Dillons First Fiction Award, and *Miss Webster and Chérif* (2006), which was shortlisted for the Commonwealth Writers Prize. She is currently Professor of Contemporary Literature at the University of Manchester. Her critical work includes a collection of essays on writing, theory and contemporary literature, *Writing on the Wall* (2002). Her most recent novel is *The Strange Case of the Composer and his Judge* (2010).

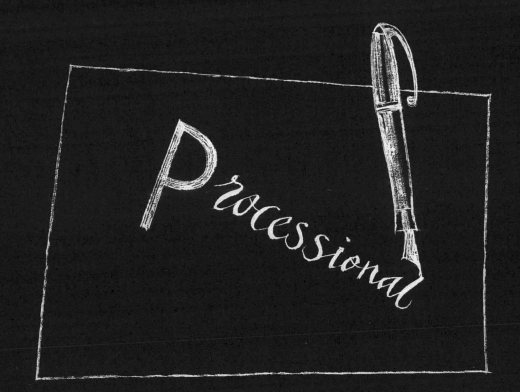

Processional

1970

Ian McEwan

I graduated from the University of Sussex in the summer of 1970. At that time in England it was still possible to feel, if not to argue, that the chief concern of serious literature was moral and that its riveting complexities, especially in novels, were mediated by choice. What imaginary people chose to do or failed to do marked their destiny and settled their hash, with the author handing various ethical rosettes out along the way.

At the age of twenty-two I considered myself to be five years into a scholarly apprenticeship that had come adrift, and I was feeling restless. I had had an intense sixth form at a boarding grammar school – I'm one of those writers who feels his conscious adult life began under the magic spell of his English master – and had continued more vaguely and eclectically at university. Now all that was over and I had a degree, and I was beginning to understand that unlike Oedipus or Coriolanus or Lord Jim, I myself had never really chosen anything at all. I hadn't even made an interesting mistake. I was convinced that my life had not yet begun. Writing, 'being' a writer, that was still a vague and intensely private ambition – the usual idle dreams. I had a clearer notion that the last thing I wanted was regular employment, and that it would therefore be a good idea to remain a student. I wanted to be in a town where no one knew me and I could start again.

I had been accepted at a couple of universities to do a PhD, but the relevant government department mercifully refused to fund me and offered instead a year's grant to study for an MA anywhere I wanted. I liked the 'anywhere' more than the 'study'. If literature was a stately conversation conducted down the generations, then I was bored with merely listening. I wanted to join in. But like many young would-be writers I had no urgent subject matter.

I'd made a few stabs at greatness during my final undergraduate year. I proudly kept a notebook. I'd written a long Yeatsian poem about circus animals, though whether they deserted or revolted, I don't recall. I had composed one of the worst radio plays ever written, about a saint who is so good he stinks, and everyone who comes across him, what with the world being so corrupt, is compelled to vomit. There were two other plays, equally useless, and I had also started a novella called *The Man Who Hated Pain*.

The summer began and I had still not made an application for an MA. I went to the Aldeburgh Festival on a scholarship, worked in an ice-cream warehouse in Brighton, and spent the remaining weeks of the summer in Italy with my girlfriend. By the time I came back in September all my friends were fixed up with jobs or further study. It was time to make a choice. I went to stay at my parents' house on an army base near Middle Wallop and tried to think myself into a job. Teaching? I couldn't face it. Advertising was supposed to be a creative world, but I had absorbed a little of Arnold and a lot of Leavis and I loathed adverts with a high-minded passion. The Diplomatic Service? The support of the Wilson government for US policy in Vietnam had more or less finished off that possibility for me, though I still had fantasies of myself in a dishdasha, fluent in Arabic and desert lore, a gentleman scholar and man of the world.

I had brought with me a dozen university prospectuses and I thumbed them sceptically, fully aware that a course description is a literary sub-genre, enlivened by unfalsifiable half-truths and unredeemable promises – advertising. For all that, I was struck by the offer of full immersion, in Norwich, at the University of East Anglia, in post-war American and British fiction, with some literary theory on the side, a dose of comparative European nineteenth-century literature, and the option of handing in at the end of the year 25,000 words of fiction in place of an academic mini-thesis.

Norwich sounded just like that 'anywhere'. American novels suited me, and there was the extraordinary offer of the fiction, so out of place in a university prospectus. I knew and liked the work of Malcolm Bradbury and Angus Wilson, who would be overseeing the MA. In a single, unprominent and understated paragraph my discontents and longings were addressed. A dream life was on offer. I made the first important conscious choice of my adult life and picked up the phone.

Within a minute I was talking to Professor Bradbury himself (the world was emptier and easier then). I explained that I'd read about the MA with the fiction component. He explained that no one had applied, that in this, its first year, the fiction side of the course had been closed down. It had never got off the ground.

I suggested that my phone call was a sort of application and he suggested that I send him my fiction. In the same breath he invited me up for a chat. For the next two weeks I sat in the spare bedroom of my parents' house and while my sunburn flaked wrote two short stories. I remember nothing of them beyond my assumption that single-spaced typing looked more serious. And I don't remember much about the chat either. Essentially, I was in.

Norwich was further away in those days. The train took forever, there was no motorway, the car-owning revolution was years ahead. The city I moved to in October 1970 appeared peaceful, clean and gratifyingly obscure. I arrived with my ambitions focused: I would do the academic work, for it accounted for four-fifths of the course, but I was here to write fiction. I knew no one in the city, I had made my choice, and real life could begin.

And it did. The year I spent in Norwich was the luckiest and one of the most productive in my life. My Sixties began. I made important, enduring friendships, and some tortuous, transient ones. I discovered the north Norfolk coast. I took mescalin. In a rented room on the Newmarket Road, and later, in a terraced house on Silver Road, I wrote thirty stories between October and June.

In the first few weeks of that autumn term I moved around like a character in my own unwritten novel, not Lord Jim exactly, but my own man at last, in control of a narrative that murmured incessantly in my inner ear. *He moved to a forgotten town and took a room in a big house. That night he put fifty sheets of paper on the table, took up a pencil and promised he would not leave until he had finished a short story.*

In fact I worked into the dawn, so excited by the romance and heroism of it all that at intervals I could not write at all. *He paced the narrow room, biting on his knuckle.* The following day I typed up the completed story – it was called 'Conversation with a Cupboardman' – and delivered a carbon copy of it to Malcolm Bradbury's office.

A week later we met up in the Maid's Head for a very quick half-pint. He did not inquire whether I was mentally ill or out to shock him, and I took his equanimity entirely for granted. His few remarks were technical, and vaguely encouraging. He was mostly interested in getting me to describe what I was trying to do. I didn't really know. The story seemed to have written itself.

'I like it,' he said at last, unemphatically. 'It might be publishable. But let's not think about that now. What are you going to write next?'

'I want to spend the year writing short stories.'

'Fine.'

'I thought I might try out a number of deranged first-person narrators.'

'Why not?'

'One's about a vile boy so anxious to lose his virginity he makes love to his younger sister.'

'Let me have it by the end of the month.'

So a pattern was set. I met Malcolm occasionally in his office, or in the corridor and once or twice in the Maid's Head. Our meetings never lasted more than fifteen minutes. He was much in demand, and sometimes elusive. Informality, muted judgement and a complete lack of interference were the principal elements of his pedagogic style. Behind it all was an unspoken but intensely radiated assumption that there was nothing quite so exciting or essential as the writing of fiction. To be the 'product' of his writing 'course' was to be the beneficiary of an absolute artistic licence and minimal guidance. It was a given that there was no subject that could not be written about. I don't think I understood the extent of my privileges until five years later, when I published the stories from that time in book form and in the press was cast in the form of a macabre ghoul.

A good deal of my time was taken up with the academic requirements. Denys Lasdun's brutal architectural dream was only a quarter-realised, but UEA was an optimistic, lively place. The seminars were intense and combative. I remember the first one I attended, when Malcolm was in his role as an academic expert in American literature and in the theory of the novel. He was a social creature and the seminar was his element.

He was in his late thirties then, and with his piled-up hair, narrow knitted tie and lopsided grin there was something of the miscreant Teddy boy about him. In a hesitant, lilting voice (so hard to place, that accent) he set out for us the course of study ahead and the various teachers, and then led us into a general discussion about the novel.

It was a brilliant session. Within minutes, it seemed, he had communicated a sense of adventure: the vitality of the novel as a form, its deep seriousness, its variety, the pleasures as well as the instruction in life it conveyed, its rich past and unguessable future. A general discussion began – a more formal version of the partying years ahead of us. Nearly all of the other students had been undergraduates at UEA. The other outsider in the seminar was Jon Cook from Cambridge, who decades later became Dean of Humanities at UEA.

Malcolm was a generous listener who laughed easily at other people's jokes. (Who can forget that delighted, whinnying giggle?) I'm sure he made us feel cleverer than we were. I was keen to impress him. We all were. I paraded my reading of Ortega y Gasset. Jon Cook appeared to be the world expert on Hegel. How tolerant Malcolm must have been. But he knew what he was about. We came away ready to start on the huge reading list he had given us.

We read Bellow, Nabokov, Burroughs, Mailer, Updike, Roth, Gaddis, a reading list whose rubric these days would have to be 'Men's Studies'. For reasons of his own, Malcolm included Borges and Julio Cortázar and they were important discoveries for me. The post-war British novel received less emphasis, but I remember John Fowles's *The Collector* making a big impression on me, as well as several novels of Muriel Spark. I heard words like 'postmodern', 'fictive' and 'faction' for the first time.

I 'compared' *Middlemarch* to *Anna Karenina*, and I handed in essays on theories of representation, but the reading lists made the lasting impression. The ambition, the social range, the expressive freedom of American writing made much English fiction seem poky and grey. To find bold and violent colours became the imperative in my stories. Touches of Roth and Burroughs crept into my writing. The struggle with influence, Malcolm told me once, was part of the pleasure of finding your own way.

There were plenty of other writers and would-be writers around, and a good deal of writing talk. Jonathan Raban had given up his academic career to write, but still returned from London regularly. Victor Sage, who had just been appointed lecturer, was starting to write stories. John Webb, with whom I shared a house, was planning travel pieces. Snoo Wilson and Clive Sinclair had graduated the year before and put in appearances. The immensely gifted Rose Tremain was living in Norwich.

In the spring term came Angus Wilson. That mischievous pink face floating above a linen suit seemed like the living emblem of the strawberries-and-champagne garden parties for which he was celebrated among his students. An opulent glow surrounded him and his friend Tony Garret. They were an incongruous couple on the concrete walkways with their carefree air of being globally well-connected.

They brought a strange light from another world – pre-war, upper middle class, bohemian, dandified, but very serious too. From Angus and Tony I understood what it could mean to perform in, to be classy in, conversation. They collected people with a passion. Angus had a particular penchant for hippy girls. He liked to exclaim loudly and fuss over their bangles and pendants. He and Tony would happily come and sit on the floor of a student flat and perform.

Angus was the reader I had in mind when I wrote a story called 'Disguises', but I'm not certain that he ever said much to me about my stories, except to tick me off once for homophobia (another new word), and to imply that I was to inherit the spirit of nastiness represented by his famous short story 'Strawberry Jam'. I was invited to dinner at their cottage in Suffolk, where Angus did imitations, gossiped and told outrageous stories spiked with comic cruelty. On one occasion, just as I was leaving I overheard him tell another guest that I was a *writer*. For a long time afterwards I lived in the glow of that remark.

When I came back to Norwich after a long absence in Kabul, I slipped into one of his seminars. Without breaking flow, he waved me into a chair. 'Dear boy, we must get you some Arts Council money.' He was Chairman at the time. 'How lean and brown you are. Now, Dickens was already treating the anti-Americanism of his predecessors as something of a racket...'

In the summer Alan Burns became the university's first writer-in-residence. He was a lawyer who had written some critically successful experimental novels that were not widely read. I have the impression that his time in Norwich turned his life around; he gave up the law and became a Creative Writing teacher. He gave me a paradoxical warning: not to be influenced by writers I had not read. He gave me Beckett's early stories, *More Pricks than Kicks*, and also the trilogy. I immediately understood what he meant. I was being 'unconsciously influenced'. I was becoming enslaved to cadences whose origins I did not know. It was a useful note.

This surrounding literary community continues in Norwich to this day: 'a significant climate around writing', as Malcolm described it somewhere. I know very few novelists who have not been to the University of East Anglia to read. It was largely through Malcolm himself – along with Jon Cook and his colleague Christopher Bigsby – that Norwich gained its international reputation as a place where writers and would-be writers alike are treated well. To create, round the business of writing, a community that is essentially friendly is a large achievement.

Such are the tricks of memory that when I think back on those times, the people I knew appear in perpetual good moods, their voices unusually loud, their gestures wildly exaggerated. The city itself was in a good mood. By 1971 the Sixties had spread up across the fens to take the town. There was, of course, an ersatz, second-hand quality to this new atmosphere. Somewhere in my archives is a hand-out inviting the citizenry to attend a 'smoke-in' in Chapelfield Gardens, where, it was earnestly predicted, clouds of cannabis smoke would envelop and confound the 'fascist pigs'.

At the end of the year Malcolm sent one of my stories to *Transatlantic Review* and it was accepted. By then I had written most of the stories that were to make up the volume *First Love, Last Rites*. More than any lesson – or the benefit of a 'course' – had been the simple fact of having been taken seriously. During the Seventies the UEA course established itself. I don't know how I would have got on in the tougher, more paranoid milieu of twelve or fifteen competitive colleagues. I might well have faded out, and this was the extent of my luck in 1970 – to have had it all to myself.

In the late Seventies Angus and Tony used to lend me their remote Suffolk cottage for months on end while they were in the States. As for Malcolm, we met from time to time at the British Council conferences he was chairing. Like Howard Kirk, the academic Machiavel of *The History Man*, Malcolm liked a good party. Just as that novel is structured round social gatherings, so were the literary gatherings over which he presided. A Cambridge college, a German monastery set in a desert of potato fields, a disintegrating Polish palace, were some of the settings for the best intellectual revels of the Eighties and Nineties.

But music, dancing and sex were not conspicuous ingredients. The business was talking and drinking – complementary human pleasures in which Malcolm took serious delight. The last seminar of the day completed, writers far from home with nowhere else to go, a delicious freedom in the air, limitless wine – these were the preconditions for a long journey into the night across unknown territory.

During these colloquia, Malcolm's tentative, judicious style granted a licence to younger writers. He was fair, so we could be savage. As a critic he lacked the killer instinct. He was a celebrator, rather than a destroyer, of reputations. However late it got, he'd be one of the last to get to bed. What he relished was a conversation with a direction, a beat. Gossip was fine too.

Another bottle is opened. A certain writer, so someone says, no longer does interviews. Only press conferences. Publicity hunger versus reclusiveness bring us to Pynchon, until the fatwa against Salman Rushdie in 1989, the world's most hunted writer.

'Inflated, whimsical, a world view stifled by paranoia,' someone says recklessly.

Malcolm hears this out, then defends. 'Only to a certain cast of English mind. To some novelists paranoia is not a disabling mental condition, but the motor of ingenious plot-making.'

By way of Melville, through Kafka, we arrive at an eminent contemporary novelist. The consensus among the young around the table is that her sentences are no good. 'Cliché-rich, unrhythmic, no surprises.'

'Therefore, she is no bloody good at all.'

Malcolm champions her. 'It's true up to a point about the sentences, but there's a certain kind of writing that gives pleasure through its design, its architecture. In the geometry of these moral schemes there's a beauty that no individual sentence can yield.'

Can a good novel be written badly? We've been around this before. *And who are today's best sentence-makers?* Malcolm makes the case for Martin Amis by means of some exquisite examples he has by heart. Two weeks before, Martin has given Malcolm a finely executed pistol-whipping in the *Observer* for his novel *Rates of Exchange*. The critic remains scrupulously detached from the workaday resentments of the novelist.

Just two years before his death at the end of 2000 I had an encounter with Malcolm that still haunts me. In the dazed hour immediately after winning the 1998 Booker Prize I was surrounded by excited voices and pulled from press conference to interviews, and from crowded rooms to answer questions in television trucks and radio cars. At some point I lost the Booker publicity people, or they lost me, and I stepped through a door by mistake into an empty hall. I went through another door, and found myself in a long, straight, ill-lit corridor.

Coming towards me, from some distance away, were Malcolm and his wife Elizabeth. We approached each other as in dream, and I remember thinking, half-seriously, that this was what it might be like to be dead. In the warmth of his congratulatory embrace was concentrated all the generosity of this gifted teacher and writer. His artful reticence and his passion for literature transformed my life.

Ian McEwan (*b.* 1948) received an MA in Literature at UEA in 1971. His first published work was a collection of short stories, *First Love, Last Rites* (1975), which won the Somerset Maugham Award in 1976. Since then he has published many novels including *Enduring Love* (1997), *Amsterdam* (1998), which won the Man Booker Prize, and *Atonement* (2001). His most recent novel is *Solar* (2010).

This is the Gig

Anne Enright

For a long time, when asked about Creative Writing courses, I said that no one taught me anything at UEA. This, strictly speaking, was true. I could neither spell nor punctuate when I left, had vague ideas about how a paragraph might be constructed, and I used words like 'denouement' with the greatest contempt. At least I had heard them, I suppose. But though I had not been taught anything, I did learn a lot: this is a nice distinction but a crucial one. Writing is learned from the inside out. It is not a subject like geography that can be doled out in parcels of information. Writing is a discipline and, as with any discipline, whether spiritual or physical, the doing is everything. No one can do it for you.

The job of the teacher in these hazy, dangerous circumstances is to feed the student and to keep her safe. Angela Carter did the first, with a scattering of photocopies, musings and anecdotes (she never mentioned my work, I think), and Malcolm Bradbury did the second, by smiling a lot, and liking books, and keeping quiet (I don't think he ever mentioned my work either – I might be wrong). The other students did mention my work; they had various opinions about it, but that was fine, because Malcolm was there to like us all, and keep us safe.

Both my teachers died when I was a baby writer. I didn't miss Angela much when she went, even though it was her work that had called me to UEA in the first place. I miss her now, though – quite keenly. It came to me recently, how the world would be so much better if she were still here.

I was with a good bunch in East Anglia, but they couldn't make the place less flat. Being an artist, I had no money and, being an exile, I had severed all my connections to home. I suffered slightly from an idea of the Irish that was prevalent in Middle England in the 1980s, not that I was dirty-lazy-drunk-and-stupid (chance would be a fine thing), but that I could write, because that's what Irish people did. I myself was of the contrary opinion. I did not write like any other Irish person I had read. Also, in fact, I didn't think I could write at all.

Of course, in the grand scheme of things, I was a wonderful writer. I was destined and marvellous. These things were very clear, they just were not clear on the page. In fact, to be honest, there wasn't very much on the page – if by 'page' you mean that white sheet of paper with words on it, or not. I had scraps and fragments, little rushes of stuff that might actually be OK. There were phrases and headlines in different-coloured marker stuck to the walls. I had intimations of the most fabulous book, with very few intimations of what it might contain. The only idea I had was this large idea of myself as a writer. I was like a balloon – the bigger my ambition, the less there was inside. And balloons (to overstretch the metaphor) are liable to burst.

This is how the day went at UEA. I would get up sometime after midday and meet the other students in the refectory. Louise Doughty was in my year, and Mark Illis, Fadia Faqir and others who have published since. It was a friendly group. We were chatty and supportive of each other when we met for lunch. This was always, for me, a ham and coleslaw roll. The others would have been up since eight, and some of them took a proper meal. They had all, without exception, written 500 words before noon. Some had written more. After lunch they might suggest a walk (I think I went, once) or plan an event at the weekend. Sometimes these events would be exciting: too much red wine at Malcolm and Elizabeth's; a couple of agents down from London; Anthony Thwaite in a green velvet smoking jacket; some literary women who looked terribly, terribly middle-aged. Sometimes they would be dull: two halves of lager and a game of pool in the student union, then home to bed, because there were 500 words to be done, early the next day.

All years are different: some are wild and wrongheaded and disastrous and wonderful, and some are not. For me, all the drama of that year happened in my head.

I never worked in the morning. I started at 4 p.m. and went through to 4 a.m. Or I might go from after dinner until dawn. I didn't see a lot of daylight. Every time I counted my words the number had shrunk (this remains true of my work). I sat at the desk all night and lost words. I got up the next day and met people who ate properly and went home for weekends and made it, one chapter at a time, through the book they had somehow decided to write.

By springtime I was working on a novel that took place simultaneously in three different centuries. It was also written in three different styles – you might even say three different languages, all of them versions of English. I have never been psychotic (I know, how can I tell?), but I have had a glimpse of it: sitting in a breeze block student room, reading Lacan and ignoring the walls, with their messages, all written in different-coloured pen.

When I fell apart, over the Easter break, I was set back to rights with great kindness by some of my fellows, who could mend me a little, but not mend my book – because writing is learned from the inside, and there's no one who can do it for you, much as they might want to help.

The book went in the bin (a few box files sitting on my bottom shelf) and I went home and started to write for real. I learned all the hard things at UEA – difficulty, incapacity, failure, humility, the importance of working more on the page than in your head. Now when I hear of people taking a year off to write, I worry that a year might not be enough. You must fail as a writer for much longer than that, I think, before you know what failure is and what use you might make of it. I didn't realise, when that first book fell apart, that every book falls apart. That this is the gig. You sit there and watch your word-count drop, and you hold your nerve. I have survived this process now many times. But the first time was the worst, and I was lucky to be among friends.

Anne Enright (*b.* 1962) received her MA in Creative Writing from UEA in 1987. Her novel, *The Gathering*, won the 2007 Man Booker Prize, and her most recent novel is *The Forgotten Waltz* (2011).

A Traumatic Process

Louise Doughty

I don't remember the writing. That is the scary part. I know that during the year I spent at UEA, from September 1986–7, I wrote reams and reams of the most appalling drivel, all produced with the utmost seriousness of purpose. But I don't remember doing it and can't recall what it was about: a love affair, I think, misunderstandings, the north-south divide…

What I remember is the drinking. I remember that myself and the other writing students often went to drink beer and play pool in the graduate students' bar, where I discovered I was a hopeless tactician but had an eye for a pot. Sometimes, during these games, our talk would fall to writing. The conversation would go something like, 'I can't work out whether to keep the eighteenth-century narrative or stick to the contemporary one – was that a red or a yellow just went down?' These games were highly competitive. We argued about whether the white had just clipped the black, or the usefulness of extended metaphor. We got quite shirty. Towards the end of the evening one of us would put 'Time After Time' by Cindy Lauper on the jukebox to remind us that we liked each other.

The writing fellow at UEA at that time was the poet Paul Muldoon. He didn't teach us – our tutors were Malcolm Bradbury and Angela Carter – but we hung out with him socially, and occasionally he would join us in the bar. One such evening turned famous. Myself and another student, a young Irish woman called Anne Enright (now whatever happened to her?) ended up going back to Paul's small house in a terraced row on campus. He poured us wine and we talked about our novels. Not only did he listen to our ramblings with great patience but, every now and then, he disappeared into the kitchen and reappeared with small snacks on plates, like a bartender. We left at 8.30 a.m. the next morning, having spent all night at his dining table explaining the problems we were having with narrative drive. As we hollered, 'Tha-anks, bye-ee!!' from his front steps, the net curtains all along the terraced row twitched.

On another occasion, at a party in someone's house, Anne and I ended up each with one elbow planted on a wall, while Malcolm stood between us, sucking ferociously on his pipe and telling us what he really thought of us. Us, that is, not our writing. 'You…,' he said, pointing the end of his pipe in my direction, 'I often come to you first when we are discussing someone else's work, because you always begin with, *what I really liked about this was*…Once you have said it, no one else needs to and we can get on with the criticism. Now *Anne*…' Anne was famously blunt, but brilliantly, incisively so. The obvious star of the course, she was also its best critic.

Malcolm went on to observe that we often thought similar things of other students' work but put it in very different ways, and that both ways were essential to the group dynamic. We were thus anointed good-cop and bad-cop – although Anne was never a really bad cop, not a throw-you-against-the-wall bad cop. It just felt that way when she was being absolutely right about your work.

There were workshops and seminars as well as the parties, but many of the useful things I learned at UEA came outside them. I learned about the camaraderie of writers, and how important it is in the psychological battle against the strange and isolating task of writing novels for a living. I learned to shut up and listen when people were critiquing my work, even though I thought they were talking bollocks, and how to listen with my intellect rather than my ego. I learned that emotional stamina was essential. All this seems obvious, in retrospect, but it wasn't obvious at the time, a fact attributable partly to my youth and partly to the state I was in before I arrived in Norwich.

I had graduated from Leeds University two years previously, at the age of twenty, with a degree in English Literature, a huge overdraft and an ambition to be a writer that far outweighed my immature abilities. I had absolutely no idea how to write a book, so I signed on the dole and trotted to the university library at 9 a.m. each morning, where I found a desk in a deserted basement area, through which no one but the occasional cleaner ever passed. I sat down with a biro and a pad of lined, A4 paper and began my first novel. It was called, variously, *My Buried Life*, *Simon's Morning* and *The Burial* and was about a library clerk and his battle with loneliness. The grand denouement consisted of the clerk – whose name was Simon – buying a goldfish. Simon hopes for friendship, but the goldfish does not reciprocate. It dies. Simon commits suicide.

I remember thinking, quite seriously, that it would take me around three months to write and that it would be published soon thereafter. I also thought it was a masterpiece. To my mind, no one had yet written a serious fictional investigation of the issues of loneliness, alienation and suicide. Well, maybe Kafka, Beckett and B. S. Johnson had taken stabs at it, but I was going to show them how it was really done.

After a year, the dole people caught up with me, predictably and justifiably enough. This was the mid-Eighties. I was put on something called the Community Programme, a grown-up version of the infamous Youth Opportunities scheme. The Community Programme had been created so that the 'long-term unemployed', a category I now fell into, could be taken out of the statistics by being 'employed' in a variety of low-paid, part-time jobs for which the state would pay, regardless of whether or not the individual concerned was qualified for or interested in whatever post they were given. If you refused, your benefit could be withdrawn. In return for receiving slightly more than my dole money, I agreed to become a schools liaison worker for a local branch of what was then called The Spastics Society. My job was to visit nearby schools and give talks in assemblies to improve disability awareness, and spend one day a week helping out at a school for children with severe handicaps, a stupidly important task for someone who was given no training whatsoever.

In the meantime, I tried to keep my writing going, although it was going very badly. Briefly, I attended an evening class at the local Workers' Education Association institute. The tutor was unpublished and read from her own work each week, so we could comment. My fellow students were all retirement age and all women, but for one small, unsmiling man who dominated proceedings with his opinions. When it came to my turn, I read out loud from *The Burial*. A deathly hush followed. The tutor was silent. The wall clock ticked. Eventually, the small, unsmiling man leaned forward over his desk to peer at me, my student earrings and Oxfam clothes, and said scathingly, 'Are you one of them there "Ban the Bomb" types?'

It is fair to say that at this point in my writing career I was very close to becoming the sort of person who bothered other people on buses. I had no money, no prospects and my writing was going so badly I wasn't even submitting it anywhere. I had even failed at being unemployed. This is one of the things I remember most clearly about those days: the feeling that somewhere out there, there was a world which real writers inhabited, but from which I – for a variety of reasons – was destined to remain excluded.

Part of this was geography. At that time, everything literary seemed to happen in London, which may have only been 200 miles down the A1, but felt as remote as the moon. It was also political. In the North of England at the height of Thatcherism, everything was political: the Yorkshire Ripper, Loadsamoney, the miners' strike. The north-south divide was very real and there were many thousands of people in Leeds feeling every bit as alienated as I was and with far greater cause.

It was economic, too. 'Why don't you move to London, then?' A friend asked me breezily. Well, for a start, I didn't have the train fare. (When a friend and I wanted to go to a party in Southampton, we hitchhiked, in February, in the snow.) My parents would have lent the fare to me if I had plucked up the courage to ask, but what then? What the hell would I do when I got there? I was too insecure, depressed and timid to go anywhere unless some external factor helped me get there.

That's what I remember about being an aspiring writer: the isolation, the feeling of remoteness, the lack of options. The other is the constant, grinding scorn with which my aspirations were regarded by friends, family and – well, almost anyone you care to mention. During the first winter of this period, I went to Sheffield for a pub gathering to celebrate the birthday of a student friend. Towards the end of the evening, a mutual acquaintance called John, who was doing teacher training, asked me what I was up to now. I made the mistake of telling him, and have never forgotten his supercilious sneer.

'God!' he exclaimed, grinning with genuine mirth. 'You must have a really big head to think *you* can write a novel.'

'I want to be a writer,' I confessed to the nice lady from the dole office, as she processed my Community Programme paperwork. She looked at me sympathetically, over her glasses.

'You know,' she said gently, 'I think one of the benefits of the Community Programme is, it gets people out of the house.'

When I finally applied to do the MA in Creative Writing at UEA it was, by then, as much about desperation as ambition. My application consisted of a section of *The Burial* and a précis, the pretentiousness of which now makes me blush to the roots of my hair. I believe I drew a circle at the top of the page and wrote something like, 'This is the shape of the thing.' Knowing I wouldn't get on to the course (who in their right minds would let *me* on?), I also applied for a place teaching English as a foreign language in a school in Sicily. As far as I was concerned, it was either that or spend the rest of my life on remedial employment schemes. By then, it had sunk in that writing a brilliant first novel and being published was going to take a little longer than three months.

In preparation for running away to Palermo, I began to study Italian, but got no further than *un bicchiere di vino bianco, per favore*, when a letter arrived from UEA. I was so convinced it was my rejection that it went unopened for two days. When I finally slit the envelope, the letter and my jaw dropped open in the same instant. I had been accepted without interview.

I still don't know why this happened, although someone at UEA later told me that Angela Carter reviewed applications and liked people who were quirky and could talk about narrative structure. Maybe the circle did the trick. It seemed such a bizarre and unlikely outcome that I arrived in Norwich the following autumn convinced there had been some sort of administrative error and that on the first day I would be approached by a stern man with a clipboard, who would tell me they had meant to offer the place to a Louis Doherty and could I please exit by the back door as soon as possible.

I didn't know it at the time, but I was lucky not only in the fact of my acceptance but in the timing of it. Malcolm Bradbury and Angela Carter were running the course and the Dean of the school was Lorna Sage, but despite its illustrious staff, in 1986, the course was not nearly as well known as it is now – Creative Writing itself was still in its infancy, and controversial. The most famous graduate was Ian McEwan, but Kazuo Ishiguro was three years away from winning the Booker for *Remains of the Day*, arguably the point at which the MA started to receive the kind of publicity and renown it has now. Malcolm was later kind enough to refer to our year as a vintage year – along with Anne Enright it produced the novelists Mark Illis and Fadia Faqir – but nobody would have guessed that when we all gathered for our first meeting. Malcolm introduced himself and said, 'We will be discussing two writers each week.' I thought by writers he meant Jane Austen or Virginia Woolf. 'You will have to submit your work to the office for photocopying.' Oh, I thought. He means us. He means *me*. It was the first time anyone had ever referred to me as a writer.

Contrary to the reputation he came trailing after *The History Man*, Malcolm proved to be the most gentle, boffinish sort of professor, sincerely interested in encouraging new writers and forgiving of our many failings. His outward kindliness belied a steely intellect, though, and his comments on our work were both astute and articulated with a clarity that cut through our egos like an épée through tissue paper.

Our individual tutorials in the summer term were with Angela Carter. By then, I had already abandoned two novel ideas and was struggling badly with the short stories that would form my MA dissertation. Sessions with Angela were fraught, but the fault was all mine – she was shrewd enough to spot a student in trouble and her advice often consisted of her gazing at me in a benign and enigmatic manner, while I tried – blatheringly – to justify my failures. It was a traumatic process. After one tutorial I emerged in tears and made my way over to the office of one of the administrative staff who had befriended me, a lovely warm lady who made me a coffee and handed me a box of tissues. She surmised, understandably but wrongly, that Angela had been mean to me.

'The thing is, my dear,' she said in hushed tones, 'what you have to ask yourself is, who *is* Angela Carter? That thing about the man who turned into a wolf – well it's not what *I* call literature.'

Eventually, with the help of my fellow students, I realised that if I was serious about this writing malarkey, then I would have to stop crying in the ladies' lavatory after every workshop or tutorial (sometimes during) and settle down to working very, very hard. I cringe at the thought of my prose style then, and cringe at the thought at how devastated I would have been if my friends had been honest with me – but everyone was kind, and subtle, and I gradually worked out what was wrong with my writing myself, which was equally as devastating but in a more productive way.

What would have happened if I hadn't got my place on the course? I don't know. Wanting to be a writer was a miserable, uncertain business and it seemed to go on forever, both before and after UEA. After the course I moved to London and worked in a series of temp jobs before finally managing to establish myself as an arts journalist and publish my first novel in 1995, eight years after graduating from UEA and ten years after I began that first novel about the library clerk.

I would like to say that I would have become a professional writer without UEA, but the truth is, I doubt it. I was too much of what my teenage daughter calls a *sad-weirdo-loser-type* person to do it without a supportive structure. Even after the course, after I moved to London, in the long years of living in damp rented rooms and scraping a living with bar work, secretarial work, whatever came to hand, I would sit on the a bus on a wet grey day and stare out at passers-by walking along the pavement, and picture myself being interviewed by a national newspaper or rehearse my acceptance speech for a literary award. Then the wind would chuck a handful of rain against the window and I would remember that I was a part-time secretary with no money who had been trying to be a writer for years. At such moments, it was bitter to contemplate the depths of my deludedness.

This was the worst thing about wanting to be a writer. It wasn't the lack of food or clothes or friends or stability – it was the fear that I was mad. Those fears persisted before, during and after the course, but at least at UEA I was able to spend time with others who shared them – and ultimately, this is what I remember most about my time there: the kindness and support people showed towards me at a time when I needed kindness far more than they could ever have guessed. I still don't know how I managed to get my place on the course, and I still don't know whether it was Angela or someone else who spotted a glimmer of something interesting in the pretentious tosh I was writing at the time, but I do know that I probably owe my career to that person and the course that Malcolm Bradbury and Angus Wilson founded.

Louise Doughty (*b.* 1963) received her MA in Creative Writing from UEA in 1987. Her first novel was *Crazy Paving* (1995), which was shortlisted for the John Llewellyn Rhys Prize. Since then there have been five other novels and one work of non-fiction. Her most recent novel is *Whatever You Love* (2010), which was shortlisted for the Costa Novel Award and nominated for the Orange Prize.

The Dusty Piano

Tracy Chevalier

I first heard about the MA programme in Creative Writing at UEA from a 1993 *Guardian* article by Louise Doughty, recalling her year there and how it helped her develop as a writer. I came across the article as I was flipping through the newspaper on my way to work, part of my somnolent commuting ritual, where articles were fodder that passed the time but did not stick.

Something must have stuck, though. When I got to work – as an editor at a reference book publisher – my boss came up to me before I'd taken off my coat or had any coffee and began talking about something I hadn't done and should have. As she went on and on, a thought suddenly came to me: 'I gotta get out of here! I'm going to do that Creative Writing MA at UEA.' An idea I'd never consciously had, at least as an adult – to become a writer – in a moment of decaffeinated pique became a plan.

Some writers say they must Write Or Die. I am not one of those. Becoming a writer was not my singular goal when I was growing up. I remember at various times wanting to be, yes, a writer, but also a librarian, a teacher, a psychiatrist. Books were one of my favourite things, though, and I always liked the idea of being involved with them somehow when I grew up.

At university I pinpointed publishing as a practical correlative to writing, and in my twenties I became an editor. Writing was a persistent itch I scratched at night and on weekends, but slowly and inconsistently. By thirty I had just half a dozen finished short stories, with one published in a fiction magazine that went bust before it could pay me the modest fee.

There were eighteen of us in the UEA Class of 1993–4. For the most part people were in their early to mid-twenties, just a year or two out of university, with a sprinkling of us a little older. We met every week to read and discuss one another's work in progress, led by Malcolm Bradbury one term, Rose Tremain the next. These sessions were the heavy lifting of the course, the only real demand made on us. It was a tricky environment: we wanted to be honest about others' work, yet our own work would also be exposed to the treatment, and we feared being too cruel, as they might be in return. And frankly, all of us were more interested in our own writing than in others'. We read others' work and commented on it only because we wanted them to do the same to ours.

The sessions were a sometimes bewildering mix of brutality and boredom. Malcolm Bradbury was a lovely man, but he took a laid-back approach to class dynamics that allowed some voices and attitudes to predominate. By the time Rose Tremain took over, the tone had been set. Though she did her best to mediate, some took the criticism of their work badly, because it had been presented to them badly. I suspect a couple of the students were so bruised by these sessions that they never wrote again after finishing the course.

To my surprise, years later one of the class members told me they were always relieved when I spoke up. 'At last, some sense,' they used to think. Perhaps it's that I'd already had experience as an editor handling academic contributors to reference books, and had learned how to be kind and firm at the same time. Also, criticism needs to be practical – here's the problem, how about this solution? If it's abstract or waffling, it won't stick. Maybe, though, I was just better at hiding my boredom.

Once I had read a bit of everyone's writing and seen them all in action as both critics and defenders of their work, I used to sit in class and play a game: if I were a publisher, whom would I offer contracts to? Excluding myself from the contestants, I admit I guessed right quite early on as to the two who would go on to publish solidly. It was based not just on their work, but on the way they approached writing. Rather than writing all night before the deadline, fuelled on caffeine and alcohol, or recycling old stories (one fellow student admitted to me at the end of the course that he had written nothing new during the whole year), these two worked steadily. Indeed, they treated it the way I do now, as a job – a fun job, but a job nonetheless, with deadlines and discipline.

I think it's no surprise that the three of us from that year who have made careers in writing were older and hence used to working to deadlines and answering to bosses. Those just out of university showed flashes of brilliance, but lacked discipline and rarely took on board criticism. There were also at times breathtaking displays of arrogance. 'If you don't understand my writing, that's your problem,' a fellow student told me. Sorry, my friend, but that is *your* problem. No contract for you, and don't wait around for that Nobel Prize you feel is due you.

I wouldn't say it was a glorious year. To me UEA was a bleak, often rain-swept campus, with few places that raised the spirits. I was thirty-one, with a mortgage and a fiancé in London. I couldn't bear living in a dorm or a clapped-out student house. So I commuted, renting a room for two nights a week, and spending most of my time on campus in the library or at the Sainsbury Centre for Visual Arts, where I sat amongst Modiglianis and Francis Bacons and Polynesian masks. I went for walks in the rain around the artificial lake, explored the old lanes of Norwich, visited the cathedral, drank a lot of tea at the central university cafe. Then I fled back to London to write.

But it wasn't an unhappy year, either. Indeed, doing the MA was a turning point in my writing life. I felt like I was learning to play an instrument I had only ever messed around with before – the dusty piano no one has touched in years, the guitar with the broken string in the corner. I would not say my writing improved because of what I did at UEA. I did not write a better sentence after one of those painful critical sessions. My sentences got better because I wrote thousands of them. In other words, I practised. Six novels in, I still write dud sentences, every day. But I have got better at ferreting them out and fixing or cutting them. (Two mottos I write by: Less Is More; and, When in Doubt,

Cut It Out.) Once you've written enough sentences, and cut out the bad ones, there's usually something left that's halfway OK.

Would I have practised the dusty piano if I hadn't gone to UEA? I doubt it. It is very difficult to write when you're working full-time, or are a full-time parent. I have huge admiration for people who manage to produce anything worthwhile under such circumstances. The MA course gave me the time in which to think and write, the deadlines and built-in critical audience I did not feel prepared to create for myself. It got me started, showed me how to set up my life around my writing, rather than my writing around my life. And once I had that piece of paper saying I'd got an MA I felt more able to do it for myself. The idea I had for a novel during that year – when before I'd never had the time to think up an idea big enough to fill a book – I could then take forward and make central to my 'normal' life. I wrote part-time and worked part-time for the next three years, then had my first novel published, and I was on my way, sucked into the enjoyable machine of writing-as-job.

Always I am asked if Creative Writing can be taught. The spark can't, no, but the practising can – and you need both to write well. I have no idea where the spark comes from; none of us does. But the practising, the discipline, really started for me at UEA.

Tracy Chevalier (*b.* 1962) received her MA in Creative Writing from UEA in 1994. Her first novel, *The Virgin Blue* (1997), was followed by *Girl with a Pearl Earring* (1999), which was made into an acclaimed film. There have been four subsequent novels, including, most recently, *Remarkable Creatures* (2009).

The Five Per Cent That Matters

Glenn Patterson

Towards the end of 1981 I was working in a bookshop in Belfast, where I had the dubious distinction of being that year's youngest and weediest in-store Santa. That year's big-selling books (I was also keeper of the bestseller list) included Salman Rushdie's Booker Prize winner *Midnight's Children*, which I hadn't read, and Evelyn Waugh's *Brideshead Revisited*, which I had, and the serialisation of which was the year's most-watched television drama. The award for most controversial television drama, meanwhile (i.e., the one with most nudity), undoubtedly went to *The History Man*, adapted from Malcolm Bradbury's comic novel of 1970s campus life. (I hadn't read *The History Man* either. Waugh, Hemingway and Orwell were my passions that year.)

An old school friend, back from university in England, called at the shop one day. He was looking for a book published by Picador. This was not a surprise. Everyone who went, or had ever thought of going to university in 1981 was looking for Picador books. They were the antithesis of pocket-sized, the print equivalent of a twelve-inch single. You not only read Picador books, you could be sure to be seen to be reading Picador books. I knew the book my friend was looking for, but I didn't know the story he told me about its author. According to my friend, this guy went to university for three years and did absolutely nothing. His lecturers never even saw him. At the end of his final term, he was called to give an account of himself. *Where had he been all this time?* For answer he threw a pile of paper on the table. His stories. The university authorities were so impressed by them they gave him a first-class degree and the stories were instantly published.

The book in question was *First Love, Last Rites*, the author Ian McEwan and the story my friend told me was the first, garbled, account I had heard of the MA in Creative Writing at the University of East Anglia, taught by the author of *The History Man*, Malcolm Bradbury.

I was getting a bit fed up in my bookshop in Belfast. I thought I could do nothing for three years as well as anyone else. I thought (who had at that stage written a handful of poems and a single story, 'A World without Oil, How Could We Cope?') that the very least I would produce in that time was a collection of short stories. I filled out the standard British universities entrance application. I put East Anglia down as my Number One choice, actually my only choice. I left the boxes for second, third, fourth and fifth choice blank.

Fortunately (back then I would have said naturally), I was accepted. Unfortunately, I still had only the haziest notion of the difference between BA and MA. The following October I found myself one of several score undergraduates being inducted for 'prelims' in the university's School of English and American Studies. I remember a lecture on Dickens, delivered by a lecturer lying prone on a table because of backache. I remember a session where we paired off and walked around a large room, guiding our blindfolded partners by a series of cries and whistles and clicks. I remember wondering whether Ian McEwan had had to go through a postgraduate version of this. I remember the only thing I wrote for the first three weeks were daily (and sometimes twice and thrice daily) letters home to my girlfriend.

I decided it was time I put a bit of effort into doing nothing. Without telling anyone in the university, I went back to Belfast for a week. On my return I discovered my name on a white board at the entrance to the School of English and American Studies. 'Has anyone seen this student?' The last student whose name had been written up on the board had turned up dead. Suicide. The university authorities were understandably concerned about unexplained disappearances. I reported to my student advisor. He told me frankly, the way I was going, doing nothing, I was going to fail English prelim. I was going to have all the time I wanted to spend in Belfast.

I did enough, just, to get through that term and the next. I even had a go in my spare time at writing a stage play (it was dreadful; I'd only ever been to the theatre once) and a screenplay (a little better, though every second of the ninety minutes was filled with dialogue). And then, at Easter in my first year, I learned that Malcolm Bradbury had decided to offer, by way of experiment, an undergraduate writing course the following autumn. Even more surprisingly I wrote, from nowhere, a decent story. More than decent, good. (I had been studying Hemingway's Nick Adams stories and been greatly impressed by the opening of 'In Another Country': 'In the autumn the war was always there, but we did not go to it any more.' My own story, about two young Belfast boys in hospital, began 'In the morning Kevin would stop crying.') Bolstered by this I put my name down for the undergraduate writing class. Mine was, in fact, the first story presented in that class. Malcolm Bradbury liked it, and the other story I wrote, later in the term. It was the beginning of an association that was to last for nearly 20 years.

When eventually I was accepted on to the MA in Creative Writing, in 1985, I was the first former undergraduate to have made the transition. Or at least, joint first. Timothy Wilson, who was also accepted on to the course that year, had been an undergraduate with me. I hadn't known him all that well, though I knew, as everyone did, that he had had his first novel accepted for publication while still in his final year. *The Master of Morholm* was a historical novel with a strong element of romance. Tim was twenty-one, fond of snooker and cider, hardly a stereotypical writer of historical romances. He roomed in a house overlooking one of Norwich's largest graveyards. Dark-haired, somewhat gloomy of speech, and like most of us in those post-punk years given to wearing nothing but black, he enjoyed getting on to buses and asking to be dropped at the cemetery.

The MA when Tim and I started it was fifteen years old, though there had been no students at all for two years after the first student, McEwan, had completed the course. It had been set up by Malcolm Bradbury, along with fellow novelist and lecturer Angus

Wilson, both of who had experience of Creative Writing courses in the United States. (In the introduction to *Class Work*, an anthology of work from the MA, Malcolm traces the tradition of American writing courses as far back as the 1890s.) My misapprehensions about the course, back in the days when I worked in the bookshop, were only partly due to my own ignorance. There were only two other universities in the whole of the UK offering Creative Writing. As a discipline, it was still not widely known about. In 1985 Kazuo Ishiguro was a recent graduate. Within four years he would win the Booker Prize and interest in the course – and applications to it – would rise sharply.

I have no idea how many applications there were the year I did the course. Besides Tim and me, there were four students taking the MA. Three were paying their own way, taking breaks from (in one case, leaving altogether) careers in business or journalism. I was getting a grant from the Belfast Education and Library Board, which in practical terms was at least as important to my future prospects as the course itself. For a full year all I had to worry about was writing.

That and my health, maybe. It was still possible then to smoke in seminar rooms. At least half of us MA students smoked. Malcolm himself was a famous pipe smoker. Between emptying it, packing it, lighting and relighting it, he rarely had the pipe out of his hand, unless he was in the company of cigarette smokers, in which case he would set it down long enough to smoke the odd gifted fag. When my own work was being discussed I more or less chain-smoked.

The format of the course was simple. Each Thursday two students would hand in a story or a chapter from a novel in progress to be photocopied for collection by the rest of the group in time for the weekend. The following Wednesday, at two o'clock, we would meet, together with Malcolm, and talk about the submitted work. (Years later, when I was back at the university as Creative Writing Fellow, I discovered that Malcolm picked up the students' writing barely an hour before the class began – a mark, I decided, hearing him talk in his usual insightful way, not of his lack of application, but of his experience. After so many years and so many students, there was little he hadn't seen or couldn't instantly connect with.) We would break up at five, each piece having been discussed for approximately an hour and a half. That's all we did: talk. I say 'that's all', because already back then there were murmurs in the literary pages of a Creative Writing School Style, as though we were being taught to write in a particular way, as though we were being formally *taught* anything. But it was the fact of being talked to by Malcolm Bradbury as a writer (a less-experienced writer, certainly, but a writer nonetheless) that was the big breakthrough for most of us.

On the first day he told us that 95 per cent of what we would hear said about our work would be of absolutely no use to us. The trick was being able to identify the 5 per cent that mattered. He meant, of course that, try as we might to be objective critics, our observations about a piece of work would be coloured by simple personal taste. And our personal tastes were as various as those of any randomly selected group of six writers ranging in age from early twenties to late fifties might be expected to be. And then, too, part of the reason for taking the course was to find out, sometimes in the very act of speaking, what we thought about writing as a discipline, a calling, an approach to life. (Developing a personal aesthetic, we said.) We were bound to come out with some stupid things.

Early on, someone told me how much they envied me my ready-made subject, coming from Belfast. I was outraged that anyone could think this way, but secretly regarded some of that student's work as inconsequential. Another student I made fun of for hosting a party, during which he produced his work and began reading to the guests. I hid in the toilet. He had a bookshelf there – a thing you never came across in working-class houses, perhaps because it made too explicit the fact that you actually *sat down* in there, for a *considerable time*, perhaps because there was always someone banging on the door asking were you nearly done. Anyway, this bookshelf had on it a copy of Camus's *The Myth of Sisyphus*: like an intellectual VD notice, I thought, and (of course, being in my own way every bit as desirous of attention as my host) told everyone I thought, though in fact if I'd known anything then of the myth I might have reflected that Sisyphus was not an inapt symbol of the task we were engaged in as aspiring writers.

I acquired a regular writing routine. My girlfriend and I were living in a house close to Norwich train station with three other recent graduates, Tookey, Chufty and Spike. The household interests were, in no particular order, music (the Birthday Party, the Pogues, Cameo, James Brown, Eek-A-Mouse) weed, the Gong Show, sleeping with the people you weren't strictly going out with, cooking (our motto was Wasted But Well-Fed), football, cricket on the radio (if you've never tried it you'll never know), literature, pool, snakes and Red Stripe lager. Being so close to the station we tended to have a lot of casual visitors. If we were lucky they might even be people we knew.

I had a box room to work in. I had an office cast-off electric typewriter to work on. (An elder brother, a policeman, had sent me the money for it when I was accepted on to the course. If he ever came up to see it, I thought, and paused to look at the interesting plants in our back porch, we were all nicked.) The carriage return was so heavy that every time I started a new paragraph I had to wedge my legs against the desk legs to keep it from collapsing. My girlfriend was saving to do a master's course of her own by waitressing in the Norwich franchise of a well-known steakhouse chain. I started work in the morning when she left the house for her day shift and stopped when she came home. If she was working nights, too, I would sometimes go back to work after dinner. Mostly I went to the pub next door and spent a precise seventh of my weekly beer budget.

I wrote two more short stories in my first term, one of which I resubmitted in revised form. They were OK, but I felt a little as though I was coasting. I thought more and more about writing a novel, but I was daunted. I needed an extra push to help the boulder over the hill.

Then, finally, I read *Midnight's Children* for a literature exam that all us Creative Writers were obliged to sit. I understood as never before that the novel was the form best able to tackle the subject – Northern Ireland, its history, its agency in the everyday lives of its inhabitants – I wanted to tackle. An agreement on greater cooperation had just been signed between the British and Irish governments. One hundred thousand Protestants had taken to the streets of Belfast in protest. My housemates and I watched on television as politicians ranted and a sports shop was looted. It was possibly while wondering, as a Northern Irish Protestant myself, how to account for this (even though I didn't agree with it) that I began to plan the novel I would write.

And there was another factor. Since Angus Wilson's retirement, Malcolm had shared the teaching of the course, term about, with Angela Carter. Angela had a formidable reputation as a writer and a critic. She had been at the forefront of British experimental fiction since the 1960s. *The Sadeian Woman*, her study of Sade's writings, was one of the staples of 1980s English curricula, while her reworking of fairy tales, *The Bloody Chamber*, had recently been made into a film directed by Neil Jordan. Her book reviews in the *Guardian* newspaper, meantime, were witty, intelligent and combative. We were all a bit scared of her in advance, to be honest. And I was first in line to hand in work to her when classes resumed after Christmas.

In the course of the Christmas vacation my brother reminded me of a neighbour of ours, an IRA member, who had blown himself up planting a bomb. He was sixteen at the time. The following day graffiti was painted on a wall near where he had lived: *Patsy Quinn Rest in Pieces.*

The line stayed with me on the long boat and train journey from Belfast to East Anglia. By the time I had arrived back in Norwich I had decided that this (with the name changed) would be the last line of a novel. It carried echoes of Yeats: things fall apart, the centre cannot hold. I tried to imagine back from this an opening line. It would be, I decided, the exact opposite, an act of creation as opposed to apocalypse. I decided to adapt another first line, the mother and father of all first lines, Genesis 1, verse 1, and put it into the mouth of a teenage boy who appeared to live on a rubbish tip:

'In the beginning,' said Francy, 'was the dump.'

The first chapter did not go down particularly well with my fellow students. (I was not entirely sure about it myself.) One, in particular, objected to the fact that the teenage boy did indeed appear to live on a rubbish tip. Was this the case, he wanted to know, and if it was the case, was it likely? Angela Carter gave what I was to discover was a characteristic laugh-cum-exasperated sigh. But when the reader opens a book, she said, as though it were self-evident, he enters into a contract with the writer. The writer's only obligation is to be true to the rules of the world he has created.

Did I say earlier that I don't remember being taught anything while on the MA? I was wrong. Every time I sit down to start a new book I remember hearing this for the first time. And of course like all truths it *was* self-evident the moment after it was spoken. It was the encouragement I needed to carry on with the novel.

I wrote through the spring and into the summer. Classes ended. Our grade for the year would be determined by a dissertation of 15,000 words of fiction to be submitted at the end of September. Throughout July and August Angela travelled up from London once a fortnight to see us one-to-one. Afterwards, I would sometimes share a taxi with her into town. She recommended authors to me: Peter Carey, Bruce Chatwin ('but you'll probably hate him'). More than once she gave the impression that she had doubts about the MA course, the increasing emphasis, as she believed, on turning out writers who would be published as soon as possible after graduating. We would get out of the taxi at the station from where I would walk up the hill to the party house and she would catch the train to London.

What strikes me looking back, and despite Angela's concerns, is how far away London and by definition the publishing world seemed to us MA students. (Tim, of course, already had his publisher.) I can only remember encountering one writer not actually teaching on the course, when the American novelist Robert Coover, a friend of Angela's dropped in to have a chat. Certainly there were no swarms of agents waiting to pick us up, or off.

When the course ended, I had the 15,000 words required for my dissertation and another 20,000 words besides. Angela told me that if the rest of the novel was of the same standard as what she had already seen she would recommend it to her publisher's, Chatto & Windus. It was hardly unqualified support, but it was something to hang on to in the midst of much change. The landlady of the house I had been sharing had decided to sell up. My girlfriend was moving to London; most of my fellow MA students left Norwich. A couple of times, calling at the university, I bumped into the new year's intake of creative writers. They were friendly, even invited me to one or two of their parties, but not surprisingly I was not one of their group. I began to worry that I hadn't written enough during my year on the course, that I had somehow missed my chance. And too, my grant had run out. I took a couple of part-time jobs, one in a cocktail bar, one in a bookshop, to earn some money and leave myself time to write. I didn't write.

That Christmas I had a phone call from Malcolm Bradbury. He was having a party for the MA students; since I was still in the city would I like to come along? Again, in future years, these parties would become famous (I saw one well-established editor turn into a gauche teenager at the prospect of going), but the only person from the world of publishing in attendance that Christmas was Michael Shaw, Malcolm's own agent and a close personal friend.

I had been suffering from a virus and had just that day discovered that it was OK to drink while taking the antibiotics I had been swallowing soberly for the previous week. I drank more than I should have, which is to say, about what I normally drank in such situations. I think I was the last person to leave Malcolm's house. Michael Shaw (who was staying there that night) listened politely while I gabbled at him about the novel I was writing and invited me to send it to him if I ever finished it. When eventually I woke next day I resolved (1) not to drink like such a maniac in future, and (2) to finish writing the damned book.

I took the completed manuscript to Michael Shaw's office by hand the following April. (I knew little about publishing, but like everyone else I had heard about the slush piles of unsolicited manuscripts.) That morning I retyped the title page (the working title was *Dog Bag*) and called the book *Burning Your Own*.

A week later Mike rang me. He was going to try to place the book for me. I rang Angela. Within days I was talking to Carmen Callil, managing director of Chatto & Windus. She was keen. She invited me back to London to meet her and the entire Chatto editorial team, including the poetry editor, Andrew Motion. They had all typed up their comments and observations, but told me, whether I chose to take them on board or not, they were publishing my book the following spring.

I stuffed the comments in my pocket and went out and drank like a maniac.

(Aw, come on. One resolution out of two isn't bad.)

Angela stopped teaching on the MA a short time after *Burning Your Own* was published, though she continued to lend her support to me and other former students, like Anne Enright from the year after me, whose work she had been fond of. She continued to give me advice about writers and books. Forget Don Delillo (I was reading *Libra*), E. L. Doctorow was the important writer of the American Left. On one occasion she interviewed me live on stage at the Institute of Contemporary Arts, where, as she must have predicted, the audience consisted of people who would not normally give an unknown writer like me the time of day, but who would turn up to see Angela Carter read her shopping list.

She invited me to dinner at her house with Paul Bailey and Kazuo Ishiguro, for despite being a published writer now myself, I still felt a little distant from the whole London publishing scene. (My dealings with agents and publishers were conducted by telephone and day-return train tickets.) How distant became clear at a party my first paperback publishers threw, to mark their tenth anniversary, in Covent Garden in the late autumn of 1989, shortly after I had moved back home to Belfast. All the writers there seemed to know one another; all the non-writers seemed intent on filling their pockets, bags, shopping trolleys practically, with as many of the free books on display as they could fit…and filling themselves with free drink, of course. I was at one with them on this. I got dreadfully, maudlin drunk. About midnight, I phoned Angela. I'm not a writer, I told her. I hate the publishing industry. She told me to get in a taxi and come over to her house. (This was a woman with a young son, who rose in the morning at normal young-son time.) We sat talking into the small hours. The next day, she took me with her to the announcement of the *Guardian* Fiction Prize. She introduced me to publishers like Margaret Busby, Marion Boyars, John Calder. These were people, she said, who really cared about literature and I wasn't to forget that they existed, too.

I said goodbye to her on the street outside the theatre where the prize had been awarded. I said she must come to Belfast to read. I never saw her again. Angela Carter died of cancer a few weeks before the publication of my second novel, *Fat Lad*, at the start of 1992. Later that year I returned to UEA as Creative Writing Fellow.

The MA group had grown to around a dozen. Curtis Brown had just set up an annual scholarship for the best applicant. It was now possible to do a Creative Writing PhD. I asked one Phd student why he would go to the expense of financing himself for the three years of his doctorate, when he could simply write a novel in that time. Because with a PhD, he said, I can go to some place like Canada and open up my own Creative Writing School.

As the Creative Writing programme had grown, so had the volume of the sniping at Malcolm. To hear some of his critics, you would have thought that the MA was being run for the greater glory of Malcolm Bradbury. Malcolm, by this stage, was approaching sixty. As well as a novelist and critic, he was a prolific writer for television, adapting Tom Sharpe's *Porterhouse Blue*, Stella Gibbons's *Cold Comfort Farm*, and scripting the popular detective series *Inspector Morse*. The obvious comeback to those who suggested he was teaching Creative Writing for reasons of self-promotion was: why would he bother?

I was talking to him in the corridor outside his room one day. (As Creative Writing Fellow I had the office next door.) We were trying to remember when the Northern Irish writer Deirdre Madden had been a student on the course. Was it the year before me, or the before that again? Malcolm ducked into his room and reappeared a few moments later with a bound dissertation. It was Deirdre's.

'She was the year before you,' he said.

I asked him how he happened to have her work to hand, nearly a decade after she took his course.

'It's all in there. Yours, too,' he said, and showed me the shelves where he kept every piece of work that had been submitted to him for assessment down the years.

The Christmas party seemed much more organised. A number of publishers had travelled up from London, including my own editor, the 'gauche teenager' referred to earlier. I knew, from chatting to some of them in the days leading up to it, that the students were equally nervous. One or two appeared to be treating this, rather than the course itself, as their big chance to impress. And who could blame them after all?

As befitted my new position of responsibility, I got drunk rather more slowly than normally, not that anyone was in much of a state to appreciate my restraint by the end of the night. I went on from Malcolm's to a party at one of the students' houses. They swapped stories about who they had talked to, what had been said. All thought the night a great success. Only one of that year's group, to the best of my knowledge, has subsequently published widely, which ought to explode the media myth that such social contacts invariably lead to six-figure, multi-book advances. Then again, it only takes the emergence every few years of a writer of the calibre and profile of, say, Toby Litt to keep the myths about the course alive.

Malcolm retired from teaching at UEA in 1995, the year that Toby Litt graduated, twenty-five years after Ian McEwan did. He was succeeded as Professor of Creative Writing by the poet, novelist, biographer and former Chatto & Windus poetry editor Andrew Motion.

I still saw Malcolm from time to time at events organised by the British Council, whose New Writing programme he was heavily involved in. Late in 1998 I received an invitation to tour Germany with a 'team' of writers led by Malcolm. (There was another team touring the country in another direction under the leadership of A. S. Byatt. I imagined us meeting, like the Sabres and the Jets, high-stepping, finger-clicking down the neon-lit streets of Essen or Chemnitz.) On one of our last nights, in Hamburg, Malcolm sat until late in the residents' bar with Adam Thorpe and me, telling stories, of how for example, as a student in the early Fifties, he had wangled interviews with Ezra Pound and T. S. Eliot.

Talking next morning, Adam and I agreed that it had felt like the handing down of a tradition, from one generation to the next; as if, simply by listening, we had been made to feel inducted into the larger narrative of twentieth-century letters.

I was by this time teaching an undergraduate Creative Writing course of my own at Queen's University in Belfast. When, a couple of years later, Queen's decided to set up an MA in Creative Writing and were looking for an external examiner from another university to ensure quality control it seemed natural that we should turn to UEA and Andrew Motion. I started teaching the MA in late September. The official launch, though, was scheduled for November. Andrew had agreed to travel over for the event. Two days before he was due in Belfast, I woke to the news that Malcolm Bradbury had died in Norwich, aged sixty-eight, of complications arising from a lifelong history of respiratory problems. We phoned Andrew, said we would understand in the circumstances if he cancelled, but Malcolm's funeral was not for several days and he decided to come as planned.

And so the launch of our MA in Belfast became a celebration, too, of the first of its kind, set up exactly thirty years before in Norwich. A few weeks later I bumped into the Belfast comic novelist John Morrow, who knew all about my UEA connections.

'I see the Old Master's dead,' he said.

He meant it in the sense of former teacher, of course, but he was right in the other sense, too.

This year, as last year, I began my MA course by telling the students what Malcolm told me, that 95 per cent of what would be said would be of absolutely no use. I hope they are as pleasantly surprised as I was at the end of the course to find how wide of the mark that is.

Glenn Patterson (*b.* 1961) received his MA in Creative Writing from UEA in 1986. His first novel, *Burning Your Own* (1988) won a Betty Trask Award and the Rooney Prize for Irish Literature. He is the author of six other novels, including, most recently, *The Third Party* (2007). His eighth novel *The Mill For Grinding Old People Young* will be published in 2012. He currently teaches on the MA in Creative Writing at Queen's University Belfast.

A Norwich Butterfly

John Boyne

My spiritual transformation took place in Norwich; it was there that, like an emerging butterfly, I was first conscious of my wings.

Leo Colston, the young narrator of L. P. Hartley's *The Go-Between*

In January 2005, exactly ten years since I had been a student on the Creative Writing MA at the University of East Anglia, I returned to Norwich as Writing Fellow, teaching on the undergraduate writing course, and acting as a resource to those on the MA who wanted their work read and discussed by a published novelist.

There was a certain symmetry to returning after a decade away. Ten years before, our class of twelve – seven men, five women – had played a parlour game night after night. Who, we wondered, ten years hence, would be a full-time working novelist? Going on past statistics we settled on four with an assured literary future, a mere third of our number, but who those four might be changed with each different story or fragment of a novel submitted to class.

After settling into my flat on campus the night of my return – it was snowing, I remember, heavily – I headed to the Grad Bar to enjoy a pint of beer at cheap student rates once again. I carried with me an advance copy of another graduate's new novel, *Never Let Me Go* by Kazuo Ishiguro, and thought about the other eleven students with whom I had spent a chaotic year during 1994 and 1995, wishing that they were there with me too, and wondering where they all were now.

We had been right about our statistics; a decade along, Richard Beard, Janette Jenkins, Toby Litt and I had published fourteen novels, two collections of short stories and a work of non-fiction between us. But many of the other eight were missing in action – this was pre-Facebook days, of course – and whether or not they were even still writing was open to conjecture.

I felt sad to be there without my old crew, nostalgic even. That year, my twenty-third, when I had first come to Norwich had been a turning point in my life. I arrived brimming over with self-confidence, a cocky kid who'd published a few short stories in magazines or newspapers, and left with a conviction that although writing mattered to me more than ever, I had no idea what type of writer I really was. I arrived young and naive – I'd never lived outside Dublin before – and left, horrified to be returning to my boring life in Ireland. I arrived with a plan to write short stories and left with perhaps no more than half a dozen, and they weren't very good anyway. Oh, and I arrived straight and left gay – thanks, UEA!

I remember my interview for a place on the course. I flew to London, took a train to Norwich and a bus from Thorpe Station to the campus. I remember the bus turning a corner and a brief glimpse of the university between the trees. I remember Jon Cook and Rose Tremain asking me questions about what I wrote, and why I wrote, and what I wanted to write, and feeling a growing certainty that I was making a mess of the whole thing, that every word coming out of my mouth was utter nonsense. I'd read *Restoration* and *Sacred Country* and liked them very much; Rose was the first real writer I had ever had a conversation with and I felt a little overawed. I remember walking to the lake after the interview and sitting there for a while, cursing myself for not being more articulate, only realising then how much I wanted to attend UEA, how much I wanted to be part of this course. I remember swearing to myself that I'd have another go next year and I'd be ready then. I'd know what to say. I remember walking past the English department on my way to catch the bus back to the station and Rose sweeping down the stairs in a red coat.

'Oh, I'll put you out of your misery,' she told me. 'You got in.'

I could have kissed her. I probably should have.

My memory of our classes leaves me feeling bewildered and embarrassed. We met every Wednesday afternoon, sitting in a horseshoe formation around Malcolm Bradbury, who was due to retire once he was finished with us. He seemed almost bemused to find us there every Wednesday, waiting for him, as if he couldn't quite believe that this whole Creative Writing lark, initiated by him twenty-four years ago, had thrived for so long. Occasionally, he would even remember our names. One student made sure to arrive first every week, just so he could sit on Malcolm's right hand and whisper sweet nothings in his ear. Malcolm looked at him with wry amusement, as if he had encountered his type on twenty-four previous occasions.

At first we were all polite, treating each other's work with kindness and consideration. We were *deeply moved* all the time, or *profoundly affected*, or professed ourselves *startled by the depth of such a vivid imagination*. I remember commenting that a certain story was filled with a wonderfully energetic energy, which made Malcolm close his eyes and clench his jaw, as if I'd just dragged my nails across the blackboard. If we found a flaw we simply wondered whether it might not be reconsidered, although we admitted that we were probably wrong to even suggest it, that such remarks merely testified to our own shortcomings, rather than those of the nascent genius whose work we were discussing.

Such politeness lasted about a month, and then the knives came out.

By November we were deeply disappointed by stories that seemed derivative of the work of famous writers. The dialogue sounded like nothing we ever heard in real life. The characters were clichéd and overwritten. And really, must we go on reading these endless tracts about the stupidity of religion, or the defiant spirit among the women gathered on Greenwich Common, or the traumas of young girlhood in Brooklyn? Wasn't life really too short for all this tedious nonsense? A suggestion was made to one student that she might be better off pursuing another career choice, needlework perhaps. Or taking the veil. There were tears, walkouts. Threats. And then afterwards, back in the arms of our most faithful attendant – the Grad Bar – we would make up, friends again for another seven days.

We invented strange games that both amused us and made a mockery of what we were there to do. The men began wearing suits and ties to class. We submitted work with photographs printed on the title pages showing each of us as babies. We competed to see who had slept the least the night before class, who had vomited that morning out of anxiety, who had considered throwing all their clothes off and drowning themselves in the lake, rather than face the vindictive criticisms of their classmates.

Once, a fellow student and I hastened to another's flat, fully convinced that we would find him hanging from a light bulb. He wasn't. In fact, he welcomed us in and offered us tea. Then, if I remember correctly, a row ensued.

And yet, despite all our nonsense, some good work was produced. Two students received offers from publishing houses while still on the course. Others were taken on by agents after Malcolm's annual house party, an evening of naked ambition, where agents and editors descended upon Norwich and where we, the current crop, would target a Person Known To Be Someone Useful and engage them in conversation about the novel we were writing and whether or not the Person Known To Be Someone Useful might like to take a look at it, just a few chapters perhaps, the first one even, a couple of scenes if time was of the essence. We weren't there just to write, after all; we wanted to begin our careers. We wanted someone to tell us that we might *have* careers.

I had been writing since the age of about fourteen, fascinated by the art of storytelling, the complexity and elasticity of words. I'm forty now and have published seven novels, plus two more for children, and around seventy short stories. A day doesn't go by when I don't write. ('Every day,' Malcolm would insist. 'Even Christmas Day.') But the only time over the last quarter century when I *didn't* write was in the year immediately following my graduation from the course. For when I left, despite having come to understand that there was no limit to the amount of things I could write about, and despite having been awarded the Curtis Brown Prize towards the end of the year, I felt that the course had only taught me a few things that really mattered: that you cannot be a writer unless you have found your own distinctive voice, that you cannot tell a story unless you have a reason to tell it, and that you cannot write a novel unless you understand the power that novels have in the first place.

And so I stopped. I went home to Dublin. I worked in a bookshop. And I read and I read and I read. And then, sometime during 1997, I had an idea for a novel that would become my first book, *The Thief of Time*. And I started to write it. And I've been writing ever since.

Every day. Even Christmas Day.

In some ways, the hardest part of doing the course was leaving the course. There was a protective atmosphere to UEA; we were encouraged to write, in fact we *had* to write as we had deadlines, submission dates, a clear schedule to follow. We were writers because people called us writers and because we were writing. We were a collective. A gang of twelve. And then it was all over. And we were out.

But now it was 2005 and here I was in Norwich again. *The Thief of Time* had been published. So had *The Congress of Rough Riders.* And *Crippen. Next of Kin* was due out in a few months time. I was writing full time. I was a novelist; I didn't have any other job. There were copies of some of my books published in languages that I couldn't read. I had cracked America, and even Robbie Williams didn't seem able to do that. I wasn't selling very many books, but it seemed churlish to expect commercial success. Being allowed to publish was surely enough. It was certainly enough for me.

I set myself a few tasks when I arrived at UEA the second time around. I wanted to be a *good* teacher. I could remember what it was like to feel intimidated by the pressures of the course, and to feel lost among students who seemed so much more confident and literary than me. I wanted to find the students who were struggling and encourage them; the quieter voices, in my experience, were usually the most interesting ones. And one other thing: I had a manuscript in my bag which had just been accepted by my publisher, but which was still a bit of a mess and needed a lot of editing and re-writing during the months ahead.

The novel in question was a short, 50,000-word book, written for children – the first time I had ever written for children – about a nine-year-old German boy whose family move away from their Berlin home to a concentration camp, where the boy's father is taking up the position of Commandant. The boy – Bruno – would meet another boy there – Shmuel – and the novel centred around their growing friendship and their gradual discovery of what was really taking place around them.

It was called *The Boy in the Striped Pyjamas.*

I laid the pages out on my desk and resolved to make this book as good as it could possibly be over the following months. And then I got to work.

The first morning I entered my undergraduate classroom, I think I felt more nervous than any of the students. There were about fifteen of them, all aged around nineteen, and I began by asking each one in turn what they were reading at the moment.

'I'm working on a thesis,' said one. 'I can't read right now.'

'Most of my time is spent with my band,' said another. 'I haven't read a book in ages. I'm more of a writer than a reader, to be honest.'

'Stephen King,' said a third.

'I see,' I said, surprised that they did not seem more engaged with contemporary fiction. 'So how many of you are actually reading a novel right now?'

Three hands went up.

'And how many of you, ten years from now, would like to be published novelists?'

The number of hands increased five-fold.

'All right,' I said. 'I think we have a lot of work to do here.'

As time went on, to my relief, I found that the students in my class were actually a highly literate and rather creative group. They experimented in their writing, didn't care if they fell flat on their faces, and were thoughtful and encouraging to each other in their weekly criticisms. I grew fond of them and believed that at least three or four had the potential to be writers. Real writers, I mean. Writers who wouldn't throw in the towel if the literary world didn't embrace them instantly.

And then I met the MA group.

Of course they were older. Of course they were a little more self-conscious about the fact that they were this year's group of Chosen Ones, with one eye on the prize and another on the statistics. (Those statistics never go away; they just change slightly with each passing year.) They also seemed to be deciding whether or not they approved of me. A few made it a point of principle to let me know that they had never heard of me or any of my books.

'Who publishes you?' one asked me that first evening as we sat in the Grad Bar and they gathered around, silently judging me.

'Random House,' I said.

'Too commercial,' came the immediate reply.

'What are you working on at the moment?' asked another.

'A children's book,' I said, brightening up, for that children's book might have been a long way from finished, but I felt that I was on to something special with it.

'I'm sorry, did you say a children's book?'

'Yes, that's right.'

She looked around at the other students, who seemed equally perplexed. It was as if I had just admitted an unhealthy interest in children, rather than in simply writing for them.

'Yes, well,' she replied, opening her mouth, realising she had nothing further to add and so, sensibly, closing it again.

'Why, what are you working on?' I asked in reply, trying to salvage the situation.

'Oh, that's an awful question, don't you think?' she said, making me feel seedy and voyeuristic for having the vulgarity to ask it. 'I can't explain in just a few trite sentences. It's rather complex. Rather personal. It's quite…' (and here it came; I knew the word would appear at some point over the course of the evening) '…organic. I'd rather not talk about it.'

'But you asked me,' I pointed out.

'Yes, well,' she repeated. 'It's just because I'd never heard of you, that's all.'

Not a good start.

But then, as the months passed, they would knock on my door and offer a story or a few chapters from a novel, and I discovered that they, too, were a rather talented bunch after all. (The interview process might not always work perfectly, but it does dig up a few gems along the way.) And in reading their work, I began to analyse my own anew; in recognising flaws that devalued the piece as a whole I could see where I might fall victim to similar errors. I've always found that the teaching of Creative Writing classes can be just as instructive and helpful for the teacher as it is for the student, and that was certainly true of my experiences in both roles.

During much of 2005 I worked and re-worked *The Boy in the Striped Pyjamas*. While in Norwich I took part in a public reading with a couple of other novelists and decided to read from the work-in-progress, something I never do, but I was anxious to see how an audience would respond to the material. I read for about ten minutes at the theatre in UEA and afterwards, during the question-and-answer session, a hand was raised and a point made regarding the merits of historical fiction. One of the novelists on the panel with me was withering in his contempt for novels set in the past, stating that there was nothing to be gained by looking towards history, as if contemporary themes could not be explored in a novel that wasn't set in the present day.

Tell that to William Golding, I muttered. Or Robert Graves. Or Kazuo Ishiguro.

My work, more by chance than design, has been almost entirely set in the past, but I have tried to bring a sense of the contemporary into the novels, both through theme and character. In writing about the Holocaust, as I was in *The Boy in the Striped Pyjamas*, I was exploring one of the most difficult and emotive topics in history, and doing so from an unusual perspective: I'm not Jewish, after all, and nor was my central character. Would readers feel that in directing sympathy towards the plight of the young German boy in the novel I was somehow detracting from that of the Jewish characters? (Many would, in fact, and would tell me so in no uncertain terms at public events over the years that followed. I can't be responsible for how you feel, was my standard reply. And besides, you *should* feel sympathy for Bruno. He hasn't done anything wrong, after all; he doesn't deserve the fate that awaits him.)

The youngest survivors of the Holocaust – boys and girls who were Bruno and Shmuel's age – are now nearing the end of their lives. Society makes sure to keep their voices heard – organisations such as the Shoah Foundation, based at the University of Southern California, have been scrupulously collecting the testimonies of survivors for many years – but fiction writers are often less comfortable with dramatising these events. Adults are well represented in the literature; when it comes to the stories of the children, however, there are fewer records available to us.

Truthfully, it's a difficult subject for any novelist to approach. It's presumptuous to assume that from today's perspective one can really understand the horrors of Auschwitz or Bergen-Belsen or Dachau, although it's the responsibility of any writer who chooses to base a narrative in such places to uncover as much emotional truth within that desperate landscape as he or she possibly can. In doing so, one looks for the best way to tell the story, and I felt my themes could best be explored through the eyes of a child.

The slow but determined breakdown of society has always been fertile ground for novelists, and by focussing on the involvement of very young children at such times, either as victims or perpetrators, participants or bystanders, I had the opportunity to focus directly on specific aspects of these moments, while ignoring certain issues which, from a purely technical point of view, were surplus to requirements. William Golding famously made the young protagonists of *Lord of the Flies* pre-pubescent, as the scourges of adolescent sexuality were not the concern of that novel and could therefore be jettisoned from the novel's boys in a way which would have been impossible had it been a group of adults left alone on that island.

I remember being tremendously moved as a child by Ian Serailler's *The Silver Sword*, one of the few children's novels to which I returned as an adult, when I was surprised to discover how much I had missed in my original reading. I recalled a story of great friendship between four children, and the heroics of their leader Jan in particular; what I discovered was a brutally effective tale of innocents left to survive in a Poland torn apart by the war. However, the fact that I didn't know much (as a ten year old) about concentration camps or genocide didn't detract from the story for me originally; if anything, it kept it alive in my head and made me want to rediscover it at a later date, aware that there were many things in there that I wanted to know more about.

Perhaps this is a good aim for a novelist writing a book for young people about difficult subjects. I've been asked many times whether *The Boy in the Striped Pyjamas* is a suitable book for children to read and my answer is that, while there will certainly be some elements of the story which they will not understand as much as others, my hope is that they will reach the end of the book sufficiently moved by the narrative, and sufficiently identifying with both Bruno and Shmuel that they will be left asking questions, wanting to know more, needing to keep the subject alive.

It goes without saying that the issue of writing about the Holocaust in a children's book is a contentious one, and any novelist who tackles it had better be sure about their intentions before they begin. For me, it seemed the only respectful way to deal with such a subject was through innocence, using the point of view of a rather naive young boy who couldn't possibly understand the horrors of what he was caught up in to tell the story. For, after all, that naivety is as close as someone of my generation can get to the dreadfulness of that time and place. *Why am I here?* Bruno wonders in his head. *What happens in this place? Why are there so many people on the other side of the fence?* Simple questions, perhaps, but at a basic level, aren't these the questions we still ask? A simple *Why?* And perhaps that's the job for any writer, to keep looking for answers, to make sure those questions continue, so that no one forgets why they needed to be raised in the first place.

I spent much of my second-time-around at the University of East Anglia sitting at my desk overlooking the rabbit-filled hills, playing with every sentence of that novel, asking myself questions about them, deleting some, editing, adding more. I completed the novel there and handed it over to its new life, which at times seemed to grow in an unexpected and – yes! – even organic way.

But it was a joyful time. Norwich and the University of East Anglia stay with me; a city I think about often, a campus I always long to revisit. Perhaps it's no surprise, then, that when I next explored the subject of war in fiction, this time the First World War in my most recent novel *The Absolutist*, I decided to set half that story in the city itself. A young man and woman in 1919 – one a traumatised veteran of the trenches, the other the sister of a young soldier who has been shot as a conscientious objector – wandering the streets over the course of a day, describing their lives to each other in the shadow of Norwich Cathedral, recalling their relationships with his friend, her brother, as they sit over meat pies and pints of ale in the Murderers Public House, reliving the trauma of war and the devastation of a loved one's death as they cross a bridge over the Yare and make their way towards the central market.

It was a pleasure to be in Norwich again, even if this time it was just in the pages of a novel. But then it was the pages of novels, the desire to write them myself, that had brought me to the city in the first place, fifteen years earlier. It was fiction that led me to the University of East Anglia, where, like Leo Colston, I was first conscious of my wings.

I have a lot to thank it for.

John Boyne (*b.* 1971) received his MA in Creative Writing from UEA in 1995 and returned as Writing Fellow in 2004–5. He is the author of seven novels for adults, including, most recently, *The Absolutist* (2011), and two for children, including *The Boy in the Striped Pyjamas* (2006), which was made into an award-winning film. His novels are published in over 40 languages and he has won several international literary awards.

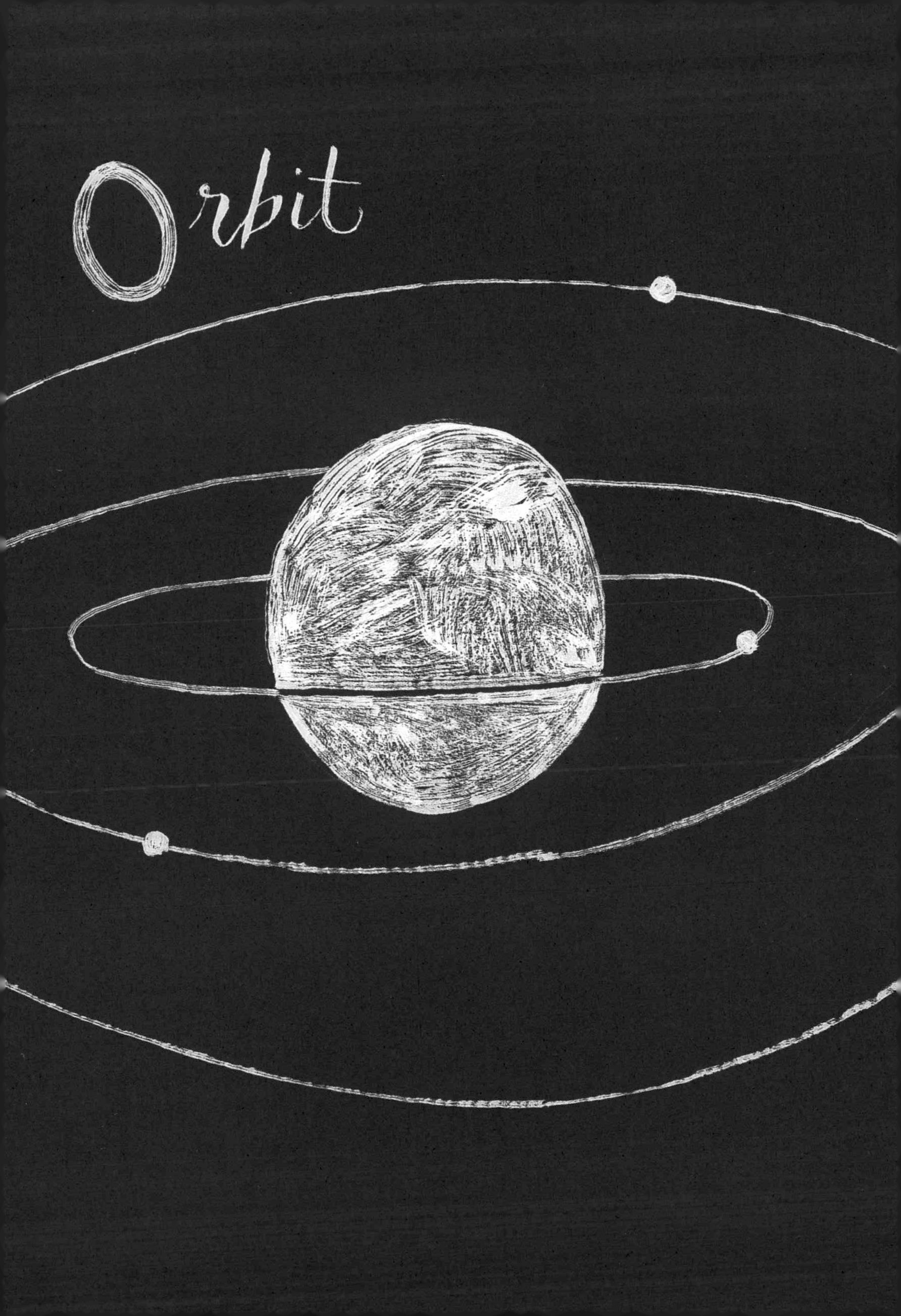
Orbit

On the Ghan

Susan Elderkin

I remember the precise moment it happened. The alarm was set for 5.45 a.m., because we wanted to be awake for dawn.

We'd boarded the train the previous afternoon in Adelaide and spent the first few hours travelling through wheatfields. By the time we reached Port Augusta it was already dark; we'd spilled out on the platform and sniffed the spice of eucalypts in the warm night air. We were full of anticipation: we'd be waking to desert in the morning.

We didn't sleep much. In the middle of the night the temperature plummeted. We were in the economy, or Red Kangaroo, car and seemed to be the only ones who hadn't thought to bring sleeping bags and pillows. We had, however, thought to smuggle on board three bottles of red. We persuaded the conductor to take a glass and after that he turned a blind eye.

It was still dark outside when the alarm went off. Drowsily, we watched the sky pale to grey before taking on a taint of yellow and then, just as a tiger's eye of astonishing liquid gold appeared on the horizon, we saw a mob of grey kangaroos – twenty or thirty of them. They were hard to pick out at first. Paralysed, staring at the train, they blended with the murky landscape behind.

Then they took off, bounding untidily away, big ones and small ones, like out-of-sync rubber balls. As they disappeared, the sun cracked into being and the flat plain was splayed out in all its beautiful orangey-pinky-rusty brilliance – a colour I've struggled to capture in a single word ever since.

I took out my notebook and started to write. I wrote about a boy, Billy, who spent a lot of time watching kangaroos, even trying to jump like them…

Inspiration is a funny thing. There's no knowing when it will strike, how long it will last, when it will go away. On this, my first trip to Australia, it lasted – at peak levels – for several months. The result was my second novel, *The Voices*.

Now, six years later, I am back on the Ghan (Australia's long-distance sleeper train). This time I'm doing the journey in reverse, from Alice Springs to Adelaide. I wonder what will happen? Does inspiration strike twice? I find myself hoping I'll come across the American tourists Nancy and Dexter, who take the Ghan in my book, loudly telling the entire carriage how much they liked Adelaide because the streets were so clean – just as Billy, wasted and smelling to high heaven, comes crashing down through the carriages looking for trouble.

I even fantasise I'll see Billy himself standing on the side of the track as we go past, taggle-haired and teetering on the verge of madness, snagging on my gaze with his grey-blue eyes, recognition flashing between us.

Of course, nothing like that happens. Even before the train has left the platform at Alice, I know it's not going to be anything like as good as last time. I'm here by myself, not with two girlfriends and three bottles of wine. A guest of the Australian tourist board, I'm now in Gold Kangaroo class, not Red. This means I have a cabin to myself, complete with fold-down bed, fold-down sink and fold-down toilet. A stewardess, Ashley, has come to ask whether I want tea or coffee with my morning call, whether I want the 'Sunset' or the 'Moonlight' sitting for supper, breakfast at 'Daybreak' or 'Sunrise'. Last time breakfast was a jar of Vegemite scooped out with a finger. What's going on?

All this luxury is very nice, of course, but it strikes me as unlikely that inspiration will come to me in Gold Kangaroo. I prefer to be among everyday folk when I'm researching a book, overhearing snatches of ripe, local vernacular, watching the way working men's jeans bag at the butt, the way their bellies wobble when they throw back their heads to laugh.

I leave my cabin and march down the carriages, through umpteen Gold Kangaroo sleepers, through the dining car, through more Gold Kangaroo sleepers, until, some ten minutes later, I arrive at the door of Red Kangaroo. This is where I belong, where stories exist.

But the door to Red Kangaroo is locked. I knock on the door. I shout. Two Japanese girls, also caught on the wrong side, explain in broken English that the door is going to be unlocked once the train starts moving. I sit down with them to wait. We're in a buffet lounge, and the blinds are all down to keep it cool, so there's nothing to see. The train starts moving.

'Don't you want to see the landscape?' I ask.

They nod. I show them how to wind up the blinds and we go round the entire carriage, gleefully winding up the blinds. Sun pours in. The untidy burbs of Alice trundle past.

'Oh!' they gasp, kneeling on the seats and staring out avidly, and I feel a stab of envy. They are seeing it all for the first time; they have their child's eyes still. For me, this is all familiar. I have lost my child's eyes for Australia.

The conductor comes along and I explain that I'd be really grateful if she could find me a spare seat in Red Kangaroo. She looks at me weirdly, but duly unlocks the door. I rush in eagerly, only to find that the carriage is full of backpackers fast asleep on their pillows, even though it's only 2 p.m. So much for the local, everyday folk.

'Changed your mind?' the conductor says with a wry smile.

Dispirited, I begin the long walk back to my lonely cabin.

'At Port Augusta,' I wrote in my notebook that first time, 'we stopped and got out on the platform. Cicadas. Smell of eucalyptus. It's dark. There's a windmill lit up by a street light, white blades spinning. A big tin sign that reads: It's a Farmer's Union Iced Coffee or It's Nothing.' Once the journey started, the entries in my book become more disjointed – random pieces from a vast and uncapturable jigsaw.

'Huge big black crows sitting in a line,' reads one. 'Clouds like claw scratches in the blue,' says another. 'Rusted shell of car turned on back like dead beetle,' reads a third. 'Dead-looking, leafless trees. Spiky, dead-looking, scrubby things beneath.' And then: 'Fantastic, wonderful nothingness! Fran the nanny at Heather's sister's house in Adelaide, when we asked if the Ghan was any good, said: "Yeah, if you like looking at nothing." I wanted to say, "Nothing is my favourite thing."'

And, back then, it was. I found the flat red expanse, the space, the eye-stretch to the horizon, breathtakingly beautiful. This time, alone in my Gold cabin, I find myself looking out the window, seeing desert, then turning back to my book. Had it really become just 'desert'? I may have lost my child's eyes, but surely now a new relationship with Australia was supposed to take over – less naive, less excited, less superficial. I look again. Instead of dead trees and scrubby things, I now see mulga scrub and spinifex mounds. I see red earth that is red because it lacks calcium and without calcium the iron is not tied up. I end up not writing anything.

I decide that a relationship with a country goes through the same phases as a relationship with a person. To begin with you love blindly, at full pelt, hungry to find out everything about the other that you can. Then, for a while, everything becomes complicated – you know things you wish you didn't, things you don't fully understand. And then, if you get through that, you wake up one morning and find you love the other because you know them, and not because you don't.

I decide that Australia and I are in the middle phase. The country is not always beautiful to me any more. I understand it in some ways, and not in others. But if I get through this stage, I'll be bonded for life. That's when I'll write about it best.

By 2.30 p.m. I've given up philosophising in my solitary cabin and am sitting in the Gold Kangaroo bar with a cold Victoria Bitter. To my delight, there are two fine Aussie beer guts sitting opposite me, wobbling with the judder of the train beneath striped T-shirts. Their owners are sitting side by side drinking their beers out of stubby holders they've brought with them specially, their backs to the fine blue-grey saltbush flashing past. Around us, polite, boring conversation is going on: 'The reason Australia's so good at sport…', '…rather remain under a monarch than be a bloody republic…', '…really think they should cull more crocodiles…'

By 5 p.m. I'm having a wonderful time. I've met Justin, a Chinese-Australian freelance photographer; Rebecca and Gwen, a mother and daughter from England; Cindy, a single mum from Melbourne, travelling with her three-year-old daughter; another pom called Jason who works in finance in Sydney. At six, Gary the train manager comes to give a talk about 'the legendary Ghan'.

Gary has only been speaking for two minutes when one of the bellies starts heckling him about the fact that the bar has run out of Crownies (Crown Lager, a classier brew than VB). 'That's because we drunk them all on the way down from Darwin,' the second belly points out, but the first is not to be mollified. 'I think it's lousy they ran out of

Crownies. We paid $1,800 per person for this trip, and we want to drink the beer we like.' Gary goes on with his story, but the heckling continues, and eventually Gary goes over to the bar and unearths one last Crownie.

'I'm going to give it to the person who's heckled me least,' declares Gary, boldly.

He finishes his talk and hands the Crownie to Jason, the pom. There are cries of outrage. I sit back and hope for a riot. But then: 'Oh, give it to the pom, it's warm anyway,' says the big belly, and peace is restored.

I go to 'Sunset' supper with Cindy and afterwards we reconvene in the bar. Jason is surrounded by bellies, being slapped on the back, his VBs bought for him. It turns out he had had the bartender put the Crownie in the fridge, and when it was cold he gave it to the first belly from Darwin. Clearly a pom who knows how to survive in this country.

At 5.45 a.m. my alarm goes off. It's completely dark outside. I keep the light off and sit up in my pyjamas, waiting for the land and the sky to draw apart. Bits and pieces of the previous night's conversation come back to me. Something I said to the mother and daughter from England. Oh God! I'd been waxing lyrical about Adelaide.

'You can be up in the hills among towering eucalypts and cockatoos, or driving through vineyards, or down on the unspoilt rugged beaches, lined with wooden beach shacks,' I'd said. 'You can leave your car unlocked when you park and no one steals it. And everywhere is really, really...' Oh God! Had I really said it? Clean?

And suddenly I realise I'm living proof that the characters in a novel are all just different aspects of its author. I hadn't bumped into my characters on the train, but then I hadn't needed to. It had been me swaying down through the carriages, banging on the door and making a scene. It had been me whanging on about boring old Adelaide. It had been my eyes looking back at me through the window saying yes, I am the one that sings everything up, everything comes from me. Inspiration is not out there but in here. It doesn't matter whether you're in Gold Kangaroo or Red.

I shower and dress quickly. I don't want to miss 'Daybreak' breakfast. Cindy and her daughter are already there, tucking into bacon and eggs. Across the aisle are two Japanese men wearing khaki waistcoats with twenty-five zip-up pockets.

'Grape,' the waitress is saying, indicating the carton of juice. They stare at her blankly. 'Grape,' she says, over and over, a little louder each time. Behind them the sunrise is vivid, streaks of red and orange and yellow. This time there are no kangaroos.

Susan Elderkin (*b.* 1968) received her MA in Creative Writing from UEA in 1994. Her first novel, *Sunset Over Chocolate Mountains* (2000), won a Betty Trask award. The following year she was listed as one of twenty-one 'Orange Futures' women writers for the twenty-first century. Her second novel, *The Voices*, was published in 2003, in which year she was also named as one of Granta's Best of Young British Novelists.

Elaborate Cure

Andrew Miller

A novel is a collection of anxieties held together, more or less well, more or less interestingly, by the chicken wire of plot. In writing my last novel, *Oxygen*, I had a radiant collection of new and long-term worries to choose among.

In the year I began the book, I was living in Dublin and suffering from breathing difficulties – a sense that I could not take a deep breath, could not fully open my lungs. I was sent to the hospital for tests. I blew into tubes. They X-rayed me. They put me in a capsule like an old-fashioned bubble car and tested me for allergies. I didn't react. I was well.

Go home, they said, and try to relax. Had I been overdoing it recently?

I said I was trying to start a novel.

That'll be it, they said. Half the city was trying to start a novel – a novel or a collection of poetry. In Dublin hospitals, breathing difficulty brought on by the birth pangs of creative enterprise is an acceptable and probably common diagnosis. But I'd started novels before (and finished them) and had felt fine. I wanted a second opinion and found a Chinese clinic where a professor from Beijing, a chain-smoker without the least command of English, drilled me with little pins – including one between my eyes – leaving me recumbent on the couch while he went into the corridor to top up his nicotine levels.

The clinic was makeshift: three cubicles with thin board walls that stopped a foot below the ceiling. Whether I liked it or not – and I liked it – I was privy to the confessions of my fellow patients, who, through the interpreter, told the professor the story of their bodies, their quest for wellness, their dark misgivings. It was an ideal situation for a novelist: pinned to a couch, listening to the secrets of strangers. It became half the reason for going there and reminded me of something I already knew, but often forget. That everywhere there are possibilities.

The pins seemed to help, the pins and the tea I had to brew twice a day, a bog-brown infusion of such astonishing bitterness I could only swallow it by lining my mouth with honey.

It wasn't just me, though. There seemed to be an epidemic of breathlessness. Half my friends – not writers at all, but regular people, social workers, computer programmers, doctors for Christ's sake – carried little inhalers in their pockets. Oxygen levels in the cities are slipping. Oxygen bars are opening in fashionable malls in America. And lack of oxygen (ischemia) is what kills us all.

I kept drinking the tea. I wrote about people who struggled for breath. I think I sometimes wrote whole paragraphs without breathing, as though swimming the length of a pool underwater.

Then I left Dublin, that rainy, melancholy city, and moved for a time to Paris, because if writing is about anxiety it is also about promises you make to yourself at the beginning of it all. To be a writer in Paris! There – the city of light – the book was lost and found again (every book has a point of crisis it must survive, a moment when it appears impossible).

The last quarter of *Oxygen* was written in England. I was temporarily homeless. I stayed with my parents in Bath and set up a little writing space, like a priest's hole, at the end of the garage. I wrote among bunches of dried flowers, bags of golf clubs, boxes of wine. I was already overdue on the delivery. It was winter. There were patterns of frost on the window. One by one my characters arrived at their appointed places. On the last day I wrote for nine hours, pressed save, sat back and breathed in from my teeth to my toes.

Two and a half years sweating over a book! Elaborate cure.

Andrew Miller (*b.* 1960) received his MA in Creative Writing from UEA in 1991. His first novel, *Ingenious Pain* (1997), won the international IMPAC Award. Five other novels have followed, including *Oxygen* (2001), which was shortlisted for the Booker Prize and the Whitbread Novel Award. His most recent novel is *Pure* (2011).

Losing My Voice

Andrew Cowan

Like a person's 'presence', a writer's 'voice' is a tricky thing to pin down. When James Wood characterises Saul Bellow's prose as 'jivey and broken and rapid', or speaks of Dickens's 'bounciness', he isn't describing the sound they make so much as the rhythms they move to, conceiving of 'voice' as something more kinetic than aural, which relates on some level to their way of being in the world, their attitude towards it, and this implies a particular perspective on things, which will influence the themes a writer is drawn to, and the ways in which those themes are treated.

Many of the epithets we use of 'voice' are suggestive of personality or character, and so incline us to apply them equally to the person of the writer. In the precision and particularity of her noticing, and the scrupulousness of her describing – her resistance to familiar formulations, to the already seen, the already said – the writer expresses a point of view, a singularity of seeing, a sensibility, and this has a moral dimension. The integrity of the writer's engagement with language – and so, by ready implication, with life – will either ring true or false to us.

We may have to listen very hard, though: almost as hard as the writer. My own, somewhat unbouncy way of being in the world draws to me certain themes – principally 'loss' (e.g., my third novel, *Crustaceans*) and what Richard Ford calls the 'normal applauseless life of us all' (my fourth novel, *What I Know*) – but while my engagement with these themes determines the things that I notice, and the ways in which I describe them, I can never be quite certain that I'm noticing accurately enough, or describing clearly enough, that I'm tackling loss without becoming mawkish, or describing the quotidian without becoming boring. However hard I listen, I can never quite *know* whether or not I'm ringing true. My own voice, in that sense, eludes me.

And faced with the anxiety of *not knowing*, with the inherent unreliability of words, my habitual defence is to reach after the consolations of formal patterning – assonance, alliteration, half-rhyme, metrical and rhythmical riffs – and to place all of these in the service of a particular cadence that plays in my mind whenever I attempt to fix any words on the page.

It's an insistent cadence, always there, and much of the effort of writing for me is dedicated to an obsessive, compulsive pestering of the page to find the exact words – or the exact combinations of words – that will allow me to express a particular thought or image or feeling in tune with this tune in my head. And if I can't find the exact rhythm – the exact cadence – then that thought or image or feeling must often remain unexpressed.

Which can be frustrating, since it seems – sometimes – that I can no more rid myself of this rhythm than I can rid myself of myself. My identity is in some way bound up with the aural aspect of voice, and this makes the experience of being translated, in particular, oddly perplexing: how can these foreign words, written to this foreign grammar, possibly sound at all like me? How can this first sentence, which I remember labouring over for weeks, continue to carry anything like the same cadence? And – most odd and perplexing of all – in the case of the Japanese, Korean and Hebrew books that bear my name, how can this baffling script carry even the slightest remnant of the sound of me? For all I know, in Hebrew I sound just like Saul Bellow.

One advantage of working at UEA is that I am daily in the ambit of both the MA in Literary Translation (MALT) and the British Centre for Literary Translation (BCLT), which has recently allowed me to explore the possibility of finding my voice in a variety of other languages, including German, Italian, Spanish and Japanese. As a writer-in-residence at the BCLT's annual Summer School, for instance, I was able to participate in the efforts of the Italian workshop group as it dedicated itself to the task of achieving not just a translation of the first few pages of *What I Know*, but a translation of the 'melody' of those pages, my eventual role being to adjudicate between the students' competing 'equivalences' of the rhythms of my sentences.

I listened, and what I heard in each case was a version of Italian whose metre and patterns of repetition, whose phrase-lengths and punctuation pauses, sounded uncannily (though intermittently) familiar, but which – I was told – fell on their native Italian ears as ever-so-slightly accented, as *foreign*. This, paradoxically, lent the translation a certain authenticity – it sounded somehow subtly 'English' – whereas any hint of foreignness in the original would have been a measure, for me, of its inauthenticity, and so of its failure.

What I Know is the first person narration of a humdrum private detective called Mike Hannah, who discovers, at the age of forty, that he 'knows' a great deal about the private lives of strangers, but is a stranger to himself, that he has amassed any number of facts about other people, but has achieved very little in the way of self-knowledge. And so he turns the technology of his trade upon those closest to him: he begins to investigate his family and friends, hoping to discover what constitutes a 'life', to understand what makes his own life tick.

Self-revelation is therefore key, and Mike Hannah's narrative of self-scrutiny and self-discovery centres on issues of authenticity or identity – which in part finds its expression in my authorial attempt to achieve a *trueness* of tone in the telling. But while the Italian translation succeeded in so far as it was able to ventriloquise 'Englishness', it was never an intention of the original to ventriloquise a 'character' or 'type' that might be labelled, let's say, 'forty-year-old humdrum private detective called Mike Hannah'.

His 'character' is an effect of the text, of course, a construct, and is revealed in the choices he is represented as making and in his reflections upon those choices, but the voice in which he 'speaks' is only minimally inflected by indicators of class or region – or even profession – and is only secondarily intended to represent his personality. How Mike Hannah sounds is, above all – and to a degree that undermines my own faith as a teacher in the distinction between author and narrator – a function of the authorial voice. The phrasing is as much the authentic expression of Andrew Cowan as it is of Mike Hannah.

Throughout my time with the Italians there were passionately argued alternatives for both the sense and the sound of Mike Hannah's narration, and what I realised as I listened to their discussions was that here was an equivalence of sorts for the process of writing, for the endlessly tiring tussle with language that Don DeLillo calls 'the old, slow water-torture business of invention and doubt and self-correction'. Clearly translation was as effortful and arduous and conflicted a process as writing, but clearly, in one respect at least, a translation into Italian (or any other Western European language) is relatively unproblematic in that much of the cultural and conceptual luggage will carry more or less straightforwardly over. My collaboration with a Japanese translator on the MALT programme, however, has revealed to me the difficulty of rendering almost any English into Japanese without the need for potentially cluttering contextualisations, irrespective of the problem of capturing a particular author's cadence or 'melody'.

A professional, experienced translator of contemporary English fiction and non-fiction, Yoko Shimada wanted to test the notion of a 'simpatico' translation founded on congeniality and proximity (she wouldn't usually meet or even talk to her authors) by attempting a translation of my novel *Crustaceans*, while based for a year at UEA. Her progress was premised on frequent impromptu meetings in which she would challenge me to account for the intention behind every phrase and to explain the wider resonance of every noun (or so it seemed), and though at first I floundered, I did eventually arrive at an understanding of what I'd been up to, and was able to communicate this to her. But the cultural gap was there from the outset; it was there on the spine of the book.

Crustaceans is called *Crustaceans* partly because I liked the seaside sound of the word, this being a novel set in a seaside resort. The word also has iconic significance for the narrator in that it's the first word he imagines teaching his newborn son to pronounce: they will go beachcombing, he anticipates, 'gathering shells…raiding rockpools for crabs'. And it has thematic significance because the narrator, struggling with his son's subsequent death, retreats into himself, into his shell.

But it seems there's no comparable word in Japanese for 'crustaceans', nothing that sounds like waves breaking on shingle *and* carries the same colloquial connotations of emotional reserve *and* can be found in most people's standard vocabulary: the nearest equivalent is a specialist, zoological term that might – at its most economical and musical (it does at least alliterate) – translate back into English as 'aquatic arthropods'. And what applies here – before the book is even opened – applies equally elsewhere in the novel, the problems posed for Yoko being typified by this seemingly simple sentence:

> My kitchen – a sink, drainer and Baby Belling cooker – was built into a recess to the left of the chimney-breast, a slatted partition to hide it.

Possibly in Italian – or in French or German or Spanish – 'Baby Belling' would similarly fail to signify, though the context might guide the reader towards a good enough understanding; saving which, a native brand of appliance might be substituted. But in Japanese there is no concept, either, of the contextualising 'chimney-breast', and what I realised when Yoko asked me to account for this sentence was just how far my choices had been governed by sound, far more than I'd been fully conscious of when writing the book. Her task then was many-sided, for whatever solutions she might arrive at for the sense of this sentence, there would remain the problem of achieving an equivalence for the alliteration of 'Baby', 'Belling', 'built' and 'breast', and the near-rhymes of 'recess' and 'breast', 'partition' and 'kitchen', 'drainer and 'cooker'.

This semi-conscious attachment to musical patterning is everywhere in my work, I've come to realise, a simple example from *What I Know* being found in these two sentences: 'I am a private investigator, and business of late has been slack. My wife is a teacher of maths.'

Conversationally, the Italians suggested, a more natural way for my detective to express himself here would be, 'My wife is a maths teacher.' But this alternative failed to present itself to my mind in the writing, and the reason, I'm sure, is because it wouldn't have allowed me to arrive at those two tidy phrases of eight beats and the end-line assonance of 'slack' and 'maths'.

Such habitual tidiness is one reason why I will never, regrettably, sound like Saul Bellow – in any language – but the experience of engaging with translators in trial situations has brought me closer to an understanding, I think, of what my 'cadence' consists of, and confirmed me in the suspicion that my real challenge as a writer is not actually to achieve on the page the cadence that plays in my mind, but to arrive at some other rhythms, some less familiar patterns – and indeed this was the intention behind my latest, as yet untitled novel, which is set in 1916 and derives from dozens of transcripts of tape recordings I made while working as an oral historian some twenty years ago.

If I wrote *What I Know* partly because I thought I knew how to do it (which lends the title an ironic inflection, an acknowledgement of my failure to free myself from the security, or shackles, of my usual method and style) this novel-in-progress was conceived partly out of frustration with the limitations of what had become the overly familiar sound of me. Derived from dozens of individual, characterful voices – each of them distinct, all literally *spoken* – the effort to achieve the singular, literary voice that might accommodate or alchemise them has forced me to stretch to some significantly longer sentences and a far greater complexity and flexibility of cadence. And possibly this confirms, as one of my Italian translators suggested, that the real effort is not so much to translate into words the rhythms I move to, but to resist those rhythms and reach after some different tunes, to rid myself of a few of my habitual riffs and invent some new ones. Possibly the real challenge for any writer in fact is not so much to find a voice, but once having found one, to lose it.

Andrew Cowan (*b.* 1960) is Director of Creative Writing at UEA. A graduate of the MA in Creative Writing (1985), he has also been Royal Literary Fund Writing Fellow at the university. His first novel *Pig* (1994) won a number of prizes, including the Sunday Times Young Writer of the Year Award and a Betty Trask Award. Three other novels have followed, of which the most recent is *What I Know* (2005). He is also author of *The Art of Writing Fiction* (2011).

The Dogged Imagination

James Scudamore

One statement you can trust is that you have to want to do it more than anything else in the world. Beyond that, every 'rule' you think you have established for yourself is subject to change from one project to another. You have to listen to the demands of the work, and different pieces will want to be written in different ways. One novel might pin you to the wall and force you to spill the beans as fast as you can, while another might leach through you slowly over time, to be tapped from your pores at intervals, like sap.

Either way, the best stuff surely happens when the writer is held to ransom, and a good test of whether or not you're writing the right thing is whether or not you could give it up even if you wanted to. It should be there when you close your eyes. If the finished article is going to be any good, and if you're going to have the patience required to finish it properly, then it has to spring from an idea that grips you so firmly that you don't have a choice in the matter. You don't have your ideas – your ideas have you. It's that oft-cited Nabokovian 'throb' – an irresistible pull towards somewhere you know, or feel, that there is gold.

It might help to think of yourself as a navigator. You're finding your way around, just like the reader. The difference is that you're the first one in, which means that you're the one who has to write it all down. The talent is in how you listen. And this should be a comfort for at least two reasons. First, it means that you shouldn't worry about losing ideas: if an idea wants you badly enough then it will keep coming back to bite. Second, it means you can improve. You're not a god – you're a hostage. If a negative reaction stings because you sense it might be justified, then you can berate yourself for nothing more than being a bad listener, and try to *fail better* next time around. (On the other hand, of course, if you are positively received, then remember that all you did was to be stubborn and to listen prudently, and don't let it go to your head.)

One skill you can't really do without, then, is that of being able to recognise a good idea. Assuming you are listening well, you will know soon enough if something isn't going to fly. If you can't shake it, and nothing can stop you wanting to get it down, and to worry away at it until it becomes something you can live with, then you have a dogged imagination, and it's probably going to be okay. Then all you need are the guts to start again if it doesn't come out right the first time. To escape the clichés of the imagination – the received ideas and the worn narrative ruts. To keep going until it's good – or at least, until it isn't bad.

The thrill of imaginative writing, whether your goal is to test the limits of language or to reach fine kernels of emotional truth, whether your lodestars are image and symbol or character and story, is that it is happening all the time. You walk around in the real world, interacting with it if necessary, while its counterpart is secretly nurtured. The constant, quiet machinery of this process affords a warm, clandestine thrill. And then there's the exhilaration of smuggling from one world to the other: of seeing or hearing something that seems to have escaped from your imagination and must be repatriated with all speed.

You often read about writers having special notebooks or pens they like to use. For what it's worth, my advice would be to fetishise the sentences, not the paper. Chew them over. Take off somewhere quiet to spy on them. Regard them in different lights, from different angles. Shine a torch on them in the middle of the night. Squint at them when you're hung over. Scribble them on the backs of envelopes, then live with them for a while. Keep the original envelope in case that version was the best one (as it so often is). And retain at all times your trust in the idea that is leading you, even if you can't really define it. Take Kundera's view that 'if the novel is successful it must necessarily be wiser than its author', and be reassured that you may not know the answer to the question, *What am I writing about?* until quite late in the process.

However early that question is answered, it should not be the starting point. You can always tell when it was, because the result, however well engineered, will have the dry whiff of contrivance. It will be writing that bellows what it is about, because it will result from the pursuit of what someone once thought was clever, and not from the stubborn refusal of an idea to go away. Think of the old explanation as to why a cathedral was less beautiful than the Alhambra – that while the former looks as if it is desperately struggling up towards the heavens, the latter seems to have been conferred on the world from above.

The dogged imagination, which is really just an attempt to describe elegantly a kind of stubborn, creative monomania, should keep you topped up with another crucial ingredient, which is confidence. You need to be able to ride out those moments when it feels like an obscure, minority pursuit, get over them, and see every thinking non-reader as an opportunity. Of course, if you have the kind of temperament I'm talking about, none of this will matter much to you, since you'll have no choice but to do it anyway. Because as I said at the top, one statement you can trust is that you have to want to do it more than anything else in the world.

James Scudamore (*b.* 1976) received his MA in Creative Writing from UEA in 2004 and returned as a Visiting Fellow in Creative Writing in 2009. His first novel, *The Amnesia Clinic* (2007), won the Somerset Maugham Award and was shortlisted for the Costa First Novel Award, the Commonwealth Writers' Prize and the Dylan Thomas Prize. It was followed by *Heliopolis* (2009), which was longlisted for the Man Booker Prize in 2009.

My Failed Novel

Nam Le

A few years ago I wrote a novel. It took me over four years, and came in at more than 700 pages. It was the hardest thing I'd done – the best thing I was capable of – and it wasn't good enough. I threw it away. A few years on – a few months ago – I published this book, a collection of short stories. Immediately I noticed that most of the reviews made reference to my age – or, more to the point, my youth. I'm twenty-nine (a veritable babe in this field where forty and fifty year olds are routinely described as 'young'). Though this reflexive age-checking was clearly positive in tone, I had misgivings about what I took to be its bass-line assumption: that the work of younger writers was typically somehow lesser, or hollower, somehow preparatory or provisional; that with age came the wisdom – or, failing that, the lived experience – from which lasting fiction was made. Absurd, I thought. What lived experience could older writers (many of whom I knew to lead unremarkable, sedentary lives) possibly attain that couldn't be imagined, inferred or extrapolated by younger writers? And wasn't that the crucial charge of all writers? To look through – and beyond – their own circumstance? Why, in any case, was it assumed that writers got better with age? Wasn't the canon full of writers who'd busted out of the gate with their best work (Golding, Heller, Ellison, Marilynne Robinson, not to mention whole slews of poets)?

The only thing worse, it seemed to me, than being praised for achievement despite my youth was being forgiven failure because of it. Besides, with my failed novel behind me, I felt like a veteran.

The irony is that looking back now I've come to believe my first novel failed, of course, because I was too young to write it. What I mean by this I don't fully know. Might I feel the same way, in time, about this book? I don't know that either. What I know, at twenty-nine, is this: writing is hard, and it is slow, and its condition is failure. Everything I've written has fallen short of its ideal conception; I know this will be as true when I'm sixty as it is now. What's more, I know I'll only get a handful of failures: we writers have to face the finiteness of words fitted to time the same way we all, eventually, have to face death. Still, I'm excited. I'm young. I have nothing and no one to answer to. My failures are mostly ahead of me. And as long as I believe that I can get better, that the last thing I wrote was the best thing I was capable of, and that the next thing will be the hardest yet, then that's enough. No, more than enough – it's everything.

Nam Le was born in Vietnam in 1978 and raised in Australia. He was David T. K. Wong Writing Fellow at UEA in 2008. His book of short stories *The Boat* has been translated into fourteen languages and won many prizes, including the PEN/Malamud Award, the Australian Prime Minister's Literary Award and the Pushcart Prize.

My Japan

Kazuo Ishiguro

Kenneth Baker's Belmont Press published in 2000 a deluxe limited-edition book, Early Japanese Stories, *comprising three short stories from my 'UEA period', rather wonderfully illustrated by Eileen Hogan. What follows is the introduction I wrote for that volume. At the time I was concerned primarily to describe my relationship to Japan as an imaginary landscape. Reading it again now, I feel it also gets down, pretty accurately, the essence of my experience as a UEA Creative Writing student.* KI

More than twenty years have passed since I wrote the stories that follow. All three, as you see, are set in Japan, and concern only Japanese characters. But already, by that time, I'd ceased to be particularly Japanese.

If you'd come across me then, that autumn of 1979, you wouldn't easily have guessed my origins. My features would have looked Japanese, yes. But I had hair down to my shoulders, a drooping, bandit-style moustache, a raggy beard. The only accent discernible in my speech was that of someone brought up in the Home Counties of England, infected at times by the languid, already dated vernacular of the late hippy era. And if we'd got talking, we'd most likely have discussed rock music, football, or perhaps the year I'd just spent working with the homeless in London. Had you brought up Japan, asked me about its culture, you might even have detected a trace of impatience enter my manner as I declared my ignorance on the grounds that I'd never set foot in that country – not even for a holiday – since leaving it at the age of five.

I had that autumn arrived with my one suitcase, a guitar and a portable Olivetti typewriter in Buxton, Norfolk – a small village with an old water mill and flat farm fields all around it. I'd come to this place because I'd been accepted on a one-year postgraduate Creative Writing course at the University of East Anglia. The university was just ten miles away, in the cathedral town of Norwich, but I had no car and my only way of getting there was by means of a bus service that operated just once in the morning, once at lunch-time and once in the evening. (But this, I soon discovered, was no great hardship, since I was rarely required at the university more than twice a week.) I'd rented a room in a small house occupied by a youngish man whose wife of two years had just left him. No doubt, for him, the house was filled with the ghosts of his wrecked dreams – or perhaps he just wanted to avoid me; in any case, I wouldn't set eyes on him for days on end. In other words, after the frenetic life I'd been leading in London, here I was, faced with an unusual amount of quiet and solitude in which to transform myself into a writer.

My little room, furthermore, was not unlike the classic writer's garret. The ceilings sloped claustrophobically – though if I stood on tip-toes I had a view, from my single window, of ploughed fields stretching away into the distance. There was a small table, the surface of which my Olivetti and an angle-poise lamp took up more or less entirely; and instead of a bed, there was on the floor a rectangular piece of industrial foam that would cause me to sweat in my sleep, even on the bitterly cold Norfolk nights.

It was in this room that I examined carefully the two short stories I'd written over the summer, wondering if they were too dreadful to submit to my new classmates. (We were a class of six that met once a fortnight.) At that point in my life I'd written virtually nothing else in the way of prose fiction, having earned my place on the course with a radio play rejected by the BBC. In fact, having previously made firm plans to become a rock star by the time I was twenty, my literary ambitions had only just made themselves known to me. The two stories I was now scrutinising had been written in something of a panic, in response to the news that I'd been accepted on the course. One was about a London adolescent who poisons his cat, the other about street fights in Glasgow (where I'd spent some time as a community worker). They were not so good. I started on another story, about a suicide pact, set like the others in present day Britain. Then quite suddenly one night, during perhaps my third or fourth week in that little room, I found myself writing, with a new and urgent intensity, about Japan – about Nagasaki, the city of my birth, in the last days of the Second World War.

This, I should point out, was something of a surprise for me. Today, the prevailing atmosphere is such that it is virtually an instinct for any aspiring young writer of mixed cultural origins to explore his 'roots' in his work. But that was far from the case then. We were still a few years away from the explosion of 'multi-cultural' literature in this country. Salman Rushdie was an unknown with one out-of-print sci-fi book to his name. Asked to identify the leading young British author of the day, most people would have mentioned Margaret Drabble; of older writers, Iris Murdoch, William Golding, Anthony Burgess, John Fowles were prominent. Foreigners like Gabriel Garcia Márquez or Milan Kundera were read only in tiny numbers, their names meaningless even to keen readers.

Such was the literary climate of the day that when I finished that first Japanese story – 'A Strange and Sometimes Sadness', the first in this volume – for all my sense of having discovered an important new direction, I began immediately to wonder if this departure shouldn't be viewed as a bit of self-indulgence; if I shouldn't quickly return to more 'normal' subject matter. I remember it was only after considerable hesitation I began to show the story around, and I remain to this day profoundly grateful to my fellow students, to my tutors, Malcolm Bradbury and Angela Carter, and to the novelist Paul Bailey – that year the university's writer-in-residence – for their determinedly encouraging response. Had they been less positive, I would probably never again have written about Japan. As it was, I returned to my room and wrote and wrote. Throughout the winter of '79–'80, and well into the spring, I spoke to virtually no one aside from my fellow students, the village grocer from whom I'd buy the breakfast cereals and lamb kidneys on which I existed, and my girlfriend (today my wife), who'd come to visit me every second weekend. It wasn't a balanced life, but in those four or five months I managed to complete one half of my first novel, *A Pale View of Hills* – set also in Nagasaki, in the years of recovery after the atom bomb – as well as the third story collected here, 'A Family Supper'. (The other story, 'The Summer after the War' was written a little later in 1982, just after the publication of *A Pale View*.) I can remember occasionally during this period tinkering with some idea not set in Japan, only to find my interest waning rapidly.

Those months were crucial for me, in so far as without them I'd probably never have become a writer. Since then, I've often looked back and asked: what was going on with me? What was all this peculiar energy? My conclusion has been that just at that point in my life I'd become engaged in an urgent act of preservation. To explain this, I'll need to go back a little.

I had come to England, aged five, with my parents and sister in April 1960 (my father was a research scientist) to the town of Guildford, Surrey, in the affluent 'stockbroker belt', thirty miles south of London. The photographs taken shortly after our arrival show an England from a vanished era. Men wear grey V-neck pullovers with ties, cars still have running boards and a spare wheel on the back. The Beatles, the sexual revolution, student demos, 'multi-culturalism' were all round the corner, but it's hard to believe the England we first encountered even suspected it. To meet a foreigner from France or Italy was remarkable enough – never mind one from Japan.

Our family lived in a cul-de-sac of twelve houses just where the paved roads ended and the countryside began. It was less than a five-minute stroll to the local farm and the lane down which rows of cows trudged back and forth between fields. Milk was delivered by horse and cart. A common sight I remember vividly from my first days in England – something I registered as an exotic feature of this country – was that of squashed hedgehogs on the roadside, tucked neatly into the gutter, awaiting collection.

All our neighbours went to church, and when I went to play with their children, I noticed they all said grace before eating. I duly attended Sunday school, and before long was singing the *Magnificat* and *Te Deum* in the church choir. (I was to become, aged ten, the first Japanese Head Chorister seen in Guildford.) I went to the local primary school – where, of course, I met only English children – and from when I was eleven, travelled by train to my grammar school in nearby Woking, sharing the carriage each morning with ranks of men in pinstripe suits and bowler hats, going to their offices in London. By this stage I had become thoroughly trained in the manners expected of middle-class boys in the Home Counties of those days. When visiting a friend's house, I knew to stand to attention the instant an adult wandered into the room; to ask permission before getting down from the dining table.

But all this time, I was leading another life at home with my Japanese parents. At home there were different rules, different expectations, a different language. (To this day, I speak to my parents in an appalling version of Japanese peppered with English words and phrases.) My parents' original intention had been that we return to Japan after a year, perhaps two. In fact, for our first eleven years in England we were in a perpetual state of going back 'next year'. As a result, my parents' outlook remained that of visitors, not of immigrants. They'd often exchange observations about the curious customs of the natives without feeling any onus to adopt them. And for a long time the assumption remained that we children would return to live our adult lives in Japan.

Accordingly, efforts were made to keep up the Japanese side of our education. Each month a parcel would arrive from Japan, containing the previous month's comics, magazines and educational digests, all of which I'd devour eagerly with or without my parents' assistance. These parcels ceased some time in my teens – perhaps after my grandfather's death – but my parents' talk of old friends, relatives, episodes from their lives in Japan, all kept up a steady supply of images and impressions. And then I always had my own store of memories – surprisingly vast and clear: of my grandparents, of favourite toys I'd left behind, the classically traditional Japanese house we'd lived in (I can still reconstruct it room by room), my kindergarten, the local tram stop, the fierce dog that lived by the bridge, the child's chair in the barber's shop equipped with a special toy steering wheel.

What this all amounted to was that as I was growing up, long before I'd ever thought to create fictional worlds in prose, I was busily constructing in my mind a richly detailed place called 'Japan' – a place to which I in some way belonged, and from which I drew a certain sense of my identity and my confidence. The fact that I'd never physically returned to Japan during that time only served to make my own vision of the country more vivid and personal.

Hence the need for preservation. For by the time I reached my mid-twenties – though I never clearly articulated this at the time – I was coming to realise certain key things. I was starting to accept that 'my' Japan perhaps didn't much correspond to any place I could go to on a plane; that the way of life of which my parents talked, that I remembered from my early childhood, had largely vanished during the 'economic miracle' years of the Sixties and Seventies; that in any case, the Japan that existed in my head might always have been, to a large extent, an emotional construct put together by a child out of memory, imagination and speculation. And perhaps most significantly, I'd come to realise that with each year that went by, this Japan of mine – this precious place I'd grown up with – was getting fainter and fainter.

I'm now sure that it was this sense, that 'my' Japan was unique and at the same time terribly fragile, something not open to verification from outside – least of all from the 'real' modern-day Japan – that drove me on to work in that room in Norfolk. What I was doing was getting down on paper that world's special colours, mores, etiquettes, its dignity, its shortcomings, everything I'd ever thought about the place, before they faded forever from my mind. It was my wish to rebuild my Japan in fiction, to make it safe, so that I could thereafter point to a book and say: 'Yes, there's my Japan, inside there.'

A book. I soon went on to publish two of them – novels – set in 'my' Japan: *A Pale View of Hills* (1982) and *An Artist of the Floating World* (1986). After that, perhaps, I felt my Japan was no longer so tentative; for certainly, from my third novel – *The Remains of the Day* – onwards, I've felt little urge to use Japanese themes or settings. But the short stories from those days had never, until now, found a secure home. For those of you interested in such things, this is their publishing history.

'A Strange and Sometimes Sadness' first appeared in a now long-defunct literary magazine, *Bananas*, in June 1980. It was later included in *Faber Introductions 7: Stories by New Writers* (1981). 'A Family Supper' first appeared in another extinct journal, *Quarto*, sometime in 1980, and was later anthologised in *The Penguin Book of Modern British Short Stories* (1987). 'The Summer after the War' appeared in *Granta* (issue 7) in the spring of 1983. Now here they are, after all these years, beautifully illustrated and bound together for the first time – a *book*, to which I can point and say, yes, there's my Japan, safe inside there.

Kazuo Ishiguro (*b.* 1954) received his MA in Creative Writing from UEA in 1980. His first novel was *A Pale View of Hills* (1982) and since then he has published five other novels, of which the most recent is *Never Let Me Go* (2005). He has been shortlisted four times for the Booker Prize, winning it in 1989 for his novel *The Remains of the Day*. He has also written screenplays, including *The White Countess* (2005).

The Scientific Anglian

Jeremy Noel-Tod

Dr Johnson's observation that 'a man will turn over half a library to make one book' is one of the best mottoes I know for UEA's emphasis on Creative Writing as an extension of literary studies. Half a modern library, of course, is too much information even for the most encyclopaedic genius. Scaling down across the centuries, a small second-hand bookshop may now be more like the kind of personal research environment that Johnson had in mind.

This, at least, was true for me when I wrote my PhD on T. S. Eliot's *Four Quartets* (1944), a work whose mid-century celebrity makes it a set text on shelves stocked by the libraries of retired lecturers. As well as books related to Eliot, I also collected hand-annotated copies of the poem itself, with their evidence of private scholarship and reflection: 'cf. Keats' imitation of Chaucer'; '?? The Crucifixion'; 'weak [wavily underlined]'; '[asterisked passage] Daddy's favourite'.

Communing with the readership of the past is one of the bookshop's attractions for the prospective writer. It is a living encounter with the posterity that Eliot imagined in an essay written just as he was starting out, 'Tradition and the Individual Talent' (1919). Assuming a voice of prophetic authority, the young poet asserts that 'existing order' of literature's 'monuments' will be 'modified by the introduction of the new (the really new) work of art among them'. Success, however, will only come to the writer who is able to 'develop or procure the consciousness of the past'.

'Procure' is an encouraging touch for the browser of brown paperbacks. The second-hand bookshop, by combining the historical range of the university library with the transient availability of the high-street chain, embodies Eliot's conception of literary tradition as a time-honoured yet provisional entity. Its 'simultaneous existence and... simultaneous order' is always shifting about, promising one day to find room for the book that you make from the gaps that you leave.

Ten years ago, living in Norwich as a freelance writer with a lot of free time, I was often in second-hand bookshops, turning them over for ideas (Eliot also speaks encouragingly of the 'necessary laziness' of the creative writer). Browsing the bargain boxes was as much a ritual as keeping a notebook. The following piece describes a shop which seemed to have found room for almost every faded Penguin under the sun. Eventually, I realised it was a subject itself.

SORRY, WE ARE CLOSED AT PRESENT said the sign, hung in a glass door sprayed with cracks. But despite the opening hours chalked up on a black, cat-shaped board in the window (11.40–5.40), *The Scientific Anglian*, Booksellers and Scientific Consultancy, 30–30a St Benedicts Street, Norwich, was closed for good.

It looked as though it might have been shut for years. The two large display windows were more strewn than stocked. A stranded, bleached copy of *The Hidden Places of Nottinghamshire* curled up in the left bay, covered with nuggets of plaster. Nearby lay an electric razor, plugged in, and a cat-shaped draught excluder. The overlapping, mirror-backed shelves of an almost empty display rack chopped the neck from my pygmy reflection. In the top corner of the window, a suspended pair of riding boots promised *Three Shelves Of Horse Books*. The only evidence of recent intervention was a clock showing the right time and date. In the right window, a lamp like a ship declared on its sailing shade *We Buy Books*. *Inside Is Like An Aladdins Cave Of Hardback Books* said another sign. Growing on the flaking front of the upper storey, two buddleia bushes shook purple spears over the street.

In fact, the shop had only just, grudgingly, shut down. Until June 2002, Norman Peake (no relation to Mervyn the novelist, despite local rumour), its 81-year-old proprietor, could be seen standing at the door, picking out change for customers from the pockets of his suit. He was legendary for knowing his way around the medieval city of his stock – its towers, alleyways and dens. Browsing by oneself, however, was something like taking an eye test on an assault course.

Driff's, the defunct guide to Britain's second-hand and antiquarian bookshops, described the shop as it was in the mid-1980s:

> Much declined from its former glory, not always poss to get upstairs, depends on owner's mood. He is alleged to be related to Mervyn Peake and the place is very Gormenghast. Perhaps he is Mr Flay. Dislikes dealers espec this one! The day I was there somebody had thrown a brick through the window. I already have the alibi prepared.

We Are Not Members Of The A.B.A. (the Antiquarian Booksellers Association) declared a yellow sign set in a neon hoop in the doorway's upper light: *Lapidemus Igitur Norvicences Cornices* (*Let Us Therefore Throw Stones at the Norwich Crows*).

During the few years I knew it, *The Scientific Anglian* was perhaps most reminiscent of Mr Krook's Rag and Bottle shop in *Bleak House* – where, Dickens says, 'everything seemed to be bought, and nothing to be sold'. After my visit last year, I realised that I had unguardedly put down, and not picked up, a volume of the *Sphere History of English Literature*, just purchased from Oxfam. Inevitably, when I went back, it was nowhere to be seen – a small titbit to an insatiable maw.

Perhaps Mr Krook's fate in *Bleak House* – spontaneous combustion – was at the back of the mind of the fire officer who finally insisted that the fuel-crammed premises cease trading, several years before its octogenarian owner had reckoned on retiring. Now, instead, Mr Peake was busy transferring the stock from his other Norwich property – an estimated 250,000 books, bought at auction and lured in by the ship-lamp over the years – to the St Benedicts premises, where he said that he would continue to live, with his cats, after selling off the contents.

The shop's curious name, painted in white Gothic script on black across the shop front, was originally a combination of targeted messages. When Mr Peake moved to Norwich, the UEA – a mile or two away – was also about to open for business. It was expected at that time to specialise in agricultural studies, including geology. The 'Scientific' set out what he thought would be his stall; the 'Anglian' answered the charge that he was a 'foreigner', despite having been born in Essex. (A Norwich crow had told him that only Norfolk and Suffolk were really 'Anglia'.) After thirty-five years in the city, there was now an occasional Norfolk inflection to his speech: 'nearboy'.

Peake studied geology during the Second World War, but ended up working as a chemical engineer. He continued with geology as a hobby, and visited Norfolk on holidays, particularly at Easter, when the low spring tides allowed him to pursue his study of the chalk layer. He became an expert on chalk in the county, which was then regarded, academically, as 'Cambridge's back garden'. In 1960 he published the first account of Norfolk chalk, a work for which he 'visited every conceivable hole in the ground, even rabbit holes' – 340 in all – and explored the chalk tunnels dug under Norwich.

After that, Peake was regularly sought out to advise on the problems posed by these tunnels. In the early twentieth century a sleeping couple were suffocated when their house dropped into one overnight. More recently, a bus sank into the road where another caved in beneath it. One of his last commissions saw him lowered down three 150-foot holes in a cage, armed with a telephone and chisel, by the developers of the Castle Mall shopping centre.

He retained his passion for the substance. The basement of his shop was, he told me, solid chalk towards the bottom. And there was a building site up the road where they had just reached the chalk in their excavations. 'I shall probably go and have a look at that tomorrow evening.'

We talked in the middle of the front part of the shop, Mr Peake parked squarely in the main gangway, while I sat on a stool in the narrow entrance to the Earth Sciences section. Short, white-stubbled, with thick, square glasses and various surviving teeth, he was dressed in an old tweed suit, dark-blue shirt and brown floral tie. Describing the geological underworld of Norwich, he sketched invisible diagrams with his finger down the spine of a cookery book called *Creative with Cream*. Behind him the labelled shelves ascended from *Giles* annuals to *Nuclear Power – Weapons*.

During the Cold War, Peake was a member of CND and the National Peace Assembly. He also belonged to the Communist Party. When his employers were taken over by an American company in the late Sixties, he decided to quit his chemical engineering job, fearing a McCarthyite witch-hunt.

He started the shop in 1967, moving up from Sussex and acquiring the Victorian premises from a greengrocer. The earlier name, *Walkers Stores,* is still visible, spaced down the seaweed-green tiles on either side of the Art Deco-era shopfront. In the Sixties the kiosk at the back, where regular customers came to settle their accounts, was still in place. Mr Peake recalled with relish a notice inside it on the subject of *How to Sell Bacon.* This featured a labelled dissection of a pig and a note advising the grocer, in case of maggots, to cut out the rotten area and sell as quickly as possible. Now the back room of the shop was dominated by a handsome wooden cabinet once intended for the sale of geological specimens – a sideline which fell through.

The Scientific Anglian was originally on three levels. The basement closed first, in 1974, when the ceiling was ruled too low to serve as a shop. The upper floor went next, in 1985, when two schoolboys started a fire by stacking open books face down (Mr Peake demonstrated with a copy of *Biggles in the Orient*) and inserting a firework beneath. It was shut for having no fire exit. Fire regulations finally closed the remaining ground floor, for lack of a rear exit, and for high shelves where over-reaching browsers might collide fatally with the fluorescent lights.

Even though the low piles of books once set out on the floor itself had been hustled away in an unsuccessful attempt to appease the safety inspector, the ground floor was still chock-a-block. The strange counter which ran down the centre of the shop was originally part of Walker's Stores, its low, deep, slanted shelves – designed to display biscuit tins – packed with paperbacks. Around the walls, in amongst the bookseller's wooden shelves, the grocer's sturdy slices of marble were still visible, strata in the shop's own geology.

The narrow ways between the tall shelves were awash with printed matter, other matter and dust, all monitored by a system of angled convex mirrors. In one of an infinite number of corners I found a squash racquet in a plastic bag, an orange safety helmet, a book on *The Rise of Modern China* and an ancient *Midland and Great Northern Railway Ledger.*

Between floor and shelves was an uncertain region of casual storage, an unstable moraine of (among other things) sunglasses, photographic slides, string, a scarf, a roll of brown tape, flat caps, maps, rust-speckled aerosols, shoe polish, sheet music, bulldog clips, a belt-buckle, a Real Ale beer mat, a large scrap of floral pattern wallpaper, a badge which demanded *Dogs Not Bombs,* and a cat-food tin. Immaculate, outdated local bus timetables were kept in a pocket on one side of a bookcase, marked *Do Not Remove.* A pile of leaflets advertising dog racing years ago at Great Yarmouth Stadium lay on a lower shelf.

I asked about the plastic dinosaur skeleton suspended above our heads. Mr Peake explained that he liked to decorate the shop with symbols relevant to each section. There was a miniature ship's wheel in the Nautical section, pressure gauges from a steam train for Railway, a desiccated crocodile's head for Natural History, a cardboard cut-out Kodak girl in a bright yellow bathing suit for Photography. The dinosaur represented Earth

Sciences. A bulbous anti-Zeppelin bomb was bracketed to the War shelves. These visual aids to navigation were, however, of less use in the latter years of the shop when – due to an increase in the average book size for certain subjects – the stock they represented gradually drifted to differently proportioned shelves.

Everything was labelled with little lettered stickers, black on white. The signs they composed had a distinctive humour – a mixture of irascibility and courtesy. A bulb dangles from a shelf in a little metal bowl-shade, the back of which barked *More Light? Just Ask.* One, below a genuine bee smoker – a conical contraption, dark with age, and fixed to the end of a book case – declared: *We Regret That There Are A Number Of B – – Smokers Who Still Do Not Use The Ashtrays Which We Have Provided.* It was, Mr Peake said, a 'rather terrible joke', although a metal ashtray, decked out with bright orange stickers, was accordingly provided – something else which must have given the fire officer palpitations.

Past the undecorated Poetry section ('I couldn't think of a symbol to represent Literature') was a doorway which led into a corner bricked from floor to ceiling with *Everyman and Similar* titles. On the left a high square-paned window, veiled with dust, let a little prematurely aged light in from the street. Where the walls met, thick gossamer wefts connected the window to the books. To the right, stairs led to the upper floor through a ravine of books. Near the ceiling, an ear-like fungus extruded itself from a hardback copy of *The Silence of the Lambs.*

The shop was in an undeniably decrepit state, but its owner remained alert and active, despite a violent robbery seven years ago, which left him unconscious in a pool of blood. At some point, he told me, he would have to find the time to write a scholarly note to accompany the 'Eel Pritch (Suffolk Pattern)', which he was donating from his walls to a nearby museum.

A potted lecture. Eel-pritching was carried out in glass-bottomed boats by men who speared the eels in the mud with 'pritches'. Pritches had backward-pointing barbed prongs, which made it impossible for the eel to wriggle off. The practice was outlawed in the early years of the twentieth century. This long forked thing was, said Mr Peake, the only example known of a commercially sold eel pritch, which were previously supposed to have been supplied directly by the blacksmiths to the eel-catchers. But his specimen's thick black enamelling was proof of passage through an ironmonger's, where paint was applied to prevent rust. Mr Peake bought it at the auction of a city-centre shop's contents.

He seemed to have been a keen collector of local oddities over the years. Hanging next to the pritch was a strangely shaped ceramic grid, which turned out to be an unusual example of an insulator for laying electric wires, patented by a Norwich firm before gutta-percha was employed.

As I took my leave, Mr Peake said, 'My life has been so full of unusual things, if someone asked me to write an autobiography…well, it would fill a book.' This prompted him to recall a witticism once lettered upon the Autobiography section: *More Fiction Upstairs.*

(And which reminds me, now, to mention that his History section started, decisively, *From 1066 – Earlier With Archaeology.*)

Peake's cynical, non-conformist humour was also evident in the handwritten account of the shop's battle with health-and-safety officials over the years, entitled *FIRST FLOWERS – LAST STRAW* and sellotaped to the split glass of the door. It ended with the municipal motto, *NORWICH – A FINE CITY.* But fine had been crossed out, and safe pencilled drily above it.

The shop is now a men's outfitters.

Jeremy Noel-Tod (*b.* 1978) is a Lecturer in Literature and Creative Writing at UEA. After growing up in Norfolk and Norwich, he studied at New College, Oxford, and Trinity College, Cambridge. A well-known writer on poetry in the national press and literary journals, he runs a poetry blog, *The Lyre,* and is the new editor of *The Oxford Companion to Modern Poetry.*

'Is There an East Anglian literature?'

Jeremy Page

With its fine weather and fertile soil, East Anglia has always grown its fair crop of writers. Its seclusion, literary tradition and abundance of nature provide ideal germinating conditions for creative work. Writers are, currently, thick on the ground. But – as with the region's other produce – does East Anglia's literature also have its own distinctive flavour?

In a foreword to *A Distant Cry*, a collection of short stories from East Anglia, Louis de Berniers wrote "There is not a coherent, identifiable East Anglian literature." Clearly it is often a writer's sole aim and duty to be as individually voiced as possible. But the unique physical elements that draw writers to this region also tend to be the same elements that inspire the work they then produce. They leave their trait, leading to a distinctive creative output, often readily identifiable. In this essay I shall illustrate specificities of East Anglian place, season, nature, traditions and community. I believe it is by understanding these elements, and spotting their influence in the region's literature, that we might begin to notice East Anglia's literature as having notions of cohesion.

A sense of place is fundamental to the writer. For Malcolm Bradbury, writing about Norfolk, place is one of two things: "sometimes our place is our real subject, the basic material we work with, providing our vision, setting, landscape and theme. Sometimes it is a culture which stimulates our writing and lets it happen." But perhaps more pertinent than place itself, is the extraction of the unique essence of the landscape that has inspired the writer, making its own particular connection. For East Anglia is a very particular landscape.

Without the great mountain ranges, deserts or savannah wildernesses of other continents, it may seem that as a nation we have been robbed of having wild frontiers to write about. Yet we do have the sea. The coast is our literary frontier, beyond which is an ancient and wild environment, and throughout our history it has inspired some of the best of our nation's writing. But unlike the hard fortress-cliffs of Cornish granite that butt against the Atlantic, East Anglia's edge is peculiar: it is porous, eroding, soft and malleable. It shifts from year to year with the tides, and in many locations the sea is held back by the merest of obstacles – a sand bar, a gravel spit, or dunes bound with marram. Why the sea does not simply roll over a land that is often at its level or even a few feet below seems to make little sense. As a frontier, it can often not be defined, and it is this unique character that's often seen in the region's writing. A sea's presence that can be felt, but sometimes not reached, is a mysterious presence. An element beyond reach, it seems tailor made for narratives of mystery, isolation or ghost story. In Julia Blackburn's *The Mermaid*, set on the Norfolk coast in the 1600s, a body traverses this frontier when a mermaid is found washed up. Throughout the story, it is the strangeness and otherworldliness of this coastal divide that is used to ignite the local community, reflecting itself in myth and folklore/paganism and religion/curse and fertility. Story arrives on the tide line of the shore, it washes up, like it did at Norfolk's Winterton, where Robinson Crusoe was first shipwrecked, or at the quayside, as with John Skelton's *Bowge of Court*.

Effectively, of course, the sea does often overrun the frontier, and it is this pull between the wilderness and the land which creates a very particular tension. Nowhere is this more evident than the most iconic of East Anglian frontiers – the saltmarsh. Scoured by a relentless wind and criss-crossed with an intricate labyrinth of creeks and channels, it is an often impenetrable border. It floods, it disorientates, and it inspires a particular type of East Anglian character, represented in its literature. In Susan Hill's *The Albatross*, this borderland is the home for the misfit, the outsider. In my first novel, *Salt*, I also explored this specific frontier, writing about characters who were on land, but at sea, living in a hinterland between the two elements and marginalised from them both. Between the sea and the land I found an imaginative territory that was free and exotic. For others, the saltmarsh is a place of infinite isolation and, with its dangerous flows of creeks and tides, a place of psychic peril. In Hill's *The Woman in Black*, the saltmarsh and tidal causeway are the barriers to rescue, allowing the flourishing of an intact supernatural presence.

Labyrinths to lose you, barriers and dead ends to isolate you, East Anglia has long been associated with the ghost story. In M.R. James's tremendously spooky *A Warning to the Curious*, it is the coast itself that has to be protected, utilising the three crowns legend of Aldeburgh. You disturb this delicate balance at your peril. Sparsely populated and full of perceived dangers, the East Anglian coastline is, for many, a coastline of fear.

The tidal feature which is most synonymous with East Anglia is the estuary. From the silt-fjord labyrinth of the Essex coastline, to the outpourings of the Suffolk and Norfolk rivers, these are the giant mouth-lung features that rhythmically suck in and expel the wilderness of the sea, twice each day. For the writer the estuary provides a landscape that has the duality of drought and flood, a changeling landscape that is held in continual balance. In Richard Mabey's *Home Country* this tension reflects not just his spirit, but the spirit of the region at large: "I sometimes wondered if the closeness of these unstable edges of the land was part of the secret of Norfolk's appeal to us, a reflection of a half-conscious desire to be as contingent as spindrift ourselves."

The coast is about dead ends, where characters are often portrayed metaphorically or – in some instances – literally washed up. But we can also see these dead ends in many of the other typical East Anglian landscapes. In Broadland we see the same watery half-world of the estuary, but with the added enclosing aspect of more traditional environments where one could become lost: the wood, the marsh, or the fen. For Arthur Ransome, the Broads were the Arcadian idyll for a liberated childhood. But for others – and more commonly – Broadland is a confusing landscape where roads are cut off, or re-routed, at all times liable to isolate the characters and communities that find themselves there. The closer you are to the actual open water, very often the more tangled and impenetrable the land becomes. As a result, it is a bespoke landscape for narratives where characters will be haunted, isolated, or bewildered. In fact, it is very difficult to contemplate setting fiction in the Broads without it being a ghost story, as M.R. James, L.P. Hartley and many others have realised. Or, at least, a good place for a jolly satisfying murder, for example, C.P. Snow's *Death Under Sail*. The components of the landscape are too irresistible: remote, unlit, pathways strangely orbiting the few places of open water, in many ways the Broads might be considered as similar creative territory to the outer-space narratives of science fiction. Quite literally, at Hickling Broad, no one can hear you scream.

In character terms, Broadland's qualities lean towards being the perfect location to travel to when your relationship has broken down – we might consider Rose Tremain's *The Shooting Season* as a fine example, where a former husband visits a woman whose life is held in the balance. Alternately the broads are a good narrative choice as a place to stay, if you never had the chance of a relationship in the first place.

The waterlogged world of the Norfolk and Suffolk Broads has its dry counterpart in the Breckland, another of East Anglia's unique landscapes. Once, much of the region was covered in this way, with gorse, heath and forest. In Robert MacFarlane's *The Wild Places*, he writes 'lying just off the Suffolk coast is a desert,' meaning the barren shingle spit of Orford Ness. But the same could be said for the huge swathes of Breckland, where its poor soil and the fact it consistently has the lowest rainfall in Britain means it's as close as this nation gets to having its own desert. Gorse is the Norfolk cactus, and within its spiked corrals there is a similar sense of enclosure and impenetrable nature that we had with the tangled fen around the Broads or the labyrinth of creeks that surround the estuary and cover the saltmarsh. Breckland's wilderness, with its poor dry sandy soil, is virtually worthless to the arable farmer, so has remained largely unchanged over millennia, ever since Neolithic miners dug for flint nuggets in the chalk. For the writer, this allows a near perfect opportunity to view into the past and connect with the communities that once lived there. As a result, many of the narratives set in Breckland feature the literal discovery of ancient remains – Roald Dahl's *The Mildenhall Treasure* is about the unearthing of Roman silver igniting a farmer's particular greed and isolation from his community. John Preston's *The Dig* sets its characters against the archaeological discovery of the Sutton Hoo ship burials. Treasures, unearthed, are often the catalysts of East Anglian literature, and have produced some of its finest thoughts, too: the unearthing of Roman burial urns was the origin of Sir Thomas Browne's philosophical *Hydriotaphia, Urn Burial*, written in Norfolk.

For Malcolm Bradbury, "a landscape comes to life through what has been written in it." It is impossible to consider the landscapes of the region, and their effect on the writing produced within it, without detailing its most extreme variation: the fen. Often considered to be brutal, industrial in its cultivation, divided by the rigid geometry of power lines, water channels and poplar wind-breaks, on first impressions it might seem unrelated to the soft amiable meanderings of the rest of the region's landscape. But a closer look reveals that it, too, relies upon the same sense of isolation and claustrophobia that exists elsewhere. Here, we also get dead ends, with the fenland droves (roads) stretching for miles in perfect straightness, only to end abruptly with the apparently non-sensical dissection by a drainage ditch. As with the coast and estuary, we have the same beguiling relationship to water and its confusing behaviour: in the Fens, the drainage channels are often higher than the surrounding fields, and when one is passed, a second river is revealed, even higher – a series of watery flyovers that make very little reasonable sense, until you discover that the field you have been in is actually below sea level, and should ordinarily be considered part of the seabed.

Surrounded by such confusing and isolating pressures, it is not surprising that the narratives set in the Fens tend to have these issues very much at their core. Ian McEwan's *First Love, Last Rites* combines the isolating stagnation of a fenland town with aspects of sexuality, desire to escape, failure and hope. Graham Swift's *Waterland* is similarly built around issues of seclusion, sexual angst and inescapable history. Trezza Azzopardi's *Remember Me* features the evacuation to a fenland farm to elaborate her themes of loss and displacement. My own novel, *Salt*, uses the Fens around the Great Ouse to highlight the issues of entrapment, exile and cyclical behaviour. It's a simple equation: small isolated communities plus large bewildering landscape equals unregulated growth of psychological anguish. It is also the perfect breeding ground for suspicion and secrecy. In Edward Storey's *No Other Word for it*, the closed fenland community is explored through the lens of murder and scandal and the effects of wrong accusation. In Sylvia Townsend Warner's *The Maze*, the same sense of isolated community is evoked, but this time with the theme of 'unearthing' that is noticeable in Breckland writing, or the triple crowns legend of *A Warning to the Curious*, this time dealing with issues of fen/soil fertility and the suggestion of black magic.

In many ways, the fen is an anti-landscape. It is an absence where, without gradient and other usual definable features it can feel as though the true landscape has been scraped away. But what is left behind might be considered as so much more – a 180° view of the sky. Noticeable in nearly every example of writing emerging from East Anglia – from short stories to novels, genre writing to nature writing – are descriptions of the region's famed skyscape. It is almost as though the sky is the super landscape that floats above the region, passing through all the narratives that are set beneath it. In *Salt*, the clouds were read by characters who lived on the saltmarsh below them, very much as though the clouds were characters themselves.

Related to the width and breadth of the East Anglian sky is the quality of its light. I have lived in London for nearly twenty years, but when I begin to write I invariably return to my roots, starting with the soft-greenish watery glow that exists in corridors along East Anglia's rivers and estuaries. It seems to be the meditative fertile light out of which any narrative might emerge. The Norfolk light, notably, is remarkable. It is highly particulate in nature, meaning there is a dustiness to it that colours the sky in curious ways. At a certain angle to the setting sun, a pastel lavender glow occurs. Under the harvest sun, a floury haze shimmers above the crops, the shadows pool under distant trees in shades of blue. In winter, the light seems ionised, made of pure ozone, blowing straight off the sea to bend the trees. Light is rarely missed as a descriptive opportunity for East Anglian writers, and it repeatedly shines off the page. In Trezza Azzopardi's *Winterton Blue*, Anna tries to recreate the searing brilliance of the Norfolk coastal light, and ends up throwing glitter at a wall.

Common, too, is the sense of season. It would be atypical for a text to be set in East Anglia without mention of its particular time of year. And seemingly more prominent than fiction set in many other locales, season in East Anglia is very much associated with aspects of the natural yearly cycle: spring is correlated with aspects of fertility; summer is of abundance, harvest and surplus; autumn finds its correlation with slaughter and winter with a pared-down bleakness. Rose Tremain's *The Shooting Season* is as much about the ashes of a former relationship as it is about the wider context of an autumnal slaughter, whereas for John Fowles, writing in his foreword to *Mehalah*, the Essex marshlands will forever be 'set to the key of winter.'

Nature, oppressive or benign, challenging or rejuvenating, is a constant presence in East Anglian literature. In Elspeth Barker's *Carborundum* a woman literally moves into the trees, living in a tree house for thirty years after her wedding day failed to happen. Her home is boarded up, still with wedding presents in it, but nature has saved her. Richard Mabey's *Nature Cure* is also primarily concerned with the ability to reconnect with the restoring qualities of East Anglia's natural environment which, in turn, references another writer who tried – and failed – to balance mental depression with nature's cures: the fenland poet John Clare.

It is not a coincidence that the region is *the* home for the finest writers in modern nature writing. Richard Mabey, Roger Deakin, Robert MacFarlane, Mark Cocker and Patrick Barkham have all been based in East Anglia, have set seminal works there, and their ancestry can be directly traced to the many Victorian rector diarists and rural life commentators that preceded them, all the way back to Sir Thomas Browne.

It is ironic, in an area often characterised by such isolated and static communities, that much of the region's wildlife is migratory. Birdlife, in particular, regards East Anglia merely as a stopping-off ground on global flyways. But even this behaviour seems to have found its counterpart in East Anglian fiction. In W.G. Sebald's writing, in particular *The Rings of Saturn*, we repeatedly find a narrative which is rooted, or searching for rootedness, alongside a migratory imagination which permits Sebald's unique visionary roaming of place, time and memory. The author, rooted, the imagination in migration.

Malcolm Bradbury saw writing "as a constant intersection between the local and the universal, things near-at-hand and events far away." For him, East Anglia's spaces provided the lack of distraction that enabled a freely roaming creative imagination. We might suggest a similar process was at work with Sir Henry Rider Haggard, who wrote *King*

Solomon's Mines and other exotic adventures from a Norfolk background, in so doing inspiring a whole new genre of 'lost world' literature. One lost world, inspiring another. In my second novel, *The Wake*, a similar pattern emerged where the protagonist, stuck on a boat among the tides of the Deben estuary, was able to create a diarised fiction of a life he might have had and a journey across the Southern states of America. George Borrow, another Norfolkman, had a similar agenda, roaming Europe in his literature – only he made the mistake of satirising Norwich, and duly managed to get his works burned there.

Without the populace flow that has invigorated many other areas of the country, East Anglia is far from being a backwater, as these examples suggest. It's a region where 'thought' has gravitated towards for many centuries. As Malcolm Bradbury wrote of Norwich, it was always "a place of learning, cultural activity, religious and political dissent. It too felt itself close to the continent, and was always enriched by 'Strangers.' The many Huguenots, and emigres from the French Revolution, joined with some of the great, often dissenting and reforming local families – the Frys, Bacons, Barclays, Gurneys, Martineaus – to make it one of the key regional capitals." As a result, it spawned a whole tradition of writers from Anna Sewell, Amelia Opie, George Borrow and Harriet Martineau to the multitude of writers who live there today.

Assimilation, of all these voices, but the famed 'separateness' of the region has always persisted. Across the centuries, literature set in or inspired by East Anglia notoriously depicts static, unchanging communities. Some of these communities have been the subject of detailed observations and dissection themselves. Take Ronald Blythe's *Akenfield*, upheld as a seminal work of English rural writing, or the oral histories of George Ewart Evans working in Suffolk, Parson Woodforde's diaries of village life, or George Baldry's *The Rabbit Skin Cap*, detailing an impoverished upbringing that is nonetheless richly abundant with nature and closeness to the cycle of the seasons. Charles Dickens used Yarmouth (which he described as 'the strangest place in the wide world') as a key setting for *David Copperfield*. Perhaps most famously is George Crabbe's *The Borough*, set in Aldeburgh at the start of the nineteenth century, which, due to the static nature of the community it portrays, is still largely valid today.

Writers are conduits of their environments, and it is the nature of these East Anglian communities that repeatedly suggest fertile narrative themes. Static communities are often superstitious, as seen in the stories of M.R. James, Julia Blackburn's *The Mermaid*, or Sylvia Townsend Warner's *The Maze*, and as their populations rarely change, tradition is largely intact. Many of the oral traditions and myths of previous centuries are still remembered today and in East Anglian literature they are very commonly revisited and reinvented. Take the myth of Black Shuck, for example, the mysterious ghost dog of Blythburgh and other coastal locations. It is largely considered to have been the catalyst of Arthur Conan Doyle's *The Hound of the Baskervilles*, has continually been spotted in a multitude of written, musical and fine art variations, and is still being revisited today, most recently in George Szirtes' *Shuck, Hick, Tiffey*. In a region where stories have traditionally been handed down, and often kept alive with pub storytellers and the like, it is not surprising that fiction itself has essentially become folklore, able to be revisited and refashioned for a modern age – for example, the extraction of the Peter Grimes story from George Crabbe's *The Borough* into Benjamin Britten's opera.

Static communities are also by nature suspicious – of change, and of outsiders. And it is the depiction of insiders versus outsiders that is perhaps the most common and notable trait of much of East Anglian literature. In Susan Hill's *Mr Proudham and Mr Sleight*, a woman renting a house near an odd and possibly gay old couple becomes fascinated by them – and the gothic wax models they make. Esther Freud's *The Visit* features a woman connecting with the country partly through her investigations into a foreign (German) history. It exposes problems in her own life, and an alienation from a London world which is increasingly intrusive. D.J. Taylor's *Passage Migrants* features a birdwatcher becoming obsessed by an exotic visitor – a woman holidaying in Sheringham. Ali Smith's *The Accidental* has a stranger joining a family on holiday, with troubling consequences. In all of these examples we can identify one of two things: either characters are brought to a crisis by visiting East Anglia on holiday (i.e. behaving unusually away from home), or they are brought to crisis as a result of misunderstanding or being affected by the tensions between those who arrive (outsiders) and those who stay (insiders). This has long been the case as a narrative model in East Anglian literature – take Arnold Wesker's play *Roots*, where a cosmopolitan London life is juxtaposed with an agrarian world, or M.R. James' stories, where usually a visiting naïve gentleman scholar stumbles upon a local mystery, or L.P Hartley's *The Go Between*, which straddles the worlds of turn of the (20th) century class division in Norfolk. However, it might be argued that the traditional narrative models of landed gentry living alongside a local working population have now been superceded by narratives concerning second home owners arriving in local communities, written about by Esther Freud, Penelope Lively, DJ Taylor, Ruth Rendell, Henry Sutton and Terrence Blacker, among others.

Writers react to their environments in a multitude of ways. It would be wrong to suggest that literature created in East Anglia is always readily identifiable and cohesive. But environment is so closely linked to inspiration, and inspiration to expression, that we should be keen to identify and react to the traits that the creative journey has left along its way.

The region is a frontier, a shore where writers and – by extension – their characters are able to assess the amassed experience of their lives. In Kazuo Ishiguro's *Never Let me Go*, Kathy ends the novel in a Norfolk field, "thinking about the rubbish, the flapping plastic in the branches, the shore-line of odd stuff caught along the fencing, and I half-closed my eyes and imagined this was the spot where everything I'd ever lost since my childhood had washed up."

The image of a storm beach is a pertinent one, because East Anglia has this quality at its core. Sticking out into the North Sea, bordered on almost three sides by cold water, it is a region that naturally collects, both writers and their material. As Malcolm Bradbury put it, the region serves as 'patron, producer and muse.' East Anglia, as muse, has clearly proved itself across the centuries, from the mystic writings of Julian of Norwich to Sir Thomas Browne, and is still reinventing itself today in the cultural literature hubs of the University of East Anglia and Norwich. It is as vast as you want or need it to be, it is total isolation, it is on the way to nowhere, it is surrounded by water, covered by water, below water, below a thousand acres of sky, too. It is everywhere you look and it is, oddly, invisible: more of a state of mind than an actual, tangible reality, shifting its influence from writer to writer, from age to age, but always leaving its trace.

Jeremy Page (*b.* 1969) received his MA in Creative Writing from UEA in 1994. He returned as Visiting Writing Fellow in 2009 and since then has continued to work as an associate tutor at the university. His first novel *Salt* (2007) was shortlisted for the Commonwealth Writers' Prize for Best First Book. It was followed by *The Wake* (2009) which won the fiction and poetry award at the East Anglian Book Awards and was shortlisted for the New Angle Prize. As well as writing novels, Jeremy worked for many years as a script editor for film and television.

Dust, Like Pollen

Rebecca Stott

There are a few books to which I return again and again. I have recently moved them together on to a single bookshelf above my desk: Melville's *Moby-Dick*, George Eliot's *Middlemarch*, Sterne's *Tristram Shandy*, Conrad's *Heart of Darkness*, Henry James's *Turn of the Screw*, Elizabeth Bishop's *Collected Poems*, Wallace Stevens's *Harmonium*, W. G. Sebald's *Rings of Saturn* and *Emigrants*. They are not favourite books as such; they are books that goad; they not only say *See, all of this is possible, see what can be done, if you are bold enough*, but they know things that evade me. I reach for them at the beginning of the day sometimes when the words won't come, opening randomly, whispering a sentence or two to feel the sentences against my tongue. I return to them because I want to know what they know.

What is it that Sebald's two strange books know exactly? I open them for many things – the beauty of the prose, the strange mixture of memoir, travel writing and history, the narratives that loop, the sense of perpetual erosion and decay, the melancholy poetry of it all, the effortless audacity. But, as a historian, most of all I come back to be reminded of the paradox at the heart of all history writing, that whilst we might pursue the dead, quarry out the past, try to connect and order fragments and search out ancestors, family trees and origins in archives and record offices, meanwhile the papers, records and photographs are perpetually turning to dust in our hands.

Sebald describes the restless, impossible pursuit of the dead in a passage in *Emigrants*. He has been searching for his long-dead great-uncle, the gambler Cosmo Solomon, and his lover-valet Ambros Adelwarth, across the cities of Europe for some time: 'I was looking for Cosmo and Ambros night and day,' he wrote.

> Now and then I thought I saw them disappear into an entry or a lift or turn a street corner. Or else I really did see them, taking tea out in the courtyard, or in the hall leafing through the latest papers, which were brought early every morning at breakneck speed from Paris to Deauville by Gabriel the chauffeur. They were silent, as the dead usually are when they appear in our dreams, and somewhat downcast and dejected. Generally, in fact, they behaved as if their altered condition, so to speak, were a terrible family secret not to be revealed under any circumstances. If I approached them, they dissolved before my very eyes, leaving behind them nothing but the vacant space they occupied.[1]

Sebald describes the vacant space that haunts all writers who work in the archives – the quarried object or the elusive dead flicker down corridors and in and out of files and sometimes entirely disappear. The archives eventually *come to an end*.

Sebald's work is full of dust and the creatures of dust: moths, mites and worms. In *The Emigrants* he describes arriving at the sanatorium in Switzerland where Ambros once lived, only to find that the institution's archives had long since been destroyed, not by officials, but by mice, as the principal explains:

> They took over the madhouse when it was closed and have been multiplying without cease ever since; at all events when there is no wind blowing I can hear a constant scurrying and rustling in the dried-out shell of the building, and at time, when a full moon rises beyond the trees, I imagine I can hear the pathetic song of a thousand tiny upraised throats. Nowadays I place all my hope in the mice and in the woodworm and deathwatch beetles. The sanitorium is creaking, and in places already caving in, and sooner or later they will bring about its collapse. I have a recurring dream of that collapse [...] before my very eyes, infinitely slowly, and a great yellowish cloud billows out and disperses, and where the sanatorium once stood there is merely a heap of powder-fine wood dust, like pollen.[2]

Wood dust is not really 'like pollen'. They are both powders, yes, but wood dust is dead matter returning to the earth, whereas pollen pollinates; it is fruitful. It disperses and inseminates; it brings things to life. In Sebald's hands historical source material – photographs, archives, records, files, memories – both disintegrates and pollinates; nothing entirely disappears; everything is turning into something else. The shorelines of East Anglia coastline are being eroded, battered by the sea and wind, but the land doesn't disappear, it just moves somewhere else. The dead don't disappear either; they linger, they return.

When Hilary Mantel won the Man Booker prize in 2009 with *Wolf Hall*, and went on to win the new Walter Scott prize for historical fiction in 2010, she went on the road. She gave eloquent lectures to crowded auditoriums. She explained how she worked – the archives, the records, the mounds of evidence and books she read, the notebooks she filled with minute facts and details. She talked about labour and scholarship, but she also talked about ghosts. She implied that in some important ways her work was a kind of clairvoyance as well as excavation or detective work. She bravely reasserted the powers of the visceral, spoke about the persistent presence of the uncanny in the process of historical discovery. For reviewers, this self-analysis – the co-presence of facts and ghosts – has sometimes proved a disconcerting juxtaposition.

Mantel's writing teems with ghosts – flickerings on the stairs, hallucinations of taste or smell and unaccountable voices. It is disconcerting, often uncanny. While writing *Beyond Black*, her novel about a suburban middle-aged psychic who is hounded and assaulted by ghosts she wishes would leave her alone, Mantel clearly drew on autobiographical experience.

'I am not perturbed,' she writes in her memoir, in a passage in which she described having once seen her stepfather's ghost. 'I am used to seeing things that aren't there. Or to put it in a way more acceptable to me – I am used to seeing things that "aren't there".'[3]

Those inverted commas tell us – with a glint in the eye – that Mantel does not doubt that the things she sees, though they are – apparently, reportedly, rationally – not there, are distinctly *there*.

Although Mantel's writing is freighted with material objects and thick with sensual detail, one feels that the world she describes might easily disappear at any moment. Her consistent use of the present tense, sustained through the 650 pages of *Wolf Hall*, suggests that she is conjuring something for us, like a soothsayer, a shaman or a clairvoyant. There are shades of George Eliot here, who began her first novel – a historical novel, *Adam Bede* – by introducing herself as a sorcerer:

> With a single drop of ink for a mirror, the Egyptian sorcerer undertakes to reveal to any chance comer far-reaching visions of the past. This is what I undertake to do for you, reader. With this drop of ink at the end of my pen, I will show you the roomy workshop of Mr Jonathan Burge, carpenter and builder, in the village of Hayslope, as it appeared on the eighteenth of June, in the year of our Lord 1799.[4]

But whilst we may rarely feel any ghostliness in George Eliot's novels, Mantel's use of the present tense throughout *Wolf Hall* makes us feel that if she stops concentrating, stops being the medium through which we see these images, it might all disappear:

> It is a spacious chamber with a high carved bed; his eye flickers over it. In the candlelight, the bed hangings are ink-black. The bed is empty. Henry sits on a velvet stool. He seems to be alone, but there is a dry scent in the room, a cinnamon warmth, that makes him think that the cardinal must be in the shadows, holding the pithed orange, packed with spices, that he always carried when he was among a press of people. The dead, for sure, would want to ward off the scent of the living; but what he can see, across the room, is not the cardinal's shadowy bulk, but a pale drifting oval that is the face of Thomas Cramner.[5]

Historical fiction can recreate the materiality of the past, bring it back out of the darkness, the archives and the libraries, reconstruct it for us solidly, as Mantel does with smell, taste, sound, colour and texture; it puts us on the ground so that we can sit on a velvet stool in a Tudor bedroom as Henry VIII anticipating the arrival of his cardinal, walk around it, open drawers and look through windows, but it can do much more than this. It can simultaneously freight and flicker its reconstruction of the past to remind us of the paradox at the heart of all historical writing, that paradox that forms the melancholy refrain at the heart of all Sebald's work – that the past must be recovered and yet can never be recovered.

In *On Histories and Stories* the novelist A. S. Byatt suggests that the proliferation of historical novels over the last fifty years has been stimulated by a rise in self-consciousness in historical practice. The more we take for granted that we cannot know the past, she writes, the more we tell ourselves it is another country, the more we reiterate the anxiety that ideology blinds, that all interpretations are provisional and that therefore any interpretation is as good as any other; the more we tell ourselves that history is a form of the sublime, the past becomes something to be approached but never reached, increasingly desired but impossible to touch. It is this sense of epistemological unease, Byatt argues (a compulsion to know the past that springs from a sense of the impossibility of that knowing) that provides the key to the flowering of the historical novel in the last fifty years.[6]

But if we are seeing a return to narrative in history writing at the beginning of the twenty-first century, a renaissance in the historical novel, as well as a new attention to the problems of knowing in history writing,[7] we are also seeing historical narratives which attend more closely to the precise and particular distillations of micro-histories, to material objects that show how, in the words of the philosopher of space Gaston Bachelard, 'the miniscule, a narrow gate, opens up an entire world. The details of a thing can be the sign of a new world which, like all worlds, contain the attributes of greatness. Miniature is one of the refuges of greatness.'[8]

Though, as a literary historian, I had probably long understood some of the provocative paradoxes of writing history, I only felt them for the first time a few years ago when I came across a strange drawing: a cross-section of an eyeball suspended in a tangle of handwriting. It provoked me into writing historical fiction for the first time. Isaac Newton had drawn it in one of his notebooks; it described an experiment he had undertaken in the dark of his rooms in Trinity College Cambridge in 1665. Determined to find out if pressure on the eyeball affected how we see colour, he had bought a wooden needle called a bodkin from a Cambridge market stall; back in his room he had inserted it into the back of his own eye socket. After repeating the experiment several times, he blinded himself. It took three days for his eyesight to return.

Looking into Newton's drawing was like opening a Pandora's box. Once opened, I couldn't get the lid closed on it again. All manner of ghostly images issued from it. I could see the young Newton in his rooms in Trinity College – the unmade bed, piles of books and paper, diagrams spread out on the floor amongst discarded food – a young man reading so much that he often forgot to eat, spinning from one experiment to another, sleepless, his mind racing. I could smell it: the fug, the unwashed clothes, the damp, the tallow smell from the candle smoke, wood smoke from the fire.

The audacity and singlemindedness of Newton's experiment shocked me. What if he had punctured his own eyeball that day? What if he had just put a little too much pressure on point r, just a little too much curvature onto the surface at t? What if he had ruptured one or both of his eyeballs or stared at the sun so long that his vision failed to return? He must have been possessed, I thought, so driven that he was prepared to put a wooden needle into his own eye, *just to know*. He began to seem a kind of Faust figure, the man who wanted to know certain things so much that he had been prepared to sell his own soul to the devil and suffer the consequences. The drawing had drawn me into its orbit. It knew things and pointed a way forward. It created a fierce new curiosity, a desire to know what this drawing knew about human ambition and the dangers of curiosity.

What I had begun to see was, of course, what W. G. Sebald knew: that the only way to understand this historical object, this gate opening into a new world, was to join fiction to non-fiction. Sebald once talked about reaching this turning point. When he had been solely an academic, he told interviewer Chris Bigsby, 'I constantly came up against a borderline where I felt, well, if I could go a little bit further it might get very interesting, that is, if I were allowed to make things up. That temptation to work with only very fragmentary pieces of evidence, to fill in the gaps and blank spaces and create out of this a meaning that is greater than that you can't prove, led me to work in a way which wasn't determined by any discipline.'[9]

I think I have come to understand what Sebald means by that phrase 'to create a meaning that is greater than that you can't prove'. I couldn't prove much about Newton's comings and goings in Cambridge in 1666, at least not in any detail, but I did know that I was reaching for a meaning that was greater than any footnoted fact. Only a complete freedom of form would allow me to explore the connections and webs in Newton's drawing, to try to unearth feelings as well as ideas, and to understand a history that tangled out from a room on Trinity Street in Cambridge to London, King's Lynn and Venice. That experiment became a novel called *Ghostwalk*, a story about Faustian over-reaching, a ghost story that was at the same time heavy with material objects. The story was all in the drawing of the eye: it spoke of the dangerous consequences of curiosity; of obsession and the dark arts; it told me about a man who was prepared to risk anything, even his own sight, even his own life in what was after all a plague year, in order to better understand nature's secret laws.

I cycled to Newton's college rooms, only a quarter of a mile from my own study in Cambridge; I stood still in the street outside amongst the passing shoppers, students and cyclists, listening. I walked across the patch of lawn beneath Newton's window that had once been the clipped hedges of his physic garden. I listened at the foot of the worn stone staircase that twisted down from his rooms and into the college courtyard. I retraced the daily web of paths he walked between his rooms, the staircase, the refectory, the chapel, the garden, the market and St Mary's Church. I searched the library for seventeenth-century maps and prints.

In the dust of libraries and rare books rooms, the seventeenth-century college room began to open out into a city. Dust had begun to behave like pollen. The world immediately beyond Newton's rooms in that summer of 1666, I discovered, the world beyond the shutters, outside the frame of the drawing that enclosed the intimacy of his private experiment, was devastated by bubonic plague. It was the first of two plague years. In the summer of 1665, when Newton began these experiments, the university authorities, expecting the mysterious sickness to arrive from London, where it had killed tens of thousands, and fearing the worst for the university town, had closed the colleges and banished the students and tutors to the country.

In Trinity College during a plague summer, there was no food to be had; no laundrywomen; no bedmakers. The city councillors had ordered all the entrances and exits to the city to be sealed up; everyone passing through the city gates had to be fumigated. On street corners, men tended fires slaked with lime in the hope that smoke and fire would drive out contagion. Every now and again the carts that rattled past Newton's window carried bodies and the sick out to the pest houses on the outskirts of the city. Everywhere Newton walked he would have overheard people taking about death, the Book of Revelation and the four horsemen of the apocalypse; preachers claimed that the plague was divine retribution; God was punishing his people. Newton heard the sounds of those plague carts and he smelled those fires slaked with lime. Smoke from the city streets drifted into his room with the sunlight. It covered everything in a film of dust.

I discovered that one of Newton's prisms, a three-sided wedge of glass about eight inches long, sits in a cabinet in the tiny Whipple Museum of Science in Cambridge, a prism that Newton used to split and refract light as it passed through those shutters. It had several chips along one side as though it has been dropped or thrown. To buy that prism, Newton recorded, he had walked to Stourbridge Common from Trinity College, along a path that the Newmarket Road follows now, with precise questions about light and colour lurching around in his head, his eyes sore from the series of optical experiments he had already begun.

My collection of curiosities – which now included the gatehouse of Trinity, the staircase up to Newton's rooms, the patch of lawn where Newton had once grown botanical herbs in a physic garden beneath his window, the drawing of the eyeball and the prism – told stories about alchemy, plague, glassmaking, the birth of modern experimental practices and scientific networks which, as they cohered around that scene in Trinity in 1665, were all connected. They demanded completion. Discovering the connections might mean finding a new way of seeing Newton and understanding this important corner of the seventeenth century, this moment of enlightenment.

Over and over again, I kept coming to the end of the archives as I tried to bring the collection of objects together and excavate their individual histories. I read books on seventeenth-century English and Venetian glassmaking practices, on plague, alchemy, on industrial espionage. I wrote to historians and they confirmed that there was nothing more to be known about glassmaking or about the impact of plague in the seventeenth century, nothing more to know than I already knew. *Where do you go as a historian*, I wrote in a notebook at the time, *when the archives come to an end?* What do you do when you come to the end of what is footnotably knowable? Where does speculation become justifiable as a way of bridging the gap? At what point might the objects demand a story that begins in the archives, but does not end there?

Ghostwalk is fiction, yet it is also, to the best of my ability, true to that moment in 1665, true to that collection of objects and their connections to each other and to that secret, fuggy-smelling, self-fashioned laboratory and the man who put a needle into the back of his own eye socket. The picture in the notebook knew something that Christopher Marlowe also understood in 1604 when he wrote *Doctor Faustus* – that sometimes you would risk your own life just to know something once and for all, that curiosity is dangerous and deeply seductive. When the archives come to an end, a storyteller, using a different set of tools, might then be able to pull those objects together across the darkness. A novelist might pick up the missing pieces where the historian might have been forced to abandon them. Yes, Max, yes, W. G. Sebald, exactly: dust is sometimes just like pollen.

1   W. G. Sebald, *The Emigrants* (London: Vintage, 2002), p.122–3.

2   Ibid., pp.112–3.

3   Hilary Mantel, *Giving Up the Ghost: A Memoir* (London: Fourth Estate, 2010), p.1.

4   George Eliot, *Adam Bede* (London: 1859), p.1.

5   Hilary Mantel, *Wolf Hall* (London: Fourth Estate, 2009), p.274.

6   A. S. Byatt, *On Stories and Histories: Selected Essays* (Vintage, 2001), p. 67.

7   On the return to narrative in history writing see the collection of essays in Geoffrey Roberts (ed.), *The History and Narrative Reader* (London and New York: Routledge, 2001).

8   Gaston Bachelard, *Poetics of Space*, trans. Maria Jolas (Boston: Beacon Press, 1994; first published 1957), p. 155.

9   W. G. Sebald in *Writers in Conversation: With Christopher Bigsby* (Norwich: AMC Publishing for the Arthur Miller Centre for American Studies), vol. 2, p. 152.

Rebecca Stott (*b.* 1964) is Professor of Literature & Creative Writing at UEA. Her first novel *Ghostwalk* (2007), which was shortlisted for the IMPAC award, was followed by *The Coral Thief* (2009), which was a BBC Book at Bedtime. She has also published three non-fiction books, including *Darwin and the Barnacle* (2003) and *Oyster* (2004), as well as academic books on Victorian literature.

Questions I Never Asked My Creative Writing Tutors

Lynne Bryan

In 1984 I was living in Bowthorpe, on the outskirts of Norwich, sharing a flat with an entomologist who was conducting complex experiments with aphids; I had no interest in aphids. I had a BA in Humanities from Wolverhampton Polytechnic, where the future Booker Prize-winner Howard Jacobson – terrifyingly articulate – had urged me in a seminar room in the back of the stands of Wolverhampton Football Club to voice my thoughts on Hamlet; I had had no thoughts, not in Howard's terrifyingly articulate presence. No interest in aphids, no thoughts about Hamlet, just one desire: I wanted to be a writer, not unpublished but the proper published kind. You could say I was focussed or a bit mad, perhaps both.

To Malcolm: What was it that made you want to be a writer?
To Angela: Would you say that men want to be writers for different reasons to women? And does this type of question annoy you?

It was mid-September. I had a novel in draft about a very thin girl who was inclined to show her breasts to strangers. I had saved a year's worth of wages from my job as a sorter in a film-processing factory. I was ready. I was readying, spending most days in Bowthorpe's dental surgery getting my front teeth fixed as I waited to take my place on UEA's MA in Creative Writing, to share my novel with nine other students and my tutors, Malcolm Bradbury and Angela Carter. I was nervous and gauche, a young twenty-three. I expected the MA to rescue me somehow. I expected the MA to turn me into one of *Granta*'s next 'Best of Young British Novelists', because hadn't it managed that with previous students, such as Kazuo Ishiguro and Ian McEwan?

To Angela: What do you think of these statistics?
'Best of Young British Novelists 1983' – 14 male writers, 6 female
'Best of Young British Novelists 1993' – 14 male writers, 6 female
'Best of Young British Novelists 2003' – 12 male writers, 8 female?
And does this type of question annoy you?

I hadn't been interviewed for the course. I'd been accepted on the strength of my work in progress. I'd won writing prizes and had received a small arts grant. I'd achieved much more than any of the other wannabes I'd met in the many writing groups I'd attended. I should have had bags of confidence, but I was nervous, gauche, and allowed myself to feel intimidated, almost immediately.

To Angela: How can I become as confident and as persuasive as you? Do you ever doubt your own abilities?

I was the worst kind of student. I made excuses. It wasn't my fault. It was the room where we workshopped our manuscripts with Malcolm, the oblong room – with the line of office chairs and Malcolm sitting behind a desk, smoking his pipe – which was too grey, too corporate. It was Malcolm's pipe smoke: it fogged the brain. It was having less time to write because the course had a critical component, which had to be completed and completed satisfactorily.

To Malcolm: Will taking a module in post-structuralism really help me with my writing?

It was the guests Malcolm invited to speak to us.

To Malcolm: Do all agents wear bow ties?

It was the tiny things in our work that Malcolm chose to focus on.

To Malcolm: Why is it so objectionable to split an infinitive?

Yes, I was the worst kind of student. Pressing the self-destruct and not prepared to accept responsibility. I wanted so desperately to become a writer – the proper published kind – but the MA required of me more exposure than I was able to risk back then. When it was the turn of other students to share their work I splurged my opinions on to their scripts – too hurriedly, with little consideration of my fellow students' feelings – yet when it came to voicing these comments in class, I couldn't. Just as in Howard Jacobson's seminars, I had shaken my head and refused to speak. Then when I gave my work to the class for their verdict I wouldn't accept – even hear – any criticism of it, no matter how delicately worded. I wanted – foolish for any writer at any level – my readers to go away.

To Angela: How do you stop yourself from shaking those students who are wasting your time?
To Malcolm: Does teaching interfere with your own writing?

It was a dreadful year for me. I'd been given an opportunity and knew that I was squandering it. I was with a bunch of people who cared so much about writing that one had moved from Italy and another had risked her marriage to take part in the course. I also had two experienced, kind tutors who were reading and thinking about my work, but I couldn't value their experience…

To Malcolm: What would you say are the key differences between writing scripts and writing novels?

…same as I couldn't recognise their kindnesses…

Angela gave us individual tutorials in Malcolm's office. On our first meeting she reached across to take a ruler from Malcolm's pen pot. The ruler was expandable. She played with it a little. Smiled.

'Lynne,' she said, 'do you think Malcolm measures his penis with this?'

To Angela: Why has it taken me so long to realise your cock joke was not about you wanting to embarrass me, but was your way of putting me at ease?

I missed my chance to know my tutors not only as writers but also as people.

To Malcolm: Your leg's in plaster and you are on crutches and yet you still manage to work the lift and smoke your pipe at the same time – how?
To Angela: What do you and Lorna Sage talk about when huddled together in the grad bar? You're always laughing. Do you tell each other cock jokes?

I missed my chance to thank them.

To Malcolm: Do you know I hadn't a clue about pastiche until you explained it to us?
To Angela: Do you know that more than two decades on I will be giving my writing students the same advice you gave me, particularly those students who write from the perspective of the angst-ridden introvert? 'Remember, there are doors and there are windows and, no matter how preoccupied, your characters will need to use both.'

Lynne Bryan (*b.* 1961) received her MA in Creative Writing from UEA in 1985. Her first book was a volume of short stories, *Envy at the Cheese Handout* (1995), which was followed by two novels, *Gorgeous* (1999) and *Like Rabbits* (2002). She has been an associate tutor on the English with Creative Writing BA at UEA and has also given courses for the Continuing Education department of the university.

My Brush with Radical Chic

John Spurling

In the late Fifties and early Sixties most of the territories in the British Empire became independent, while Britain itself took a kind of Dominion status in the burgeoning but more surreptitiously controlled empire of the United States. This new subordinate role – often sweetly called 'the special relationship' – was necessary economically, because of our enormous financial debt to the United States after the Second World War; militarily and politically, because of the constant threat from the expanding communist empires of Russia and China; and technologically and culturally, because in the post-war world most things new and dynamic tended to come from across the Atlantic. Nearly all the European countries, after all, had either been crushed by Hitler or crushed with him.

For young people in Britain – those who had experienced the war, but played no active part in it – the psychological effect of dwindling from one of the masters of the world to the new master's dependant was complex and confused. Enjoying our new freedom from responsibility, we became almost hysterically frivolous; resenting our loss of status, we became angry – chiefly with our own political leaders and the whole traditional 'Establishment' of our society; and, combining both frivolity and anger, looking about for some more attractive alternative to unlovely American commercialism, we lurched politically leftwards and tried to believe, many of us, in the Marxist utopia.

It is easy to forget now and hard for later generations to imagine how seriously intelligent people then took this delusory and destructive ideology. I remember being bewildered when a fellow student at Oxford in 1959 asked whether I was 'committed'. Committed to what? But that was my own naivety and ignorance. Of course, he meant committed to radical socialism. A decade later that meant virtually to revolution, by violence if necessary. Like so much in Sixties Britain – the new sexual candour, the women's miniskirts, the men's long hair and flared trousers, the ubiquitous mockery and satire, the explosion of noise in popular music – this political extremism, publicly displayed in marches and demonstrations and clashes with the police, was a form of dandyism, a way of showing-off and trying-it-on and frightening the older generation.

In other Western-bloc countries more severely damaged by the war – France, West Germany, Italy and Japan – political extremism did seem for a time to have roots in reality and in the late Sixties and Seventies sprouted into various terrorist organisations, whose heroes were Marxist men of violence like Trotsky, Guevara and Mao and whose members were often middle-class intellectuals and students. In this country only Northern Ireland provided the genuine inequality and oppression to match the talk.

But although there was no serious danger of revolution here, it often felt as if there were, and the atmosphere was so charged that for any youngish person working in the arts, literature, the media or the universities to admit to being at all right wing was an act of rare courage or folly. It might gain you a few assignments as a controversialist in the media, but it would almost certainly spell creative unemployment and an indelible reputation as a 'fascist'. Of course, this cultural dictatorship of the radical Left was nothing like as rigorous as that of the Artists' and Writers' Unions in communist countries. There was no question here of imprisonment, exile to a Russian gulag or a Chinese rural work-camp, confinement in a psychiatric ward or execution. But it was potent nonetheless, because the comrades or their fellow-travellers were highly active in all the cultural organisations, and if you were not judged to be one of them you missed out on grants, subsidies and commissions, as well as the best opportunities for your work to be seen or read at all. Some of these 'committed' people were sincere believers, others – this being showbiz – were only timeservers, 'champagne socialists', subscribers to 'radical chic'.

My first play to be professionally produced, *MacRune's Guevara (as realised by Edward Hotel)*, satirised 'radical chic' and, in the immediate aftermath of 'Che' Guevara's death in South America and the student riots in Paris in 1968, confronted the whole question of violent revolution. I began writing it while Guevara was still alive and reported to be leading a revolution in the Bolivian jungle, but by the time it was performed, in February 1969, he was known to be dead. It was produced in an experimental season at the Jeannetta Cochrane Theatre by the still newish National Theatre, with a starry cast, including Robert Stephens (MacRune), Jeremy Brett (Che Guevara), Derek Jacobi (Edward Hotel), Jane Lapotaire, Ronald Pickup and Charles Kay. It was directed mainly by Frank Dunlop, with some help from Robert Stephens.

The play was summarised by the *Financial Times*'s theatre critic B. A. Young as

a piece of satirical 'theatre of fact' as trenchant as it is comic. MacRune is an unsuccessful painter; in his dying days, he scrawled on the walls of his bedroom a life of Che Guevara in graffiti. The play is a dramatised version of this life, but filtered through the mind of the dramatist, a self-satisfied young man named Edward Hotel, whose ideas are as unMarxist as MacRune's were Marxian, and who keeps popping up to explain what's going on. Mr Spurling has arranged his piece as a series of episodes parodying established forms – the musical, the drawing-room comedy, the television melodrama, and so on. It uses lots of straight quotations from Che, often so manipulated as to seem inhuman or silly. Two morals emerge cogently: one, a hero is no more than you make of him, and two, principles are less important than men. The play is funny and wise.

Most of the reviews were equally encouraging. John Barber, the *Daily Telegraph*'s critic wrote:

The technique of this witty play recalled to me one of Che's own maxims: 'Constant movement, absolute mistrust, eternal vigilance.' The author does not commit himself:

he moves with speed from mistrust of all Che stood for to an eloquent statement of his romantic appeal. Draw your own conclusion, if you can [...] Like the writers who have influenced him, Pirandello and Borges, the new dramatist dazzles the audience with the speed of his transitions.

'Taken as a whole,' wrote Irving Wardle in *The Times*, 'the play offers a cunning answer to the question of how the theatre can treat subjects whose vitality lies less in recorded fact than in popular myth.' Sheridan Morley in the *Tatler* called the play 'a complex, elaborate and ambitious kaleidoscopic portrait of an unknown but famous man', and remarked that 'if the National do not soon put *MacRune's Guevara* into their repertoire at the Old Vic they will be cheating themselves of the best new play to have come their way since [Tom Stoppard's] *Rosencrantz and Guildenstern are Dead.*

The play did go into the repertoire at the Old Vic (the National's own theatre was not yet built), but in a truncated form, so as to occupy only half an evening, in tandem with Maureen Duffy's one-act play *Rites*, and for only seven performances. The reason for this was that the National Theatre's artistic director Laurence Olivier was baffled by its unconventional structure ('Cut it to the bone!' he told me in an uncomfortable interview in his office, and could not understand that the 'bone' of the play was precisely the number and variety of its viewpoints). For anything new or out of the ordinary Olivier relied on the judgement of the National's dramaturge, the critic Kenneth Tynan, who, as the doyen of 'champagne socialists', had naturally disliked it from the beginning. One of the rebellious actors inside the play complains to the supposed author, Edward Hotel: 'This play is in terribly bad taste. Putting on stage a man who is a hero to millions, only just dead. And you make him out to be some sort of mad gangster.' Most of those words came out of Tynan's own mouth, when he tried to stop the play's director Frank Dunlop from performing it in the first place.

The irony was that Tynan himself was at that very time himself involved in the production of a play in the West End, the German playwright Rolf Hochhuth's *Soldiers*, whose thesis (for which there is no historical evidence) was that Winston Churchill had conspired during the Second World War to murder the Polish leader General Władysław Sikorski. So Dunlop observed that Tynan didn't seem to mind travestying 'a hero to millions', so long as he was right wing. Tynan replied that Hochhuth's play was 'serious', whereas mine was mocking and laughing. He was either unable to see or more likely saw only too clearly that *MacRune's Guevara* was aimed less at 'Che' Guevara than at people like himself.

Soon after its British premiere, *MacRune's Guevara* was due to be performed in Stuttgart, West Germany, and again ran into a confrontation with 'radical chic'. It had been bought by the director of the Württembergische Staatstheater, a pupil of Bertolt Brecht called Peter Palitzsch, who had left East Germany and taken refuge in the West, where he retained his socialist principles but drove a Porsche, wore expensive suits and spent his weekends in a charming hunting-lodge in the Black Forest.

In the autumn of 1969 I flew to Stuttgart for rehearsals and was whisked straight from the airport to the theatre's green room. The whole theatre company was assembled there, together with a German-speaking serviceman from the nearby American airbase as interpreter, and it turned out that they had decided not to perform the play after all. Palitzsch, who had very little English, had been seduced by the play's title and the fact that the British National Theatre had performed it, but had not understood the subversive contents until his dramaturge translated the text into German. In Germany, however, theatre companies were better unionised and more democratic than in Britain and could not be ridden over roughshod by their directors. Indeed, I think that unsatisfactory directors were easier to get rid of than unsatisfactory actors. So I was to be given the opportunity of explaining my play before it was dumped. I argued for some three hours that it was by no means anti-Guevara, even if critical of some of his methods and supporters, that plays were not improved by being hagiography or propaganda, and that I hadn't forced the play on them, it had been bought by their director.

The upshot was that I won over the actors, though not Palitzsch himself, and that the dramaturge, Jörg Wehmeier, who very much liked the play, would direct it. But no one in the company was willing to play the supposed author, Edward Hotel, whose views seemed altogether too right wing. So they hired an actor from the commercial theatre in Berlin, whom they virtually ostracised throughout the production – he did have rightish opinions – making the reality behind scenes extraordinarily close to the fiction of the arguments between the author/director and his cast on stage.

Rehearsals began and went well, Palitzsch was distant but friendly, and even got me to write an essay for the programme of his next production, Oscar Wilde's *The Importance of Being Earnest*. But meanwhile he had slipped copies of my play to the students of Stuttgart University and notices had appeared on their boards warning of this right-wing infiltration of a good socialist-orientated theatre; and on the first night several rows of seats in the stalls were filled with students knowing the text and primed to barrack. The actors responded with courage, humour and steady nerves. They were completely loyal to the play, which they had grown to like, and they fought the claque in the audience from start to finish. The scenes in which the actors inside the play rebel against the supposed author/director, Edward Hotel, allowed them from time to time to appear to be taking sides with the students' claque.

It wasn't quite a riot, but nearly so, and the stolid German bourgeoisie of Stuttgart in the front stalls were completely bewildered. The actors won through to the end, when I had to appear with them on stage, as was the custom in German theatres for authors at premieres, and although the boos perhaps outweighed the applause, it was an exhilarating experience. The critics, writing at much greater length than their English counterparts, hated it, and it was not kept on for more than a few performances.

MacRune's Guevara was later produced in many other countries and did not, so far as I know, meet the same hostility anywhere else. In 2006 I attended its most recent performance off-Broadway in New York, by the small, extremely energetic Mirror Theatre Company – young actors to whom 'Che' Guevara meant little more than a face on a T-shirt. Nearly forty years after its first performance, the play's 'boneless', kaleidoscopic structure, its odd combination of romanticism with satire, of charismatic hero with self-deceiving worshippers, still worked and had not dated. But it has never been revived by the National Theatre or any other state-subsidised theatre in Britain. Tynan's writ, it seems, still runs.

John Spurling (*b.* 1936) was Henfield Writing Fellow at UEA in 1973. Besides *MacRune's Guevara,* more than twenty-five of his plays have been performed on stage, radio and television over the past three decades, including *In the Heart of the British Museum* (1971), *The Death of Captain Doughty* (1973), *Racine at the Girls' School* (1992), *Heresy* (2001) and *A Household in Hove* (2002). He was art critic of the *New Statesman* from 1977 to 1988. His published plays include *MacRune's Guevara* (1969) and *The British Empire, Part One* (1982). He has also published two books of criticism, *Beckett the Playwright* (with John Fletcher, 1972, 1978, 1985), and *Graham Greene* (1983), and three novels, *The Ragged End* (1989), *After Zenda* (1995), and *A Book of Liszts* (2011).

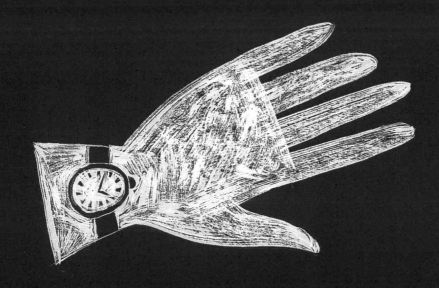

Ambit

Afterword

David Lodge

What follows was first published as the afterword to Liar's Landscape: Collected Writing from a Storyteller's Life *by Malcolm Bradbury (Picador, 2006). Edited by his son Dominic Bradbury this volume comprises pieces of Malcolm's fugitive journalism and memoirs, some unpublished stories, a section of an unpublished novel, autobiographical memoirs, and other fragments of unfinished work in progress. References to 'here', 'this book', 'this collection' etc, in what follows all refer to* Liar's Landscape. DL

Malcolm Bradbury was my first real 'writer-friend' and also the closest, although after the first few years of our relationship we were physically separated, most of the time, by the distance between Birmingham and Norwich, which until the construction of the A14 was one of the most tedious journeys in England.

In 1961, aged twenty-six, I was in my second year as Assistant Lecturer in English Literature at Birmingham University when the Head of Department, Professor Terence Spencer, decided that we ought to have a specialist in American Literature, and accordingly advertised for one. I remember being in his office one day when he showed me an application for this post from a man just a few years older than me, called Bradbury, currently an extra-mural studies tutor at Hull. He had an impressive CV, and a number of interestingly varied publications to his name, including a novel, *Eating People is Wrong*, which I had heard of though not read.

'I don't think we need bother interviewing anybody else, do you?' Spencer said nonchalantly (heads of departments enjoyed the power of feudal barons in those days) and I readily agreed.

I was the only teacher in the department under forty; I looked forward to having a colleague of the same generation, and one who seemed to have the same ambition as myself, of combining an academic career with creative writing. I had published my first novel in 1960, and Malcolm his in 1959. Naturally, I read *Eating People is Wrong* before he arrived in Birmingham, and naturally he read *The Picturegoers*.

We quickly became friends, as did our wives. We found we had a lot in common, in educational background and in literary taste; but there were also marked differences between us which showed in our respective novels. I was a Catholic, in those days a fairly orthodox one, and a Londoner; Malcolm's roots, in spite of some early years in Metroland, were essentially provincial, and his values were those of secular liberal humanism. These differences can be traced through our respective literary oeuvres, but are more obvious in some books than in others. If our 'campus novels' were sometimes confused in the minds of readers (a phenomenon Malcolm amusingly alludes to in his 'Wissenschaft File'), and we were both on occasion congratulated on writing each other's books, that was partly because we had the same kind of experience to draw on, and found that we perceived the academic world with a similar sense of humour.

Edith Wharton, writing in her memoirs of her friendship with Henry James, says, 'the real marriage of true minds is for any two people to possess a sense of humour or irony pitched in exactly the same key, so that their joint glances at any subject cross like interarching searchlights.' I often had that experience with Malcolm, long after he left Birmingham, when our eyes would meet after a remark or anecdote overheard in some conference bar or senior common room, as if silently to say, 'Toss you for it?'

But it was his influence and example that first encouraged me to develop a vein of comedy in my work, which in my first two novels was restrained by a soberly realistic technique. The third one, *The British Museum is Falling Down*, was dedicated in part to 'Malcolm Bradbury, whose fault it mostly is that I have tried to write a comic novel.' A crucial part of that influence was collaborating with him, and a Birmingham undergraduate called Jim Duckett whose talent Malcolm quickly spotted, on a satirical revue in the *Beyond the Fringe* mode, commissioned (again through Malcolm's initiative) and performed by the Birmingham Rep in 1963. I have written elsewhere about how much I learned from that experience, and what fun it was – indeed I am not sure that writing was ever such fun again.

Malcolm was a great collaborator, and a somewhat fantastic account of his early enthusiasm for that form of literary composition is included in this volume. I do not know whether it was literally true that he and his friend Barry Spacks would bash away simultaneously at their typewriters until one called out 'Stuck!' and then change places and continue each other's stories, but it is a wonderful image, both sublime and ridiculous, of collaboration overcoming the frustrations and anxieties of the creative process.

Malcolm responded to the stimulus of other people's ideas and could often see in them possibilities of which their originators were unaware. I remember an instance of this that happened shortly after he came to Birmingham. I had found in a local second-hand bookshop a copy of a light romantic novel, by a completely forgotten novelist, published in 1915, called *Nymphet*. That is the familiar name given by the hero of the story to an eleven year old girl who facilitates his eventual union with his beloved. It is also, of course, the generic name bestowed by Humbert Humbert on the eponymous heroine of Vladimir Nabokov's celebrated novel *Lolita*, published forty years later, which was generally thought to be the only application of this archaic word in modern literature. It was possible, by close reading and interpretive ingenuity, to see beneath the innocent sentimental surface of *Nymphet* the unconscious representation of an adult man's erotic attraction to a pre-pubescent girl, and to regard it therefore as some kind of precursor of Nabokov's masterpiece. It seemed to be an idea worth writing up, and I accordingly did so, and sent my essay to a few magazines – without success. I showed it to Malcolm and he offered to rewrite it and split the fee if he placed it. Being hard up at the time, I agreed.

Malcolm transformed my straightforward essay into a personal anecdotal piece in a humorous, self-mocking style which he had honed in contributions to *Punch*, and sold it under the title of 'Nympholepsy' to the American magazine *Madamoiselle*, which paid a great deal more than *Punch*. Pocketing my share, I was impressed – and perhaps a little piqued by his achievement. I began to write humorous anecdotal pieces on my own account, and managed to publish them here and there.

Malcolm had a pragmatic, professional commitment to writing which was contagious, and I suspect that my literary output might have been significantly different, and narrower in focus, if I had not met him at a formative stage of my career. It was this basic, inexhaustible appetite for the craft and business of writing which, among other qualities, made him in due course such an inspiring teacher of younger writers. When I first met him he already seemed to cover the whole waterfront of possible authorship, from the most austere literary criticism to popular journalism, adjusting his style effortlessly to the medium and the moment. And he was always thrifty with ideas, aware that they do not grow on trees. (In 1988 I encountered 'Nympholepsy' once again, much elaborated, revised and updated, in a chapter of *Unsent Letters*.)

When Malcolm was lured away from Birmingham to the University of East Anglia in 1965 I was in America on a fellowship. Had I been at home I should certainly have tried to dissuade him from moving, though in retrospect it was probably essential for our individual development as writers that we should separate. The confusion of our names and identities in the public mind would have increased exponentially if we had remained colleagues for much longer. More importantly, it was necessary that we should have different experiences to write about. *Changing Places* and *The History Man* both appeared in the same year, 1975, and both were about the same basic phenomenon – the global radicalisation of universities in the late Sixties/early Seventics – but observed in quite different places and fictionalised in quite different ways.

Changing Places, incidentally, was turned down by three publishers before Malcolm suggested I should send it to his own publisher, Tom Rosenthal at Secker & Warburg, who accepted it, after which my fortunes as a novelist improved steadily. My editor at Secker was the inimitable and irreplaceable John Blackwell, who soon took over Malcolm, too, and to whom Malcolm paid eloquent tribute in an obituary essay reprinted here. Writers who are in the same field are inevitably rivals to some extent, even when they are friends, and many authors would hesitate to invite such a friend to join their own publisher's list, but Malcolm's gesture was typically unselfish. Of course, it gave a further excuse for people to merge our identities in the conceptual compound novelist, Blodge…

Malcolm himself agonised about leaving Birmingham, where he was very happy. He told me that on the day when he finally, definitively, irrevocably had to make up his mind, he went out with two letters in his pocket addressed to the University of East Anglia, one saying yes, and the other saying no. Just in time to catch the last post, he mailed the one that said 'No'. The next day UEA rang him up and said, 'You don't really mean it, do you?' And he agreed that he didn't, and so he went to Norwich. I was reminded of this anecdote when reading 'Honoured', in this volume, about his hesitation over accepting the offer of a knighthood, and how he couldn't remember, ten minutes after posting the reply form, whether he had ticked 'Yes' or 'No'. In fact, Malcolm hated to say no to anybody, as many people discovered to their advantage – publishers, newspaper editors, TV producers, British Council officers, conference convenors, and secretaries of literary societies. This trait partly accounted for the extraordinary variety and range of his literary output, which is reflected in the contents of this book.

I am particularly interested in the fragments of autobiography it contains, especially of his childhood, which was uncannily like my own in many respects. We were both children of the war and the Blitz, traumatically separated for a time from home and parents, dimly aware of a vast historical drama being played out in which our little lives had been caught up with unpredictable consequences. It made both of us, I think, temperamentally somewhat prone to anxiety, cautious in the conduct of our adult lives, and grateful for the opportunities which opened up in peacetime for the first beneficiaries of the 1944 Education Act. Like Malcolm, I went to a grammar school (a state-aided Catholic one), funded by passing the eleven-plus, and my parents, like his, had to be convinced by the headmaster that it was a good idea for me to apply to university, rather than to leave school at sixteen and start earning my living. A few years later I think both of us would have been encouraged to apply for Oxbridge, but because his father would not countenance a third year in the sixth form, he went to the University College of Leicester, while I didn't even consider an alternative to my local university, and went to University College London, commuting from home. As Leicester took the London University exams in those days, we pursued essentially the same syllabus, and later both of us obtained London MAs – then a two-year research degree.

It is interesting to speculate what difference it would have made to our subsequent careers if we had gone to Oxbridge. I suspect he would have adapted to it better than I, and he might have stayed on to become a don. In later life he enjoyed the occasional sojourn as a visiting fellow at Oxford, and for many summers chaired an annual seminar for foreign academics and writers run by the British Council in a Cambridge college. He always seemed very happy and at home in these settings – the smooth lawns, gravelled paths and ancient buildings soothed his spirit, and the ritual of hall and high table appealed to him – but the redbrick University College Leicester, housed in a converted lunatic asylum, provided more useable copy for a first novel in the Fifties. (After all, a brief visit there had inspired Kingley Amis to write *Lucky Jim*.)

Though politically he was slightly left of centre (and a staunch SDP supporter during its brief life), Malcolm was at heart a kind of liberal Tory, or Tory liberal, rather like E. M. Forster, one of his favourite novelists, valuing tradition and pastoral life, tolerance and civility, distrusting modernity and the revolutionary desire for change. These preferences became more overt in his later work. In the essays collected here, especially those on East Anglia, the North Yorkshire coast, and Scotland, the past, as inscribed in landscape and architecture, is always treated with respect and nostalgia, while the impish satirical asides are directed at everything that is modern, trendy and commercial. In one of the funniest pieces a fictional character from the past, Robinson Crusoe, is brought back to suffer the indignities of celebrity in our media-dominated culture.

Another English novelist whom Malcolm particularly admired was Evelyn Waugh, a kind of Tory anarchist, and like Waugh he revelled as an artist in features of the modern world which he deplored as a human being, because they provided such rich material for satire. 'Convergence' is a gem of this kind, evoking the babel or bedlam of a multicultural conference taking place in the commercialised paradise of Hawaii, by simply (though it is not at all simple to achieve) letting us hear the different voices of the hosts and participants using and abusing the English language in their various ways.

Most peoples from everywhere come through here these days, because we're a great stopover, and so our population has every kind of ethnic source...In my poem, we have the pear blossom passing across the face of a fixed star. Then, in despair, the girl spreads the hair in her armpits, and the wind carries her away...Excuse me, sir, I should like to point to a falsie in your argument...It seems so weird, says the girl, being here without John. He's had to stay on in New York City. He teaches a course on the enjoyment of death.

The way this last speaker's isolated remarks and questions unfold a little plot, threaded through the polyphonic babble, is typically deft.

Bathos, broken English, the comedic clash of cultures – this piece is recognisably the work of the author of *Rates of Exchange* and *Dr Criminale*, but there are other examples of Malcolm's fiction in this book, two very early and one very late, that are quite different in style. 'A Week or So in Rome' and 'The Waiting Game' are interestingly dark stories, apparently set, and probably written, in the Fifties, in both of which a relationship (marriage in one, an affair in the other) seems to fail because of some chronic inadequacy in the male partner. The ways in which being 'abroad', on holiday, ostensibly to enjoy oneself, can actually exacerbate the tensions and resentments between a couple are well portrayed. There is some comedy in 'The Waiting Game', especially at the beginning, but none at all in 'A Week or So in Rome', which is especially hard on the male character.

In one of his essays Malcolm records that he conducted a WEA course on French existentialism in Nottingham as a young man, and there is a kind of bleak fatalism, a pervasive *nausée*, in these stories, and a tendency to gnomic generalisation in the narrative discourse ('love is partly disgust, I would swear') that suggests Malcolm did for a while genuinely feel the appeal of the fashionable Parisian philosophy of the day. One wonders whether he tried to publish these stories, and if so, when; and if not, why.

Questions also hover around the fragment of the novel he was working on at the time of his death, which gives its name to this volume. *Liar's Landscape* is, tantalisingly, just a little too short for us to be able to complete it. There is a long historical prologue, about the exploration and appropriation of North America by Europeans in the eighteenth century, which is interesting and informative, but makes us impatient for the story to begin; and even when the hero, Chateaubriand, finally makes his entrance, it still doesn't really begin, or more accurately it keeps beginning over and over, sometimes at the end. Clearly the author is playing a game with the readers' expectations of what constitutes a novel, and there is a continuity in that respect, and in others, with his last completed work, *To the Hermitage*, published in 2000, just six months before he died. That novel was about the Enlightenment *philosophe*, novelist and encyclopaedist, Denis Diderot, focusing on his residence at the court of Catherine the Great of Russia, but their story was spliced with another one, about the author himself, in modern times, embarked on a cruise which is a kind of conference on Diderot, a tale full of farcical incident, caricatured pedantry and humorous digression, like Sterne's *Tristram Shandy* (to which Diderot paid the compliment of imitation in his *Jacques le Fataliste*).

In *Liar's Landscape* there is the same combination of a historical central character and a modern authorial perspective, but those elements are more closely interwoven. The voice of the authorial narrator, situated in a bit of old Norwich quaintly called Tombland, blends in counterpoint with the voice of the author of *Memoirs from the Other Side of the Tomb*, quoted or impersonated. Chateaubriand had an extraordinary life, full of adventure, narrow escapes, love affairs, political intrigue, and literary fame – enough material for a half-dozen novels – and we get some sense of the rich possibilities of his story in the flowing, allusive, doubly-voiced discourse of *Liar's Landscape*:

> He…has served Napoleon, been to Egypt, toured the Orient, celebrated the revival of Christianity and faith. Now he's Monsieur Romanticism, Vicomte Gloom, the French Byron, the Parisian Pushkin, author of many books. Later he's made French ambassador to Britain. His fame is great, his loves and lusts are many, the steaks of his famous chefs are the talk of the town. One day a black-dressed lady, Lady Sutton, recent widow of an admiral, calls at the Embassy seeking assistance: she wants some help and preferment for her two sons. She asks if he happens to remember her. 'Yes I remembered Miss Ives! I took her by the hand, made her sit down, sat down by her side!'

This is the daughter of the vicar of Bungay in Suffolk, whom Chateaubriand met when he was a penurious refugee from the revolutionary Terror, passing under the name of Monsieur Coburg, and she was only fifteen; whom he tutored and admired and might have married, if he hadn't inconveniently been married already. It's a charming, poignant tale, and it may well have been what first attracted Malcolm's attention to Chateaubriand as the possible subject for a novel, because it began in a place, and a house, now owned by the novelist

Elizabeth Jane Howard, which he knew well ('I was there for dinner only last night').

The experiences of Chateaubriand in England alone would have made an enjoyable historical novel of a familiar type, filling out the known facts with imagined emotional and psychological detail, but if Malcolm had intended to make this story the centrepiece of his *Liar's Landscape*, he would surely not have dealt with it so summarily at the outset, squandering much of its narrative interest in a few vivid paragraphs. The historical prologue suggests that the core of the novel would have been Chateaubriand's adventures in America as a young man, but it is impossible to be sure. The whole fragment is in effect an extended, teasing, discursive prologue to an absent story. There is a particular poignancy in the hero's admission, near where it breaks off: 'It's the story of my own life and death we are all waiting for, and I fear in my usual fashion I'm delaying things a little too long.'

In the case of *Furling the Flag*, the other unfinished work of fiction in this volume, at least we can discover how the story was going to develop, and end, by referring to the television script on which it is based, which was never produced but is printed in its entirety here.

Television drama was an important part of Malcolm's professional life as a writer, and it is appropriate that it should be represented in this collection. He was one of the first English literary novelists to embrace the medium enthusiastically, and he kept faith with it throughout his career, in spite of many frustrations and disappointments. In the late Sixties and Seventies the Drama Department at BBC Pebble Mill in Birmingham was something of a powerhouse of innovative production; Malcolm made contact with the people there while he was in Birmingham, and maintained it after he left. The first fruit of this association was a 'Play for Today' in 1975 called *The After-Dinner Game*, which he wrote – typically – in collaboration with a colleague and friend at the University of East Anglia, Christopher Bigsby. It was a studio play, as most TV drama was in those days, rehearsed like a stage play and then recorded on video by a multi-camera method in twenty-minute 'takes', which had to be aborted and done again from the beginning if anyone fluffed their lines.

I went along to Pebble Mill at Malcolm's invitation to watch this tense, complicated, collaborative operation, impressed by – and a little envious of – his involvement in it. The experience kindled in me a desire to get involved myself one day, though it was many years before that came to pass. The technology of video-recording evolved rapidly in the meantime, allowing for a movie-like flexibility in shooting and editing, which was more compatible with novelistic narrative than the inherently theatrical studio play.

An early example of Malcolm's grasp of the medium's possibilities was his adaptation of John Fowles' story 'The Enigma', which I greatly admired (it was enhanced by a brilliant cameo performance by Nigel Hawthorne). He went on to make many successful adaptations of other writers' work (e.g., Tom Sharpe's *Porterhouse Blue* and *Blott on the Landscape*, Kingsley Amis's *The Green Man*, Stella Gibbons's *Cold Comfort Farm*), but not his own outstanding novel, *The History Man*, transmitted by the BBC in 1980. Instead it was very ably, and faithfully, adapted by Christopher Hampton as a four-part mini-series, and it turned out to be one of the seminal television dramas of the Eighties, making Anthony Sher into a star, and giving the novel a kind of second life, with a much bigger readership.

When the novel was first published in 1975 it was a daringly subversive take on the radical orthodoxies that then held sway on university campuses, but by 1980 Mrs Thatcher was in power, the Left was in ideological retreat, and right-wing pundits greeted the televised *History Man* with glee as a vindication of their views. This was something of an embarrassment to Malcolm, as one may infer between the lines of his essay 'Welcome Back to the History Man', though he enjoyed the new level of fame it brought him.

His next novel, *Rates of Exchange*, set in the imaginary East European state of Slaka, was published (and shortlisted for the Booker Prize) in 1983, and in due course Malcolm was commissioned to adapt it himself as a serial for the BBC. Two weeks before principal photography was due to start (in Hungary), the project was cancelled, due to a dispute or crisis over budgeting in the BBC's Drama Department.

Only someone who has been involved in television production, and knows how difficult it is to get a major TV serial 'green-lighted', and has some idea of the countless rewrites demanded of the screenplay-writer even after that point has been reached, can begin to imagine the depth of Malcolm's disappointment. Many writers would have given up the medium in disgust, but characteristically he soldiered on – pausing, however, to relieve his feelings in a satirical novella called *Cuts*. And, again characteristically, he found a way to use some of the apparently wasted work much later.

In the years that followed this setback, Malcolm wrote several original and ambitious serial 'tele-novels' about subjects of topical significance. *Anything More Would Be Greedy* addressed the enterprise culture of Britain under Thatcherism. *The Gravy Train* was a carnivalesque satire on political intrigue and corruption in the bureaucracy of the European Economic Community (as it was known in those days), and had the novelty of being funded by a consortium of TV companies in several European countries, with a multinational cast. It won a 'Golden Nymph' award for Best Mini-Series at the Monte Carlo Film and TV Festival. A few years later Malcolm wrote (and I suspect proposed) a sequel in which some of the same characters were sent to an East European country to experience the political and economic upheaval that followed the collapse of communism. This was *The Gravy Train Goes East*, and the country was, of course, Slaka.

A pivot of both these mini-series was the character of Spearpoint, the British diplomat (played by the accomplished Ian Richardson, who specialised in such roles), his impeccable manners and dignified professional persona contrasting comically with the mayhem and mischief in which he becomes embroiled. Spearpoint is also the central character of *Furling the Flag*, which would have completed a trilogy. This was a risky television venture, because (to adapt Karl Marx's well-known epigram) it attempted to anticipate as farce what was about to occur as history: the handover of Hong Kong by Britain to the Republic of China in 1997. Perhaps time ran out; at any rate, like so many scripts 'in development' it was never produced. Some while later Malcolm began to turn it into a novella, somewhat in the style of *Cuts*, and to my mind it reads very well and entertainingly. But by now it was tied to an historical event whose outcome was known, and on to which it would have been difficult to graft the original comic plot; so perhaps the script is not, after all, a reliable guide to how the novella would have developed and ended.

All these television scripts, and many others (both produced and not produced) which I have not mentioned, took up a great deal of Malcolm's writing life; and some of his literary friends regretted the displacement of so much time and energy from the novels he might have written instead. The income the screenplays brought in was, of course, an incentive to continue writing them – Malcolm always got a pragmatic Johnsonian satisfaction out of making money by his pen – but I do not believe that was the real reason. There was also the satisfaction of reaching a large audience through television – with one episode of *Inspector Morse* or *Dalziel and Pascoe* he might reach more people than the readership of his entire output of novels – but he knew as well as anyone that most popular television drama is perceived by the audience as the product of its stars rather than its writers, and the specificity of each episode is quickly forgotten.

That was not the real reason either. Essentially I think he just found the fun and busyness of being involved in this medium irresistible: the stimulus of collaboration, the challenge of problem-solving, the thrill of visiting a set or location and realising that all this expensive, complex activity had been brought into being by one's own words. He wrote expressively about this in the introduction to a little book in which the scripts of his first three television plays were published:

> Where novels are fictions that exist between two imaginations, that of the writer and the reader, the television play activities an enormous actuality. Directors say goodbye to their children and block out months in their diaries. Actors…commit themselves to roles and impersonations that will keep them standing cold on street corners or huddled in bleak church halls for extended periods of their lives…Planes are chartered, houses hired and then totally refurnished to make them into something quite different, streets in the centres of great cities are blocked off, caterers with steaks assemble, men with booms chat up girls with make-up…writing television plays is really a very long way from writing novels, where none of these things happens at all, and the invented world stays within the reasonable comfort of one's own head; and they are actually a strange way of stepping out from the imagined into what some people might mistakenly call the real world. Television plays are an activation of many types of onscreen and offscreen behaviour, generating a complex pattern of enacted images, shaped by both the social and the ever increasing technical sophistication of those images. Writing a television screenplay is an act of profound self-instruction in the grammar of inventive writing itself, a process in which one is simultaneously trying to guide and shape the massive fleshing out of the imaginative drives that set writers to work in the first place, and testing out the possibilities of

narrative sequence and development, the growth of image and sign, in a collective situation with developing collective laws.[1]

This book belongs to a genre that used to be called, rather lugubriously, 'literary remains', though being by Malcolm Bradbury it is not at all lugubrious in effect. It is a book for readers who already know and love his work, and cherish every bit of it; who will be grateful that a substantial amount of his fugitive journalism has been preserved, engaged by the autobiographical memoirs, and fascinated by the unpublished stories and fragments of unfinished work-in-progress. His son Dominic's Foreword explains movingly how the book evolved, 'to explore the art, craft and life of the writer and commemorate the work and passions of someone who lived a storyteller's life to the full'.

In February 2001, some two months after Malcolm's death, a memorial service was held in Norwich Cathedral which drew a huge crowd of people from the many different walks of life which he had shared during his career – writers, academics, actors, directors, producers, journalists – as well as family and friends from far and near. I was invited to speak on that occasion, and I have incorporated some of the things I said in this Afterword. Let me end with the conclusion of my address on that occasion:

> Another writer-friend gave me a desk diary at the beginning of last year, with a handwritten passage or sketch by a writer or artist on every page. The text for the day of Malcolm's funeral, which I attended, Monday 4th December, had in one sense an uncanny appropriateness. It was contributed by the Irish novelist Brian Moore, who must have submitted it not long before his own death, and it was a quotation from Roland Barthes's essay on Chateaubriand. As many of you will know, Malcolm was working on a novel about Chateaubriand when he died. The quotation is: 'Memory is the beginning of writing and writing is, in turn, the beginning of death.' But if I understand that statement correctly – and Barthes is an elusive writer – I don't really agree with it. It has always seemed to me that writing is a kind of *defiance* of death, because books live on after their authors have gone. Certainly the greatest consolation we have for Malcolm's passing is that we can re-experience his company, his character, and his life-enhancing sense of fun, through his books. But that is not the same, of course, as a living, breathing, laughing friend.

---

1   *The After Dinner Game: Three Plays for Television* (Arrow, 1982), pp. 11–13.

David Lodge (*b.* 1935) is a leading British writer with more than thirty titles to his name, beginning with *The Picturegoers* (1960). His novels include *Changing Places* (1975), *Nice Work* (1988), *Therapy* (1995) and, most recently, *A Man of Parts* (2011). He has also written stage plays and screenplays, and many books of literary criticism, including *The Modes of Modern Writing* (1977), *The Art of Fiction* (1992) and *Consciousness and the Novel* (2003). Emeritus Professor of English Literature at Birmingham University, he continues to live in Birmingham.

Influence

Anne Enright

I met Angela Carter in the spring of 1987 when I was a student and she a tutor on the MA in Creative Writing at the University of East Anglia. My work had, over the course of the previous winter, gone from bad to worse. I was twenty-four, I had no idea how to live in the world, let alone write about it; and the self, who was supposed to produce some kind of narrative by the end of the year, seemed an increasingly unlikely entity; fugitive and fragmented. I functioned well enough, though the whole business of being Irish in England seemed to me old-fashioned and, in tiny ways, ghastly. People thought I was amusing, in an Irish sort of way: and I suppose I was. Perhaps I should have written about this: the Irish in Britain are the least storied version of 'Irish' there is. But as a postgraduate student in 1987 there was already something soggy about the problem; the lines of power had gone a little slack. Besides, I may have left Ireland, but I had not exactly moved to England. I went over on the ferry and back on the ferry, from one place I didn't want to live, to another place where I didn't want to live, and it didn't really matter what accents people had.

If I dream about Samuel Beckett, he is always sitting on that ferry. Glass of Guinness. Stone-coloured trench. I see him there and I say:

'Hi Sam.'

I had a room with unpainted breeze-block walls, and no money, and a truly terrible bed. My work was not going well. I did not know why. It was not that I was distressed – I had often written when in distress. In fact, a little breaking open, a little falling apart, a tincture of four in the morning, used to work quite well, for me. Emotion was not the problem, it was the fact that I could not make the shift from emotion to story, or not on the required scale.

I don't know if stories do come from feeling – perhaps it just feels that way. Certainly the inability to write is a very emotional state. I don't know if stories do come from feeling – perhaps it just feels that way. Certainly the inability to write is a very emotional state. The shift from feeling to fiction is a necessary thing, it is the reason I need to write. But the more you need, the less you get, and this was the cruel truth I learned in that room in East Anglia.

I recognise the problem now in students and strangers who talk about inspiration, who ask, 'Where do you get your ideas from?' Something about their faces – the intensity of them – there is a thing they don't understand how to do, and they really, really want to do it. As if a story were a natural, pre-existing thing, like a bird, and not a built object, like a plane.

Is this the source of the rage against fiction; as sometimes evinced by fiction-makers themselves? You must make it up, but not too much, you must use language, but curtail its possibilities and avoid its pleasures. You must not use metaphor, for example; be sparing with simile, avoid adverbs like the plague, use adjectives sparingly, you must not use long words; you must not show off, nor let language show off, you must be humble and tell the truth and not make anything up, except the Everything that you make up, and this Everything, though fictional, must be in some higher sense True.

The rage against fiction, like the fashion for realism, moves around, but it is hard not to see desire under the puritanism of the project. Why else do critics get so cross? If they did not yearn so much for the grace and gift of it, why would they spend so much time saying that the novel is dead, the way God used to be dead? Why else do people get angry with writers – people who, after all, just sit in a room, making things up?

Or not making things up, as I was doing in that room in East Anglia.

Where do you get your ideas from? I worked all the time, but there was no shaft of light. No deep knowledge surfaced, like a new thing, from the depths of my mind. I did not wake inspired. I had fragments, bit of this and that, but if the words came from anywhere, it was from a point over my left shoulder, like a taunt. I was twenty-four. I do not think that I was entirely well.

Into this mess Angela was to descend, wings fluttering, silver hair floating and little shoes – perhaps they would be red – clitter-clattering on the floor.

I don't think she would agree with anything I have just said, by the way. The psychoanalytical model I am using here – all this talk of need and flow – is that of the child at the breast. The underlying assertion is that the infant who cannot invent, who cannot make things up, is, in the absence of the mother, bereft.

Also, if you think about it, this talk of grace and gift is very religious, (not to mention the shaft of light). I mean it is a Christian or perhaps Neoplatonic view of what a story is and does, and it begs all sorts of lies about essence and transcendence. Angela Carter was a socialist and a materialist; she was also a woman who was profoundly suspicious of all this mothering malarkey, so you will appreciate that even as I claim her as an influence, I have not been influenced *enough*, as my own words show.

So I will try, as I remember my sad, 24-year-old self – too clever and too stupid to write – I will try to avoid words like 'balm', 'blessing', 'inspiration' (I really don't believe in inspiration) and all ideas of 'authenticity' (a word which I find truly oppressive) or 'soul'. Also 'belief', of course, which fiction, like religion requires, albeit in smaller doses, and which – let us not forget – the reader is absurdly eager to supply.

I bought my first books when I was thirteen years of age, after I won a book token in a school radio quiz. It was a substantial amount of money and I was allowed into town, alone, in order to spend it. I looked at every volume in Books Upstairs in the Georges Street Arcade in Dublin and ended up with three paperbacks: *The Greek Myths* by Robert Graves (volumes I and II) and *The Pillow Book of Sei Shōnagon*. This last is a commonplace book written by a woman in the tenth century court of the Heian dynasty in Japan. I thought it was wonderful. I read it countless times. I was entranced by the beauty and formality of her life; the kimonos made of seven layers of silk, the pathos and compulsion in her relationship with the aesthetic; the plum blossoms, the snow, the leaf drifting on water. I was also hypnotised by the elegance of her sex life: men who appeared from behind a screen, left before dawn and sent a poem in the morning. 'My sleeves are wet with tears.' There were no children, or the children disappeared, and the fates of other women, and of men, too, were mysterious and inevitable, and always sad.

After this, a lot of the fiction I read was translated from the Japanese: Mishima, Endo, Tanizaki, though I missed Oe, for some reason, and Murakami did not come along until I was grown up. If you ask what an Irish schoolgirl was doing reading Japanese literature in the late 1970s, then you cannot know what Ireland was like in the late 1970s, and I for one do not have the energy to tell you. It was, perhaps, as Shelley wrote and I transcribed on to the green vinyl cover of my school folder (just above some Led Zeppelin lyrics), 'The devotion to something afar / From the sphere of our sorrow.'

This 'afar' was only cultural. The erotics of Mishima and Tanizaki may have been, in their formal perversity, stark and satisfying to a teenager whose very informal culture had no 'erotics' at all. But even so, their stories stayed close to a world I could recognise. There was no great strain, I mean, between the real and the surreal as flowered later in the work of Murakami. Japanese mimesis is close enough to any other kind. After eight hundred quiet pages, Tanizaki's 'The Makioka Sisters' ends with a minor episode of diarrhoea one of the characters suffers on the train into Tokyo. At the age of sixteen I closed the book thinking that I did not know where I had just spent the last week of my reading life, but it might as well have been Kansas.

Reading your way into a culture may be, as an exercise, the opposite of Orientalism, but I knew that I wanted something foreign when I bought those books, or something that would tell me how to be foreign, which is to say how to be lonely in a more interesting way. This adolescent cultivation of my otherness is familiar to us all. It is also a traditional writerly stance.

Angela Carter went to Japan on a Somerset Maugham scholarship in 1969, and then returned and stayed for two years. Her novel *The Infernal Desire Machines of Dr Hoffman* was written over the course of three months, on a Japanese island where she was the only Westerner. She says in her collection of essays *Nothing Sacred*: 'I wanted to live for a while in a culture that is not now nor has ever been a Judeo-Christian one, to see what it was like. In Japan I learned what it is to be a woman and became radicalised.'

It is possible that Japan did not change Carter so much as make her more like herself. Because she did not understand the language, she says, 'I started trying to understand things by looking at them very, very carefully, in an involuntary apprenticeship in the language of signs.'

Japan, her friend Lorna Sage, wrote, 'completed the work of the Sixties' for Carter. It confirmed her sense of strangeness. 'I can date to that time,' Carter wrote, 'in the summer of 1968, my own questioning of the nature of my reality as a woman. How that fiction of my "femininity" was created.' The answer lay in the mirror, and in the mirror of society's gaze, which, in Japan, was more clear for being unfamiliar. It is in the eyes of strangers that she sees and welcomes her estrangement.

The children flock to her window in wonder, and she hears 'the rustle of innumerable small voices, murmuring the word: *gaijin gaijin gaijin* (foreigner).'

There is no Japanese word which roughly corresponds to the great contemporary European "identity",' she writes, 'and there is hardly an adequate equivalent of the verb "to be"'. Ideas of the individual and the collective are differently constructed, so the ego plays by different rules. On Japanese streets the cosy and the clean coexist happily with the drunken and pornographic. Even the body is seen differently, she says (though she does not ask if it is differently inhabited). Carter delights in the fact that 'no one told the Japanese that the human form was supposed to be divine'. Her essay on the art of the irezumi tattoo, which she calls 'one of the most exquisitely refined and skilful forms of sadomasochism the mind of man ever divined', one in which bare skin 'incorporated into the overall design, acquires an appearance of artificiality'. 'In Japan,' she writes, 'the essence is often the appearance.'

Sometimes Carter seems in thrall to the artificial. It is a conjuring thralldom, however, an invocation. It is as though, by looking long enough and hard enough, she can bring the image alive. She is interested in the surface of the mirror, and in the membrane between the artificial and the organic that is the tattoo. Skin is the substance that turns 'meat' into 'flesh'. It transforms the brute and mortal, and births it into the sexual and deathless world of the sign.

The book of stories she published after her sojourn in Japan deals directly with the confusion between the self and the mirror. In 'Reflections' a woman kisses her image to find that 'these mirrored lips of mine were warm and throbbed…When my eyes opened, I had become my own reflection, I had passed through the mirror and now I stood on a little cane-seated, gilt-backed chair with my mouth pressed to an impervious surface of glass.'

This book of stories *Fireworks* also contains the first piece I read by Angela Carter, photocopied and handed out for a seminar when I was a student at Trinity College Dublin.

'The Loves of Lady Purple' is a story of a puppet and her Asiatic puppet-master. The puppet is constructed for only one role: in a sense she is Lady Purple, a prostitute whose talents 'verged on the unspeakable'. She may even have been the petrification of a once living whore, 'whose kisses withered like acid and whose embrace blasted like lightning'. This 'quintessence of eroticism' comes alive at the kiss of the puppeteer and, acting out her role one more time, sinks her teeth into his neck and drains him. The newly living doll wonders 'had the marionette all the time parodied the living or was she, now living, to parody her own performance as a marionette?' and she leaves the fair to enter the carnal world.

I did not like the story much at the time – the transformation, although exciting, was not transcendent enough for me, perhaps – but there was something about the story that made it available for plagiarism. I mean, the counters were thrown so freely down for you to pick up and discuss and, ultimately, use. The conversation had begun. It is this fine carelessness that makes Carter such a hit in universities, even now. She bares the mechanics of the story, she gives you the tools. She liked writers, she said, like Poe and E. T. A. Hoffmann, 'who dealt directly with the imagery of the unconscious – mirrors, the externalised self, forsaken castles, haunted forests, forbidden sexual objects'. She likes to put the clutter of the unconscious outside, on the page where it can be seen and manipulated. This externalisation is in itself liberating and interesting, and somehow telling. It is, besides, so much easier to make things up, with elements that are already 'made up' when you encounter them. The challenge (of which Carter was deeply aware) was to make these images not just move, but also live, and this is a problem which her work restates over and over again.

'The puppets of the Bunraku,' she says in an essay about Japan, 'are the most passionate in the world.' Still, it is difficult for the reader to make the same investment in wood and strings, no matter how ardently they are described. You might even say that the baroque beauty of the descriptions is partly to compensate for, or to animate the fetishised object at the centre of her tale. This animating function is later taken over by the burlesque energy, that moves and makes antic the performers in *Nights at the Circus* and *Wise Children*. But there is a difference between energy and freedom, between movement and life. For this Carter needed another shift or lift, a transformation that is organic, and therefore, you might almost say, true.

But it is difficult to pity Lady Purple in her voracity, either as wood or as flesh. I wonder why so many of her images – in this instance, that of the perfect and perfectly destructive prostitute – are either taken from or written into some version of the male unconscious? Even if he were not male, the puppet is a product of his imagination and we are outside the circle. Who is the reader supposed to be, the puppet or the puppeteer? With whom are we supposed to empathise?

It is this refusal to invite our empathy that makes the story political. 'For me,' Carter said, 'narrative is an argument in fictional terms.' When we come to the end and the puppet becomes flesh, the reader's empathy runs back through the story. We see ourselves as puppets, we realise something about our lives. The pity we feel is for ourselves as images, and distorted images, of desire. This pity for the image is everywhere in Carter's work. I wonder is it a kind of forgiveness? It feels a little like the pity we accord the religious icon, and also owes something to camp: the way we see divas at their most heroic as their beauty fades.

Or am I just too much of a fuddy-duddy for Lady Purple? It was when she was in Tokyo that Carter first picked up the Marquis de Sade by chance and the story owes much to his novel *Juliette*. The masochism she saw in Japanese society interested her, in the way the formality of Shōnagon's sex life interested me. I was going to say that I had not yet, when I read this story, accessed my inner Juliette, but I never did find her – how could I, when Juliette can only exist from the outside?

'In the looking-glass of Sade's misanthropy,' Carter writes, 'women may see themselves as they have been and it is an uncomfortable sight.' But surely, the only thing to be seen in Sade's mirror is the face of Sade.

Here I am, bleating for essence, demanding it, in Carter's playground of mirror and sign.

The Sadeian Woman is a kind of shadow text for *The Bloody Chamber*. Both books were published in 1979, after many years in which Carter wrote without being much heard. This surely added to the iconoclastic impulse behind it. *Well, maybe they'll hear this.* It has not been popular with feminists, and no one else would want to read it. Go, Angela!

It is as though she put all the problems and traps in one text, and the transformations and solutions in the other. Pornography and fairy tale are both anonymous forms, and it is tempting to confuse the anonymous with the democratic, natural or archetypal. Sade's figures of Juliette and Justine hold a fascination for Carter, but they have all the dullness of pornography, too. There is no development. They are born, not made. They enact, but do not change. De Sade's pornographic project failed to be truly revolutionary, Carter says, partly because he cannot break the taboo against the mother, and the father's authority – his imagination – continues to reign supreme.

Sade's work with its relentless mirroring, the either/or of Juliette and Justine, vice and virtue, sadism and masochism, thesis and antithesis, this endless flipping of the coin, was a great influence on Carter. You might say it was a statement of the problem her fiction sought to solve. The reader begins to miss the third term: some idea of synthesis, metaphor, transformation, change.

The Bloody Chamber is a book of transformations. I read it as course book in Trinity College English Department in, perhaps, 1983 – which was pretty quick off the mark. The first transformation in the Bloody Chamber is of the folk tale; she turns the traditional narratives on their heads, turns them inside out. The characters are different admixtures of the human and the bestial: a child is reared by wolves, there is a werewolf, a talking cat. Along with these hybrids and confusions, there are full metamorphoses: the beastly cat becomes a man, the frightened girl a fabulous cat.

The excitement I felt reading this collection has never left me. It was what I needed to read. It made great sense. This was the proper relationship between a writer and her culture. Carter made ideas manifest and available. She expressed something that had been waiting to be expressed, and in doing so effected cultural change.

I applied to the MA in Creative Writing because of this book and because of *Nights at the Circus*, which deals with a flying woman, Fevvers, who is a hybrid as much as a transformed being. I realise – I get it down now from the shelf – that it was given to me by the man I would leave to do the course, which leave-taking was surely a large part of my sadness in that room in UEA. We had both been working in the theatre in Dublin. When we were still students – shortly after I read 'The Loves of Lady Purple', in fact – I had written and staged a series of three monologues about performers. He played a puppeteer, whose doll – I forget what happened to the doll, she came alive I suppose. He forgets, too. He says, 'There was something about him sticking his thumb in her head and it was like a strawberry.' So much for old work. The second monologue was from an Elizabethan boy actor, who tells the story of how Shakespeare fell in love with him, all in lines directly lifted from Shakespeare's plays. The last monologue was from a contemporary artist, who, as part of a performance piece, cuts off two of his fingers.

Imitation may be the sincerest form of flattery, but even though Carter thought that travesty was all right in its way, I am shocked at the way I just took her ideas and wrote an inferior version of them, without the slightest qualms.

The posture of the writer talking about great and previous writers is both grovelling and self-aggrandising. To claim influence is to say that you are good enough to absorb what you need from a writer, and to spit the bits you don't need back out again. I know I am using another maternal model here, but I get fed up of male writers talking about Joyce, old father, old artificer, slaying him in an Oedipal sort of way only to find him still standing.

I never bothered much with the posture of influence: in my own work I use whatever helps at the time. For this I have Carter herself to thank: she was only ever influenced for fun. And though I find it difficult, writing about her now, when I was a student my admiration for her work was direct and easy. I had not yet spent twenty years disappointed with my own books. Having done precisely nothing, I felt myself to be, in all the ways that mattered most, her equal, and I neither worshipped her nor wanted to do her harm.

Perhaps I am doing both now. What surprises me about these monologues, which were my first pieces of fiction, is that all of the characters were men – though one of them was in drag and, of course, there was the puppet. These days I find it quite difficult to write men. Carter used a male point of view in her early novels and shifted towards a female perspective in the later work. If Angela were alive – this is a game I sometimes play – if Angela were alive, what would she write now?

But if her influence is painfully obvious, so is my need to get clear of it. The performance artist cuts off two of his fingers in an attempt to break through the mirror of the fourth wall. Skin is a kind of costume, as Carter well knew. Perhaps this is why she never wrote for the stage. Actors' bodies are very intractable. The strangeness of theatre, for me, of seeing my lines happen on stage, was 'the word made flesh'. The physical fact of actors excited me; the fact that, like Shylock, if you prick them they will bleed. It was clear from the very first that the answer to the problem of the mirror lies for me in the body; or in the fragmented body. But clearly, I did not have to meet Angela Carter in the flesh. With that one story, 'The Loves of Lady Purple', a story I claimed *not to like*, she had made me sit down and answer; she had called me to write.

I have a theory about Creative Writing courses. When people say that they turn out writing students who know what the mechanics of writing fiction are, and how to put a book together, how to produce a synopsis and make it look good – even though it is clearly a simulacrum and not a living, breathing book – they forget one thing. The rise of the writing course tracked, almost exactly, the rise of the word processor. The generation that graduated from the new writing courses was the first generation that could move things around easily, check their spellings and make things look good before sending the manuscript off in an envelope. Perhaps we are blaming the wrong kind of machine. My tutors – Malcolm Bradbury was the other – did not teach me a thing about how to construct a book. They said vague things about agents and publishers. They were more interested in us doing real work than in our getting ahead.

I knew nothing about Angela Carter's career when I arrived to be her student. I had never read a newspaper review in my life. It did not matter to me how long it had taken her to be recognised, when I had recognised her immediately. Even the idea of 'career' was strange to me, when a book was such an absolute object. This act of recognition happened, like everything else that happens between the writer and the reader, one to one.

Angela Carter sat in a room and, one by one, the students knocked on the door and went in. They also came out again. In the same order. And one by one.

We were supposed to meet six times, but I only remember two. I think she missed one session and I certainly missed another; there might have been talk of making up the time in London, but I don't know. She was forty-seven, which is the age I am now. She had a six-year-old son. She had published *Nights at the Circus* the year before and at the time was possibly working on *Wise Children*, which was to be her last novel.

There is nothing less interesting than abandoned manuscripts. They are worse than last week's horoscope. I can't describe the book I worked on that year. It was, if you can bear to listen, about sleeping with the enemy. It was about Cressida. It was about Colley Cibber's daughter Charlotte Charke, an actress who, according to me, played Cressida in not Shakespeare's, but (for reasons that must have been historical) Dryden's bastardised version of the play. Part of this section was written in makey-uppey eighteenth-century stage dialogue. Everything kept splitting up into threes. I may have set part of the book during the actual siege of Troy, but I am not going to admit to this, because that would be too embarrassing. There was a modern section also told by an actress, who opens the book with a description of Juta Mai. This was a nineteenth-century geisha dance form that I had seen at a theatre festival in France. The narrator describes the dancer's costume, her tiny movements: she tells how the actress holds in her eye a tear that is always brimming, but never falls.

We were all very tense. The student ahead of me came out of Angela Carter's office, made a big face and hurried away. I went in. Angela Carter sat beside, rather than behind a desk. On the edge of it, facing back at me, were the pages I had submitted, with a handwritten a note from her on the top sheet. She indicated the pages with a graceful hand.

She said, 'Well, this is all fine.'
And then we talked of other things.

If the question was in the mirror, then the answer was in the eye.

This was the problem that obsessed me in the spring of 1987.

'The eye, is it the mirror to the soul?' says one of my fruity eighteenth-century thespians.

'It is an orifice, rather,' says Charlotte Charke. 'In brief, Sir, it is a hole.'

I stayed up late, reading Lacan. No wonder I was mad. I wrote out big chunks of it in my notes:

Bear with me through this difficult process, he says, talking about the Mirror Stage, whereby 'the being breaks up, in an extraordinary way, between its being and its semblance, between itself and that paper tiger it shows to the other…something that is like a mask, a double, an envelope, a thrown-off skin'.

The shift from feeling into fiction was a shift from being into an image of being, from inside to outside. 'To break out of the circle of the *Innenwelt* into the *Umwelt*,' Lacan wrote – and at the time I understood this, too – 'generates the inexhaustible quadrature of the ego's verifications.' I think he meant you fall apart a bit, when, as an infant, you see your image in the mirror. It is also possible that you have to fall apart a bit in order to make fiction; that making an image of yourself is a kind of falling apart. And that the resulting image is always too coherent and rigid – what Lacan called 'orthopaedic'.

The problem of the mirror is more than political, it is fundamental to the creative act. But it is also political. When Carter says that in Japan she learnt what it is to be a woman, she meant she learned what it is to be seen as other. It's a visual thing. This confusion of 'to be' and 'to be seen' makes me unhappy, in the same way I am unhappy when Carter holds up Sade's mirror, as if the reflection were true.

The separation of essence and appearance freed Carter into a world of invention; she is, besides, more than capable of having her cake and eating it, of moving from the fetishised and mechanical to the living and organic. What is metamorphosis, after all, this complete change from one shape into another, except a celebration of essence?

Here is something else from my notes of that spring: a verse by Aragon, quoted by Lacan in his *Écrits*.

I am that poor thing, a mirror
that might reflect but still can't see
our eyes are empty – to the error
of your absence –

The mother, Carter says in *The Sadeian Woman*, is mirror to the daughter. The most transgressive thing that Carter ever wrote about was Sade's tale of the rape of Mme de Marcival by her daughter. The revenge of the daughter is terrible. The mother is not only raped but infected with syphilis, after which her organs of generation are sewn up. Carter's syntax goes awry during her account of the rape. She starts to write 'we' instead of 'they'. It is the kind of passage that has to be held at a distance and read at speed, so perhaps this is why the copy-editor missed the error.

'The theory of maternal superiority,' Carter writes in the introduction to the book, 'is one of the most damaging of all consolatory fictions, and women themselves cannot leave it alone, although it springs from the timeless, placeless, fantasy land of archetypes where all the embodiments of biological supremacy live.'

Sometimes I envy the feminists of the Sixties and Seventies their iconoclastic clarity. The shock of the object. The object speaks back. And I regret that my own work is so enmired in the problem of the self and of the body – and not the body as object or image, but the seeing, desiring, penetrated, pregnant, mortal and happy body: also the fragmented body, the body that contains the eye.

If Carter's work stepped into the mirror, my own is an attempt to step back out again. But there is no doubt I still meet her in the glass.

The most important thing I have to say about Angela Carter is that she was kind to me. She read my work.

She said, 'Well, this is all fine.'

Then we talked about Kabuki versions of Shakespeare, a subject of great interest to both of us at the time. Her note about my impossible novel was, when I read it outside in the corridor, deft and enthusiastic. For another session she brought a photocopy she had made of Henryson's *The Testament of Cresseid*. She asked me what would happen after I left the course, and where I was going to live. I said I was going back to Ireland.

'Why?' she said. By which she meant, 'Whatever for?'

'For a man,' I said.

And once, I think, she understood that I meant a particular man, rather than just an Irishman, she said, 'Oh, all right then.'

Anne Enright (*b.* 1962) received her MA in Creative Writing from UEA in 1987. Her first novel *The Wig My Father Wore* was published in 1995. Since then she has published four other novels, including *The Gathering*, which won the 2007 Man Booker Prize, as well as books of short stories, essays and non-fiction. Her most recent book is *The Forgotten Waltz* (2011).

Open Questions

Marina Warner

What follows is the introduction to Moments of Truth: Twelve Twentieth-Century Women Writers *by Lorna Sage (Fourth Estate, 2001).* MW

The word 'glamour' comes from grammar, and Lorna Sage, who combined wit and panache with a scathing dislike of sloppiness, embodied this paradox to the full.[1] In her now classic memoir *Bad Blood* she tells us how, when she began learning Latin, she instantly loved it, could do it, wanted to use it; language was a refuge, and the place she wanted to be was in her head, with literature her companion. So she was grammatical – and she had glamour.

Lorna Sage's thinking about writing affected a whole generation of writers, publishers and, not least, readers. It's difficult to communicate how exhilarating it was to be read by her, to be the object of her attention, to be spared her satirical wit and win her praise – to be *rated* by her. It first happened to me with my second novel *The Skating Party*. Terence Kilmartin, a great friend of hers, for whom she regularly wrote some of her deftest criticism at a vintage time for the *Observer*'s literary pages, suddenly confided that she had been eloquent on the book's behalf on a prize they were judging. News of her interest in it came as a real parting of the rain clouds. She was interested in me and, as it did for others who were lucky enough to be in this position, this interest fired me up, made my writing feel worthwhile.

But Lorna was never cosy: her partisanship was tempered by irony and words like malicious, cackling, mocking, freakish, profane, figure in her vocabulary of praise. She finessed a rare position: she cultivated the English literary talents of scorn and scepticism and utopian bile without becoming a rancid Swiftian; her misanthropy was lightened by humour, by glee, by genuine, infectious pleasure. Certain moods of melancholy, certain bleak and ghastly states were meat and drink to her; she used the phrase 'cosmic irony' about Edith Wharton, and the concept wasn't a stranger. She valued 'a good hater'. Yet, at the same time, she had a rare laugh: a wonderful, rich, deep, complicit chuckle, which came readily bubbling up, even when she was suffering atrocious effects of illness.

In the major extended essay about Simone de Beauvoir included here, Lorna Sage wonders: who is Beauvoir speaking for? Whom or what does she *own* – own in the sense of acknowledge as her own? Thinking about post-war feminism and *The Second Sex*, Lorna puzzled over, not the mirage of matriarchal lineage, but the possibility of owning and owning up to another constituency, which was female in gender, feminine in practice, applicable generically to the enterprise of living as a woman, inside and outside texts, yet respectfully particular in every individual case. With Angela Carter, her close friend, ally, comrade-in-arms and fellow sufferer – from human folly as well as shortness of breath – she wanted to reconfigure the 'we' women could use. They were, both of them, profoundly impatient with claims to niceness and motherliness, to goddess revivals and myths of 'wimmin'. Angela Carter provocatively co-opted the Marquis de Sade to her quest for female freedom;[2] Lorna Sage, coincidentally, was looking for its polymorphous possibilities elsewhere, in women who wrote. They both wanted to forge a new kind of 'us'.

This collection of essays about twelve women writers was sifted from her spirited and prodigal output by Lorna before she died in January 2001; she discusses Edith Wharton, Jean Rhys and Jane Bowles, among others, concluding with her friends, Iris Murdoch, Angela Carter and Christine Brooke-Rose. Introductions to reprints of classic works such as Virginia Woolf's *The Voyage Out* and Katherine Mansfield's short stories, combined with longer journal articles, shape her incisive, original take on the interplay between text and person, between the life and the work; the reader can watch Lorna Sage's thinking through the all-important twentieth-century relationship of memoir and invention, record and fabrication.

Lorna Sage began a life in criticism as an advocate of postmodern fabulism, exemplified by the playful allusiveness and textual games of Italo Calvino in *The Castle of Crossed Destinies*, Angela Carter in *Nights at the Circus*, Umberto Eco in *The Name of the Rose* and Christine Brooke-Rose in her nimble, witty metafictions. Her critical sensors were tuned by days and nights of years of continual, voracious, scrupulously fine reading: at her memorial service in April 2001 Victor Sage, her first husband, recalled with dry wit marathon sessions during which Lorna would, for example, 'do Scott', that is, read the entire oeuvre of Sir Walter Scott, one book after another, including titles long forgotten. Lorna was hyper-acutely calibrated to the way a book lies – in more senses than one. As a critic, she's alert to the unspoken resonances between lines, and the wider rings of thought spreading beyond them. She continually startles her readers with the sensitivity of her attentiveness to implication, to the ellipses in her chosen subjects' sentences, to the way she hears the full chord and its harmonic overtones, not the single notes, and can follow their reverberations. In a tribute to Angela Carter after her death in 1992, for example, she quotes Angela reminiscing about her brother and her younger self, wondering how 'such camp little flowers as ourselves emanated from Balham via Wath-upon-Dearne…' Lorna takes the thought and, with characteristic verve, places it far beyond Angela's slightly defensive self-mockery, on the vertiginously larger, subtler emotional map of *Zeitgeist* and literature after Modernism, when she comments, 'This is not about nostalgia, but connects with a quite different contemporary sensation: of coming at the end, mopping up, having the freedom of anomie.'[3]

In the 1990s, when she was writing these essays, Lorna was responding to the rise of the genre now widely referred to as 'life-writing' with a fresh set of questions and rereadings of writers whom she already knew well. Memoirs, confessions, testimony, diaries and even travel journals were swelling the category, beyond all expectation, in the decades following the proclaimed 'Death of the Author'. Barthes's celebrated essay had become a manifesto for a critical generation, but far from disappearing from the text, the author was rising, like the indestructible undead, and haunting literature far and wide, blurring the boundaries between fact and fiction, memory and imagination. Autobiography was displacing the novel, it seemed, as the prime literary vehicle of human experience. The work of W. G. Sebald, for example, one of Lorna Sage's colleagues at the University of East Anglia, cannot be classified along any former lines: the stories in *The Emigrants* and *The Rings of Saturn*, though aesthetically highly fictional in tone and execution, are convincingly recounted as events in the life of the writer, posited as genuine memories. At the same time, readers hunger to know if a story is true, and they respond differently to the play of the author's presence between the lines if they can be persuaded this is the person to whom this really happened. As Adam Phillips has remarked, 'Today we value truthfulness, not truth.'[4]

Lorna had a special reason besides wanting to probe the territory where fiction meets memory: she was writing her own memoirs. Some brilliant early instalments of *Bad Blood* had memorably appeared in the *London Review of Books* years before she managed to finish the book, which wonderfully revealed her literary gifts to a much wider public. *Bad Blood* is extraordinarily evocative, richly remembered, brave, very funny, sharp, poignant, gallant, packed with character – and characters – an adventure story of reckless youth, experiment and escape. She lived to see its success: the *Daily Telegraph* reviewer said it 'encapsulates the experience of a generation. This is not just an exquisite personal memoir, it is a vital piece of our collective past.' Mary Beard, reviewing in the *Times Literary Supplement* wrote that the description of Valma's attempts 'to make gravy is one of the best accounts of domestic melodrama that I have ever read'. It was a surprise bestseller and won the Whitbread Prize for Biography. Telling the story of her family and upbringing, Lorna shows us – and we need reminding – that literature really can make something happen: books here became her voyage out, her forged papers out of a childhood hell. She was such a scalpel-sharp reader and such a fierce advocate of certain writing, because she saw that literature and language are catalysts in the making of experience, not simply passive precipitates.

Bad Blood draws on the remarkable diary kept by her wicked grandfather, the 'Old Devil', the philandering vicar, of his days and nights, his ups and downs. Lorna wanted him to get into print, perhaps because he had called her after a heroine from a book – Lorna Doone – perhaps because he'd shown her the world inside books (even though in his own library he'd blacked out the titles as 'a precaution against would-be borrowers'.) The diary becomes the stake between grandfather and grandmother: she finds it and threatens to show it to the bishop. That way she holds him to ransom, and he – well, he then has a cast-iron excuse to let things carry on the way they are. Even the most secret of documents speaks to someone to a purpose, Lorna knows, and autobiography – the wide range of what Dutch historians call 'ego-documents' – fashions and re-fashions the self, in dialogue with imagined interlocutors, even if those imagined receivers are one's own future selves. The subjective 'I', the literary first person, has become a troubling ghost, there and not there, imagined or actual, dwelling in any number of texts, not least of *Bad Blood*; Lorna Sage writes here about one of Christine Brooke-Rose's novels, *Next*, in which the characters have stopped using the pronoun 'I' because they own nothing, have no home, belong nowhere. You have to have all these coordinates to be a person who can speak for yourself.

Yet such a new emphasis on truth-telling sets a challenge to invention, to fabrication and to impersonation and performance, all the energies that leap in the fantastic, fairy-tale and postmodern fictions that Lorna had so brilliantly interpreted and advocated. Lorna's argument gradually develops through the essays in *Moments of Truth*, that you can't have the work without the life or, more pointedly, the life without the work, nor the work or the life without the art. In other words, the grammar without the glamour. And she was going to pursue this theme in another book, to be called *Writing Lives*, to show that 'the "heroism" and representativeness of writers' life-stories [are] aspects of the decay of classic literary realism…'

The title Lorna chose for this collection of essays – *Moments of Truth* – interestingly shifts Woolf's epiphanic 'Moments of Being' away from the felling-of-what-happens (the Modernist enterprise) towards truth-telling, and the knowing-what-happened, in the sense of revelatory events that make a difference, that cause a shift to take place. Lorna returns again and again to a key concept in Beauvoir's thinking – the idea of *mauvaise foi* or bad faith, which the French writer loathed, and diagnosed in bourgeois and clerical hypocrisy, in lyrical, confessional manifestations in writing, in short, in any public show of virtue, literary, social, religious and personal. I think there may be an echo of this phrase in the title of Lorna's memoir, but with a twist – because the phrase 'bad blood' both claims and rejects her inheritance, it revels in it as a badge of honour and at the same time relishes the irony that with all this family stuff behind her, she escaped, she stopped the stain – the so-called stain – seeping. She was a bad girl, perhaps, but she could also tell when something was in bad faith. In *Moments of Truth* Lorna Sage has discerned a pattern in the way women writers of the last century made their exits from bargains involving bad faith – both on their part and on the part of others.

The book is a sequel to her *Women in the House of Fiction* (1992), but it engages more tenaciously with the issues of determinism in life and realism in literature, to probe the roughness and porousness of the female ego that texts are busy picking, unpicking, weaving, unweaving. The mesh that holds someone in social, economic and above all emotional obligations could be as sticky and strong as a pupa, if you like, but it could also be abruptly torn and cast aside. She traces these moments through the writings, quoting, for example, Christina Stead saying 'another fatal idea that belongs to the bourgeoisie, that there's something sacred inside which if you dig out it will make you an original…There's nothing inside.' Of one of Jane Bowles's characters, Lorna comments, 'Miss Goering disinherits herself, in short, and becomes and adventuress and a serious lady. That is, a woman who turns her true character into an open question.'

It is also surely relevant here that Lorna's own experience of time changed as her illness – asthma, emphysema – got a more and more unshakeable grip on her. She was looking back to see where she had come from, and it prompted her to inquire more closely into the play of light – and shade – from personal histories on Jean Rhys's way of looking at men, at Violet Trefusis's comedy of manners in high places, on Djuna Barnes's eccentric bohemia. Her subjects emerge in all their singularity – her word – as people living in time and place, but in continuous conflictual dialogue with their given circumstances, as the young Lorna herself was, growing up in Hanmer on the Welsh borders. Was she attracted to fatality? Or does some terrible boozy, hacking nemesis keep coming after women writers? Lorna loathes sentiment and even romance; she doesn't focus on issues of self-destruction or premature demise, and she never reads the works backwards through their makers' deaths, because that would fall into the mythographers' sticky clutches.

Instead, through close individual studies of other people and their writing, Lorna gradually pieces together another way of telling the story of modern literature in which writers aren't acting in character or bearing out behaviourists' and functional anthropologists' theories of nurture, but making themselves up as they go along: becoming new beings made of words, like one of Arcimboldo's allegories, creating their own 'profane interiorities'. As Lorna traces her subjects' features, the collection becomes a stimulating, original, idiosyncratic portrait gallery or private pantheon, almost in the manner of the baroque literature about amazons, angels, winged griffins and demons that was one of her first loves (one of her early essays was about Milton's *Comus*), when books were published with titles such as *Galerie des femmes fortes* and Bess of Hardwick commissioned embroidered wall hangings of mythological and biblical heroines. She liked my own study of allegorical female figures, *Monuments & Maidens*, perhaps for this reason, that they represented a huge and mighty female host who could be marshalled to a new cause.

Recognising women of spirit also provided a guiding principle for *The Cambridge Guide to Women's Writing*, a huge undertaking that Lorna Sage edited single-handedly from 1992 to 1998. Original, electric, witty (an unusual attribute of a reference work), it came out the year before *Bad Blood*; the two works, at opposite ends of the literary spectrum, embody Lorna's distinctive contribution to the debate about literature and gender. The *Guide* ranges far and wide over the globe, including all literatures in English from every epoch and in every genre, even traditionally relegated forms such as children's writings, fairy tales, romance, science fiction, slave memoirs, essays. Characteristically, it never bends the knee to pieties or precepts, from whatever source; Lorna's own style of criticism sets a pace for the contributors, close to the 'lightness' and 'quickness' and 'exactitude' singled out as literary qualities by Calvino in his *Six Memos of the Millennium*, published just after his death.

Heroism here lies in discovering a voice and speaking up: *Moments of Truth* listens in, filters out interference, picks up the individual resonance. Lorna herself continued to treat all problems of interpretation as open questions: doubt, scepticism, dissatisfaction keep her reading and her writing crackling with energy. It's characteristic that in her *London Review of Books* review of Jeremy Treglown's biography of Henry Green, the last piece Lorna wrote, you can hear her impatience with the reticence, even silence at the centre of Green's final compact with life: 'Asked for his opinions on the world, he'd tell people one should sit as still as possible, try not to go out. He didn't actually talk helpfully to interviewers…he simply adopted a parody of the correct language.'[5] This stance could provide 'protective colouring' for survival, a stratagem Lorna Sage understood well from characters in Jean Rhys; but none of Lorna Sage's female subjects ever used it as a literary manoeuvre or beat this kind of retreat – least of all herself.

There's a wonderful photograph, among many such in *Bad Blood*, showing Lorna at the Coronation Day Parade in 1953; even dressed as Little Bo Peep, with beribboned crook and apron and scrip, her trimmed straw hat's subtly cocked and there's a defiant light in her eye (she will get into Arcadia, she will confront the Faerie Queen). Later, at the time I first met her, she put paid to all the typecasting sneer and scoffing commonly compacted then into the term 'female academic'; with her long slender transparent hands, her elegant feet, her blue eyes, her husky, torch singer voice, and her liking for being driven about in her husband Rupert Hodson's large squishy leather-upholstered motor, she pioneered proof that you could be brilliant and learned and incisive – and blonde. The week she died, when I was asked to write a tribute for the *Independent* obituary page, I remembered meeting her by chance in Florence one time, and how she'd reminded me then of Beatrice, who, with her own luminous Botticelli tresses, guides the poet through the nine fixed spheres towards the stars while disquisitioning with occasional severity, and flashes of impatience, on everything from poetry to astronomy to theology as she does so.

1   It was Angela Carter, I think, who first told me this odd scrap of etymological lore.

2   Angela Carter, *The Sadeian Woman* (1979), reprinted New York: Penguin, 2001.

3   'Death of the Author', *Granta* (1993), p. 240.

4   In conversation with Frank Kermode and Marina Warner, at PEN, March 2001.

5   Landlocked', *London Review of Books* (25 January 2001).

Marina Warner (*b.* 1946) is a writer of fiction, criticism and history; her works include novels and short stories, as well as studies of art, myths, symbols and fairytales. Since 2004 she has been a Professor in the Department of Literature, Film and Theatre Studies at the University of Essex. Among her non-fiction books include *From the Beast to the Blonde: On Fairy Tales and their Tellers* (1994) and *Signs & Wonders: Essays on Literature and Culture* (2003). Her novels include *The Skating Party* (1982), *The Lost Father* (1987) and *The Leto Bundle* (2001).

Angus Wilson's Lost Legacy

D. J. Taylor

Sir Angus Wilson (1913–91) became a part-time member of UEA's English department on its foundation in 1963. His first question at interview was 'Would the position be pensionable?' He became Professor of English Literature in 1966, and retired from university teaching in 1978. During his time at UEA, Wilson published three novels: Late Call *(1964),* No Laughing Matter *(1967) and* As if by Magic *(1973). The majority of his work is out of print.*

Of all the reputations forged in the crucible of the literary 1950s, Angus Wilson's has been the most subject to fracture and neglect. Kingsley Amis's *Lucky Jim* (1954) is still regarded as one of the decade's key texts; William Cooper's *Scenes from Provincial Life* (1950), which has some claims to have set the whole Fifties bandwagon rolling in the first place, gets regularly reprinted; but the author of such gems in the Eden-era diadem as *Hemlock and After* (1952) and *Anglo-Saxon Attitudes* (1956) is as dead as the passenger pigeon. There is no getting away from this collapse in the Wilson share price, for its effects could be glimpsed throughout the last decade of his life. An *Observer* seventieth birthday tribute, written by his former UEA colleague Lorna Sage, noted that his early novels were 'slipping mysteriously out of reach'. As for the later work, Jonathan Raban – another UEA trusty – maintained that *Setting the World on Fire* (1980) had 'fright written on its every page – fright at not moving in the right circles...in the centre of things'. After thirty years of being in the swim and of the moment, an habitué of the Royal Society of Literature reception, an ornament of the TV book show and the high-culture colloquium, Wilson spent his long, dementia-cushioned twilight washed up on the beach of literary fashion by a tide that would never return. A collected edition of his works, urged on Penguin by a gang of admirers in 1992, was a spectacular flop.

The descent would have been less flagrant had not the peak from which the victim plunged been so very lofty. In his long essay 'The Novel as Pastiche: Angus Wilson and Modern Fiction' (reprinted in *No, Not Bloomsbury*, 1987) Malcolm Bradbury – a third UEA *convive* – practically lays the compliments on with a trowel. Wilson, we are immediately told, is 'one of the great figures of our age'. Furthermore, 'when we consider the tiny handful of recent British writers who can be claimed as major, as of long-term importance and lasting representativeness, then Angus Wilson is clearly one.' As well as being a grand literary eminence, our man was also, in his day, a hot public property. His occasional irruptions of temperament – he was a great flouncer-out of dinner parties and exchanger of sharp words on judging committees – were reported like the tantrums of a minor film-star. ANGUS WILSON WALKS OUT shrieked a bold-type *Evening Standard* headline from April 1960, after Wilson had briskly vacated a PEN dinner at the Café Royal where the top-table seating plan did not, alas, include himself. Touchy, vain, pitilessly self-absorbed – a persona that Margaret Drabble's admiring *Angus Wilson: A Biography* (1995) never quite manages to dislodge – he took himself, as Anthony Powell noted when hearing of his death, 'very seriously'. Yet at some point in the 1970s and 1980s, the reading public, if not the critical praetorian guard drawn up before it, simply lost interest. The reputation had walked out. And unlike the distinguished novelist quietly seething on the pavement in Regent Street it would never be invited back.

What went wrong? There are two standard ways of accounting for what might be called 'Charles Morgan Syndrome', the chastening spectacle of a writer, wildly celebrated in his day, whose posthumous, or pre-posthumous, prestige crumbles incrementally to dust. The first explanation is a finite relevance, the subjects that the writer chooses to write about somehow not commending them to the bookshop browser of twenty years hence. The second is collective critical delusion – the cracking up, by persons in positions of cultural influence, for reasons best known to themselves, of a reputation that posterity will judge to be inflated. In Wilson's case, neither of these diagnoses seems to fit. No doubt some of the furniture of his Fifties novels, its New Towns, its earnest secondary school headmasters and its bantering chat, is showing its age. On the other hand, nothing could be more pertinent to the early twenty-first century agenda than the liberal-humanist dilemmas they set out to advertise, that series of immensely subtle variations on the eternal question of how far we tolerate something that, once conciliated, will cease to tolerate us. As for the collective critical delusion line, the testimony of a room-full of grand literary panjandrums from Bradbury to Kermode insists that he was world-class. They can't *all* be wrong.

Inevitably, all this leads us back to the particular qualities that Wilson's admirers detected in him. Bradbury's essay claims that, among other triumphs, Wilson 'has brought about the possibility of a substantial, a compassionate modern fiction of moral urgency and historical power'. He has also apparently 'humanistically re-oriented the traditions of the past'. One could argue for quite a long time about the precise meaning of a phrase like 'humanistically re-oriented the traditions of the past'. Yet Bradbury's real point has to do with a 'moral toughness' that not only alerts the characters caught up in it to the sometimes devastating consequences of responsibility and self-knowledge, but starts to undermine the fictional form that surrounds them, so that what starts out as a halfway realistic depiction of modern life then changes into a tantalising modern grotesque. Drabble's encomium, laid out in the preface to her biography, makes the same claims in only slightly less lapidary language. Above all, she assures us, Wilson demonstrated 'that it was still possible to write a great novel'. Consequently, he found himself 'exalted as the only writer capable of carrying on the great tradition of serious moral fiction established by Dr Leavis…He was the repository of hope.'

Great traditions; serious moral fiction; 'repositories of hope'…It doesn't perhaps need Drabble's invocation of the Sage of Downing to establish that this is ultimately a Leavisite context, in which whatever is being written about in a novel gradually assumes the status of a moral inquisition – that old Leavis line about literary values being much less important than judgements about life. And certainly the moral atmosphere of the early Wilson novels is uncannily distinctive. Whereas individual behaviour in, say, a Kingsley Amis novel can sometimes seem to be merely expedient – one acts as one does to avoid trouble or to appear in a flattering light, to trump the villain or grab the girl – *chez* Wilson it is a source of constant agonising. 'Fairness and truth are my greatest difficulties in life,' remarks the narrator of 'More Friend than Lodger', a short story collected in *A Bit Off the Map* (1957). This is not only an unobtrusive flagging-up of the piece's principal themes, but also a declaration of procedural intent, the reader being given notice that Wilson, in the same way as Anthony Powell, knows that his characters' inner lives are not only extraordinarily complex and extraordinarily vital to them, but governed by impulses that are well-nigh mythological in their scope. Like Powell, again, Wilson is an impresario of the personal myth, the characters who makes sense of their lives through constant accretions of illusory baggage, always ripe to be exposed for what they truly are. 'There won't be so much time and I've been able to clear up so pitifully little of the mess,' progressive Priscilla wistfully declares in 'Such Darling Dodos' (1950). 'Oh, my dear,' her elderly Catholic cousin lobs back, 'if you're going to constitute yourself charwoman to the world.' In the end Wilson is something more than a moralist: he is a broker of moral possibility. He is also, to go back to Bradbury, a shape-shifter, a protean literary mage, a fusspot and a self-conscious link between the old-fashioned novel of historical exactitude and the rougher beast, its hour come at last, that came shambling towards the jungle of 1960s academe to be born. None of these roles, as his later career demonstrates beyond doubt, was at all easy to sustain.

Meanwhile, what are the books – the early books, anyway – about? A preliminary list might include neurosis, hysteria, evil, homosexuality, embarrassment, domestic tension, 'progress', the powerful unease of a humanism that is moving towards some dimly glimpsed liberal utopia, while deeply reluctant to yield up the social privileges guaranteed to stop this utopia taking shape. Their characters tend either to be caught up in the slipstream of this progressive vanguard, stage-managing its concerns to their own private ends, or lagging miserably behind it, baffled and frustrated by a world which seems to have no place for the values they call their own. Schoolmasters; parliamentary candidates; interfering old ladies; sexually and socially ambiguous young men; bright, unhappy girls; decaying *rentier* families thrown on to Queer Street; old soaks; pompous arts world eminences; remittance men: middle-aged survivors less keen on 'getting on' than simply getting by: these are the people in whom Wilson specialises, nearly all of them precariously established in a figurative milieu of frontier settlements, state-sanctioned good works and a cultural framework robbed out of back issues of the *New Statesman*.

The particularity of Wilson's response can sometimes be rather overwhelming; the relentlessness of his detail is a social historian's index card ('Pathos was Priscilla's dominating sensation: it had led her into Swaraj and Public Assistance Committees; into Basque relief and child psychiatry clinics; at the moment it kept her on a Rent Restriction Tribunal; it fixed her emotionally as a child playing dolls' hospitals' – 'Such Darling Dodos'). It is a world of grotesque accidents with the power to shift people's lives dramatically out of kilter, a world of barely suppressed hostility, quite often breaking out into sudden acts of violence or humiliation, a world of fellow-feeling and respect for all the good brave causes, of genuine altruism and infinitely subtle calibrations of response, but also one of pain, loneliness and secret suffering, in which practically any human emotion, when subject to the gaze of what Martin Amis called Wilson's 'rheumy eye' will be found wanting, or at any rate not what it seems on the surface.

Hemlock and After (1952) – a startlingly original novel for the age of Churchill, Attlee and the Festival of Britain – brings most of these themes together in conditions of maximum claustrophobia. Bernard Sands, its late fifty-something hero, is a celebrated man of letters who, as the novel opens, has just received the go-ahead for a long-cherished scheme to convert the decaying local stately home into a 'writers' centre'. Bernard's private life, meanwhile, is built on quicksand, his public image of a happily married man ever more deeply undercut by his adventures in the homosexual underworld. The novel's pivot turns out to be an odd, voyeuristic incident in which Bernard, late at night in Leicester Square, watches a young man being arrested for 'importuning'. Although merely an observer – there is no question of his having approached or encouraged the man – Bernard is profoundly affected. 'But it was neither compassion nor fear that had frozen Bernard. He could only remember the intense, the violent excitement that he had felt when he saw the hopeless terror in the young man's face, the tension with which he had watched the disintegration of a once confident human being. He had been ready to join the hounds for the kill then.'

It is the authentic Wilson note – high-minded, right-thinking liberal man indelibly compromised by an urge he can do nothing about – and the fire of moral interrogation it sparks off leaves nearly everyone else in the book – Bernard's wife, Ella, his prospective Tory MP son, his numerous gay companions – badly singed. At the same time, *Hemlock*'s originality is not just a matter of the remorselessness of its moral logic, or its notably frank treatment of what was then becoming known as 'the homosexual question', as the air of genuine menace that steals into its depiction of stay-at-home provincial life. Mrs Curry, who at first seems merely odd and conniving, turns out to be a procuress of under-age children. One of the most sinister scenes involves a tour of her house, its walls choked with sentimental watercolours of naked children, with the tour guide supplying a running commentary ('Naughty little things, they want a smack a bot, don't they?'). But even Mrs Curry's exposure and imprisonment offer no solution to some of the moral problems her presence in the novel sets out to advertise. As a matter-of-fact little coda soon makes clear, she uses her time in prison to assemble another band of willing helpers, 'through whom she could bring snugness and cosiness to respectable lonely gentlemen'.

The release of moral energy that fills up the later stages of a Wilson novel is invariably devastating, and nearly always rendered more uncomfortable by the fact that it often takes place in public. *Hemlock*'s denouement, significantly, hinges on the uncompromising speech with which Bernard favours the celebrity audience bidden to the opening of the writers' centre. Its aesthetic consequences, on the other hand, are much less satisfactory, for they have the effect of turning the people caught up in it into bores. By far the most cumbrous passages in *Hemlock*, for example, are the ones in which Bernard sets out his moral position for the benefit of the uncomplaining Ella, shortly before dying of heart failure: self-justifying rodomontades, which leave the reader pining for a bit less moral delicacy and a bit more attention to the way in which real people really communicate with each other. It is the same, up to a point, with Harold Calvert, the widowed headmaster of *Late Call* (1964): morally engaged, keen for the human beings gathered around him to find acceptable ways of behaving in an increasingly uncertain world, a textbook pluralist always let down by his inflexibility, his lack of self-awareness, his inability to let anything around him – people, principle, custom – go without a pitched battle.

Crammed with pompous, self-aggrandising egotists, their lives sustained by an overweening consciousness of their own rectitude, most of the satellites around them ripe to be sacrificed on the altar of their personal myth, Wilson's novels frequently suffer from the sense of characters who are given too little room for manoeuvre, never let off the leash of their creator's disdain for long enough to make any serious impact. It was Alan Ross, reviewing *Such Darling Dodos*, who accused Wilson of being a 'contemptuous ringmaster', a bayonetter of 'dead corpses' with insufficient respect for his characters. If the characters of the novels are more fully realised, more 'developed' in the technical sense, then there is still the thought of a great, gothic nursery full of overgrown children fidgeting themselves into neurosis, while nanny stands vigilantly by. Master-classes in the funny-horrible and the comically overbearing, Wilson's characters also have their structural weaknesses, not the least of them a habit of degenerating into 'types' of the kind contributed by Geoffrey Gorer and Ronald Searle to Fifties-era *Punch*. Searle, it should be pointed out, is a constant presence in the Fifties literary landscape and illustrated several of Wilson's early Penguin jackets.

Late Call's chief technical resource is pastiche: a series of pitch-perfect renditions of the television soap operas and light fiction with which its heroine Sylvia Calvert beguiles her leisure. The effect of these ebullient send-ups is curiously double-edged: on the one hand, reinforcing the novel's realist grounding; on the other, sustaining this reinforcement by artificial means. But Sylvia's mediated life, seen through the lens of *Mrs Dale's Diary* and the latest middlebrow novel (and again, not without its Leavisite subtext, in this case from *Fiction and the Reading Public*) is simply a by-blow of Wilson's wider theory of characterisation, in which no one is ever solely himself, where the end in view is to show that the selves through which we live our lives are mostly imagined, and the theatricality of the whole is further compromised by the author's readiness to jump on stage to play most of the parts himself. A great relief when set against the plain-spoken straightforwardness of Amis-man, or Joe Lunn in *Scenes from Provincial Life*, Wilson's trick of never leaving his characters alone, of rarely allowing them to draw breath, of loading them with more symbolic freight than they can bear, can also be one of his most irritating habits. Significantly, it was a tendency that grew more marked in the latter part of his life, when his fiction finally broke free from its original social-realist grounding.

The Sixties experimentalists took their cue from the idea, pithily expressed by Eva Figes in a much later *New Review* symposium from 1978, that the English social realist tradition 'cannot contain the realities of my own lifetime, horrors which one might have called surreal had they not actually happened'. Wilson appears in the same collection rebutting the influence of 'trends' ('We write alone...all bandings together, whether in French style by writers themselves or as in England by accepting convenient journalistic labels which are simply labels by which novelists *seek* to feel stronger.') Already, in *The Old Men at the Zoo* (1961), he had constructed a violent and morally unstable dystopia in which he believed that he had 'got nearer to fusing the social novel with the allegorical one than ever before'. In the context of the Sixties avant-garde, his Northcliffe lectures of 1961 are oddly prophetic. His general thesis, Margaret Drabble suggests, 'was that the provincial English novel of manners was inadequate to the violent age of Buchenwald'. The English 'had tended to lock themselves in a citadel of false security', either domesticating evil or stylising it to the point where it could not be taken seriously. Come the mid-1960s, Wilson's novels are bigger and baggier, more polyphonic and ventriloquial, less rooted in particular, known environments, tricksier, denser and more devious. They are also – a fact which even admirers of his work had finally to concede – much less good.

That something went wrong in Wilson's work – dangerously and irreparably wrong – is apparent almost from the opening pages of *No Laughing Matter* (1967). The long, fabulously layered tale of another crazy, multi-sibling family, tracked through nearly half a century of English life, its hectic engagement with the paraphernalia of its time, its false trails, its labyrinthine detail, its constant interrogation of its characters' motives, can seem merely exhausting. There is far too much in it and, by the same gauge, not nearly enough. It was the misfortune of *As if by Magic* (1973) – 'a profoundly ambitious attempt at a global novel' (Bradbury) – to be taken apart, at length and without compunction, in the *New Statesman* by the young Martin Amis. And Amis, it should be emphasised, is not being malicious. He simply points out, as a young person, that the novel's attempts to discover what young people are thinking are 'hilariously inaccurate', before going on to register grave doubts about Wilson's recently proclaimed interest in experimentalism: 'Nothing in *As if by Magic* is experimental,' Amis pronounced, 'yet one suspects Wilson is using the tag merely to widen his pitying smile should anyone be gauche enough to raise questions of motivation and plausibility.' All this hurt, but Amis's essential disinterestedness is made clear by his praise of *Late Call*, which he compares to Iris Murdoch's *Under the Net* ('such transsexual novels...show us what the imagination can do without the corroboration of experience'). Wilson, deeply traumatised – the jittery letters he wrote in the months following are full of wounded *amour propre* – never forgave him.

As to why that something went wrong, more than one critic has noted an odd coincidence. Which is to say that the cracks that begin to emerge in the carapace of Wilson's talent start making their presence felt shortly after his arrival at the University of East Anglia. Jonathan Raban, in particular, believed that his time at the UEA, his exposure, however indirect, to the postmodern lords of the US campuses and the late-1960s theorising of Barth, Hawkes and co. had led him to mistake the value of his own work, to judge that his brand of 'very heightened social realism' was on the way out, and – possibly the most wounding charge of all – 'to confuse postmodernist aesthetics with a social world from which he felt he was being increasingly excluded'. Lorna Sage, on the other hand, thought the novel had widened Wilson's sense of what the novel could do, and that *As if by Magic* was 'before its time'.

Twenty years after his death, what remains? Bradbury's claim that Wilson 'shaped a significant post-war direction in British fiction' is special pleading. Kingsley Amis was far more of an influence, however ultimately malign. Certainly, his shade makes occasional appearances in the modern canon. One can see it, perhaps, in Margaret Drabble's own moral interrogations: interestingly, the recent collection of her early stories, *A Day in the Life of a Smiling Woman* (2011), shows distinct Wilson traces. The premise of A. S. Byatt's *The Virgin in the Garden* (1978), with its 'New Elizabethan' setting and its country house ripe to be turned into an art centre, looks as if it may have borrowed something from *Hemlock and After*. In a recent *TLS* review, Peter Parker drew attention to the gay signifier role played by *No Laughing Matter* (referred to cryptically as 'Angus Wilson's new novel') in Alan Hollinghurst's *The Stranger's Child*. More generally, as a flag-bearer for liberal humanism he is the link between E. M. Forster and Malcolm Bradbury, with less of Forster's equivocation and about the same amount of Bradbury's moral resolve.

As for the wreck of a once-mighty reputation, in *Angus Wilson: A Biography* Margaret Drabble seems to suggest that the neglect into which her subject fell is a consequence of a more mercantile, less nuanced society, whose readers lost interest in the kind of moral territory that Wilson had made his own. Undoubtedly, there is something in the idea of a world in which liberal anguish has lost its savour. At the same time, far more of the evidence insists that what we have here is only the age-old spectacle of a writer who, as he matures, increasingly loses touch with the things that are worth writing about, that Wilson, an adept at one particular kind of post-war novel, saw the way the critical wind was blowing and tried to write another kind of book at which he was much less likely to succeed. This is neither to undervalue his contribution to post-war fiction or to deny that without him the landscape of 1950 to 1970 would have been a much less impressive place – less scrupulous, less morally charged, less socially aware, less engaged both with fiction's materials and the form that gives them shape. Like his hero Ronald Firbank, the sheens and surfaces of his style are simultaneously an invitation and a key half-turned in the lock, a hall-of-mirrors archness which sometimes conceals the immensely serious – and thoroughly estimable – business that lurks beneath.

D. J. Taylor was born in Norwich in 1960 and continues to live in the city. He has written nine novels, most recently *Derby Day* (2011), biographies of Thackeray and Orwell and several critical and cultural studies, including *Bright Young People: The Rise and Fall of a Generation* (2007). He writes frequently for the national press and literary journals.

A Watch on Each Wrist:
Twelve Seminars with W. G. Sebald

Luke Williams

I

I want to write about the two incarnations in which I knew W. G. Sebald: first through his writing, and then through his being my tutor at UEA. When I first encountered his work, in the winter of 1999, I had recently moved to Paris, a city new to me. I had discovered my French was worse than I thought. Having arrived there with no plan, for no clear reason, I was experiencing a sense of mounting frustration and bewilderment. What was frustrating was not the *fact* of my bewilderment – I had become used to the sensation – but that I wished to articulate it, and yet had found no way to do so. I did not want simply to forget or overcome my confusion, but, through writing, to examine its complicated paths. And yet the very confusion about which I wanted to write was preventing me from writing anything much at all. Whenever I tried to set something down, my prose seemed bleak and tedious. Reading Sebald offered me a brilliant example: here was writing which spoke honestly about loss and confusion, about a world on the verge of destruction, in a voice that was itself compelling and precise. What is more, Sebald's voice seemed to recognise the difficulty, even the impossibility, of expressing that sense of loss and confusion, even as he set out to do so.

At the time I was trying to write my way into a novel. I had come to a standstill. I suspect now this was related to the books I had been reading. In my early twenties I had felt drawn to a cadre of writers who had opposed themselves to what has come to be known as literary realism: Fernando Pessoa, for instance, and Natalie Sarraute, Alain Robbe-Grillet, Georges Perec, Salman Rushdie. I had no desire to write the kind of novel which tried to imitate reality, at least the 'realism' of clock time and easy human empathy and knowing narrators, the kind that flourished in the nineteenth century and which, despite the insights of literary modernism, remains the predominant form. What I especially resisted was the characterisation in realist novels: it was true that the heroes of those tales were sometimes confused or destabilised, but, it seemed to me, only superficially; because their confusion was not really confusion, not the kind of bafflement I was experiencing, which tended to unsettle all things, all feelings, and which pointed towards silence. No, these writers created a kind of teasing befuddlement, I felt. They toyed with confusion, tamed character and made internal disorder seem ultimately quite knowable.

Books such as Robbe-Grillet's *Jealousy* or Rushdie's *Midnight's Children* were not so articulate. If they wrote about character at all they wrote of an empty vessel into which conflicting elements might be poured. They spoke of the world and its people not as repositories of meaning but as things impossible for the imagination to grasp. It was a notion to which my sense of bewilderment bore witness. So I wanted my own novel to exist in their company. But – and this is where my problem lay – I also felt tired of the empty play of character or absence of story in these books, which were at times too coolly intellectual, concerned only with abstract structural problems. They rarely gave me pleasure, and less often left me feeling emotionally engaged. What is more, I could not understand how the radical insights these novels offered up – the dissolution of character, the breakdown of language and perspective – could lead to such confident, endlessly playful books.

It was with these thoughts in mind, coupled with my feeling of isolation in a foreign city, that I discovered *The Rings of Saturn*. I read: 'Lost in the thoughts that went round in my head incessantly, and numbed by this crazed flowering, I stuck to the sandy path until to my astonishment, not to say horror, I found myself back again at the same tangled thicket from which I had emerged about an hour before.' I read: 'he was convinced that everything he had written hitherto consisted solely in a string of the most abysmal errors and lies.' And this: 'It is difficult to imagine the depths of despair into which those can be driven who, even after the end of the working day, are engrossed in their designs and who are pursued, into their dreams, by the feeling that they have got hold of the wrong thread.'[1] This sentence appears in the end-section of *The Rings of Saturn*. After nearly three hundred pages of speaking about loss and confusion in the most compelling way, Sebald admits the possibility, even the probability, of being mistaken. James Wood recognises this: 'Sebald and his characters are haunted by the incomprehensible, the indecipherable, the wrong turn. And Sebald includes his own thread, his own course, in this category.'[2] *The Rings of Saturn*, together with Sebald's other books then published in English, which I read one after another, offered an example of the kind of book I wanted to write, the kind that accommodated the radical insights of literary modernism, were haunted by those insights, and still left the reader emotionally engaged.

Some time later I returned to the UK. I got a job. I rewrote the first chapter of my novel. I was still unhappy with the result, but my efforts seemed a little less false. Though I still felt confused, writing had given me relief. I sent my first chapter to the UEA Creative Writing MA. I did not know then that Sebald was teaching on it. When I heard I was accepted on to the course, I gave up my job and prepared to move to Norwich. How strange and exciting to learn, some four months later, shortly before arriving at UEA, that I was to be taught by Sebald.

Before the first seminar I had an (as it turned out) illusory encounter with my future tutor. Around that time *Austerlitz* was being published in the UK and Sebald was to appear in London to read from and talk about his latest work. So I caught the train from Norwich on the evening of his reading, bought the book at the venue (it was not yet out in the shops) and took my place in the audience. I remember little about the event, only that Sebald, who spoke flawless English, read first from the German edition of *Austerlitz*, then had his translator read the same passage from the UK edition. Later he told the interviewer that he wrote and read in German because he feared he had a 'funny accent'. Immediately after the talk I left. I was new to London and took the wrong bus to Liverpool Street Station, and I missed my train. The next and final departure was not for another hour. So I sat on one of the station's moulded plastic chairs and opened *Austerlitz*. I read: 'When I entered the great hall of the Centraal Station with its dome arching sixty metres high above it...' I read: 'the railway passengers seemed to me somehow miniaturised, whether by the unusual height of the ceiling or because of the gathering dusk, and it was this, I suppose, which prompted the passing thought, nonsensical in itself, that they were the last members of a diminutive race.' I looked at the late passengers in their crumpled suits, many of them eating burgers from colourful boxes. Then I saw Sebald. He was standing by the ticket desk. He, too, was waiting for the Norwich train. I hid *Austerlitz* in my bag. Sebald was smoking a cigarette, which struck me somehow as odd. I took *Austerlitz* from my bag, thought about removing the dust jacket. Conscious that its author might spot me reading his book, and in truth half-willing him to do so, I continued from where I had left off. 'One of the people waiting in the *Salle des pas perdus* was Austerlitz,' I read. 'When I finally went over to Austerlitz with a question about his obvious interest in the waiting room, he was not at all surprised by my direct approach but answered me at once.'[3] I tried to force myself not to look at Sebald, who had moved to the turnstile. My dilemma was this: should I board the train as soon as the turnstile opened, before Sebald, leaving to chance our plainly fated meeting; or should I allow him to go first, stepping afterwards into his carriage, thus nudging fate in the right direction?

It is important to mention at this point that, informed by his books, I had the idea that Sebald could hardly step on to a bus or train without some fortuitous meeting. (I recalled the episode in *Vertigo* when the narrator, travelling on a bus during his quest to retrace 'Dr K.'s' 1913 Italian journey, meets twin boys who bear an uncanny resemblance to Kafka himself.)[4] I had been snared by the strange logic of these books, where coincidence, in the form of a finely patterned series of meetings and discoveries, takes the place of the conventional plot device of cause and effect. So it seemed perfectly natural, even likely, that I was to meet Sebald that evening (just as his other odd notions, notions that if taken to their logical conclusion would put in jeopardy the common understanding of the world – that, for instance, we have 'appointments to keep in the past'[5] – can seem plausible, even inevitable, under the spell of his imagination). But I was confused; I had, in fact, succumbed to the very mistake that Sebald's books, like those others which challenged literary realism, counselled against: I was ascribing to lived experience a clarity or inevitability which existed only in the falsifying narratives of the realists. For if in Sebald's prose coincidence takes the place of conventional plot, coincidence also works against itself. Events in his books are so artfully arranged that only in the non-place of fiction could such a finely patterned set of coincidences occur. I did not recognise this at the time, however; standing there in Liverpool Street Station, some two metres behind Sebald, waiting for the signal to proceed on to the platform and board the train, I continued to blend fiction (Sebald's) with reality (my own).

I didn't meet him that evening on the train, although we sat in the same carriage. Instead, I intermittently read *Austerlitz* and watched its author as he talked to a woman in a parallel seat. The two conversed animatedly for almost the entire journey, and if I felt disappointed I was not in her place, I also felt privileged to be witnessing the live process of Sebald's research (although I later discovered that this woman was one of his colleagues at UEA and had perhaps accompanied him to the talk).

The writing course was soon to begin. I was still unsure how I would react on meeting Sebald. I had spent so much time in the company of his books, had been party, as I thought, to his most intimate thoughts, that I felt nervous at the prospect of his gaze. How strange it would be to sit in class with his eyes turned on me! It is often the case that long hoped-for encounters disappoint, because they rarely match the intensity of expectation which preceded them. Certainly the experience of being in Sebald's class was different to how I had imagined it, but it was every bit as exhilarating.

II

The most economical way, I think, of conveying my experience of Sebald as a Creative Writing teacher is to transcribe an edited version of the diary entries I made during that winter term of 2001.[6]

September 26

First seminar. Each of us introduced ourselves. We spoke a little about our writing projects and our hopes for the course. Some, the more reticent, were prompted by questions from Sebald. He was friendly and curious, as I had expected, but also witty, which somehow I had not imagined him to be. When my turn came I talked for far too long. After the last student had finished speaking, Sebald said something like, 'I suppose I'd better tell you something about myself.' He went on to say that he was more surprised than anyone to find himself here, in front of a bunch of Creative Writing students, since the university had until now regarded him as nothing more than an obscure scholar of German-language literature. But his 'prose works' had recently become known to UEA, and so here he was. The upshot of these prose works having come to light, he told us, had had a second fortunate effect, which was that he was now given greater leeway at the university. The staff were happier to indulge what he called his 'eccentricities' (which he didn't go into). Best of all, he said, he no longer had to deal with the tedious administrative duties that academics are nowadays everywhere forced to carry out. He then proceeded to tell us that despite the privileges being an author can convey, at least in the university environment, there is very little else to say in favour of the profession.

You must be already slightly disturbed if your goal is to spend your lifetime staring at a blank piece of paper, he told us. What is more, the process of writing itself is often quite different from how you might imagine. Being always on your own, for instance, with your own thoughts, trying to make sense of them, being forced to constantly invent things – is this not a recipe for mental ruin? Think hard about whether you really want to be a writer, he told us, and if you decide that you do, make sure you take another job as well. Teaching is not a bad option, he said. Neither is it a bad idea to become a barrister. Best of all, he told us, is to get involved in the medical profession, because you will hear many strange stories, which later at your desk you can make use of.

What a strange introduction to a Creative Writing class! Of course, he's right. I've heard that less than 10 per cent of published writers in Britain earn more than the minimum wage. And that instances of depression and alcoholism are much higher among poets and writers. Was he trying to put us off? If so, his talk had the opposite effect. It only made me more sure I want to be a writer. Did he calculate it this way?

October 3

In our first meeting we had been told to bring a passage of writing we admired. The passages were photocopied and distributed at the end of class. I had not been able to decide between two of my favourite writers: a section from Georges Perec's *Life: A User's Manual* – a novel set almost entirely at one minute to eight – and a short story by Ingo Schulze. In the end I had chosen Schulze, a German, probably, stupidly, because I wanted to impress Sebald. We spent the whole of this second seminar looking at the passages. Mine was, in fact, the first Sebald picked out. For a moment I was thrilled. I thought that he had chosen it for its merits. It was not the case. In fact, he seemed to hate it. He tore it apart (and by extension my taste). The story was clumsy, artless, imprecise. Worse, he said, you just couldn't *see* what the author was talking about. He disliked one line in particular that went something like this (I'm too ashamed to go and look it up): 'Only when the dimpled sewer covers started to spit ice cubes up on to the road, like smoothly licked sweets, were we able to walk normally again.'[7] I can't *see* it, Sebald kept on saying. Perhaps it's my bad English, he said, but I can't imagine a spitting sewer cover. What on earth does such a sewer cover look like? No one, myself least of all, had an answer. And why, he went on, if the road was presumably covered with ice cubes, had the author highlighted this fact as the moment when 'we' (and note that he never, in fact, tells us who this 'we' are) were able to walk normally again? Wouldn't the pedestrians be slipping about all over the place? I certainly wouldn't go out on such a day, he said. I myself made a pathetic attempt to defend the story, but I could hardly speak. And I stayed mute for the rest of the class. Sebald treated every piece to this scrupulous criticism. He tore into Don DeLillo's *Underworld* for its inconsistencies of perspective. How on earth can the narrator be so sure about all the things he seems to know? How can he be in so many places at the same time? One minute, Sebald said, he's describing the Arizona desert from the ground-level view, from the perspective of an iguana, and the next from high above. In the space of a few lines he has become a bird of prey spying on the iguana, probably so he can gobble it up. Discussing a Raymond Carver story Sebald got us all to stand up and try to act out some motion the narrator's wife carried out. We had to stick strictly to the description in the text. She was doing something like taking a chicken out of the oven whilst turning to her husband and saying something about the chicken. Sebald was right. It was impossible, the way Carver described it, for the human body to move in precisely this way. He went on to say that it's very difficult, not to say impossible, to get physical movement right when writing. The important thing is that it should work for the reader, even if it's not meticulous. You can use ellipses, he said, abbreviate a sequence of actions, you needn't laboriously describe each one. Out of all the passages the only one Sebald liked unreservedly was from Jim Crace's *Being Dead*.

I'm still shocked. Sebald's point, it seems to me, was simple. That precision in writing fiction – *especially* in writing fiction – is an absolutely fundamental value. He summed up by saying that if you look carefully you can find problems in all writers, or almost all (Kafka being an exception; especially, he told us, if you look at the reports he wrote for the Workers' Accident Insurance Institute!). He told us that even those writers who have talent and scrupulousness must be on their guard against sloppiness and indulgence. He gave, as an example of sloppiness, Günter Grass, who, he said, had started off writing quite well, but had lately let his writing slip. He thought it had happened since Grass had won the Nobel Prize. Probably, he said, Grass's publisher has been too scared to edit his latest manuscripts.

I'm going to stop writing now and take a look at my chapters. I won't go to sleep until I've tightened them up.

October 17

It was uncomfortable in class today. For the first time we saw Sebald riled; not angry exactly, but agitated, even perplexed. It was clear that one of the hand-ins, H.'s, had affected him quite strongly. The story was set in an unnamed city under curfew. Food was becoming harder and harder to come by. Citizens were being shot. There was some kind of confused relationship between a man and a woman. In the end the two turned to cannibalism. Most of us liked the story. I did, too, although I think it is heavily indebted to the Peter Carey story 'Room No. 5 (Escribo)', which I read last summer. This time Sebald didn't make his usual criticisms about superfluous sentences or too many characters being introduced all at once or lack of concrete detail, but went straight to his point. There is something wrong with the way the story is told, he said. It's the voice. You are writing about horrendous things. Horrific events. Are you sure you know what you are writing about? Have you actually been to such a place? Have you yourself witnessed such horror? H. replied that she had lived in Jerusalem for nine years. That surprised him. We talked about the story some more. There really wasn't a lot to say (it is always the case that the better, tighter hand-ins get shorter crits). But Sebald wasn't willing to let it go. He said again that he had a problem with the voice, with the way the narrator approaches the horror she is describing. He told us that horror is everywhere now, there is so much of it, in all walks of life, everywhere we look. I went into my local video shop, he said. It's filled with nasty videos. A generation who have never known war is being raised on horror. Then he asked a few questions. How do you surpass horror once you've reached a certain level? How do you stop it appearing gratuitous? He answered himself. Let me get this right. You (he was addressing the whole class) might think that because you are writing fiction you needn't be overly concerned to get the facts straight. But aesthetics is not a value-free area. And you must be particularly careful if your subject concerns horrific events. You must stick absolutely to the facts. The most plausible, perhaps even the only, approach is the documentary one. I would say that writing about an appalling state of affairs is incommensurable with traditional aesthetics.

I can't quite understand Sebald's point, though I'm not willing to dismiss it. I thought at first he was reiterating Adorno's dictum that there can be no poetry after Auschwitz. It can't be, though, because all Sebald's work picks over the barbarism of the twentieth century, often focusing on the Holocaust, if obliquely. And he implied that you *can* write about such things, if only you stick to the facts. But facts are slippery, especially in times of emergency, as Sebald surely knows. So his problem with H.'s story cannot be related to her writing fiction about horrid events per se. It must lie with the way she chose to write about them. And, in fact, thinking about the story now, there *is* something gratuitous about it. That absolutely flat tone. The horror never seems to touch the narrator. H.'s point is that those who experience dreadful events on a daily basis become numbed to them. As a comment on human behaviour this may be true, and on that I don't think Sebald could argue with her. But I think Sebald's problem lay elsewhere. I think it lay deeper than his argument over aesthetics. He had had an unpleasant reaction to the story; you could hear it in his voice. For him the story had crossed some kind of line. I'm thinking of Coetzee's *Disgrace*, when David Lurie chooses to cremate dead dogs himself rather than witness workers breaking the dogs' legs so as to fit the corpses better into the cremation fire. And he chooses to do this for no clear or logical reason, but because of a private instinct: 'For his idea of the world, a world in which men do not use shovels to beat corpses into a more convenient shape for processing.'[8] I think Sebald's reaction had something similarly private about it. I think it had something to do with the fact that he has chosen as his subject unspeakable events, and it's my guess it took him a lot of thinking and self-searching to decide, in fact, to voice them. That's perhaps why he published fiction only relatively late in his life. It had probably taken years for him to feel confident enough about his form, to trust himself to approach his subject in writing. And it is now hard for him to countenance another, weaker, more common-sense method. Like all great writers, he's too involved in his own vision.

October 31

It strikes me that Sebald is not your usual UEA-type Creative Writing tutor. I always knew that. What I didn't expect was how opposed, even hostile, is his attitude to the kind of writing that usually comes out of UEA. He rarely states his hostility explicitly. And, in fact, if you were to analyse any one of his seminars you would not necessarily deduce what I am sure is a deeply felt antipathy to the flat, realist style (those confident, quirky male protagonists, the breathy girl-child narrators that are always somehow damaged, the sentiment masked as irony, the smooth metonymy, the easy generalisations) most of the class produce. Taken together, his comments and digressions, such as the one today on time ('Physicists now say there is no such thing as time: everything coexists; the artificial thing is actually chronology'), add up to a fairly sustained attack on the UEA/realist aesthetic. This afternoon he even took a swipe at Ian McEwan. We were looking at S.'s story, which follows the misadventures of an English family in a campsite in south-west France. It was a pretty good story, most of us agreed. Sebald was enthusiastic about it, too. He said what he liked best was the detail. The focus on camping equipment: the different types of tent poles, mattresses, stoves, the names of certain kinds of knots specific to the camping world, etc. It was for him a whole new vernacular, he said. I could translate a page of Ian McEwan in half an hour, he said, but a camping manual! That is another matter entirely. And two Sainsbury's managers talking to each other are a different species altogether.

Here's a (necessarily incomplete) list of his polemic comments so far:

I can only encourage you to steal as much as you can. No one will ever notice. You should keep a notebook of tidbits, but don't write down the attributions, and then after a couple of years you can come back to the notebook and treat the stuff as your own without guilt.

It's very good that you write through another text, a foil, so that you write out of it and make your work a palimpsest.

In the twentieth century we know that the observer always affects what is being said. So you have to talk about where you got your sources, how it was talking to that woman in Beverly Hills, the trouble you had at the airport, etc. Writing that does not acknowledge the uncertainty of the narrator is an imposture, jaded, even dangerous.

In the nineteenth century the omniscient narrator *was* God. Totalitarian and monolithic. The twentieth century with all its horrors was more demotic. We have to acknowledge our own sense of ignorance and of insufficiency and try and write with this always in mind.

I find it hard to countenance writing in the third person.

There is a certain merit in leaving some parts of your writing obscure.

Writing should not create the impression that the writer is trying to be 'poetic'.

On time: Chronology is entirely artificial and essentially determined by emotion.

Contiguity suggests layers of things, the past and present somehow coalescing or coexisting.

I think quite a few class members find his perspective hard to follow or are hostile to it. For example, P. said he did not worry about these kinds of things (I think he meant first- vs. third-person narration) and disliked 'experimental' writing generally (as if his own social-realist style is the right way and any diversion from this 'experimental'!). I think what is new in Sebald can be seen in the way he himself dealt with the issue of realism. His writing mostly eschews realism, not just in its structural radicalism but in that he seeks a kind of verisimilitude of the nether world. Isaac Babel once said of Tolstoy that if the world could write itself, it would write like him. It strikes me that if the dead were to write themselves, they would write like Sebald.

November 21

By all means be experimental, Sebald said today in class, but let the reader be part of the experiment. Write about obscure things, but don't write obscurely. This advice brought me up short. I think my own writing suffers on this account. I am too ready to pack my writing with obscure facts, oblique references, and I want everything to be tricksy. Plus, I'm always having to mask the essayist in me. This is exactly the trap that Sebald, in his writing, (mostly) circumvents. What marks him out is his ability to blend the essay form with the purely fictional. His books leap (and it *is* a leap, since so often the fiction takes over in a passage of flight, often in a dream-sequence when the narrator flies above both the landscape and his own rational thoughts) into the fictional. He rarely makes the mistake, as I do (and others in the class whom his writing has influenced), of believing that obscure information or antique objects have charm in themselves. He never transposes raw facts into his texts. If he did they would read as still-born. I must keep this in mind. Information is not appealing merely because it's authentic. I must remember that in my novel information, however interesting in itself, cannot be regurgitated without having been touched by the alchemy of fiction.

December 5

This afternoon in class I had a bizarre momentary vision of Sebald. It was one of those seminars when everyone seemed tired and distracted. The story we were discussing was poor. It concerned an autistic child and his mother's attempt to come to terms with the affliction. It was clunky and depressing. You could hear the 'grinding noises' (Sebald's phrase) of the plot. And the discussion was rambling, too, going nowhere really. At one point, as he sometimes does, thrillingly, Sebald started talking at length. He told us about his boyhood hatred for the 'old Nazi' who gave him zither lessons. He told us about his Austrian friend who had graphomania. He told us that Princess Diana regarded the Windsors as nothing other than a bunch of German upstarts. At one point I started looking at my classmates. I thought about how we had been thrust together in this class. I thought about how raw the crits could be, how I had read about some very private things, how some of the criticisms had bordered on personal attacks. I thought about the very different personalities in the class and how most of us were in some way nutty. Some with ambition. Some with neuroses. Some with jealousy or past hurt. And some were just odd looking. Sebald was still talking. He was telling us about a writer called Ödön von Horváth, who had escaped Germany when the Nazis came to power. I looked over at the window. It was raining outside. I could hear the drops tapping against the glass. Horváth, Sebald told us, was exiled in Paris, where he consulted a clairvoyant, who warned him to steer clear of the city of Amsterdam, never to ride on trams, on no account to go in a lift, and to avoid lightning at all costs. Horváth took this advice very seriously. At one point I stopped looking at the faces of my classmates and instead watched Sebald. He was leaning back in his chair. His legs were stretched out in front of him, his body a long diagonal. His eyes looked up at the ceiling and the round glass of his spectacles reflected the strip light. Both his hands were placed on the back of his head; together his arms made a coat-hanger shape, a pair of 'V's. Horváth, Sebald was saying, despite all his precautions, was one day walking on the Champs Elysées when a branch fell and killed him. Sebald continued to talk, perhaps he was telling us more about the writer Horváth, perhaps he had moved on to something else. But I was no longer following him, because I'd noticed something strange. He was wearing a watch on each wrist. On his left wrist he wore a cheap digital watch, face up. On his right an analogue watch, its face turned round to the underside of his wrist. The rain continued. Sebald talked on. But I wasn't following him. I kept looking at the watches on his wrists. Why two watches? Why one digital and one analogue? Why was the analogue watch turned face down? I didn't know.

III

Less than two weeks after this last diary entry Sebald was killed. Someone read about it in the local paper and the news travelled quickly around the class. Shocked, we tried to give his death a meaning. Someone suggested (ridiculously) that it was appropriate that Sebald, who was happiest whilst travelling, had died on the move. We all vowed to keep our essays with his hand-written comments on them. I wanted to find a reason for his early, incomprehensible death. I wanted, hopelessly, to read his next book, which he had mentioned once or twice in class. I thought about the few times I had spoken to him personally. It was tempting to think that he had singled me out among the students, but it wasn't true.

These last years I have thought about his death quite a bit. I have read, and thought about, his writing even more. I recently found a passage from Kierkegaard. It said something about it being one thing for a life to be over, and quite another for a life to be finished by reaching a conclusion. Though, of course, it is over, there can be no conclusion to Sebald's life. It is too easy to think in terms of conclusions. To do so is to give his life false meaning. It would be to ascribe to muddled existence a clarity it can never have. Like my mistake that evening at Liverpool Street Station, it would be to confuse fiction (Sebald's) with reality (his own).

1   W. G. Sebald, *The Rings of Saturn*, trans. Michael Hulse (London: The Harvill Press, 1999), pp. 171, 7, 283.

2   James Wood, 'W. G. Sebald's Uncertainty', in *The Broken Estate: Essays on Literature and Belief*, (London: Pimlico, 2000), p. 284.

3   W. G. Sebald, *Austerlitz*, trans. Anthea Bell (London: Hamish Hamilton, 2001), pp. 5, 6, 7.

4   W. G. Sebald, *Vertigo*, trans. Michael Hulse (London: The Harvill Press, 1999), p. 88.

5   W. G. Sebald, *Austerlitz*, trans. Anthea Bell (London: Hamish Hamilton, 2001), p. 360.

6   I have edited the diary entries to make them clearer and so that the focus is on Sebald. I have also integrated some notes that two fellow students, David Lambert and Robert McGill, wrote during the seminars and handed to our class after Sebald's death. I am grateful to them both.

7   The passage is from Ingo Schulze, *33 Moments of Happiness: St Petersburg Stories,* trans. John E. Woods (London: Picador, 1999). It in fact reads: 'Not until the dented sewer covers began spitting ice cubes up on to the sidewalks like well-licked pieces of candy was our normal gait restored to us.' p. 255.

8   J. M. Coetzee, *Disgrace* (London: Vintage, 2000), p. 146.

Luke Williams (*b.* 1977) received his MA in Creative Writing from UEA in 2002. His first novel is *The Echo Chamber* (2011). He contributed a chapter to *Saturn's Moons: A W. G. Sebald Handbook* (2009).

cademy

Saffron

Paul Muldoon

Sometimes I'd happen on Alexander and Cleopatra
and several of their collaborators
tucking into a paella
tinged with saffron, saffron thought to be a cure
for scabies, bloody scours,
fires in the belly,

skin cancer, the ancient pestilence of Sumer,
not to speak of Alzheimer's
and plain old melancholy.
I'm pretty sure things first
started to look bleak in 1987 at the University
of East Anglia

where I was introduced to the art of the lament
by Ezekiel. His electric fire's single element
was an orange ice lolly.
He made me think I might lose my spot
as number one hod-carrier in Mesopotamia,
a role that came quite easily

now I lived in a ziggurat
overlooking a man-made lake and sipped sugared
water with a swarm of honeybees.
Though A Flock of Seagulls
were scheduled to play the Union, there had been an icicle
in my heart since Anubis,

half-man, half-jackal,
had palmed me off on Ezekiel
for ritual embalmment.
He claimed A Flock of Seagulls were a one-hit wonder,
desert flowers left high and dry
on the polder. Anubis refused to implement

the Anglo-Irish Agreement.
He also told me the church clock in Crimond
had sixty-one minutes
to the hour. Ezekiel, meanwhile, was convinced
that Creative Writing, still in its infancy,
would amount

to a bona fide
academic pursuit only if students weren't spoon-fed
but came to think of literature
as magical rather than magisterial.
Saffron itself was derived from the three stamen-tufts of a sterile
crocus that, ground, were often adulterated

with turmeric. An icicle was formed
precisely because it would repeatedly warm
to the idea of camaraderie,
then repeatedly give in to chilliness.
I took comfort from the insistence of the anchoress, Julian,
on the utter

necessity of sin for self-knowledge, a theory I'd have to tout
to the Hare Krishna devotees
who'd sworn off sex outside procreation in marriage.
Sometimes I'd see one, late at night, in saffron robe and topknot,
stranded at a bus stop
on the outskirts of Norwich.

Paul Muldoon (*b.* 1951) held the UEA Writing Fellowship in 1987. He published his first collection of poems, *New Weather*, in 1973. Many other books have followed, including *Mules* (1977), *Why Brownlee Left* (1980), *Meeting the British* (1987), *The Annals of Chile* (1994), *Moy Sand and Gravel* (2002), for which he received the Pulitzer Prize for Poetry, and *Maggot* (2010). Since 1987 he has lived in the United States, where he is the Howard G. B. Clark Professor in the Humanities at Princeton University.

Faking It

Martyn Bedford

So you are leaving the theatre, your mind boggled by the performance of one of the world's most spectacular illusionists, David Copperfield, when someone sidles up alongside you like a pimp. 'Psst, I know how he does it.' 'Does what?' 'That magic malarkey.' You're hooked, drawn into the whisper of a shared secret. The 'pimp' tells you how Copperfield makes that railway carriage levitate and disappear, how he walks through a wall, how he survives bisection by electric saw, how he causes the Statue of Liberty to vanish. The revelations should be thrilling. But by the time he has finished revealing the tricks of the trade of the Trade of Tricks you are, in every sense of the word, disillusioned. The show is spoiled, the magic rendered mechanistic. You feel cheated.

Except, of course, that it isn't. And you don't.

When you pay to see an illusionist you are entering into an unspoken, unwritten contract. You both know it isn't 'real' magic, but for the purposes of entertainment and amazement the performer acts as though it *is*...and does it so brilliantly, so bafflingly, you're just about ready to believe it might be magic after all.

Traditionalists, like Copperfield, stick close to this deal, keeping the curtain tightly drawn across the true nature of their act. With other illusionists a different kind of agreement is on offer. There are those, like Uri Geller, who claim to possess real psychic abilities – that their 'effects', as they are known in the trade, are not tricks at all. Then there are those such as Derren Brown who, in interviews and on stage, make no pretence that what they do is magic; while he stops short of revealing exactly how he does his tricks, the fact that he *is* tricking you is part of the patter, part of the act. The double act Penn & Teller take this to its logical conclusion by building their show around the performance of an illusion, followed by a repeat demonstration, explaining the methodology step by step.

Whatever type of contract the performer and audience enter into, however – and regardless of whether we are wowed by the magical effects or the skill and ingenuity of the fakery, or both – the 'show' is essentially the same: each illusion is a story and, like any storyteller, the illusionist aims to hold us spellbound.

When I had the idea for my novel *The Houdini Girl*, about a professional conjuror involved in a duplicitous relationship, I hadn't made this connection between stage magic and the art of storytelling. But as I researched my protagonist's trade and pondered the associated notions of deception and illusion which underpinned his story, I was struck by the similarities between the magician's craft and that of the writer or, indeed, anyone who uses artifice to entertain or enlighten. As the American illusionist Ricky Jay says, 'The magician is supremely honest. He tells you he is going to deceive you, then lives up to his word.' For magician, read playwright, TV dramatist, film director, actor, novelist.

The most obvious parallel between magic and fiction is the contractual one – the suspension of disbelief. Fully aware that the story is invented and the characters aren't real people, the performer and audience set forth, hand in hand, into the land of make-believe. A world where the novelist makes the false seem true and the reader is happy to be duped. Of course, many writers – from Laurence Sterne to the Modernists and postmodernists – have taken the Derren Brown or Penn & Teller line and made the fact that they are telling a story integral to the story they are telling. But readers who venture out into *that* wild landscape merely retrieve their coat of suspended disbelief from a different hook. Fiction or metafiction, a story is still being told, a pact is still being brokered.

So, there exists a kind of collusion between artist and audience. But fiction also shares certain practical similarities with magic in the way that its story – its 'effect', if you like – is constructed and performed. Sometimes, for example in crime fiction, this analogy isn't too hard to make: the creation of a puzzle for the reader to solve, the withholding or disguising of vital information, the false trails that misdirect a reader's attention, the *ta-daaa* moment of revelation. Even in a 'literary' novel, however, or one driven by character and theme rather than plot, the author will often present dual narratives: the one being played out at the surface and the other one (or more) concealed beneath. If the text is the conjuror's flourish, the percussive flash from the tip of a wand, then the subtext is the sleight of hand being enacted, unseen, behind the puff of smoke. Story and meaning, we might call them. Our eyes are drawn to one and we are left to fathom out the other.

What arises from this is an inevitable tension between the creator of the artifice and those for whom it is created. In *Our Magic,* co-written in 1911 by the top British illusionists of their day, Nevil Maskelyne and David Devant, the authors state:

> Tricks and dodges are of comparatively small importance in the art of magic. At the utmost they display inventive ability, but nothing more. The effect – and the effect alone – produced by the use of such invention, is the consideration of real importance. The general public, however, tend to the notion that magic consists merely in puzzles to be solved and challenges to the audience's acuteness. To the magician, the 'secrets' are little more than are, to the actor, the wigs, greasepaints and other make-up and costumes…the art of the magician, like that of the actor, depends on matters far higher than mere appliances and processes.

Here we find another connection between magic and fiction – our desire to know the secrets of their creation. When we watch Penn & Teller explain the workings of their illusions or those of other magicians, we are satisfying a natural curiosity to find out how it's done. To un-baffle ourselves. If we are bamboozled by a Derren Brown TV show, we can fire up our PC and surf one of the numerous online forums set up to discuss – and disclose – the tricks behind his mind-bending trickery. This is nothing new. Harry Houdini, the greatest illusionist and escapologist of them all, used to publish the secrets of his feats in a monthly magazine. Earlier still, in 1584, the *Discoverie of Witchcraft* described the techniques of legerdemain, so that its practitioners would be protected from false accusations of satanic practices. In those days, when magic was commonly equated with black magic, the performing conjuror trod a treacherous path.

Today, when even Paul Daniels is safe from being burned at the stake, there are any number of books which claim to spill the magic beans, so to speak – including one devoted entirely to 'exposing' David Copperfield. It's the work of a Bavarian biologist and amateur magician, Robert Rau, who spent years studying Copperfield's act in order to figure out his illusions. The book – a bestseller on its release in Germany, where Copperfield has a huge following – revealed the methodology to be disappointingly conventional: the use of mirrors, lighting, concealed compartments, optical illusions and pure sleight of hand. The mainstay of stage magic for centuries.

Of course, the sheer scale of Copperfield's illusions is what raises his show above the rest. Making a smiling, sequin-costumed assistant disappear is one thing, spiriting away an eighty-foot, seventy-tonne train carriage is something else. Yet, according to Rau, the basic principle is the same. The object (woman, train, whatever) is draped in a cloth then removed – quietly, unseen – into a dark zone created by subtle use of spotlighting and black backdrops. Meanwhile, its presence beneath the cloth is stimulated by a 'jimmy' – a collapsible wire frame, which is whisked away with a flourish, along with the cloth, when the magician delivers the illusion's dramatic punchline. David Copperfield, as he would do, dismissed the revelations contained in the book as 'mere hypotheses'. The German Magic Circle accused Rau of breaking the fundamental code of magicianship by laying its secrets bare, and all in pursuit of a publicity-seeking exposé.

But what is there to expose? We know the magician operates in apparent rather than actual defiance of the laws of nature. We know he possesses great skill rather than paranormal powers. We know his illusions to be just that: illusions. In this technologically sophisticated age, does anyone watch a magic show in the serious belief that they are witnessing an actual magician – some kind of Merlinesque sorcerer – at work? Is the illusionist akin to a fraudster, to be named and shamed for exploiting his punters by raising false expectations, by claiming to be something he isn't, by presenting lies as truth?

It's a short step from tricks to trickery, and magicians – like writers – haven't always been entirely honourable. In the days of street shows and travelling fairs, conjurors were said to operate in cahoots with pickpockets, who worked an audience while it was distracted by the amazing events on stage. Another notorious rip-off is the centuries-old gambling game, Find the Lady, where you have to bet on which of three playing cards is the queen. Performed legitimately, this is a true contest between performer and punter. Its illicit version is an illusion within an illusion: you think you're testing your powers of observation against the card-sharp as he moves the three cards about the table at high speed, but it's a case of heads he wins, tails you lose…sleight of hand has removed the queen from the fray before you place your bet, and restored it as one of the 'losing' cards after he's pocketed your money.

The true magician is no trickster; there is no victim in magic as an entertainment. Indeed, the profession boasts a long history of seeking to discredit performers who use their 'magical' skills for fraudulent purposes or who pass them off as psychic or supernatural phenomena. One of the forefathers of modern illusionism – that man Maskelyne again – launched his career with an act devoted to exposing the tricks used by spirit mediums. An apprentice watchmaker and jeweller who practised conjuring as a hobby, he had been asked by a professional clairvoyant to repair a piece of apparatus. The device was designed to be attached to the medium's leg so that, unseen beneath the table, the communicative raps of lost loved ones could be produced. Outraged, Maskelyne – billing himself as a Royal Illusionist and Anti-Spiritualist – mastered this and other clairvoyant techniques and began staging mock séances. One bogus medium was jailed for three months after Maskelyne demonstrated in court how the defendant faked written messages from the dead. Houdini, famously, also had it in for spiritualists. When his mother died he employed a medium to make contact and, sure enough, the dead woman's spirit spoke to her beloved son. The only snag being that she used English – a language she could barely speak when she was alive. Thereafter, Houdini dedicated himself to rooting out charlatanism.

So, genuine illusionists are honest liars – even as they deceive us, we trust them not to rip us off. We expect much the same of our novelists. Any breach of contract goes down badly, as James Frey discovered in the furore following his admission that *A Million Little Pieces*, published as a memoir, was mostly fiction. But to pick up the thread of an earlier (and perilously long-neglected) line of argument, there is one crucial distinction in the nature of the relationship between magicians and their audience, and writers and their readers. At a magic show, we want to be captivated by the performance – by the drama of the 'story' the conjuror acts out for us with each illusion – but, perhaps more importantly, we want to be left wondering, 'How the hell does he *do* that?'

Readers don't have this same curiosity to understand the 'doing' of fiction – the writer's working methods, or the storytelling devices and techniques from which character, plot and theme materialise. Writing is not done 'as if by magic' and so, while you know you are being lied to, as Ricky Jay might put it, you don't much care to know how. The many 'how to' books on creative writing exist to help aspiring writers develop their own storytelling practice, not to blow the gaff on how Joyce wrote *Ulysses* or Rowling wrote the Potter novels. In his biography of B. S. Johnson, *Like a Fiery Elephant*, Jonathan Coe refers to the literary biographer's difficulty in recounting a subject's working methods when pretty much all of the interesting stuff occurs inside the writer's head. A very dull exposé would have resulted should Herr Rau have attempted to study a writer's 'act' in the way that he studied David Copperfield's. The observable methodology would amount to this: Stared at screen. Typed. Picked nose. Scribbled notes. Typed. Stared at screen. Bit fingernail. Drank coffee. Typed. Sighed. Swore. Checked emails. Reopened document. Stared at screen. Typed. Stared out of window. (Repeat daily for two years.)

It follows, then, that if readers show an interest in writers, beyond merely enjoying their writing, it often centres on the seemingly alchemical mental processes that give rise to stories. 'Where do you get your ideas from?' must be the most commonly posed question any fiction writer will face. Closely followed by, 'Are the characters based on people you know?' or 'Is your novel autobiographical?' (An irony which would not be lost on James Frey.) However, it isn't that the questioner wants to expose some trickery on the author's part or decipher the magic formula that produces fiction. Rather, the novel reader's curiosity is piqued by a desire to grasp that tantalisingly ungraspable of things: the workings of the creative imagination. Not so much '*How* does he do that?' as '*Why* does he do that?'

Despite this distinction, perhaps this is where magicians and novelists have most in common – in their enduring ability to mystify us. Even now, when we are surrounded by so much more high-tech wizardry in our daily lives than was the case in the days of Maskelyne or Houdini, stage magic retains its allure. A space shuttle takes off and we sit in our homes watching the event via satellite, taking this for granted. Yet a good illusionist, using age-old tricks of the trade, can still confound and captivate. It might be that modern technology is so complex, so far beyond our comprehension, that we give up even trying to understand it. We simply accept. After all, you don't need to know how an iPod, a computer, a mobile phone, a DVD player, a Kindle work in order to use one. In contrast, the workings of an illusion seem understandable, albeit teasingly poised beyond our fingertips. We may feel excluded by the technological 'miracles' of our times, but we can still immerse ourselves in the simulation of the miraculous.

An illusionist, albeit momentarily, breaks the chain of cause-and-effect which binds us to rationality. We are disoriented, and delighted to be so. We glimpse a world where logic and science, and what we've learned to be the natural physical order, have been stood on their head.

In magic, there are two things taking place at once: what seems to be occurring and what is actually occurring. We like this, we humans. This joy of mistaking the unreal for the real is at the heart of storytelling. And stories, after all, are what set us apart from the other animals. Facts tell stories, too, they explain, they make sense out of chaos. But fiction – and magic is fiction, of a kind – transports us beyond what we know to be true and into the wonderful realm of mystery and belief. As much as people crave knowledge, we also have an innate need to *believe* – or, at least, to suspend disbelief from time to time. When David Copperfield makes a train carriage disappear we know he *hasn't*, but we half-wish he had. And if some smart-arse sidles up to us on the way out of the auditorium and whispers: 'Psst, I know how he does that…' Well, that's another story.

Martyn Bedford (*b.* 1959) received his MA in Creative Writing from UEA in 1994. He is the author of five novels for adults, including *Acts of Revision* (1996) and *The Houdini Girl* (1999). His latest novel, *Flip,* for teenagers and young adults, was published in 2011. Martyn lives in West Yorkshire with his wife and two daughters, and teaches on the English & Writing programme at Leeds Trinity University College.

Why Shouldn't We?

Adam Mars-Jones

What follows was first published as the introduction to the 1993 UEA Creative Writing anthology Mafia! AM-J

Only sex education seems to cause more unease in British hearts and minds than the teaching of Creative Writing. You're going to study *that?* But that's not a subject!

Some of the unease is based on assumptions about education: surely anyone who wants to can write, using tools acquired along the way. This turns out to be largely an assumption about class, and the 'anyone' who turns incidentally acquired skills into competent practise would have to be a pretty rarefied creature.

Another unease-factor has to do with gender: a Creative Writing course sounds suspiciously supportive, amniotic, in a word *unmasculine*. How does authority work in such a setting? Is this like apprenticeship to a craft master? Do you have to make knife-boxes before being allowed to attempt a table?

Creative Writing may not be a subject like other subjects, but it is a quasi-subject, of which I have some experience as both teacher and taught. I have the distinct impression of having benefited as a student (in America in the late Seventies), and of having done no harm when I, in turn, became a teacher.

At the same time, as a student I can recall no actual item of advice that turned out to be revelatory or more than dimly helpful, and as a teacher I have no memory of passing on tips that had any sort of value except in the context of a specific piece of prose.

A 'course' of Creative Writing sounds somehow plausible, have you noticed? While no one would voluntarily refer to a Creative Writing *lesson*. The absorption of – what? – is too gradual to be compatible with the sharp outlines and one-way traffic of a 'lesson'.

The University of Virginia at Charlottesville, when I arrived there in 1978, had a good reputation for English studies and particularly for Creative Writing. There was an endowment for half-a-dozen writing studentships – the Henry Hoyns Fellowships. (There was also a Benjamin C. Moomaw Award for Oratory and an Emily Clark Balch Prize for a story or poem. The Hoyns and Moomaw, the Balch: they all sounded like diseases of trees.)

I was supposed to be writing a PhD on American literature, but I never even located the papers in Alderman Library – the Faulkner holding – which were my excuse for being in the country. Instead I 'audited' writing courses – that is, attended classes without getting credit, and without needing to take the deadlines with any great seriousness.

In what turned out to be three years in America, I took writing courses with three tutors all told. The first had a pipe and a latent stutter. His tweediness was neutralised by sportiness – serious distance running in the over-forties category he had just joined. In winter, he would enter the room where the class was held, then dive out again as if he'd forgotten something. He would come back into the room wearing a different woolly cap, and anyone who noticed this, or anyone who spotted the lime-green tennis ball in the fruit bowl at Creative Writing breakfasts, would receive the standard jocular accolade: *Your eye for detail will take you to the top of your profession.* In class he saw his role as comparable to an orchestra conductor's, a matter of balancing forces, and would doggedly defend stories no one else liked.

The second tutor let us know that he was only teaching at all because there was alimony to be paid. He was uncomfortable with the notion of having authority, and didn't want to sit in the conventional teacher's posture, facing the class. This would have been more satisfactory if the chairs in our assigned room hadn't been fixed in place, so that there was no prospect of us creating a supportive circle. Instead our teacher sat behind us all, in the back row. From there his comments, however mild, were inevitably disconcerting – but not as disconcerting as his silence when he withheld comment.

The third teacher was eminent, Southern, gentlemanly. He referred to his post as a sinecure, his reward for a lifetime's literary effort; perhaps it was a mistake to mention this to his students. I assume that's why the contribution I was making to the sinecure scheme – $387 – is burned on my brain, when nothing else from those years still bears its price tag.

This third tutor's Fall teaching was a conventional class, but his Spring teaching was like a correspondence course without the correspondence. He would spend the winter in Key West (he specified 'the heterosexual part') until his wife, who remained in Charlottesville to endure the season, was able to promise him that Virginia was once more habitable. On his return, he would spend an individual hour with each student.

Not very much of that hour was, technically, criticism. One friend reported that he had divided her stories into two piles. Pointing to one pile, he said, 'These stores' (his Memphis accent suppressed the second syllable of the word) 'These stores are good.' Pointing to the other: 'These stores are *no* good.' That – with suave elaboration – was that, for the semester's teaching.

With me he was less definite, perhaps because I had submitted a novella, not so easily divided into two piles. For most of our hour, though, we talked about London, a city he had loved in the past and whose landmarks he was anxious to assure himself were still in place.

A prankster, a weak king afraid of power, and an overcharging absentee. I appreciate that I seem to have sketched a succession of profoundly unhelpful helpers, but that was not how I experienced it. Then again, my project was not learning to write, exactly, but somehow finessing my way to self-belief, when my culture had taught me to prize only diffidence.

I was psychologically much closer to Francis Wyndham, for instance, who, after writing a book of short stories in his late teens submitted it to publishers, and when it was rejected put his ambitions on hold indefinitely, than I was to William Faulkner – who kept an elaborate chart of which magazine had rejected which story, so that he could have the sharp pleasure of resubmitting them, and having them gratefully accepted, once his name was known.

My first teacher – he of the tennis ball in the fruit bowl – was perhaps crucial to my project. His pipe made him a patriarch, but his stutter when it surfaced made him into a shy child. His authority was variable, and if his judgement went against me I would find a way to diminish it definitively.

Just as important, I wasn't taking credits and could treat deadlines relatively lightly. They were no more than impalpable nudges toward literary production. For this class I wrote my first three stories, 'Lantern Lecture' the last of them. This teacher also procured for me (though he made out that these decisions were entirely consultative) that coveted disease of trees a Hoyns Fellowship, which enabled me to stay in the States for another year.

If the other people in the class had sincerely disliked my stuff, I could always have told myself that they were, after all, *Americans*, not attuned to the nuances in which I so thrillingly dealt. But in fact adverse criticism is not necessarily as threatening as misplaced enthusiasm. To be praised for something you didn't intend, something in fact you set out to avoid, is a truer rite of passage for a writer. Thereafter you must imagine the relationship between reader and writer differently.

By the time I encountered my second teacher, he who sat behind us, I was sufficiently confident to think, not *I don't understand this method*, but *What a daft way to go about it*. Even so, the course was not a dead loss. Our teacher happened also to teach a course on 'Law and Literature in Nineteenth-Century America', and his reference to this subject irritated me into writing a novella which assumed that law and literature, in the teeth of his line of argument, were profoundly incompatible ways of looking at the world. To him, in a sense, though he read only fragments of it, I owe 'Bathpool Park'.

Even the third teacher, the winterer in Key West's respectable quarter, did no harm, since I realised I, too, could travel (writing classes were my only actual commitment), and spent Mardi Gras 1980 in New Orleans with a clear conscience.

From the University of Virginia's Creative Writing Program I was able to derive not only confidence and a regular incitement to produce fiction, but the money that translates into time. When I returned to Britain, I had a full-length manuscript to my credit, however little I expected it would be published.

It may be, in fact, that all these things – confidence, mild peer pressure, money as time – are more important than an actual teacher. Certainly groups with a shared agenda – women's groups or gay groups like the Lavender Quill Club in New York around 1980 – can manage quite well without.

But some sort of structure is most often necessary, and if there were more courses like the University of East Anglia's in this country, the hostility and embarrassment that surround the subject would – surely? – soon die away. [1]

What's the worst thing that can be said about sex education classes? That they only tell you what you already know, or else that they put you off the whole business altogether? The objections to writing classes are no more substantial. Why shouldn't people explore their natural curiosity about where stories come from?

---

1   'Ninety-four British universities now offer a range of postgraduate degrees in Creative Writing and in any one year there are usually over 10,000 short-term Creative Writing courses or classes on offer in the UK.' Giles Foden, in the introduction to this volume (2011).

Adam Mars-Jones (*b*. 1954) was UEA Writing Fellow in 1983. His first collection of stories, *Lantern Lecture* (1981), won a Somerset Maugham Award. Other works include *Monopolies of Loss* (1992) and *The Darker Proof: Stories from a Crisis* (1987), which was co-written with Edmund White. His first novel *The Waters of Thirst* (1993) has been followed by two others, *Pilcrow* (2008) and *Cedilla* (2011).

Killer Fiction

Joe Dunthorne

'All plots lead towards death.'
Don DeLillo, *White Noise*

A few weeks ago, all but one of the stories handed in to my Creative Writing workshop ended with a character being murdered. I looked around at my students, trying to differentiate between the expressions of attentiveness, those of boredom and those of impending homicide. Was that human blood or just a tea stain on my Don DeLillo handout? Why would anyone need a pencil that sharp?

Hanif Kureishi has said, 'Writing courses, particularly when they have the word "creative" in them, are the new mental hospitals…One of the things you notice is that when you switch on the television and a student has gone mad with a machine gun on a campus in America, it's always a writing student.'

In my experience, writing classes are not as exciting as he makes them sound. If my students are sociopaths then they hide their symptoms well. They generally appear hardworking and polite if, occasionally, dangerously hungover.

Of the notable campus shootings in America, I can only find one committed by a bona fide creative writing student. This was, admittedly, the Virginia Tech massacre of 2007, the most deadly school shooting in America's history. After the event, Seung-Hui Cho's violent plays – *Richard McBeef* and *Mr Brownstone* – were dissected as evidence of his mania. Stephen King, writing in the aftermath, said that if his own college writing had been analysed, 'someone would have tabbed me as mentally ill'. He suggests it's not possible to pick a psychopath out, based on their work, 'unless you look for violence unenlivened by any real talent'. In my own experiences, it's usual to discover that the reason a character is arbitrarily murdered at the end of a short story is not because of the author's homicidal tendencies but that they couldn't think of any other way to wrap things up. It's a blunter version of Raymond Chandler's advice: 'When in doubt, have a man come through a door with a gun in his hand.'

When I first started writing, I certainly leant on this easy way out; when at a dead end: kill off the protagonist. In fact, friends in my Creative Writing class christened a new poetic form – The Dunthorne – based on this tendency. A Dunthorne is easy: in the final stanza, you must surprise the reader with a sudden, unearned, needlessly ambiguous death. If at all possible, it should involve someone on a pushbike. In the poem that gave birth to this form my cyclist-narrator, eating black olives while navigating traffic, was knocked down in the penultimate line: 'The T-junction freckled with full stops.' Chilling, you'll agree. Killing off a character in this manner stems from anxiety that the story or poem is not working. It's the ejector seat of endings: *Get me out of here, this one's gonna blow!*

But that's not to say the only reason a character gets killed in fiction and poetry classes is because the word count is fast approaching. There's no doubt that plenty of students unpack their traumas in Creative Writing classes, and rightly so. The poet Roddy Lumsden has written that 'a poet confessing to mental illness is like a weightlifter admitting to muscles'. The flipside of this is that there are instances where students, if their story gets criticised for being sensationalist, protest *But it's true, it all happened.* They see their subject matter as inherently powerful – because of their experience of it – and forget to bring the reader along for the ride.

I think that, to differing extents, all writers draw on chinks in their mental health. Kureishi said that when he goes to his desk each morning to commence writing, he thinks to himself: 'Why am I doing this? Shall I commit suicide?' Writing is one of the few professions where mental illness has no stigma. If anything, the stigma runs the other way. We are led to believe that it's part of a writer's skill-set to be mentally unstable. When David Foster Wallace committed suicide during a bout of severe depression it was presented by some as a battle he had lost with his novel-in-progress. This seems to me to be a dangerously romantic view – and one that makes depression seem like a lucky source of inspiration, rather than an illness. Inspiration has always seemed like an unhelpful idea, as far as I'm concerned. It does happen, occasionally, but I can never plan for it, or try to force it – all I can do is keep writing, and try to be fighting fit for when it arrives, unannounced.

Kureishi also said Creative Writing courses foster false expectations: 'The fantasy is that all the students will become successful writers – and no one will disabuse them of that. When you use the word "creative" and the word "course" there is something deceptive about it.' In my experience of being a student of Creative Writing, few people have these delusions. Even with the MA at the University of East Anglia's track record, we knew the odds were stacked against us getting a publishing deal and, even less likely, a career.

But I remember, particularly when I started Creative Writing classes, I was surprised how many straightforward, helpful things I learnt from my tutors. I was in my first year. A tutor explained that, by putting the tag and the physical description in the middle of a piece of dialogue, I could make characters walk *and* talk, rather than just walk *then* talk,

'As if by magic,' I said, smoothing my eyebrows, 'I secured my seat on Richard and Judy's couch.'

There were other simple bits of advice. Use fewer adjectives and adverbs. Follow David Mamet's dictum that writing a scene is like going to a party: 'arrive late, leave early'.

But as my course progressed, there were less of these moments of revelation. I became jealous of scriptwriters, who, I imagined, were given all the answers on how to write a perfect script via colourful diagrams: flow charts for character development – *The Hero's*

Journey. Instead, there was the realisation that getting good at writing was mostly just hard work: practice and discussion and practice. Importantly, the MA gave me a taste of what being a writer actually involved, posing the question: did I want to spend most of my days alone?

Kureishi also says, and this I can agree with, that studying Creative Writing will make you a better writer, but it won't make you more content. 'When I teach them,' he said, 'they are always better at the end – and more unhappy.'

It's not a bad deal. As your unhappiness broadens, so does your ability to communicate it.

Joe Dunthorne (*b*. 1982) received his MA in Creative Writing from UEA in 2005. He also did his BA at the university. His first novel *Submarine* (2008) was shortlisted for many prizes, including the Desmond Elliot Prize, the Wodehouse Bolinger Prize and the Commonwealth Writers Prize for the Best First Book. A feature film adaptation of *Submarine* was released in 2011. His most recent novel is *Wild Abandon* (2011). He also featured in *Faber New Poets 5* (2010).

Writing my life

Francis Gilbert

I didn't write in depth about my life in any extended way until my mid-thirties. I was asked intermittently at school to write the odd 'autobiographical' essay, but my writing never strayed to discussing any troubling family issues. I attended two infants' schools in Cambridge, where I learnt that writing was a dangerous, stressful activity: I was frequently castigated for not being able to spell properly or write fluently. This situation did not change when I moved with my mother and stepfather to Wanstead, a suburb in north-east London. At Aldersbrook Primary School I had a succession of poor teachers who terrified me with their criticisms of my writing. I can vividly recall not showing my work to one bad-tempered teacher for a whole year, because on the one occasion I had shown him it, he'd shouted at me. He didn't notice that he hadn't marked my book. I was the victim of what Paulo Friere terms 'the banking concept of education'.[1] In *Pedagogy of the Oppressed*, Friere writes:

> Implicit in the banking concept is the assumption of a dichotomy between human beings and the world: a person is merely in the world, not with the world or with others: the individual is spectator, not recreator.

Throughout my education my teachers tried to inculcate the idea into my head that there was a 'correct' way to write, a 'correct' way to read and a distinct 'body of knowledge' that I had to learn. I was, as Friere says, a 'spectator' to them who had to absorb the necessary rules and regulations. I wasn't a 'recreator'. Because at that point I was a poor imitator, my writing never lived up to their standards. Indeed, I realise now, having read Friere, that this whole approach 'oppressed' me, making me feel 'merely in the world, not with the world or with others'.

This realisation is itself involved with a process of continuing education as a writer. I'm currently halfway through completing a PhD in Creative Writing and Education at Goldsmiths' College, University of London. Blake Morrison is supervising the creative component of my PhD, for which I am writing an autobiographical novel, *Who Do You Love?*, which is about a student love affair between myself and 'Ellida', a fictionalisation of a real person I met at Sussex University in 1987. This novel will form the main part of my submission, amounting to 70,000 words approximately. For the education component, supervised by Professor Rosalyn George, I am writing a mini-thesis, 30,000 words approximately, which is looking at my work both as a writer and teacher. I have been reading sections of *Who Do You Love?* to my pupils at the comprehensive where I teach and asking them to respond with their own fictionalised autobiographies, with a view to looking at the value of teachers sharing their autobiographical writing with pupils and how it might produce interesting responses. What follows is an adapted version of the beginning of this thesis, with an expanded section reflecting upon my time doing an MA in Creative Writing at the University of East Anglia.

Concerned about my poor academic achievements, my mother and stepfather removed me after one term from the local comprehensive when I was eleven and sent me to the local private school, Forest School in Snaresbrook. There, the 'banking system' was much more efficiently run: I learnt to 'bank content' more easily, spending long hours copying out key passages from textbooks before my termly exams. I became an expert 'imitator' of the various academic styles, achieving high grades in my O and A levels.

When I was a teenager, inspired by John Lennon, Bob Dylan, the Smiths and Philip Larkin, I quietly rebelled against such conformism by writing my own songs and poetry. It wasn't particularly autobiographical in nature, but did aim to express my feelings of anger and alienation, which were very real. No one looked at this writing except for my grandmother, who, discovering that I wrote poetry, asked to see it. She was very positive and non-judgemental. My poetry fitted more what Friere calls the 'problem-solving' approach to education: I sought out and took considerable care to find suitable images and forms to express my growing sense of alienation from the world. I spent many hours learning about the various metrical forms of poems to do this. In this sense, my journey towards aesthetic autobiography is similar to Blake Morrison's. He told me: 'I started writing poetry as a teenager. It was an escape and a rebellion. I couldn't say that I didn't emerge from traumatic circumstances, but there was an underlying disturbance. There was definitely a sense that this was a way of escaping family expectations. I never had a sense of being "I will be a writer." Poetry was a natural outlet.'[2]

Unlike him, I had a major figure, my grandmother, to encourage me during my teens and my twenties. She frequently spoke of me becoming a writer and would say that one day I would write about my family. I realise now that my grandmother and I were constantly exploring different forms of autobiographical discourse; our oral discourse was constantly verging on what Rosen terms 'framed episodes',[3] extended and polished life stories which are recounted simply for the pleasure of telling them.

My autobiographical discourse really flourished at university because I discussed my life so much with my fellow students. However, I rarely wrote about it: my time was occupied with studying and writing plays that had nothing to do with my life. I achieved a good degree in English at Sussex University. It was there that I first encountered theorists such as Friedrich Nietzsche, Jean-Paul Sartre, Roland Barthes and Jacques Derrida who really challenged implicitly held beliefs about the 'banking concept' of education: they all emphasised that the individual self constructs his or her own vision of the world.

My relationship with Ellida at university was relatively 'destructive': much of my life at Sussex was occupied with being with her and not paying much attention to my studies – or anything else. As a result, I didn't have much idea about what I wanted to do after I graduated. I had initially wanted to go and write in my grandparents' house in Northumberland after university, but, taking my mother's advice, I trained to be a teacher at Cambridge University instead. It was 1989 and the year in which the Berlin Wall fell and the Conservative's Education Reform Act was instituted. I realise now that my tutors did attempt to teach me that the 'banking concept' of education was a false notion, but they were fighting a losing battle. Brian Cox's enlightened vision of the English National Curriculum was soon replaced with a much more 'content-heavy', 'concept-lite' version by Ron Dearing.

After gaining my PGCE in English and Drama in 1990, I spent a year doing a MA in Creative Writing with Malcolm Bradbury and Rose Tremain at the University of East Anglia (UEA) – a liberating experience for me. It was the first time that I was surrounded by other writers. Many of them were quite a bit older than me – there were only three of us who were just out of college, with the rest having worked as teachers, TV producers, romantic novelists, researchers and 'caregivers'. At that time, the Creative Writing 'industry' at university was relatively small; there were only a couple of other university Creative Writing courses in the country for post-graduates. The UEA course was small with only twelve writers being admitted in my year, which was, in fact, the largest number admitted until that date. As a result of the small class, there was a real intensity and sense of comradeship to the group. There was also the sense that this was the last time any of us would be at university (for a long time) and that awareness of the fleetingness of the experience gave all of us a determination to make the thing work.

Malcolm dominated everything. Of course, his reputation preceded him; he was the author of some very successful books, TV dramas and was a prolific commentator on TV, radio and in the press. He was everywhere. His approach to the course was both practical and theoretical. Every week two writers would submit work, which was photocopied and disseminated to everyone on the course, who read it before it was workshopped. In the 'workshop' all of us sat in a circle and discussed what we liked and disliked about the writing in question, offering our suggestions for improvement. In a certain sense, this abided by 'Frierean' principles, in that the work most definitely 'came from us'; we were offered no stimuli or guidance on what we should write or the form our writing should take. It was – and is – very different from the way I teach Creative Writing in the classroom, where the dictates of the curriculum demands that the teachers set out their learning objectives, give pupils a variety of structured, short activities which lead to a complete piece of writing. In the classroom, the writing process is carefully 'scaffolded' by the teacher. With the MA it was assumed that we could all write – the application process was aimed at filtering out people who couldn't – and that we didn't need any help with improving 'our processes' of writing. Personally, I think I could have benefited from learning about structuring stories and writing in different styles.

Malcolm's great strength was that he wasn't prescriptive. He didn't say 'write about what you know', nor did he demand that you never wrote 'autobiographically'.

Nevertheless, the students quickly learned that there were certain styles of writing that he liked much more than others. Because he was the teacher and such an eminent writer, students were desperate to please him. After I submitted my first piece of writing and had it dismissed by Malcolm very briefly as 'teenage fiction', I amended my style to write something much more literary. Without a malicious bone in his body, Malcolm was always trying to be kind; when he called the adventure story I submitted 'teenage fiction' he didn't mean to upset me, but he did. This was well before Rowling and Pullman turned the form into a respected literary genre. But I could tell he had scant regard for my writing, because he barely spent five minutes discussing my work. A bitter blow. After the session I remember leaving the workshop, walking in a daze down to the lake underneath the ziggurat buildings and crying. I felt humiliated. Luckily, a few people on the course came and found me and reassured me that, really, I was a 'great writer' – the sobriquet that everyone on a Creative Writing course wants to be garlanded with. My confidence a little bit shored up, I had a go at writing in a more literary style, drawing upon incidents from my own childhood. They were more favourably received.

Malcolm gave short shrift to writing he thought was 'minor', but liked to linger for a long time on writing he liked. One such writer was Erica Wagner, who is now my wife (we married in 1993, a few years after the course finished); he would speak at length about various techniques in her writing that made it 'work' and where it might be placed as a published form of fiction. I remember him regularly rhapsodising about Erica's work, saying that it would be published everywhere soon – which, indeed, it was! Whatever you may say about him, he had a genuine 'nose' for a good writer: after all, amongst many 'finds', he discovered two of the major writers of modern times, Ian McEwan and Kazuo Ishiguro, both of whom did the MA course.

Rose Tremain was much fairer with her time; she was scrupulous about giving everyone equal amounts of attention, no matter how dreadful she thought their writing was. I think she found the whole set-up much more stressful than Malcolm; she was much more sensitive to the emotions of the writers and perhaps more uncomfortable in the role of the 'all-knowing, all-seeing' disseminator of literary wisdom. I actually found her sessions even more terrifying because she didn't mince her words; she was as unimpressed with my writing as Malcolm was and yet lingered much longer over its shortcomings. Wimp that I was, I chickened out of my individual tutorials with her in the summer term – I still regret not attending them. If only I could have those tutorials now that I am a bit better at writing. Alas, too late. Needless to say, her 'scariness' was all in my imagination.

Every year, Malcolm held a party at his large, lovely home in Norwich and invited the MA in Creative Writing students to meet many of his literary contacts: agents, publishers, TV producers and directors. It was very merry; lots of wine and lots of 'ligging' as we called it, with all of us trying to attract the eye of a publisher or an agent. The Holy Grail was, of course, to get a publisher and, if not that, an agent. I got neither, but quite a few others did. In the end, many years after the course finished, most people on the course published novels or books with respectable 'houses'.

After the course, realising that I wasn't going to make much of a living as a writer, I taught, for the most part, in various comprehensives in London. I would write in the evenings after I'd marked my pupils' work and prepared my lessons for the next day. Writing a few hundred words every night meant that I wrote five novels, none of which were published. I saw my writing and teaching identities as entirely separate: I never wrote about my life as a teacher. I didn't want to: I wanted to forget all the stresses of the classroom when I was writing. At school, being pressurised by the constraints of time and an unenlightened curriculum, I held fast on to a 'banking concept' of education; that I had a certain amount of knowledge that I had to funnel into my pupils' heads. Friere writes:

> The banking concept (with its tendency to dichotomise everything) distinguishes two stages in the action of the educator. During the first, he cognises a cognisable object while he prepares his lessons in his study or his laboratory.[4]

This is exactly what I was trained to do and am currently instructed to do: to identify learning objectives for every lesson I teach. This necessarily leads to lessons being reductive experiences that are about the teacher making sure all pupils are cognisant of what Friere terms the 'cognisable object', which the teacher establishes. As Friere points out, this is an implicitly oppressive model for education with the teacher playing the role of 'oppressor' and the pupils being the 'oppressed'.

I should add here that I, too, felt as powerless as my pupils. I, in turn, became 'oppressed' by my pupils' resistance against this style of education; their refusal to follow my commands, their lack of interest in what I had to say, their indifference to the academic material they had to learn. I gave up teaching in 1996 as a result and trained to be a journalist. Learning how to be a 'hack' helped me a great deal: it made me less precious about my writing and it steered me towards writing about my experiences as a teacher. I worked for a little bit on various newspapers and then taught part-time in Havering, writing on a freelance basis during my spare time. I found my life as a teacher an essential wellspring for my writing. I began to 're-educate' myself along lines more in tune with Friere's ideals. He writes:

> Problem-posing education bases itself on creativity and stimulates true reflection and action upon reality; thereby responding to the vocation of personas as being who are authentic only when engaged in inquiry and creative transformation.'[5]

By reflecting upon my own experiences as a teacher, I was able to craft articles and books which 'creatively transformed' my past. Whether what I was doing was 'authentic' is a moot point. My books *I'm A Teacher, Get Me Out of Here* (2004) and *Teacher on the Run* (2006) were written to communicate what it *felt* like to be a teacher in an inner-city school: to protect myself I had to fictionalise the people I had encountered, changing genders and attributes. To make the book entertaining and meaningful, I chose to dramatise key turning points. Although my writing in no way has the literary quality of the classic 'aesthetic autobiographers' that Suzanne Nalbantian critiques, her observations of their techniques could apply to my autobiographical books about school:

> The autobiographical novelists drew first from their personal everyday life, cultivating perceptions selectively which could then be transposed into their fiction. A primary facet of their art can be said therefore to be an activity of perception. Then comes the leap to what is literary. In the passage from self-observation to self-recreation, life facts were transferred to structures dictated by concepts of aesthetics.[6]

This was certainly true of my teaching memoirs. After writing very dry, factual first drafts, I found the material just didn't 'live' on the page and that I needed to highlight 'spots of time', key turning points, in order to make the reader feel what it was like to be in the classroom, to capture its excitement and terror, its joys and disappointments.

Writing about my teaching was a form of 'problem-solving' learning on many levels: an exploration of my past, a therapeutic confession, an investigation into my own motives and ideologies, a construction of my identity as a teacher and a person. Furthermore, it led me to see the importance of autobiography in the classroom; that I should be encouraging my pupils to do what I was doing in my books; to examine themselves, to look at their motives, to perceive the ways in which they 'constructed' their own identities, to identify where the problem areas were, to find ways of dealing with the stresses and strains of life. Moreover, I realised that it was the fictional techniques that Nalbantian speaks about which genuinely promote, as opposed to negate, this process of 'constructing' oneself and one's life. On the surface, this appears to be a counter-intuitive point: surely a teacher is actually encouraging pupils to 'lie' about their lives if he/she asks them to use fictional techniques such as dramatic dialogue, poetic imagery, and invented characters when writing their autobiographies?

Indeed I was fascinated when a pupil who normally didn't work hard turned in a fantastic but rather alarming autobiography about her difficult life, but said, 'But sir, I lied!' Her comments provoked all sorts of thoughts and questions in my mind which made me want to explore the ways in which autobiography is used in the classroom.

In fact, the pedagogical processes that English teachers now employ in the classroom to encourage Creative Writing are very complex. The days when English teachers just ask children to write about their holidays are gone; now they encourage their pupils to blend fiction and non-fiction, and to use film, pictures, photographs and music to enhance their literary representations of their lives. English teachers are now very conversant with the ways in which new technology can bring creative and autobiographical writing alive.

Furthermore, English teachers, like most state school teachers, are very good at encouraging pupils to assess their own work, using peer-to-peer assessment and different forms of feedback where pupils reflect seriously upon what they have achieved, what they know and what they need to know. This 'assessment for learning' approach could be more widely adopted in universities, where feedback tends to be sporadic and usually only conducted after coursework has been handed in.

This said, English teachers can be very programmatic in the ways that they teach Creative Writing, insisting that pupils meet certain 'assessment objectives' (specific goals that exam syllabuses insist must be met). This can lead to a 'box-ticking' mentality which doesn't foster a deep search for literary quality or lyrical Sensibility.

Now that I am back studying Creative Writing at university, after a twenty year gap, I can't help reflecting upon how much the publishing scene both has – and has not – changed. Many commentators have already remarked that the Internet has revolutionised publishing, but it's a point that's worth dwelling upon again and again, because it's so important. Unlike in 1990, when you had to print a book or publish an article to get anyone to see your work on a mass scale, anyone can publish anything on the Internet in the form of a blog or an e-book.

I would have certainly been very attracted to this if it had been around when I was at UEA; I'd have also liked the ability to mingle music, video and writing by making short films on YouTube and so forth. In fact, given the obsessive type of person I was, if it had been around I probably wouldn't have gone on a Creative Writing course – I'd have been too busy messing around on the Internet.

Back then, of course, the technology just wasn't there or cheap enough for people like me to construct multi-media writing; to produce YouTube poetry, to write extended fictional blogs and so forth. Now it is – and this has led to a revolution in the ways in which fiction and poetry are represented and disseminated. Teachers are aware of this perhaps much more than academics are. As a school teacher, I really encourage my pupils to make little films of their poems, to add music and to present their writing in the form of slide shows such as Prezis and PowerPoints. It strikes me that the 'forms' which writing can be presented in are changing and evolving very quickly and that it's in these 'changing forms' that the really exciting writing is happening. Why can't we have the blog novel, the Twitter short story and FaceBook poetry?

I have been shocked, though, that many Creative Writing students and lecturers at university – as well as publishers – still are obsessed by the 'old paradigm' of making their work public. At the Great Writing conference (June 2011) at Imperial College, one writer who lectures in Creative Writing at a UK university told me that you had to be 'desperate' to publish on the Internet and that being accepted by a mainstream publisher was the only serious option for a serious writer. Other creative writers then cited the fact that you get the benefit of a good editor when publishing through a big company. I've published a number of books now and I'd say that this simply isn't true: editors just don't have the time to work on a manuscript in depth any more. You actually get far more editorial attention if you publish a blog and ask the public to critique your work.

So while the Creative Writing that goes on in schools may be much more 'directed', it's also much more 'innovative' in certain ways, especially in the way that English teachers invite pupils to play and experiment with form. Creative writers are absurdly nostalgic for the days when you could publish a novel with a respected publisher and be acclaimed as a 'great writer'. Those days are going fast. The Internet is a much more democratic form; it doesn't create 'hierarchies' of literary greatness in the way that the publishing industry used to. With the Internet it's all about interactivity, engaging with your readership, moving on to the next thing, provoking discussion, mingling video, pictures, photographs and writing.

Creative Writing lecturers and students could learn a great deal from the sorts of exercises that English teachers are doing as a matter of course in schools: the pedagogical approach which focuses upon helping pupils with the processes of writing, engaging them in directed writing activities and assessing their own work. Teachers also seem more confident in taking a cross-curricular 'technological' approach to writing by encouraging pupils to mix different media with writing, producing writing in different forms, and using the Internet to publish and so forth. Meanwhile, teachers themselves could benefit from seeing the ways in which Creative Writing courses allow students more freedom to choose what to write; the emphasis on literary quality rather than meeting assessment criteria.

1   P. Freire, *Pedagogy of the Oppressed* (Harmondsworth: Penguin, 1985), p. 56.

2   Interview with Blake Morrison, 16 December 2009.

3   H. Rosen, *Speaking from Memory: The Study of Autobiographical Discourse* (Stoke-on-Trent: Trentham, 1998), p. 57.

4   *Pedagogy of the Oppressed*, p. 61.

5   *Pedagogy of the Oppressed*, p. 65.

6   S. Nalbantian, *Aesthetic Autobiography: From Life to Art in Marcel Proust, James Joyce, Virginia Woolf and Anaïs Nin* (Basingstoke: Macmillan, 1994), p. 49.

Francis Gilbert (*b.* 1968) received his MA in Creative Writing from UEA in 1991. He works as a writer and teacher and has published the following books: *I'm a Teacher, Get Me Out of Here* (2004), *Teacher on the Run* (2005), *Yob Nation* (2006), *The New School Rules* (2007) and *Parent Power* (2008). He is completing a PhD in Creative Writing and Education at Goldsmiths' College, University of London.

The Case for the Study of Creative Writing

Bernardine Evaristo

Dancers train for years to contort their bodies gracefully so that they don't look like waddling penguins or leaping elephants. Opera singers learn how to strengthen, stretch and manipulate their vocal chords to produce the most soaring, spine-tingling sounds. Visual artists spend years studying painting, drawing, sculpture or conceptual art. Tracy Emin may have become famous for her seemingly artless unmade bed, but she studied art at two colleges before unmaking it.

Like all other art forms, creative writing is also something that improves with guidance and practice. You can't teach raw talent or ambition, you can't teach perceptiveness and emotional intelligence, but you can certainly teach the rest.

In the case of fiction this might involve story structure and plot, characterisation, setting, dialogue, point of view and voice. In the case of poetry it might involve form, diction, tone, sound and imagery. One of the first things every student learns is the need to 'show and not tell': to illustrate rather than merely state or summarise. As Chekhov wrote, 'Don't tell me the moon is shining; show me the glint of light on a broken glass.'

The teaching of creative writing might not be as prescriptive as the teaching of ballet or opera where there are hard-and-fast rules on how to stand *en pointe* or how to sing at full pelt, but some rules still apply. The difference is that, because writers have a huge range of individual approaches, styles and belief systems about what constitutes good literature, many of the rules in creative writing can sometimes be broken. After all, no one ever wrecked their vocal chords or sprained an ankle just by splitting an infinitive.

Becoming a writer, however, is about more than learning a craft. Professional writers do not necessarily shine with exceptional talent at an early stage. Aspiring writers have to work hard to nurture any raw talent they do possess, discover their own magic and find their voices. They are often shocked at this as they assume that either you have the unattainable, elusive X-Factor, or you don't, no matter how hard you work.

For instance, I've been told many times by students that they don't have much of an imagination. But imagination is like a muscle: it strengthens with use. The more time you spend accessing it, the more powerful it becomes.

In 2002 I was Writing Fellow at UEA and taught Joe Dunthorne for a term on an undergraduate Creative Writing course. Joe subsequently completed the Creative Writing MA at UEA and found a publisher for his novel *Submarine*, about a boy's coming of age in Wales. This has recently been made into a film. Now I mention Joe, not in any way to take credit for his success, but to say that in a class of other very bright, talented students, what he did possess, even in his late teens, were many of the qualities that are helpful to becoming a professional writer: an openness to learning and developing craft, commitment and determination, self-discipline and single-mindedness. Other determined and talented students from that class such as Jon Stone and Belona Greenwood have also been published and/or had plays produced. They wanted it badly enough. Writing is not for the faint- or half-hearted.

Another writer I worked with was Diana Evans. Her first novel *26a* was about mixed-race twins and won the Orange Award for New Writers in 2006. After she attended a weekend workshop of mine, I informally mentored her as she worked on her novel because her writing was so promising, her prose so beautiful and the story she wanted to tell so strong. As Toni Morrison says, 'If there's a book you really want to read, but it hasn't been written yet, then you must write it.' Diana also gained an MA in Creative Writing from UEA and recently published her second novel. The remarkable thing about her is that she was never *not* going to write *26a*. In fact, she completed it while still a student at UEA. Her commitment to becoming a writer was absolute and her work ethic formidable.

From 2010 to 2011 I mentored another UEA student, Chelsey Flood, as part of the Arvon (Foundation) Jerwood Mentoring Scheme. Mentees were selected anonymously, and her writing stood out because she, too, displayed a love of language, wrote fantastic dialogue and sensitively described a young, country girl's relationship with a teenage traveller boy whose family squat on her family's property. When she graduated last summer, Chelsey already had her pick of agents and had won the Curtis Brown Prize. None of it just 'happened' – like Diana, Chelsey worked incredibly hard for it.

As Thomas Edison famously said, 'Genius is 1 per cent inspiration and 99 per cent perspiration.' And, as the American journalist Gene Fowler notoriously said, 'Writing is easy. All you do is stare at a blank sheet of paper until drops of blood form on your forehead.'

The craft of writing is something that develops over many years and needs tremendous drive to sustain it. The first major challenge is how to complete a manuscript and get it published. Once this is achieved, a second, even greater challenge then presents itself: how to keep on doing it. Published writers might appear to be 'lucky', but the truth is that no one can publish a book that's not been written. 'I'm a great believer in luck,' said Thomas Jefferson, 'and I find the harder I work, the luckier I get.'

Unfortunately, these days one often encounters students from the Celebrity Generation. They believe they can dash off a novel in a few months, get a big advance and immediately take their place in the pantheon of literati glitterati. They assume that instant global success equates to a life-long writing career. In fact, a slower climb can provide the staying power needed to keep climbing, while a rocket launch into the stratosphere usually has only one destination: straight back down.

Like all other areas of education, teaching and studying, Creative Writing is not unproblematic. A poet-teacher who believes all poetry should be quiet, visually neat, understated and oblique isn't *necessarily* going to encourage wilder, more exuberant, more experimental styles of poetry. A novelist who firmly believes that the best novels are written in plain, unadorned English, third-person, past tense is unlikely to warm to a student's work if it's flamboyant and filled with many narrators and time shifts. Writers can, of course, teach beyond their own practice, but preferences can easily become prejudices. One student told me that the novel she was working on wasn't set in any specific time period because her novelist teacher had told her this would quickly make it outdated. To which I replied, 'Oh, you mean like Dickens?' Another was told his protagonist had to be either a hero or an anti-hero. Textbook teaching. Even when students make good progress, problems can still occur if they remain with the same tutor or mentor for too long. This can lead to tunnel vision, mimicry and writing for the approval and audience of one. I prefer multiple influences – throw it all into the mix and see if something unique can be cooked up.

In workshop situations, the pressure of peer approval can also inhibit and suffocate originality. But, generally speaking, constructive feedback and discussion plays a vital role in enabling Creative Writing students to flourish. Being selective about whose opinion you trust is one thing, but if twenty out of twenty classmates tell you they can't make head nor tail of your short story, then you might want to pay attention. It's good preparation for a writer's career, developing that rhinoceros hide. No one gets good reviews all of the time, although, as John Osborne put it, 'Asking a writer what he thinks about criticism is like asking a lamppost what it feels about dogs.'

Ideally, the teaching of Creative Writing should provide structure, guidance, technique and a space to discover through experimentation. But there is no gold standard for anything in literature. Take one celebrated novel and ten independent-minded readers un-swayed by media-hype and you might get ten responses ranging from 'I hate this book so much I want to strangle the author' to 'This is a masterpiece, a work of genius, the best thing I've ever read.'

Many writers do get published without ever receiving any tuition. I know from my own experience that it isn't essential – but at the very least it can help speed things up. I'd been writing for fourteen years before my first book was published. My second book and first verse-novel *Lara* (based on my family history with roots in England, Nigeria, Ireland, Brazil and Germany and spanning 150 years) took five long, isolated years to complete – a process heavily sabotaged by self-doubt, stasis and procrastination.

To believe that you can write and might one day be published requires vast reserves of self-confidence. Lack of it can kill creativity, especially for students from backgrounds in which a sense of entitlement is not encouraged. The outsider's voice, the voice of those still marginalised in this society, is often the most under-confident. I saw this regularly in the four years I spent as a director of Spread the Word literature development agency in London. Women formed the majority of our workshop participants and, due to strategic programming and marketing, a sizeable percentage of them were black. An Arts Council report I initiated, *Free Verse*, revealed that less than 1 per cent of poetry books published in the UK are by black or Asian poets. Of course, low self-confidence isn't all that's keeping these voices from being heard. As the report revealed, the cultural bias and myopia of most poetry publishers is still a major factor in this. Nonetheless, workshops, courses and mentoring schemes are essential if the imbalance is ever to be redressed.

On a Creative Writing degree, students usually move from a position of isolation to membership of a writing community. The tuition, direction, structure and discipline of study should lay the foundations for them to continue writing alone in future; the degree is just the beginning. A good course will also enable students to appreciate literature from a *craft* point of view (as opposed to a literary theory analysis) and appreciate work that extends beyond their personal tastes. I have come across many Creative Writing students who, to my horror, admit that they rarely read any fiction or poetry other than the set books they had to study for their degrees. Questioned about her reading habits, one student asked 'Do magazines count?' Aspiring poets who don't read poetry, aspiring novelists who don't read novels – sound familiar? I became a writer through being an avid reader. 'If you don't have the time to read,' says Stephen King, 'you don't have the time or tools to write.'

In fact, we absorb how *story* works from our earliest listening and reading experiences. Young children know that a story has a beginning, middle and an end, although they can't articulate it. Try *not* finishing a good story you're telling an under-five year old. They know a story has characters, whether they are human, animal or even tank engines; and they enjoy the suspense of wondering what happens next. They want what's read to them to excite their minds, imaginations, emotions. As do we all.

At a deeper level, Creative Writing fulfils a fundamental human need for narrative. It is about communication and the means by which we understand ourselves and our lives. Through storytelling we connect the generations, we become keepers of our histories – personal, family, communal, cultural, racial, religious, national, global; we transform our experiences and transcend them. Our entire lives are narratives, too, with shape and characters, twists and turns, relationships, desires, conflict, obstacles, triumphs and eventually resolutions. Our conversations are peppered with stories, whether anecdotal or more convoluted, with elaborations, omissions, interpretations and judgements.

To study the telling of stories, therefore, is to engage with something that is integral to us. Great literature is never lightweight or trivial or 'mere entertainment' – although entertainment is also crucial to our sanity and well-being. The student gets to wave a magic wand and create worlds, characters and situations of their own choosing. To make them convincing, interesting, readable, they draw on their insights into how people think and feel, what they do and why. To study creative writing is to extend beyond the self and broaden our understanding of what it means to be human.

Graduates learn to communicate creatively, persuasively, imaginatively, articulately and with originality. Not all of them want to become professional writers, but they can still take what they've learned into whichever career they choose – as editors, journalists, teachers, press officers, marketers, advertisers, performers or even culture secretaries. Although it flies in the face of today's obsession with vocational training, there is plenty to be said for studying creative writing for its own sake, for enjoyment, self-discovery and self-expression.

In 1999 I taught a course for the British Council for rural women in Zimbabwe. Most had never written creatively before and the idea of landing a three-book deal was as foreign to them as mucking out in a pig pen is to me. Through their writing it emerged that all of them had relatives and neighbours who had died from AIDS. This was a taboo subject in Zimbabwe, but in this workshop setting it became an issue to be aired, shared and discussed. The women were able to transform a national epidemic and their own personal tragedies into individualistic, deeply felt stories. Out of suffering, came creativity and solace.

A few years later I was a visiting professor at Barnard College in New York. The young undergraduates came from privileged, sheltered, suburban backgrounds. In our first session together they wrote stories about pyjama parties and the trauma of being denied a horse as a child. I inwardly groaned as I contemplated a whole term of this, but by the end of the course they were writing carefully researched, imaginatively crafted stories set in Imperial China, Revolutionary Russia, Nazi Germany, as well as subjects closer to home. The course helped transform them from young women with limited experience of the world to young women able to see beyond their own concerns, engage with important periods of history and bring them alive in fiction. They had moved from the present to the past, the parochial to the international – they were growing up.

A course in Saudi Arabia in 2006 for the British Council was different again. When the students, all female (of course, in this segregated society), entered the class draped head-to-toe in purdah, I panicked as I wondered how the hell I was going to teach without seeing their faces. Thankfully, slowly, they started to unravel some of the layers. They were all university students but, living in a police state where literature is heavily censored and mostly unavailable, weren't your usual student demographic. It was a challenge getting them to express themselves openly, not least because they were suspicious that their fellow students would inform on them. The short stories they wrote were heavily self-censored but, even for them, studying creative writing opened their eyes to the possibility of creative freedom.

Finally, I taught an inter-generational Creative Writing course in Suffolk earlier this year. In my workshops, schoolchildren from a poor part of Ipswich and local pensioners studied together as equals. The youngest was eleven, the oldest was in his eighties and writing allowed all of them to be heard in a society that usually either doesn't take them seriously or doesn't listen. For the schoolchildren, all their most pressing concerns – anger at parents, serious dysfunction at home, homophobia, religious beliefs or outrage at social injustice – were addressed and articulated through poetry and fiction. Some of the older people had never written creatively before and trawled eagerly through their memory banks to write about the past and their experiences of love and loss. One woman who described herself, with some resignation, as 'a wife, mother and daughter', said it was the first time in decades she'd done something just for herself. She discovered, through her poetry, that not only did she have things to say that were unique to her, but she had a natural flair for writing. Her sense of her identity began to shift.

In America most published writers are graduates of Creative Writing degrees and this is increasingly the case over here, too. Creative writing courses not only help equip people with the skills needed to be a writer, but are also shaping what is being published. If we accept that literature deepens and transforms human experience, nourishes our imagination and intellect, stirs our emotions and causes us to reflect, question, expand and engage with lives and realities other than our own, then we must also accept that Creative Writing teaching plays a vital and indispensable part in the health of our national and cultural life.

Bernardine Evaristo (*b.* 1959) was UEA Writing Fellow in 2010 and currently teaches on the UEA-*Guardian* Masterclasses. She is the author of six books, including *The Emperor's Babe* (2001), *Blonde Roots* (2008), *Lara* (2009) and *Hello Mum* (2010). She co-edited the poetry anthology *Ten* with Daljit Nagra (2010), *Wasafiri – Black Britain: Beyond Definition* with Karen McCarthy Woolf (2010) and the British Council anthology *NW15* (2007) with Maggie Gee. She was made an MBE in 2009.

Listening in Restaurants

Antoinette Moses

I am in a popular restaurant in Covent Garden. At the next table a man is talking about the dearth of traditional English apples. 'Do you have any concept how many great English apples there are?' he booms and, without waiting for a reply, continues: 'Thousands, mostly pippins, raised from pips, not grafted. Most of them mongrels. Mongrels,' he tells his companion. 'Quite,' she chirps every time he pauses for breath. 'And what about Adam's Pearmain, Belle de Boskoop, the Newton Wonder?' he asks. 'Quite,' she says. At an adjoining table, a man and a woman are studying the menu. 'You must try the pheasant breast,' says the man. 'Yes?' she asks. 'It's their signature dish,' he tells her. 'It's their signature dish?' she repeats. 'Yes,' he says, 'you must try it.' '*Then* I must try it,' she says.

After dinner, I jot down these fragments of conversation in a small notebook. If a writer with a notebook was listening to one of my conversations, they might note a tendency to go off at tangents and a habit of not finishing sentences. If they reproduced this in a play, they might create a husband who constantly asks: 'What?...What?' as he waits for a conclusion that will enable the sentences to make some kind of sense. Or they might turn the overheard dialogue into a comedy sketch, such as those in which Ronnie Barker finishes Ronnie Corbett's trailing sentences with unlikely endings.

It often surprises me that so many books which aim to teach students how to write plays or scripts or a 'killer' screenplay hardly cover idiolect, if they mention it at all. There are notable exceptions: Noël Grieg's *Playwriting* has a chapter on voice; Janet Neipris writes in her study on playwriting, *To be a Playwright*, on the importance of listening to voice; and Michelene Wandor argues in *The Art of Writing Drama* that the process of writing a dramatic text should be rooted in dialogue; students, she says, need to be aware of 'differently voiced and inflected dialogue'. Generally, however, dialogue is analysed in terms of exposition, plot development and the demonstration of character. Speech is examined in relation to what characters say, and how characters speak in a play or script is rarely considered. Yet the specific way in which people utter their words is fundamental to an understanding of their personality, and an awareness of idiolect can only assist in creating clearly differentiated and rounded characters. What makes a character memorable is not merely their appearance or actions, but how they use words.

What I'm talking about here when I use the word 'idiolect' is language which is specific to the person who utters it. It is a person's individual voice, and this includes the particular verbal tics a person uses as well as what words they choose and any specific turns of phrase they favour. Within any language there are only a set number of ways in which a person can speak or write, and linguists have codified these to demonstrate the norm. The personal footprint we place on language is therefore judged by the ways in which we deviate from normative speech; in writing it is this footprint which enables forensic analysis to prove authorship or plagiarism.

Playwrights who specialise in radio plays often talk and write about the importance of having a variety of voices in a play so that the listener can distinguish who is speaking. At its most basic, this may mean having characters who have different dialects and ages, and who come from different social classes. And while it is important to remember that what you write will be played by actors, many students think that the function of dialogue is simply to tell the story and allow the actors to provide the different voices. In fact, it is the writing which determines the actors. Casting should be suggested in the idiolect created by the writer. The idiolect created by the writer, moreover, not only forms the basis for the selection of the actor, but will, according to many actors, help them discover the physicality of their role. The voice suggests the person.

There are philosophers who question whether it is ever possible to have a personal idiolect, while others argue that language, and how we use it, reveals precisely who we are. Many make clear distinctions between the idiolect of an individual and the language of his or her community, though not all agree that there is such an entity as a community which shares a common form of discourse. In relation to such considerations, I am aware that my use of the term idiolect is cavalier; it is shorthand. As a playwright I think about the characters I create in three ways: their interior and exterior perspectives (how the characters view themselves and how others view them) and also in terms of their world (where they come from and what their background is). And this is what I pass on when teaching character development. Thus, when I use the term idiolect with students, I use the term in a very broad sense, conflating it with a character's sociolect and dialect, the way in which their characters' utterances demonstrate their position in society, education, gender, nationality and region. In other words, I tell students that when creating the voice and language of a character, they need to consider person-dependent particularities in language use as well as community- or group-dependent particularities.

There is always one student, of course, who quotes Pinter's response when asked about the background of his characters in *The Caretaker* – that he had no idea at all of anything outside of what they did and said on stage. They may also cite an early interview in which he states that he does not eavesdrop on conversations. But in relation to idiolect, I tell them, this question would assume that Pinter had invented the language of his characters and that it had no context, whereas Pinter listened assiduously all his life and towards the end of his life acknowledged many of the influences on the voices he created. In order to create an idiolect for a character, every writer has to have examples of voices on which she or he can draw. Such voices inevitably begin with family and friends, and many of Pinter's early characters are based on the friends he knew as a young man in Hackney. In Michael Billington's biography of Pinter – a book I recommend to every student who quotes Pinter selectively – one of these friends, Morris Wernick, notes how Pinter 'with a writer's ear picked up words and phrases from each of us'. Pinter could not have written his play *Celebration* unless he had listened in restaurants. The couple I overheard discussing the signature dish could have come from this play. As Deirdre Burton and David Lodge have both shown in their analysis of Pinter's dialogue, much of this is extended phatic communion, where language is used to establish a social bond, rather than to communicate information or ideas. The ritual form of phatic communion, of endless small talk which is never developed, is heightened by the rhythm of Pinter's words.

For the non-writer the notion of the 'writer's ear' may sound odd: how is the way that a writer listens different from the way that anybody else listens? I would suggest that it is in that writers are listening to several things at once. We listen to the words in terms of the information they carry, but we also listen to the way they are delivered and what that tells us about the person who is talking. And we have developed a habit of listening to what is not said as well as what is said. Which is the way we have to listen to Pinter's plays which, as the actor Michael Gambon has said, 'have a surface of a thousandth of an inch and subtext of two miles'.

Learning to listen to speech, I think, begins with recording it. I cannot remember when I started to carry a notebook with me, but the earliest record I have is of an Italian family in London in 1959, which I described as 'scattered like pigeons along the Cromwell Road'. '*Mi scusi, Signorina,*' the mother said to me, 'but where is open?' A fair question to ask on a dismal Sunday afternoon in the grey London of the late Fifties when everything indeed appeared to be closed.

Fifty years later I am sitting in a café listening to three friends discussing the shortcomings of one of their boyfriends and the number of ways they use 'like': 'And he was like, "'Course I like you, babe" and I was like, "Yeah, and I like Bacardi and Coke, but it's not the same, innit?"' David Mamet, in his book *Writing in Restaurants*, which inspired the title of this essay, wrote how joy and sorrow can be displayed and observed by the writer in a restaurant; writing down snippets of conversation is merely the beginning. To create voices that carry the peculiarity of individual characters, we need an awareness of the pattern of voices, their rhythm and their music. For this, the overheard snippets of discourse are rarely adequate; a novice playwright needs to 'listen' through reading as well, and to analyse what they hear and read, to develop a writer's ear.

Listening through reading allows us to see the variety of narrative functions of voice. In *A Portrait of the Artist as a Young Man* Joyce develops the role of the narrator though the use of discourse. The narration changes from baby talk ('Once upon a time and a very good time it was there was a moocow coming down along the road') to an idiolect that is more articulate and self-aware as Stephen Dedalus grows up physically and intellectually, and at various points echoes the disparate voices of family, church and state. In Anthony Burgess's *A Clockwork Orange* the style and tone of the book are also controlled by idiolect. Here, it is the narrator Alex and his friends whose language, Nadsat, Burgess devised from a combination of cod-Russian, rhyming slang, Romany and other elements. I would argue that it is the use of this idiolect, as well as its particularity, which works either to create a bond with the reader who enjoys a sense of identification with Alex's teenage gang or to distance the reader. The idiolects of the narrators in Irvine Welsh's *Trainspotting* may be said to employ a similar function. Indeed, Derek Paget has observed how idiolect 'becomes character in *Trainspotting*' and that all the principal first-person narrators (Renton, Begbie, Sick Boy and Spud) 'have traits of speech which become a kind of recognisable signature tune for their character'. The result of these characteristic voices, he points out, is that when they talk in sections of the book, the reader can hear their 'rhythms from another perspective'.

Clearly identifiable idiolects do function as signature tunes and as useful reminders of individual characteristics. One reason why Dickens's characters work so well in adaptation and are popular with actors is the distinctive quality of their idiolects, and Dickens was well aware of the theatricality of his dialogue through his own performance of the works and because of his enthusiasm for the theatre. David Lodge has suggested that just as Shakespeare would have been a novelist had he lived in the nineteenth century, so Dickens's 'natural bent was towards the theatre'. Readers who encountered his novels in instalments would have been assisted by the memorable idiolects of his characters, an effect exploited by writers of today's drama serials and situation comedies.

In a published collection of emails about the writing of *Dr Who*, Russell T. Davies observes that one of his roles as series producer is to add 'signature dialogue', though he also is aware that all his characters speak with the same rhythm, which is essentially his own rhythm. One element of that signature dialogue is to give each of the manifestations of the Doctor a different idiolect. This has been noted by the dedicated fans of the series who comment on the different phrases and sayings that the David Tennant Doctor uses. They note that he likes to use short phrases from French and Italian, such as '*allons-y!*' and '*molto bene*'. In one episode the Doctor expresses a wish to meet someone called Alonso simply so that he can say '*Allons-y*, Alonso!' and Davies obliges him in the 2007 Christmas episode 'Voyage of the Damned'. One of the signature tunes of the Tennant Doctor is that he reinforces an observation with a personal declaration: 'It's snowing! I *love* snow!' and 'It's a cat. I *hate* cats.' He also apologises frequently. One obsessive fan has made a video of the 120 times in the series in which David Tennant says 'sorry' in the series and put it on YouTube.

Signature dialogue is only one aspect of discourse, and while we tend to consider discourse analysis as the way that linguists look at language functioning as communication, it is also practised by actors and can be a useful tool for playwrights. The technique of actioning has become well known as a rehearsal process popularised by the director Max Stafford-Clarke at Out of Joint, from a technique suggested by Stanislavsky. This exercise is a form of discourse analysis. In actioning, every utterance is assessed for its function as a speech act (a term coined in the 1970s by John Searle): a sentence, thus, can be a greeting, a warning, a reproach or an assertion. Any student of rhetoric will, of course, be aware that this is merely a reinvention of an ancient technique. 'Speaking is always *doing* something,' Peter Womack writes in *English Renaissance Drama*. 'Rhetorical utterances admonish, blame, congratulate, demand, exonerate, flatter, urge, warn.' John L Austin, who taught Searle at Oxford, calls this form of speech 'performatives'. Ordinary conversation operates on the understanding that the listener interprets the function of the speech act correctly. In a play, as in real life, the listener may always misinterpret or ignore the intention of the speaker.

One of the ways to learn to listen and analyse speech is through imitation, and the first exercise I usually give to students is to write a pastiche or parody of the fairytale 'Goldilocks' in the style of a contemporary playwright. I invariably use 'Goldilocks' because the tale is intrinsically unsatisfactory: we have no knowledge of who Goldilocks was before she entered the forest, why she was going there, nor what happened to her after she ran away at the end. There is a reason for this incomplete information: it is because, unlike Snow White, for example, the story, originally called 'The Three Bears', is not a traditional fairytale, but is a fragment of a longer tale, overheard by the Victorian author Robert Southey. It is thought that the story began as the tale of a fox, 'Scrapefoot', and Southey confused 'vixen' with the term for a crafty old woman. Southey's intruder then changed from an old woman into a small girl until, finally, in the early twentieth century, she was declared a blonde and became Goldilocks. The incomplete nature of the tale and its history gives the students creative space to play with their own version.

Writing this pastiche allows students to become aware of the 'voice' of different playwrights, as well as the ways in which they create the voices of their characters. It is also an exercise which they enjoy and therefore do well, and it provides a useful introduction to a number of dramaturgical principles. Over the years I have enjoyed reading interrogations of the bears by the police in the style of David Mamet and Sam Shepard, and uncomfortable encounters between Goldilocks and the bears in the style of Mark Ravenhill and Sarah Kane. Mrs Bear has complained through a number of monologues with strong echoes of Alan Bennett's *Talking Heads* of the problems that arise from making breakfast and then leaving it to go out for a walk. One recent script caught the way in which Bennett uses idioms: when Goldilocks has been discovered, Mrs Bear assumes that she must be very hungry and 'Well…it was action stations,' she says as she sets about her task. The most successful pastiches, however, have been those of Tom Stoppard, and one recent student created a philosophising fox, Scrapefoot, based on Goldilocks's precursor, who contemplates the existential and ontological horror of being another which is entirely Stoppardian: '…if I were to have no onlookers – if I was replaced by another player in my own story, what then? Do I exist? Or am I just some forgotten fiction?'

When students begin to think about idiolect, many of them tend to write comedy, which is unsurprising, since idiolect is accentuated and exaggerated in comic characters.

In Shakespeare we think of Polonius and Osric in *Hamlet*, Dogberry the constable in *Much Ado About Nothing* and Elbow in *Measure for Measure*. The speeches of the last two characters are notable for their malapropisms – named, of course, after Sheridan's character in *The Rivals*. Mrs Malaprop's speech is littered with examples of this particular misuse of language: 'If I *reprehend* any thing in this world it is the use of my *oracular* tongue, and a nice *derangement* of *epitaphs!*' Before Mrs Malaprop made them her own, this misuse was sometimes called a Dogberryism, and Shakespeare gave several examples to the constable: 'Comparisons are *odorous*,' he says, a joke which Shakespeare had earlier inverted in *A Midsummer Night's Dream*. When Bottom declaims that 'the flowers of odious savours sweet' he is corrected by Peter Quince ('odorous!'), while Bottom continues the joke: 'odours savours sweet; / So hath thy breath, my dearest Thisby dear.'

The function of malapropisms is similar to that of the catchphrase in creating a character's signature, so that they are easily recognisable to an audience. One of the most popular characters in *Coronation Street* was Hilda Ogden, who was characterised visually by her hair curlers and headscarf, and also became known for her malapropisms. She frequently referred to the wall-sized poster of a mountain landscape, as her 'muriel', and another famous coinage was 'the world is your lobster'. Such misuse of language remains perennially popular. The way in which one of the candidates of the recent BBC television programme *The Apprentice*, Stuart Baggs, mangled phrases was quickly picked up by bloggers and posted on the Internet. Baggs's most celebrated declaration was that he was not a one-trick pony, nor a ten-trick pony – but a field of ponies. When Del Boy Trotter in *Only Fools and Horses* announces that it is 'Good to be back on the old terracotta,' he places himself in a direct line of descent from Dogberry and Mrs Malaprop.

The tradition of misusing language was a staple of the music hall. The actress Jean Alexander, who played Hilda Ogden, claims that she developed her character of Hilda from the music-hall performer Hylda Baker, famed for her malapropisms and her use of innuendo, which was inevitably followed by her catchphrase, 'She knows, y'know!' The rhythm and idiolect of the music hall were perfectly caught by John Osborne when he created Archie Rice in *The Entertainer* and is found in Pinter as in Beckett. It also continues to resonate in the catchphrases written by television comedy writers such as Matt Lucas and David Walliams in *Little Britain* and by Catherine Tate. The catchphrase of Tate's creation, the teenager Lauren, 'Am I bovvered? Do I look bovvered?' echoed around school playgrounds a few years ago, but will, inevitably, become as dated as the forgotten catchphrases of Mrs Mopp, the office charlady in the 1940s radio show *ITMA*, 'Can I do you now, Sir?' and 'TTFN', which stood for 'Ta-ta for now.'

A character's idiolect frequently signals their status, and the use of language in terms of establishing power is one aspect which makes an understanding of its function so important to a playwright or scriptwriter. Ayckbourn has pointed out how this is one of the ways he demonstrates the status of his characters. Anthony, for example, a character in *The Revengers' Comedies*, is a man who is naturally authoritative, 'with overweening self-confidence' and thus talks in 'long measured, unhurried sentences […] – interrupt him if you dare'. Ayckbourn contrasts Anthony with Tristram Watson, 'the disastrously inarticulate junior solicitor in *Taking Steps*'. Tristram's idiolect is full of hesitation and apologies and signals his inadequacies through his speech patterns.

Many politicians are aware of the effect of the way they speak and mould it to make themselves popular. Tony Blair is, of course, the most famous example of a politician who changed his idiolect from standard English with received pronunciation to an idiolect that displayed many of the features of Estuary English with its glottal stops and frequent interjections of the phrase 'you guys' as if to demonstrate that he himself was a 'pretty straight sort of guy', as he once termed it. The political columnist Simon Hoggart once noted that a Blair speech was a like a piece of music, its aim not to inform but to create good feelings.

In order to think about discourse purely in terms of music it is helpful to try to eliminate the meaning and concentrate on the sound of the words. Many exercises I use with students have been developed from those of Noël Grieg which help students to do precisely that. These exercises have become the backbone of much of my own work on idiolect. Grieg, in his book on playwriting, includes four exercises on speech patterns and one is an exercise that requires students to think about the way a character talks in the form of a simile: this person talks like a tidal wave / a stampede of horses / a meandering river / a yapping dog, etc. Students add to the list, which can then be employed for the creation of dialogues. Another exercise I have adapted is a list of different idiolects: these include the person who is very precise and always talks in complete short sentences, the person who goes off at tangents, the habitual quoter of Shakespeare, the person who interrupts and never listens, the person who constantly apologises and the person who has one word or phrase that turns up in every sentence they use.

The degree to which personalities are embodied within idiolect and are recognisable through their speech patterns became apparent when I started to study verbatim theatre and wrote plays in this genre. Verbatim theatre is a form of documentary theatre where the dialogue is entirely or partly created from the actual words spoken or written by those who feature in the plays. When Derek Paget, who first defined the term in a landmark article in 1987, interviewed a number of practitioners working in this field, he noted the enthusiasm of the actors, writers and directors. What they enjoyed was working with what they regarded as 'the rich *textures* of ordinary speech'. Interviewing the director David Thacker about the play *Enemies Within*, Paget quotes a speech from the play in which a woman in a Yorkshire mining community talks about who was responsible for the death of her fourteen-year-old son. The speech uses the repeated local idiom 'now then' and Thacker, he relates, argues that no writer would have the nerve to employ the phrase in this context. I found the same use of repetition in a similar context when writing the play *Trash* about a mother trying to come to terms with the death of her daughter, Kelly. Like Thacker, I am certain that I would never have dared to repeat 'they wouldn't listen' so many times or find this remarkable natural rhythm. This is what the mother, Jean, says about the moment when two policemen arrive to tell her about the death of Kelly:

And one of them says to me: 'Er…Kelly is…' And I say: 'Yeah?' And he says…how did he put it? 'Kelly's in hospital.' And the other one says: 'She's passed away.' That's how it happens. Two policeman. 'Kelly's in hospital.' The other one: 'She's passed away.'
That's how it was said.
I didn't become hysterical, but I…I was repeating over and over and over and they wouldn't listen, they wouldn't listen, they wouldn't listen. They wouldn't listen to me, they wouldn't listen to me.

Many practitioners of verbatim theatre have noted how much the voice of the original person whose voice has been transcribed to form the dialogue of the play remains embedded within their speech. Jessica Blank and Eric Jensen, who wrote the anti-death-penalty play *The Exonerated*, advise future actors and directors not to contact the individuals whose stories are narrated in the play. Such contact, they suggest is, in fact, unnecessary, since their characters can be found within their words as spoken in the play. 'Over and over, we've seen completely disparate actors, after spending time with these words, unintentionally begin to channel the people they are playing, down to their speech patterns and mannerisms. It happens involuntarily and has nothing to do with mimicry or impersonation.' The transcribed words with the idiolect of those who are speaking in the play carry the particularity of the individual. Thus, the original person and stage persona become blurred, as demonstrated by the government official who was overheard asking his mother after watching and listening to himself portrayed by an actor in the play *Half the Picture*, which recreates the Scott Inquiry, 'Wasn't I good?'

Some voices have an idiolect that is so strong that it leaps from the transcription and demands to be put on stage. I feel that this is true of a woman I call Elsie (not her real name) whose letters to her husband when he was in an old people's home I inherited. Elsie had an unpunctuated, unstoppable flow of speech and writes as if talking:

You and I are prisoners, so to speak, even taxis, let alone buses that we took so much for granted are, alas, no longer at our disposal. I loved buses, whereas, correct me if I am wrong, you would sit, your eyes in front, where I sought out all avenues, the shops, the people, the people on the bus, the lady who I kept telling you, you should give her the seat, you said no, you had your shopping on it and it was frozen food and too cold to have on your lap. The lady said, after I'd reasoned with you, 'Don't worry, I've got one like that at home.' Anyway, you listened to reason, she got the seat.

Pinter, Steven Berkoff and Jack Rosenthal would recognise Elsie, as would Dickens. Indeed, she has much in common with Mrs Limper, the landlady in *Nicholas Nickleby*, who, like Mrs Nickleby herself, was based on Dickens's mother. Mrs Limper's idiolect has the ring of authenticity that comes from being based on a known voice.

My head, as well as my notebooks, are full of the accumulation of many years of conversations, as well as overheard conversations, voices whose distinct idiolects have been – or may become – the basis for characters in my plays and books. From cafés: 'Turkey or owl feathers are best for sweeping your aura. You can use chicken at a pinch.' 'I loathe Buck's Fizz, awful concoction. Squeeze me an orange and I'll drink it with pleasure and I'm always partial to the shampoo, but together – forget it.' From interviews: 'I have to punish myself. I mean if I weren't bad they'd never have done them terrible things to me.' As I continue to develop my own writer's ear, I store such snippets which will be used in the creation of future characters; with a pen and a pad always ready, I go out and about, watching and listening.

Antoinette Moses (*b*. 1946) is a lecturer in scriptwriting at UEA, having also done the MA in Creative Writing and a PhD there. She has written a number of plays, of which the most recent, *Cuts*, was longlisted for the Samuel Beckett Theatre Trust Award. She has also published many books of language-learner literature which have become set texts at schools and universities around the world.

Sensibility

Toby Litt

What follows is the text of a lecture delivered to students of the Birkbeck Creative Writing MA on 4 May 2010. TL

I don't think you're going to like this. It's probably going to hurt. If it doesn't hurt, there's a problem. As part of your coursework, you'll have read Flannery O'Connor's essay 'Writing Short Stories'. She begins by saying this:

> I have heard people say that the short story was one of the most difficult literary forms, and I've always tried to decide why people feel this way about what seems to me one of the most natural and fundamental ways of human expression. After all, you begin to hear and tell stories when you're a child, and there doesn't seem to be anything very complicated about it. I suspect that most of you have been telling stories all your lives, and yet here you sit – come to find out how to do it.

As do all of you, here in this room.

> Then last week, after I had written down some of these serene thoughts to use here today, my calm was shattered when I was sent seven of your manuscripts to read.
>
> After this experience, I found myself ready to admit, if not that the short story is one of the most difficult literary forms, at least that it is more difficult for some than for others.
>
> I still suspect that most people start out with some kind of ability to tell a story but that it gets lost along the way. Of course, the ability to create life with words is essentially a gift. If you have it in the first place, you can develop it; if you don't have it, you might as well forget it.

When, last term, I asked my students what they thought of the essay – a good, teacherly question – the first of them to speak up said, 'Well, I think she's a bit of a git.'

Although Flannery O'Connor had – of course – read none of this particular student's writing, and this student was not at all being told to 'forget it', still this student felt compelled to take the comment personally; which, I think, is exactly how Flannery O'Connor intended it to be taken.

'Forget it…' – This is not the way we're used to being spoken to, particularly nowadays. We are accustomed to being given the party line on the American Dream: 'If you believe, you can achieve.'

Flannery O'Connor is advising some of us, some of you, to stop dreaming and forget it. Forget it because you do not have the gift of creating life with words.

I'm going to return to forgetting it a bit later, but not in Flannery O'Connor's way. I should start by saying that for much of this talk you're probably going to think I'm a git, too. Maybe even a bigger git than Flannery O'Connor, because I *don't* believe that 'most people start out with some kind of ability to tell a story'. I'm going to take that away from you.

I do believe that most people start out with some kind of ability to paint wonderful, free, energetic pictures in primary colours. If you compare the paintings of three year olds to the paintings of thirteen year olds, there's no doubt that – during the intervening years – some element of uninhibited genius has disappeared. Adolescent art is always the worst art.

I will go along with Flannery O'Connor so far as to say that you were all gifted, at an early stage, with the ability to speak charmingly, innovatively. You will have said things, in trying to speak the world clearly, which came at it sideways and got it more right than clichéd adult speech almost ever does. But this haphazard charm of accuracy is something quite different to being able to tell a story. And most of the time, you were probably running round shouting 'Poo-bum-willy-fart! Poo-bum-willy-fart!', as all children do; all children who are allowed to get away with it, anyway.

Even though I've grown up to be a writer, I don't feel that, as a boy, I ever had a great, free, natural ability to tell stories. But Flannery O'Connor is quite stringent, quite determinedly gittish. All she's granting any of us is 'some kind of ability'.

I'm going to make a number of statements to you – about writing, about good writing, about bad writing. I don't expect you to agree with all or any of them, but I'd like you to listen to them as carefully as possible; because I am saying them on the basis of a belief that there are potentially good writers who nevertheless write badly – potentially good writers who have always written badly.

As an aside, I can imagine someone objecting: 'You can't just say some writing is good and some bad.' To which I'd reply, 'Yes, you can.'

Bad writing is mainly boring writing. It can be boring from any number of different causes. It can be boring because too confused or too logical, or boring because hysterical or lethargic, or boring because nothing truly happens.

If I give you a 400-page manuscript of an unpublished novel – something that I consider is made up of bad writing – you may read it to the end, but you will suffer as you do. It's possible that you have had to read 80,000 words of bad writing. The friend of a friend's novel. I have. On numerous occasions.

If you ask around, I'm sure you'll be able to find a really bad novel easily enough. I don't mean by someone who is in this room, who has taken our classes. I mean someone who has spent isolated years writing a book they are convinced is a great work of literature.

And when you're reading it, this novel, you'll know it's bad and you'll know what bad is.

The friend of a friend's novel may have some redeeming features – the odd nicely shaped sentence, the stray brilliant image. But it is still an agony to force oneself to keep going. It is still telling you nothing you didn't already know.

So, here are my propositions about bad writing – which you may still not believe exists.

Bad writers continue to write badly because they have many reasons – from their point of view, very good reasons – for wanting to continue writing in the way they do.

Writers are bad because they cleave to the causes of writing badly.

Bad writing is almost always a love poem addressed by the self to the self – even, or especially, when its overt topic is self-disgust.

Bad writing accepts that the person who will admire it first and most and last is the writer herself.

While bad writers may read a great many diverse works of fiction, they are unable because unwilling to perceive the things these works do which their own writing fails to do.

The most dangerous kind of writers for bad writers to read are what I call Excuse Writers – writers of the sort who seem to grant permission to others to borrow or imitate their failings. I'll give you some concrete examples of Excuse Writers – Jack Kerouac, John Updike, David Foster Wallace, Virginia Woolf, Margaret Atwood, Maya Angelou.

Bad writers bulwark themselves against a confrontation with their own badness by reference to other writers of the past and present with whom they feel they share certain defence-worthy characteristics.

In order to protect their badness, bad writers form defensive admirations: 'If Updike can get away with these kind of half-page descriptions of women's breasts, I can too…' or 'If Virginia Woolf is a bit woozy on spatiality, on putting things down concretely, I'll just let things float free…'

If another writer's work survives on charm, you will never be able to steal it, only imitate it in an embarrassingly obvious way. This writing will be adolescent, and adolescents lack charm – adolescents don't value charm.

Bad writing is written defensively; good writing is a making vulnerable – a making of the self as vulnerable as possible. The psychic risk of a novel such as Virginia Woolf's *The Waves* is vast – particularly for someone for whom psychic risk was so potentially debilitating and ultimately dangerous. When John Updike began writing *Rabbit, Run* all in the present tense, it was either going to be a great technical feat or a humiliating aesthetic misjudgement. (Excuse writers aren't, in themselves, bad writers; not at all.)

Good writing is a hymn of praise to everything the self feels itself incapable of perceiving.

Good writing is of necessity a betrayal of the known self, of the version of the self we believe we know, and through that a betrayal of the known world – a betrayal into truth.

What are some of the direct causes of bad writing? What are some of the good reasons people have for continuing to write badly?

I'm going to suggest four main ones – there are others, I'm sure.

1. Often, the bad writer will feel that they have a particular story they want to tell. It may be a story passed on to them by their grandmother or it maybe something that happened to them when they were younger. Until they've told this particular story (which may be what has drawn them to taking writing seriously), they feel they can't move on. But because the material is so close to them, so precious to them, they can't mess around with it enough to learn how writing works. And, ultimately, they lack the will to betray the material sufficiently to make it true.

Bad writers think: 'I want to write this.'

2. Bad writers often want to rewrite a book by another writer that was written in a different time period, under completely different social conditions. Because it's a good book, they see no reason why they can't simply do the same kind of thing again – with the characters wearing different clothes, eating different food. They don't understand that even historical novels or science fiction novels are a response to a particular historical moment. And pretending that the world isn't as it is – or, perhaps more accurately, that the world should still be as it once was – pretending this is disastrous for any serious fiction.

Bad writers think: 'I want to write this.'

3. Conversely, bad writers often write in order to forward a cause or enlarge other people's understanding of a contemporary social issue. Any attempt at all to write in order to make the world a better, fairer place – to write stories, I mean, not essays or polemics – any attempt to write world-improving fiction is almost certain to fail. Holding any value as more important than learning to be a good writer is dangerous. Put very simply, your characters must be alive before they seek justice; justice will never be achieved by cardboard cut-outs or mannequins; cardboard cut-outs and mannequins don't need justice.

Bad writers think: 'I want to write this.'

4. Bad writers often believe they have very little left to learn, and that it is the literary world's fault that they have not yet been recognised, published, lauded and laurelled. It is a very destructive thing to believe that you are very close to being a good writer, and that all you need to do is keep going as you are rather than completely reinvent what you are doing.

Bad writers think: 'I want to write this.'

Conversely, good writers think…

What do you think good writers think?

I think good writers think: 'This is being written.'

I'd like to sidestep now. You've probably heard the words 'good' and 'bad' enough for one day. Although, I'm afraid – git that I am – that they'll be recurring later.

What I'm now going to do is quote another essay by Flannery O'Connor. This one called 'The Nature and Aim of Fiction': 'In fact,' Flannery O'Connor says, 'so many people can now write competent stories that the short story as a medium is in danger of dying of competence. We want competence, but competence by itself is deadly. What is needed is the vision to go with it, and you do not get this from a writing class.'

Competence, obviously, lies in between bad and good writing. But the territory isn't as simply mapped as that. Competence can be a lot further from great than awful is. To go from being a competent writer to being a great writer, I think you have to risk being – or risk being seen as – a bad writer.

Here are a few propositions about competence:

Competence is deadly because it prevents the writer risking the humiliation that they will need to risk before they pass beyond competence.

Competence will never climb the trapeze, take a pie in the face, put its head in the lion's mouth, transfix a raging audience through wit and will and voice. Competence will never truly entertain because it will never run away to join the circus.

To write competently is to do a few magic tricks for friends and family; to write well is to run away to join the circus.

Your friends and family will love your tricks, because they love you. But try busking those tricks on the street. Try busking them alongside a magician who has been busking for ten years, and earns their living busking.

When they are watching a magician, people don't want to go, 'Well done.' They want to go, 'Wow!'

Competence never makes people go 'Wow!'

At worst, on this course, we will have shown you how to do some magic tricks; at best, we will have taught you how to be a good magician; beyond that, though, is doing magic – and that you will have to learn for yourself. For what we can't show you is how to do things you shouldn't be able to do.

By this point in your Creative Writing MA you are all far more likely to be competent writers than bad writers.

You're probably at the high-point of thinking I'm a git, now. You didn't take a Creative Writing MA in order to be told to run away with the circus. The situation isn't that extreme, is it? What's the point of saying all this if it isn't going to help – if I'm not going to give you some way of improving as a writer?

But that's exactly what I'm going to do.

First, though, I'd like to take a sidestep – from the circus to high-level physics.

One of the questions that teachers of Creative Writing get asked most frequently, apart from 'How do I get an agent?' is 'Can creative writing be taught?'

For a long time, I didn't have a satisfactory answer to this. I would say that I believed creative writing couldn't be taught, but that it could be learnt. In other words, that the process of going through a Creative Writing course could radically improve a student's stories, even though it probably wouldn't be the taught element which caused this improvement. I would say that the most useful thing for me, when I studied Creative Writing at the University of East Anglia, was to feel that I had a small audience who weren't (unlike my friends and family) emotionally committed to me as a person. I could hand in a piece of work to the class in the knowledge that they would respond without thinking they had to spend the rest of their week, or maybe even the rest of their lives, dealing with the consequences of being negative. It's a completely different feeling, knowing that you are writing for a small group of committed readers, rather than for the judges of open competitions, for skim-reading agents or work-experience people in publisher's offices. This, I used to say – the provision of an audience of peers – was how creative writing was learnt.

But a while ago I came up with what I thought was a better answer. Yes, creative writing can be taught, but only in this sense: what we teach you on the Creative Writing MA is equivalent to Newtonian physics. In other words, it's a pretty good way to do the basic jobs of dealing with matter. If you want to predict where the moon will be at a certain time in the future, Newtonian physics will enable you to do this – at least to the extent that your telescope won't be pointing in completely the wrong direction. Newtonian physics, for most things you're going to come across, gets the job done.

However, as we've discovered since Newton, the universe – including both the moon and the telescope but also your eye – the universe doesn't operate according to Newtonian physics. The universe exists on a Quantum level, and the rules of Quantum physics are often in direct contradiction of Newtonian physics. In the Quantum world, things can simultaneously exist and not exist. In the Quantum world, things can travel backwards in time. Quantum physics means matter can do things it shouldn't be able to do.

Now, transferring this over to creative writing – what we do on the MA is, as I said, teach you the equivalent of Newtonian physics. The technical stuff that we go through – point of view, use of time, narrative tone – all of this will let you find the moon, observe it, predict it. But if you want to do good or great writing – what I think of as good or great writing – you are going to have to step up to Quantum physics. And this is where the analogy between creative writing and physics starts to break down. Because whilst you can teach Quantum physics to very bright students, it's almost impossible to teach Creative Writing on the Quantum-equivalent level.

Why?

Because on that level it's ceased to be creative writing and has become just really good or great writing. And to say anything useful about that, your tutor would have to be in your head, commenting on your vague plans and your specific choices within sentences. But commentary, at this point, is probably the last thing you need. You may not even, strictly, be conscious of what you're doing. You'll just be following your developed instincts as to what seems right.

Good writers think: 'This is being written.'

To tie this in with the running away to join the circus: Newtonian physics makes the crowd say 'Well done.' Quantum physics makes the crowd say 'Wow!'

I'd like to turn now to the subject of this talk, which I've done a remarkable job of not mentioning before: Sensibility.

The reason for this is that Sensibility belongs very much to the Quantum world of writing. And, in order to reach it, I needed to pass through bad and competent writing.

The best thing I've heard said about Sensibility came in an interview between the poets John Betjeman and Philip Larkin in a documentary made in 1964 for the BBC programme *Monitor*.

John Betjeman asks Philip Larkin, 'What sort of attitude do you take to adverse criticism?' and Philip Larkin replies:

Well, I don't know [if] you feel this, but I feel it very strongly – I read that, you know, I'm a miserable sort of fellow, writing a sort of Welfare State sub-poetry; doing it well, perhaps, but it isn't really what poetry is and it isn't really the sort of poetry we want; but I wonder whether it ever occurs to the writer of criticism like that that really one *agrees* with them but what one writes is based so much on the kind of person one is, and the kind of environment one's had, and has now, that one doesn't really choose the poetry one writes, one writes the kind of poetry one has to write or can write.

Here, although he doesn't say the word, Larkin is describing Sensibility. His own disappointing Sensibility.

What do I mean by Sensibility? Is it the same thing as in the title of *Sense and Sensibility* by Jane Austen? In a way yes, and in a way no.

It was in the mid-eighteenth century that the idea of Sensibility came to prominence – as much as something to be mocked as something to be proud of. Novels were full of what my father would call 'sensitive little flowers'.

Slightly later, the Romantic poets adapted the idea of a distinctive hyper-sensitivity to the things of the world; if one had Sensibility, one would be able to react appropriately or even originally to (here's a very common example) the sight of the snow-covered heights of Mont Blanc. One might even feel moved to write a sonnet on the feelings stirred in one by the vision.

The understanding of Sensibility I'm talking about has developed from this proud Romantic notion. It's the particularity of someone's response to Mont Blanc that displays their particular Sensibility. And because we're no longer Romantics, or we try to kid ourselves we're not, this Sensibility doesn't necessarily have to express itself as appreciation of the sublimity of the natural world. W. H. Auden, for example, said: 'Apart from nature, geometry's all there *is*…Geometry belongs to man. Man's got to assert himself against Nature all the *time*…I hate sunsets and flowers. And I loathe the *sea*. The sea is formless.'

(This is W. H. Auden appearing as 'Weston' in Christopher Isherwood's autobiographical novel *Lions and Shadows*, 1938.) Here, Auden is defining himself as an anti-romantic Sensibility by aesthetically attacking the things the Romantics held dearest. Where they valued mountains, he would value disused Victorian industrial machinery. And he was doing this, he asserted, even before he became a poet:

> From the age of four to thirteen I had a series of passionate affairs with pictures of, to me, particularly attractive water-turbines, winding-engines, roller-crushers, etc., and I was never so emotionally happy as when I was underground.'[1]

Auden was unusual in having a Sensibility that revealed itself to him, and to others, even in adolescence. People like Auden end up being called geniuses. But I think it's more likely that they are people who begin working on their Sensibility very hard and at a very early age – even if they are not aware that that's what they are doing.

Which brings me, at last, to Fernando Pessoa (1888–1935) and to *The Book of Disquiet*. Although to call it a book is to make it appear more planned and finished than it ever was. If you've researched Pessoa a little, you will have found out the unimportant facts:

– that he lived a quiet life, working as a translator in Lisbon

– that he was known in his life as a poet; in fact, as more than one poet, because he wrote in completely different styles under a series of what he called 'heteronyms'

– that *The Book of Disquiet* was left unfinished by Pessoa, and that each printed *Book of Disquiet* we have is a version created after Pessoa's death by editors who have tried to put his fragmented manuscripts into readable order

– that whichever edition of *The Book of Disquiet* you have looked at, you won't have read all of it; and unless you learn Portuguese and become a Pessoa scholar you probably never will

So, why did I choose Pessoa as the required reading?

Well, I hope you will remember my earlier reference to the bad novel you might borrow, and the bad writer who had written it – the friend of a friend, 'I mean someone who has spent isolated years writing a book they are convinced is a great work of literature.'

This was Pessoa. This is how he thought of himself:

> Today's dreamers are perhaps the great precursors of the ultimate science of the future, not that I believe in any such ultimate science…Sometimes I invent a metaphysics like this with all the respectful scrupulousness of attention of someone engaged in real scientific work. As I've said before, it reaches the point where I may really be doing just that.

This was Pessoa, and he was *right* – he was writing a great work of literature.

In fact, *The Book of Disquiet* – in Creative Writing MA terms, in Newtonian physics terms, in some of my own terms – looks very like bad writing. It has many of the faults that the worst writing has. It centres on one isolated, autobiographical character who believes, against all evidence, that they are worthy of universal attention. It hardly ever engages this character with another character. There is almost no dialogue. There are very few scenes. The character is depressed and, probably to some readers, depressing. There appears to be no chance of change within his life. There is no story as such. The writing is disorganised, repetitive, seemingly directionless. The world described is limited, drab, boring.

And yet – and this is where we flip to the Quantum world and go beyond Creative Writing – and yet this is a great, endlessly readable, endlessly fascinating work of fiction.

Why?

Sensibility.

The Book of Disquiet is a book which works consistently to remove anything from itself that is neither an examination of Sensibility nor an expression of Sensibility. Take any random page and it will almost certainly contain a statement of the sort: 'I see things like this' or 'I have always seen things like this' or 'I wish I hadn't always seen things like this...'

In writing this lecture, I took a random page and found:

> When I first came to Lisbon the sound of someone playing scales on a piano used to drift down from the flat above, the monotonous piano practice of a little girl I never saw. Today, through processes of assimilation I fail to comprehend, I discover that if I open the door to the cellars of my soul, those repetitive scales are still audible, played by a girl who is now Mrs Someone-or-other, or else dead and shut up in a white place overgrown by black cypresses.

Imagine how this would be workshopped: 'Look, this is just an inert description. How about if another girl moves in above the narrator and starts playing scales, and how about if he meets and falls in love with her mother, or with her, or with the idea of playing piano himself? Make something happen.'

Pessoa is about the removal of making something happen in order to allow Sensibility to take the happening's place. In this, and in other things, he is a more extreme version of other modern writers of a similar period – Franz Kafka, Robert Walser, Bruno Schulz, Marcel Proust, Virginia Woolf – all of whom I would recommend you investigate with Sensibility in mind.

Pessoa's writing is great because, and only because, he has a fascinating Sensibility. It is a Sensibility he has cultivated, but it is also a Sensibility that oppresses and poisons him.

The Book of Disquiet is constantly summing itself up, but here is one definition of Pessoa's project: 'Abdicate from life so as not to abdicate from oneself.'

This is Quantum writing – writing that has risked total humiliation in order to pass beyond competence. It is great or it is worthless. It is doing something that it shouldn't be able to do.

So, why don't we teach Sensibility as part of the MA?

Perhaps if we had an exclusively tutorial system and ten years with each student, we could. I doubt it, though. Because Sensibility is partly about rejecting those things which can be taught – rejecting those things which others believe worth teaching. Sensibility is the difference between Creative Writing and writing – meaning good writing and especially great writing. This is why I chose Sensibility as something worth talking about at this stage of this term. If you'd heard it mentioned in Week One, it would have become just another thing to angst over: 'Oh God, not only is my use of point-of-view wobbly, but I don't have an original and fascinating Sensibility. Maybe I should forget it?'

Which brings us back to where we started, that old git Flannery O'Connor. Perhaps now she seems less of a git than she did; now that I've become the uber-git. But I hope I've supplied an explanation of her words on telling stories and on competent writing.

My definition would be: 'Competent writing is writing that lacks an interesting Sensibility.'

However, O'Connor was clearly aware of Sensibility, she just called it something else, 'We want competence, but competence by itself is deadly. What is needed is the vision to go with it.'

I think Sensibility is a better word than Vision because it not only suggests that you need to see a different world, it also suggests that you need to inhabit and create a different world.

And I've already said that Sensibility is unteachable.

Does that mean that the talk is going to end right now?

(Bummer.)

No.

Because I think that, without teaching you, I can give you some suggestions which might help you develop as a writer and, through this, develop your Sensibility.

First, you *do* need to forget it. Forget it and give up completely and forever.

Then, immediately, you need to start again, but not from where you finished before. Do try to forget where that was – for the moment at least.

Cease to attempt to be what you will never succeed in being. If you are Larkin, there's no point in you trying to be (as he did) D. H. Lawrence or W. B. Yeats. A great deal of the business of developing a unique Sensibility is to do with the failure to be X or Y, the failure to be other than one is.

I repeat, slightly altered: cease attempting to become what you stand no chance of ever convincingly being. To develop as a writer, and so as a Sensibility, there are four basic things you can do: Writing, Re-writing, Reading, Re-reading.

I wouldn't put them in this order of usefulness, though. My ranking would go something like this, from least useful to most useful:

4. Writing

3. Reading

2. Re-reading

1. Re-writing

Here, by re-writing, I also mean intensively and honestly re-reading what you have written.

These four things should be obvious to you by this point in the course. Here are a few other, less usual suggestions:

Write a list of your obsessions. Allow it to be as short or as long as it wants to be. Add to it over the following week, whenever a forgotten thing occurs. At the end of the week, go over it once more. Take out any item you think is there to impress or in any way speak to other people. Now, who does this list remind you of? Read it. Read it again. Then destroy it. A week later, repeat the exercise. You can try to remember what was on the first list, if you like, but it's better to return to the question, 'What obsesses me?' This second list, you can – if you want – keep. Perhaps it will be useful.

Take five good but not necessarily great novels quickly, randomly, from your bookshelves. Read the opening page (just that, not a word more) – the opening page of each of them. Then read just the opening page of your most recent piece of work. How do they announce themselves to you, these other writers? And how do you find yourself announcing yourself? How, if you could choose, would you like to announce yourself?

Create a pseudonym you don't care for, and begin immediately to write as that person. Don't worry any longer about whether what you are writing is good or not. Just write as energetically as you can. After a week, compare what you wrote, spontaneously-as-another, with what you wrote the week before, consciously-as-yourself. How do the two periods compare? Is one truer to you than the other? If not, why not?

Choose a writer whose work you know really well. Now, write a parody of them – exaggerating every feature of their style, but still applying it to the kind of subject matter they applied it to. A week later, reread what you've done. Where do you fail to be true to the parodied writer? Are there any gaps through which you can peek at your own Sensibility? Writers always used to learn by imitating. (The first thing we have by Keats is an imitation of Spenser.) Because when a writer puts something forwards and says, 'This is an imitation of so-and-so,' the reader looks for the places where the imitation succeeds, but more so for the places where it fails. And these failures are where the two Sensibilities fail to coincide. So they are places you can use to investigate your own Sensibility. If you were to do conscious imitations of a series of writers, you would learn a great deal about yourself as a writer.

After you have done the previous exercise, write another parody, this time trying to take the original writer's Sensibility but using it to write about something they never (to your knowledge) wrote about. If it's Hemingway, say, have your version of him write about the doings of a family of white mice or a women's institute coach trip to London to see

Priscilla, Queen of the Desert. If it's Jane Austen, have your version of her write about a mafia killing or a speed-dating event or zombies.

Well, maybe not zombies.

Stop writing your first drafts on a computer. Even if you find your handwriting unusable (because illegible, because slow), a page of handwritten manuscript will reveal more to you of your own Sensibility than the neutrality of Microsoft Word ever will. The faults of your writing are covered over when not actually exacerbated by word-processing. The stage of typing up a handwritten draft – of seeing it transform from rough scribbly letters to respectable-looking text – is very illuminating. But if the words have never been rough and scribbly they will never gain those qualities. In one way, the words will always have been public. And a feeling of privacy is one of the most attractive qualities in writing.

Also, the physical labour of writing is useful; increase rather than decrease this for yourself. By doing this (handwriting) you are inhabiting your sentences, allowing them to pass through your body in a less distanced way than if you simply type them out. Don't try to rush to the final draft; learn the difficult art of dwelling.

In all of these things, don't be concerned at all whether you are writing badly or well. Simply try to write as energetically, as committedly, as you possibly can.

I'm going to conclude with a third set of propositions. I began by trying to define good and bad writing. Then I went on to competent writing – with some side-references to running away to join the circus, busking magicians and Quantum physics. I'd like to finish by making some propositions about Sensibility. This is on the basis that great writing is writing that displays or reveals a fascinating and unique Sensibility.

A unique Sensibility begins to find things very important which the majority of others have always seen as trivial.

A unique Sensibility will find mountains which are not mountains.

A unique Sensibility refuses not to see as still important things which the majority of others believe were last year or last decade or last millennium's concern.

And original Sensibility is formed by encountering original obstacles. The great writer discovers a unique obstacle, just for herself. There are far fewer obstacles than styles or sensibilities.

Proust's obstacle: to incorporate the time of a life into a book.

Joyce's obstacle: to refer to everything all the time without a moment's cease.

Beckett's: to remove human referents as totally as possible without removing human referents totally.

Woolf's: to depict idiosyncratic minds which are yet still porous to other idiosyncratic minds.

Pessoa's: to write about no subject other than writing about Sensibility.

Where do differences in individual Sensibility originate? This is perhaps the trickiest question.

I would say that it has something to do with time.

A person's Sensibility stems from a person's unique relation to time, of which we have very few maps.

There are conventional relations to time, as expressed in fiction. Genre fiction depends on conventional relations to time. Literary fiction is a kind of genre fiction. There are also dominant relations to time, in any given literary period.

I'd say that a writer like Raymond Carver has a limiting, standardising relation to fictional time – if you imitate him too closely. The simplification of tenses, avoiding even the past perfect, and allowing the past historic to overtake all, reduces the chances for writers to display their unique relation to time.

In other words, 'She had…' predominates over 'She had had…' or 'She had been having…' or 'She hadn't been having…' or 'She might perhaps have been having…' or 'She will have been having…' or 'She would have been, perhaps, having…'

I'm not trying to encourage you to write like Henry James or Proust. Just to realise that Carver's obstacle isn't your obstacle. His time isn't your time.

Examine your unique relation to time and examine how you express it in words.

I have used enough of your time.

---

1   W. H. Auden, *The English Auden* (Faber, 1977), pp.397–8.

Toby Litt (*b.* 1968) received his MA in Creative Writing from UEA in 1995. One of *Granta*'s Best of Young British Novelists 2003, he is the author of two collections of short stories and nine novels, including *Corpsing* (2000), *deadkidsongs* (2001), *Ghost Story* (2004) and *King Death* (2010). His story 'John & John' won the Manchester Fiction Prize.

Forms

The Translators

George Szirtes

1.

Sometimes you see clouds drifting past the city,
inventions of the sky,
within which images appear then petrify
and remain there in perpetuity.

Otherwise things shift with a certain insouciance
but keep moving. Meaning vanishes
into night, into the vacant parishes
of the imagination, into a non-presence

that is positively terrifying. But there,
the clouds still loom like statues
with faces, as if one could choose
to see them suspended in imagined air.

2.

I have jumped to conclusions in my time.
What else would you jump to otherwise?
To orders? to attention? Look into the eyes
of language and you see nothing. Only rhyme

and punctuation. I have talked to ghosts
in ghost language, the solemn dead
at their jabber, hearing the music of instead,
the sigh of the wind at its last post.

I once had a mother who used at times to speak
but now I only conjure her. We carve
images into clouds so we should not starve
for lack of company. We break

the silence into pieces, syllables of space.
We are translated into ourselves. The sky
rushes at us. We observe it insouciantly,
watching clouds move, looking for a face.

3.

We have seen mirrors in darkened rooms
hunger for us. We have seen the dead
in our streets. We have felt the dread
of a face and the shapes that it assumes

in its own mirror. We owe them a shape,
all those faceless one, you and I.
We should feed them before they petrify,
before their clouds pack up or else escape.

4.

How do I know myself before I have created
my simulacrum? How are the hungry
to be fed? Listen, the sky is angry.
The gods are demanding to be translated.

George Szirtes (*b.* 1948) is Reader in Creative Writing at UEA. His first collection, *The Slant Door*, was published in 1979. His many subsequent books include *Short Wave* (1984), *Blind Field* (1994), *The Budapest File* (2000) and *The Burning of the Books and Other Poems* (2009). He has won a variety of prizes for his work, most recently the T. S. Eliot Prize for *Reel* (2004). His translations from Hungarian literature have also won numerous awards.

The Short Story

Jean McNeil

What's to be done about the short story? Writers want to write them, readers very likely want to read them, but publishers (at least in the UK) don't want to publish them. Because publishers think we don't buy collections, writers don't write them – your ordinary vicious circle, folks. What is certain is that the short story has not flourished in this culture to the extent it has in Canada and the United States. This matters for writers in Britain, because those literary forms that find success have much to do with how writers themselves flourish, and in particular with how they learn to write.

Every writer has an apprenticeship. Mine happened to take place in Canada, where I grew up and went to university. As an aspiring writer I had access to many quality literary magazines, most of them funded by either provincial or federal governments and hosted by a university English Literature department. In them I published poems, short stories and essays before attempting my first novel, aged twenty-two. Canada is friendly to the short story, in both its reading and writing culture. For a new writer to debut with a collection of short stories is expected and lauded. They even win prizes – in 2006 Vincent Lam, a medical doctor and writer, won the country's pre-eminent literary prize for his collection of short stories, *Bloodletting & Miraculous Cures*.

For the last few years I have taught a seminar course on the short story and the novella on the MA in Creative Writing at UEA. The pressing questions my students want answered are: what is involved in writing a truly good short story? What *is* a short story in the first place? And why is it not valued here?

A short story is very often defined by what it is not, namely a novel. What separates the two has less to do with length than structure, and with what I call emotional intent. The Italian writer Alberto Moravia wrote a little-known but very helpful short essay, 'The Short Story and the Novel'. In distinguishing between the two, Moravia writes that 'The principal and fundamental difference lies in the ground-plan or structure of the narrative…what we could call ideology, that is the skeleton of the theme from which the flesh of the story takes its form. The novel has a bone structure holding it together from top to toe, whereas the story is, so to speak, boneless.'

Moravia goes on to observe that in the novel the plot 'is made up of not only intuitions and feelings (as in the short story) but primarily of ideas expressed poetically but well defined'. Short-story writers, he states, have more variety, and paradoxically a broader world view than novelists. He cites the examples of two hyper-prolific writers, Guy de Maupassant (who wrote more than 800 short stories) and Anton Chekhov: 'while Maupassant and Chekhov…exhaust the variety of situations and characters of the society of their time, Flaubert and Dostoevsky are rather like those solitary birds that restlessly and loyally repeat the same significant cry.'

William Faulkner regarded the short story as harder to write than a novel. Having written a few novels now myself, I'm not so sure that's true, but there is one old adage I do believe: only exceptional short-story collections will get published, whereas there are plenty of middling novels out there.

Not that this tells us very much about the short story's essential mystery. As Moravia cautions, 'all this has little to do with the principal qualities of the short story – I mean that indefinable and inexpressible charm of narration experienced both by the writer and the reader. An exceedingly complex charm, deriving from a literary art which is unquestionably purer, more essential, more lyrical, more concentrated and more absolute than that of the novel.'

Where does this 'charm' come from? As a genre, the short story has been remarkably little theorised; the reams of opaque literary criticism studded with terms like *parole* and *récit* simply haven't been written. This means you can do what you want with it. Here's what I foreground in my class: in short stories, images, curtailed thoughts, fragments, glimpses, often make the point that explicit commentary or extended set-pieces would make in a long novel. In the short form you have to be deft, precise, observant – the magpie with the beady eye. To write short stories well, a writer must have a feel for the delicacy of the moment, which is the kernel of life, an understanding that what is left out is at least as important as what is left in, and finally a furtive quality, which I can't really put my finger on.

So why does Britain remain largely immune to its charms? The anthropologist in me takes a cultural approach to literature, meaning I see literature as a reflection of a society, an era, its concerns and desires. In Britain I detect a vaguely masochistic desire to be instructed. Big novels – big social novels in particular – might not have a single real person or emotion in them, but if they are intellectually ambitious and seek to 'tell us how the world works' (to quote Zadie Smith) then we love them – or rather, we admire them. We are impressed by novels that reflect the 'society we live in', stocked with hyperbolic personnel and plotted across large swathes of space and time. In contrast, the short story almost never seeks to instruct. It's far too subtle for that.

In 2004 a unique report on the issue was published. 'The Short Story in the UK' was funded by Arts Council England and other writing bodies. The data is a bit old now, but I think its findings are still worth consideration.

The report found that most short-story collections are bought on impulse, so visibility in shops and promotions like 3 for 2 were deemed very important. Around 25 per cent of short-story collections were bought as gifts. Virtually all of the top 100 short-story bestsellers for 2002 were from mainstream publishers, and most were written by novelists. (In 2002 the bestselling short-story writers were Frederick Forsyth and Catherine Cookson.) Advances for short-story collections were (and remain) significantly lower, on average, than for novels. The report found that short-story writers increasingly had to turn to independent publishers to get published.

Perhaps we knew this already, but the report's more qualitative findings are illuminating. The researchers talked to readers, writers, publishers and booksellers and found that 'Most readers prefer novels, partly because they can become "lost" in the world of the novel but partly because they are "afraid" to tackle a short story, feel they won't "get it" and need to be reassured that it's not such a difficult form.' To quote other interesting findings: 'the best way of all to support the prestige and profile of the short story would be to assist writers to write them'; 'While publishers continue to believe that only a novel will make a writer's name, it will be difficult for new or early-career writers to publish stories'; and 'There's no point marketing something that isn't there.' Among the report's conclusions were the need to develop a reading culture for stories, starting in schools; the need to 'rebrand' the short story; the need for an annual anthology of best UK short stories and to establish 'a new high-profile prize for short story collections'.

What I notice is that this is all about the market, rather than literature. In Britain we have a highly commercialised attitude to literature; the only way to solve the problem of the short story is prizes, money and notoriety. (You could conclude the only things anyone in Britain values are money and fame.) In Canada, I was brought up to think of literature as an art form. But that's me, the sackcloth-and-ashes purist, wandering in my own private desert.

The good news is that judging from the reviews pages of the broadsheets, and from the literary anthologies coming out of Creative Writing programmes (of which UEA's is a shining example), the short-story form remains much admired by critics, by teachers of literature, and most importantly by writers themselves. Many writers thrill to the 'high-wire act' (to quote James Lasdun) of writing a good short story: will it work? Can I do what I want to do? Where is this all going?

That thrill, and the desire to try out new ways of telling stories, are what drove me to write my collection *Nights in a Foreign Country*, published in Britain in 2001 and in Canada a year later. At the time, I had just published my first novel. I didn't know what to write next and feared that whatever it was it would lack the freshness and resolve of my first book. The collection was born out of an episodic period in my life when I was changing countries and jobs often, living in Brazil, in Central America, Mexico, encountering an array of people and situations. The story seemed the only form that could offer me the variety to test out ideas and settings. Then, as now, what thrilled me about the short story was its intensity, which does not come solely from the incident depicted – the story or the theme – but from a tight patterning of drama, symbol, motif in such a way that its dramatic tension is exposed; how everything within it is directed at a single emotional effect.

Also, by my mid-twenties, when I started *Nights*, it was beginning to dawn on me that in life we don't encounter people and situations locked in the vast web of occurrence and happenstance, as in grand social-panorama novels. People in short stories are very often portrayed caught in isolated moments. If the novel's natural territory is 'how the world works', and the novella's of memory and desire, the short story's is, I think, the turning point: fulcrum moments or short timeframes which represent a change.

Because or in spite of these qualities, the isolation and the brevity and attack of the form – Raymond Carver's advice for writing short stories was: 'Get in, get out. Don't linger.' – a writer's Sensibility is more apparent in short stories. The short form requires more control of story, and better emotional judgement, than the novel because its very brevity forces the meaning of such moments beneath the surface, where, as one critic writes, 'by the nature of its indistinctness, it gives the impression of being inexplicable'. Stories are often like photographs, blurry and indistinct, as if seen through myopic eyes or in the developing tray, gradually becoming more distinct. This sharpening of focus mirrors the process of understanding, often aided by epiphany – the moment of revelation – and of the simultaneous realisation that a moment of enlightenment is perhaps all you're going to get. The novel promises understanding. The short story generally eludes it, although somehow – and this is part of its genius – in its very evasion points to a more expansive and more honest truth.

Then there are those furtive aspects of the story I can't quite explain: my suspicion that it is an elegiac form, an unannounced elegy for what is lost or missing, not only in the characters' existences, but in all our lives. Nadine Gordimer has written that short-story writers deal with the only thing we can be sure of – the present moment. There is a loneliness to this, I think. We are stranded in the moment with our awareness that life is not that grand narrative, but more like the flash of fireflies, off and on, now here, now there, flitting through the darkness.

Like every literary form, the short story has its limitations and its weaknesses – coyness, a tendency to miniaturism, a breathy portent that calls attention to its every manoeuvre. Writers themselves tend to fall into the trap, when writing them, of an over-emphasis on craft and on perfection. Often this results in a story-by-numbers approach; we end up writing the same story over and over again. Creative Writing students love the short story because it seems to proffer the beguiling possibility that there is a 'way' to write, that the craft can be learned and perfected, and you don't need to spend ten years at your desk sawing away at some 600-page monster to do it. But the truth is the story's power lies not in craft, nor in perfection, but in the emotion that drives it.

When teaching story-focused workshop classes there is an exercise I use wherein I ask my students to write *what your character dreamt the night before the story started*. The result is writing that displays anticipation, energies and forces gathering to enact what will be an intense and concentrated effect, even if what students write will not appear in the story, like figures just outside the frame of the photograph. Dreams are, of course, mysterious and at the heart of short stories is a mystique. Joyce Carol Oates has written that 'the root of all stories is in the Brothers Grimm, in dreams; not in cameras and tape recorders'. The short story, Oates writes, is 'the dream realised'.

I find short stories harder to write now than I did when I started out as a writer. Perhaps because I am too aware – of the conventions of the genre, of the tasks it sets the writer. I lack the reckless clarity I had as a young writer. Or maybe all my ideas are simply novel-length and novel-breadth these days. I don't know.

What I do know is that I benefited from knowing virtually nothing about the form when I wrote my stories. I broke many of the rules, not entirely successfully. Now I counsel my students to read widely and consider what we discuss in class about the history, conventions and expectations of the story; but when writing their own stories I say: take risks, make the story work for you, not the other way around. The short story is a flexible, intelligent, subversive form. Dream the dream of the night before the story started. Make it yours. Make it new.

Jean McNeil (*b.* 1968) is Tutor in Creative Writing at UEA. Originally from Nova Scotia, she is the author of nine books, most recently the novel *The Ice Lovers* (2009), which is set in the Antarctic. In 2005 she was awarded a Fellowship to join the British Antarctic Survey as a writer in residence. She is currently writer in residence at the Environment Institute at UCL.

Temple of Truth

Richard Holmes

In 2001 the University of East Anglia appointed me as its first Professor of Biographical Studies – of 'life writing' as it has come to be known. The term was actually coined by Virginia Woolf to cover both biography and autobiography, 'the writing of the self'. As a discipline of creative and critical study at UEA, Life Writing was founded in 1999 by two brilliantly original and maverick dons, Lorna Sage and Janet Todd.

'Life writing has always been *suspect*,' Sage once said gleefully. 'There's always been an affinity between biography, autobiography and fiction. But so many people want to say "I was there" or "This is how it happened."'

However, Life Writing had a difficult launch at UEA. Todd moved to Glasgow in 2000 to take up another academic post. This departure was then followed by disaster. The same year the much-loved Sage published her autobiography *Bad Blood* and received wonderful reviews. She won the Whitbread Biography Prize in January 2001, then, at the moment of triumph, tragically, unbelievably, she died.

I attended her memorial celebration in April 2001. At the podium her friends, students and colleagues, openly tearful, told stories and recounted memories amid jokes. Lorna reading Cicero for breakfast; Lorna drinking too much gin; Lorna still supervising her students when she was too ill to stand. I noticed that every speaker used a carefully worded text with visual details and precise turns of phrase. It was a demonstration of Life Writing that Lorna would have been proud of.

At the reception afterwards I was surrounded by four of Lorna's mourning postgraduate students. Though evidently downcast by their loss, they soon turned to encouraging their new prof. 'We must discuss our dissertations,' they said bravely. 'Things must move on. *We must talk about lives.*'

Talk about lives, study lives, write lives. Could it be done? The popularity of the genre – with 3,500 new titles published each year – was not in dispute. Readers loved it, publishers valued it. But could it be taught? How would biography – 'the most delicate and the most humane of all the branches of the art of writing,' as Lytton Strachey once called it – survive the buckshot of postmodern jargon, the ideological damnations, the old historicism and the new reception theory, the whole terrible fiery shirt of abstract theory?

I'm exaggerating, of course. But many academics do still hate it. The author is dead, said Roland Barthes. Biography is bourgeois revisionism, said Professor Terry Eagleton. Biographers are flesh-eating bacilli, said Professor Germaine Greer. Even John Updike referred to biographies as 'just novels with indexes'. Even Samuel Johnson's friend, the learned Dr Arbuthnot, groaned that 'biography has added a new terror to death'. A generation ago the sceptics used to say: 'I studied at the university of life.' Today they would probably mockingly reverse the terms: 'I studied Life at the university.'

Well, could biography be taught? Over the past ten years I and my successor Kathryn Hughes, the shrewd biographer of George Eliot and Mrs Beeton, have striven at UEA to shape, out of our own creative practice, an academic subject. We have given it historical rigour, a textual canon for study, and a practical component of research and writing on individually selected topics. It is now fully established as an MA in Life Writing, with an accompanying creative-critical PhD programme.

These courses are shaped by three key ideas. First, that there is a great forgotten *tradition* of English biography waiting to be rediscovered: for example, Daniel Defoe on the heroic jail-breaker Jack Sheppard, Samuel Johnson on the sinister blackmailer poet Richard Savage, William Godwin on the first feminist Mary Wollstonecraft or Samuel Smiles on the great Victorian engineers.

Second, that an essential discipline is *comparative* biography, the critical comparison of several lives of the same subject, so we can see how a reputation emerges. We compare and contrast, in differences of fact, interpretation and tone, several lives of Lord Byron or Florence Nightingale or William Blake or the Brontë sisters, for example.

Third, that students are encouraged actually to *write* original biography, as well as biographical criticism. Here their subjects may be historical or quite contemporary: the Renaissance beauty Venetia Stanley (1600–33) or the feisty American singer Janis Joplin (1943–70) have both been the subjects of vivid studies. Crucially, we want our students to look outside themselves, to discover the world, to be practitioners as we ourselves are. 'Another place, another time, another identity' has become almost a motto. The MA course culminates in a 15,000-word piece of biographical writing; and in the case of PhDs (of whom a recent example is Lucasta Miller, author of *The Brontë Myth*), this can rise to 80,000 words, and the potential basis for a publishable book. Druin Burch's fine essay on John Keats and his medical supervisor Astley Cooper eventually became a notable scientific biography *Digging Up the Dead*, published by Chatto in 2007.

We happily acknowledge that – so far – UEA remains best known for its MA in Creative Writing (Fiction). But there are increasingly valuable exchanges between the two MAs: for instance, Mohammed Hanif studied on both programmes before writing his remarkable Booker longlisted novel *A Case of Exploding Mangoes* – partly inspired by a biographical essay on Plutarch's tyrants. As Updike's remarks above suggest, there are interesting tensions to explore between the two forms.

These were first revealed to me some years ago, long before I came to UEA, at that temple of adversarial truth the Law Society in London. In 1990 the lawyers and barristers arranged a debate on the various merits of fact versus fiction – in literature, rather than in court. The participants they summoned to the bar (both kinds) were novelists and biographers, defending and explaining the different aspects of their 'craft or sullen art'. Much lively evidence, both admissible and inadmissible, was introduced, culminating on a theological rather than legal note, when Anthony Burgess pronounced loudly through a dramatic cloud of cheroot smoke: 'You biographers may write the Bible – but *we novelists are God.*'

In my experience, biographers and novelists are not necessarily antagonists. We learn a lot from each other and many distinguished writers practise both forms: for example, Peter Ackroyd, Sebastian Faulks and A. N. Wilson in England; or Henri Troyat and Pierre Assouline in France. But it is true, as any bookseller will tell you, that during the 1980s and 1990s modern English biography in the hands of such scholar-artists as Michael Holroyd, Richard Ellmann or Hilary Spurling began to capture a general readership, once exclusively associated with the Fiction end of the shelves. And novelists, in turn, have become curiously fascinated with the figure of the biographer at work, as in Julian Barnes's brilliant parable of biographical misinterpretation, *Flaubert's Parrot*, or Antonia Byatt's superb Victorian saga of literary pursuit, *Possession* (which won the Booker), wherein the modern hero, heroine and villain are all more or less conscience-tortured biographers on the hazardous trail of human Truth.

So a kind of creative bargaining between the two forms is emerging, a questioning of methods and objectives, which is extremely interesting. As a participator in that Law Society debate (for the biographers) I had a few observations to offer, in a spirit of mild provocation, perhaps. There is, of course, a hard-line case against all literary biography, as a form of intrusive and unnecessary gossip. This pyrrhic position is marked by a long line of literary bonfires: the burning of Byron's journal, Dickens's letters or Larkin's diaries (shredded). It was summarised by William Faulkner, who said that biographies should consist of seven words: 'He wrote the novels and he died.'

Biographers would look at that sentence critically. To begin with, shouldn't it read: 'He (or she) wrote the novels and *he lived?*' But more than that: doesn't the whole fascination of biography lie precisely in that 'and', in the gap between the art and the life, in the difference between the 'he' who wrote and the 'he' who lived, and the light that one throws upon the other? This reply is stated with classical concision in Dr Johnson's great *Rambler* essay No. 60 on the enduring human value of biography, which all our students still read – I hope with fervour. James Boswell later took it as his guiding star for his epic *Life of Samuel Johnson Lld*, the work that truly launched literary biography in 1791.

In reality, I argued before the lawyers, good biography is less like gossip and more like justice. Novels are notoriously and brilliantly unfair to historical characters, and indeed few novelists would claim to do more than 'loosely base' their inventions on historical figures: the inner truth they seek is of an essentially unhistorical kind. Working for many years on Coleridge, I was haunted by the absurd, portly, comic, polymath caricature who booms and bounces through Thomas Love Peacock's novels, such as Mr Panascope, 'the chemical, botanical, geological, astronomical, galvanistical, musical, pictorial, bibliographical...philosopher'. I had to rescue Coleridge from that hypnotic mendacity.

Similarly, it took a remarkable biography by Claire Tomalin, a masterpiece of sympathetic detection, to rescue and bring back to life the figure of Ellen Ternan – Dickens's secret companion and mistress over many years. Previously, Ellen had only been granted a fictional half-life by Dickens (or Dickens's first biographer John Forster), disguised in the tender childlike beauty of Lucy Manette in *A Tale of Two Cities* or the cruel, taunting sexuality of Estella in *Great Expectations*. What Tomalin did so memorably was to grant Ellen Ternan justice.

What I am suggesting here is that the truth of biography is different from – not superior to – the truth of fiction. The two forms embody radically separate ways of investigating human nature. The novel is always ultimately an imaginative extension of the self, while the biography is an imaginative reaching out towards the other. The novelist has the final, absolute command over his creations, while the biographer works in subtle, historical subordination or dependence. It is a profound epistemological difference. Sylvia Plath once said that poetry was like a closed fist, while the novel was like an open hand. In this sense, biography seems to me like a handshake: a handshake extended through time, which can range in feeling from the subtlest caress, to the most exhausting kind of arm-wrestling. From Shelley to Stevenson, I have certainly experienced the full gamut of those biographical grips.

Novelists rightly argue that they can get inside their characters in ways forbidden to the biographer. Certainly the biographer is limited by his documentary sources, and even Lytton Strachey felt constrained to quote an authority for his description of Queen Victoria eating a soft-boiled egg for breakfast. As Desmond MacCarthy once said, 'the biographer is an artist upon oath'. But it is these limitations which provide the fascination and power of the form. The raw chronological data of a life can be composed into dramatic scenes, flashbacks or historical panoramas; extracts from letters can be worked like dialogue; and diaries and journals can provide the interior monologue of private thought and speculation.

Moreover, biography faces the challenge, curiously rare in modern fiction, of presenting the 'whole man or woman' in the perspective of an entire life. It continually asks that most pertinent question: how close can we really get to another person? How well do parents know children, husbands know wives, friends or lovers or simply work colleagues know each other? How well does the artist know himself or herself, and the forces that drive or inspire? Biography can also trace that most modern sense of multiplicity within personality, of all our self-contradictions and fragmentations. What novelist could present the supreme improbability of the author of *The Ancient Mariner* serving as a horse trooper in the Light Dragoons, and find the connection between the two?

Since that debate, over twenty years ago now, changes in biographical method have come and gone, along with accompanying but not entirely related patterns in publishing. The practice of 'narrative non-fiction' has provided a bridge between fiction and biography, and other new hybrid forms are emerging. As the current course description for the MA in Life Writing at UEA puts it: 'Biography is currently undergoing rapid change and reformation. Instead of the old "cradle to grave" narrative, our best writers are now experimenting with new forms and subjects. Group biographies, partial lives, and even lives told backwards are all part of the new and exciting mix.'

Over the same period, the creative and critical study of Life Writing in the academy – as undertaken at UEA and elsewhere – has grown enormously. The scholarly bibliographies for Life Writing were once wonderfully silent; now they are beginning to fill up fast. But there is still a sense in which biography remains blessedly free and untrammelled, compared to the roaring factory of academic criticism which resounds around fiction.

Perhaps what we were doing at the Law Society all those years ago was a legal or constitutional matter after all. We were making a modest declaration of independence, of imaginative autonomy, from the Old Empire of Fiction. As we ran up the flag and won the debate (but not the champagne), some of us could hear the distant chuckle of our patron saint, that sober Edinburgh citizen James Boswell, lawyer and biographer – and free spirit.

Richard Holmes (*b.* 1945) was Professor of Biographical Studies at UEA from 2001 to 2007. His many books include *Coleridge: Early Visions* (1989), which won the Whitbread Book of the Year Prize, and *Coleridge: Darker Reflections* (1998). His most recent work is *The Age of Wonder: How the Romantic Generation Discovered the Beauty and Terror of Science* (2008).

Revisiting The Novel Today

Malcolm Bradbury

What follows is Malcolm Bradbury's introduction to the 1990 edition of his anthology The Novel Today: Contemporary Writers on Modern Fiction, *which itself revisited the original 1977 edition. The later edition contained pieces by Iris Murdoch, Philip Roth, Michel Butor, Saul Bellow, John Barth, David Lodge, Frank Kermode, John Fowles, B. S. Johnson, Doris Lessing, Italo Calvino and an interview with Milan Kundera by Ian McEwan.* GF

Fiction writing, unlike reportage, eye-witness accounts or scientific descriptions, isn't trying to give information – it *constitutes* reality.
Alain Robbe-Grillet, *From Realism to Reality* (1955)

I began to write fiction on the assumption that the true enemies of the novel were plot, character, setting and theme, and, having once abandoned these familiar ways of thinking about fiction, totality of vision or structure was really all that remained. And structure – verbal and psychological coherence – is still my largest concern as a writer.
John Hawkes, in an interview (1965)

As I have pointed out before, characters are not born like people, of a woman; they are born of a situation, a sentence, a metaphor containing in a nutshell a basic human possibility that the author thinks no one else has discovered or said something essential about.
Milan Kundera, *The Unbearable Lightness of Being* (1984)

I

This is a new and changed edition of a book first published in 1977 – a collection of essays by or interviews with some of the most important contemporary novelists, British, American, European, who have commented seriously and well on both their own work and the situation of the novel today. Reprinted from various sources, the pieces represent, I believe, some of the most interesting opinions we can find on contemporary fiction. They are also concerned not just with the individual creativity of these writers, but the fact that in our age fiction has developed its own distinctive practices, its own climate, its own particular sense of direction. That, I think, has grown much more obvious to readers now than it was when this anthology was first compiled. In the last few years we have increasingly recognised the scale and achievement of contemporary fiction, and the fact that it does have its own clear character, in many ways different from the fiction of the past. The novel now has a flourishing appearance; after a period of appearing little more than commonplace, it has regained much of its stature and its artistic and intellectual interest. Many things have helped. There has been an increase in public discussion, major publishers have concentrated on it, and even the proliferation of literary prizes for fiction has done much to draw attention to contemporary talents. Perhaps, as readers, we are more prepared than a few years ago to acknowledge that we do have our own distinctive fictional tradition – a novel for our own age, the age after the Modern.

Collecting up the pieces for this book, I have assumed that there is always something inherently pleasurable and rewarding about hearing a good writer describe the stimuli, the direction and the nature of his or her creativity. Sometimes such accounts are fundamentally subjective, not surprisingly; fiction has its natural source in subjectivity. But it also depends on larger things – a broader conception of the task of the novel, of the writer's responsibility, the pressures of history on literary form, the need for the novel to discover both the world and the word anew. I find novelists at their most interesting and revealing when they are conscious that the writing of fiction is not only a psychological and aesthetic, but a social and historical, act. The novel has always been a provisional, self-questioning form; and its best practitioners have always seen part of their task as testing out the contemporary nature of the form they use. Novels are complex literary contracts made between the author and a life that becomes imaginatively real and powerful because it has passed through the public fact of a publication and a relation with its readers. They are forms of exploration, enquiring modes of knowledge, and as concepts become written words they become part of the fictional self-discovery of their own times. Like all knowledge, the novel changes with history and its own environment. It depends on its own relation to other discovering languages – those of science, philosophy, history, journalism, travel-writing, autobiography. It is altered by historical events and shifts in ideology and social and gender relations. At the same time it fights its own case for the fictional and discovering imagination amongst the ideas, the politics, the social emphases, the world views of its times. Styles transform; literary forms reshape and reorder; discovering fictions understand themselves in new ways and use new means. The novel may by now appear a traditional genre, but it is and always has been different in every age.

Indeed the word *novel* means new, and news. When in the seventeenth and eighteenth centuries the novel in Europe became a public literary genre – the 'burgher epic' – it was new indeed. From the start there was a question over its character: was it a predominantly realistic, reportorial genre, a form of biography, history and reportage, or was it essentially a form dedicated to its *own* discovery, a self-sceptical species of art? That double role remains with us, and throughout its recent history the novel has seemed to oscillate in its function. Sometimes it seems a more or less innocent affair, an instrument that expresses our delight in being told a human and familiar story, given important social or historical information, satisfied by the well-resolved plot, the engaging character, the happy ending. Sometimes it seems a radical grammar for exploring experience, consciousness, psychology, the fiction-making process itself. These two functions have always both consorted and contested with each other. In the nineteenth century much of the major fiction inclined toward the realistic, or what Henry James called 'solidity of specification'. In the early twentieth century much of it was predominantly experimental and self-questioning, a development that Henry James was also to celebrate. 'It has arrived, in truth, the novel, late at self-consciousness, but it has done its utmost ever since to make up for lost opportunities,' he wrote in an essay called 'The Future of Fiction', written exactly as the twentieth century came into existence. The self-consciousness James was pointing to marked the growing of a split between the novel as popular form or merchandise, and the novel as art. It also marked the emergence of a new experimental avant-garde, for whom the established traditions of art were over, the forms exhausted, and the age demanded something new. So there seemed to be an Old Novel, moral, realistic and bourgeois, and a New Novel, exploring the mythic and symbolic sources of fiction, its creative nature, and the gap between the word and the thing.

That change, that oscillation, has left us with two different codes for talking about the novel. One, coming from the aesthetics of realism, emphasises plot and character, setting and theme, denouement and discovery. The other comes from the new symbolist aesthetics of what came to be called the Modern Movement, and it emphasised other terms: myth, symbol, abstraction, angle of vision, point of view, stream of consciousness. The war was fought through several famous duels – between Henry James and H. G. Wells, Virginia Woolf and Arnold Bennett, Marcel Proust and Sainte-Beuve – and it represented a fundamental revolution, a Revolution of the Word, even a Death of the Novel. Certainly the Modern Novel, the New Novel, began to dispense with much of the novel's familiar realism and its dense and habitual sense of character and plot, setting and atmosphere, chronological and historical time. It probed deeper into consciousness, individual and collective, looked outward at a world that seemed less a clear material substance than a place of random time and chaotic history, and it pluralised awareness, multiplied perception, ironised narrative and looked directly into its own formal nature as art. It became an art of refined practitioners, and many of them – Conrad, Lawrence, Mann, Joyce, Proust, Stein, Svevo, Musil, Woolf, Faulkner, Hemingway, Gide, Kafka – still dominate our sense of the serious novel, our fictionalising imagination, today. Their work examines itself and discovers itself; their notebooks, diaries and essays, as well as their novels themselves, declare a new historical, aesthetic and creative intention. The novel, once thought of as a lower form, took on the character of a major literary genre, a true companion to poetry and drama.

With the modern novel there therefore came modern criticism. Henry James saw the great reappraisal as essentially an affair of practitioners, of novelists exploring and reflecting on the imaginary and imaginative worlds they sought to compose. But the growing critical movement, developing alongside the systematic study of literature, took to the study of the novel; and in time it came to seem that it was not what novelists said about it but what the critics said that constituted the only worthwhile or reliable interpretation. The critics saw a new art of estrangement and polyphony, explored what Mark Schorer called 'technique as discovery', and acknowledged the novel as a serious form of human investigation, the 'bright book of life'. They constructed the Great Traditions, wove lineages and inheritances, created complex theories of narratology, examined the nature of the text and the language of fiction. In time, they then deconstructed what they had constructed. In the process a speculative gap often began to appear between what the critics were perceiving and what contemporary novelists were actually doing; and the voice of novelists as makers and finders in their own medium began to grow smaller. It is therefore worth making the point that what modern critics and what novelists are there to do is different, though not unconnected. The critic's task is indeed to explore the history of genres, the nature of imaginative discourse, the conditions of artistic existence; it was also, once, to pursue standards of judgement, measures of seriousness, standards of taste. The novelist's business at best is to make himself or herself an exemplary creative citizen of a world which is still occurring and which needs to be named into existence, to invent the possibilities of an imaginary book in a universe that needs to find names for things. He or she works inside a convention that always has to be de-conventionalised in order to generate a new work authentic to the author and the contemporary occasion.

That is why, in an age remarkably dominated by criticism and literary theory, but not, alas, by a general aesthetic debate, it seems important to allow the author's voice to be heard in a book like this one. Selecting the pieces here, I have tried to think of them as important contributions to the practitioners' debate that, at best, should always surround the making of an art form. Such debate, of course, goes on inside the novel, in the pages of the works we read, as well as outside and around it. There are writers who prefer their books to be their own commentary, and there are writers who sometimes seem better at commentary than they are as writers. Nonetheless, somewhat muted by the prevalence of critical theory, there has been an important contemporary debate taking place among writers themselves. It has perhaps been most visible in France, where the novel is considered as a philosophical form, and in the United States, where writers have often had academic associations, and where in the 1960s and 1970s novelists like John Barth, William H. Gass and Raymond Federman did attempt some reconciliation between dominant critical ideas and their sense of contemporary literary practice. In France we heard of the *nouveau roman*, and in the United States of 'the literature of exhaustion', 'metafiction' and 'surfiction'. What these writers were very properly reaching for was the notion that we were living in a distinctive age of style, a time that the French writer Nathalie Sarraute called 'the era of suspicion' and American writers sometimes called 'postmodernism'. Whether the terms are useful can still be argued about, as we shall see. The important thing, one I have kept in mind in compiling this anthology, is that in the debate of any given era certain fundamental themes and directions do begin to emerge out of the continued variety, and that the novel in a particular period does begin to take on a distinctive historical character which audiences often take time to grasp.

II

The era of contemporary writing is still called the post-war era, though almost fifty years have now passed since the end of the Second World War and we are now approaching the end of the twentieth century or the second millennium. The forty years before that war largely made up the period in which the modern literary revolution was conducted, and it went through many movements, many phases, many reverses and upsets, as well as coming from many sources and many different nationalities. With the Second World War, that era and its literary revolution seemed to be over, and after it a shattered world had to reshape itself. Because it seemed over, the Modern Movement now began to acquire a certain clarity and shape, and the several generations of major novelists whose work had developed then took on a central position and a power over our imaginations that still continues. The post-war period has not assumed the same clarity, even though, I believe, it will prove to have a similar scale of achievement. This is partly because we consider that we still live in it, and it has the disorder of the contemporary, partly because it is not distinguished by a sense of radical revolution, and partly because its achievement has been generally more various.

So it is hard to take a general view of an age that contains the wide variety of directions we find in it. It reaches, for example, from the existentialist minimalism of Samuel Beckett and the fictions of Jorge Luis Borges, preoccupied with the status of imaginary acts and the relation between the orders of the mind and those of the universe, to the fragile, imagined worlds of Vladimir Nabokov, unrooted from conventional reality, rich in fictionality, shimmering with a potential symbolism. It spreads from the tight, object-centred, anti-anthropomorphic economy of French *nouveaux romanciers* like Michel Butor, Alain Robbe-Grillet and Nathalie Sarraute to the often contingent but always romantically vivid and highly staged world of Iris Murdoch, and to the flamboyance of Patrick White or the surreal expressionism of Günter Grass. It ranges from the attempts of John Barth to recover a literature of replenishment from an era of literary exhaustion, by modernising the narrative stock bequeathed us by great narratives like *The Thousand and One Nights* or Greek legend, to the cybernetic novels of Thomas Pynchon or William Gaddis, where the characters become comic units swamped in a technological world coded with arbitrary plots. It includes the hard, ironic black comedy of Muriel Spark and the romantic existentialism of John Fowles and the galactic fantasy of Doris Lessing. It takes in the combinatorial games of Italo Calvino and the rich storytelling invention and 'magic realism' of writers like Gabriel García Márquez and Salman Rushdie; the black feminist novel of Toni Morrison and the feminist fantasy of Angela Carter.

Indeed, the contemporary novel is now a very broad community indeed, one which includes amongst its important citizens Max Frisch and Thomas Bernhard, Christa Wolf,

Peter Handke and Patrick Süskind, Saul Bellow, Philip Roth, Norman Mailer and John Updike, Eudora Welty, William Burroughs and Richard Brautigan, Muriel Spark, Ian McEwan and B. S. Johnson, Claude Simon, Philippe Sollers, Michel Tournier, Milan Kundera, Vladimir Voinovich and Georges Perec – the list can go on and on. As our international sightlines widen, as our sense of each new generation deepens, we are constantly finding significant and central names to add to it, and that increases our sense of variety and plenitude.

Our modern writing comes out of a world that in some post-war nations saw a climate of victory, in others defeat, in others a bitter legacy of occupation. It also comes from a world divided into two camps and from a time when political fortunes and allegiances among writers have been varied, political pressures and punishments different. It comes, too, from a world that has grown larger, and many of our most interesting writers come from post-colonial nations, from countries like Canada and Australia, and from Africa and South America. It arises too from a changed world of gender relations which has seen the rise of a new and international tradition of feminist writing that has challenged the myths and prototypes of the fictional tradition. It is inevitably hard to identify broad trends, though I think there are a few markers that might give us some sense of the directions and eddies that have shaped the general pattern of contemporary novel writing.

So in the 1950s it appeared that the movement of Modernism was over, and that the novel was now returning towards a more traditional and realistic view of fiction, pressed perhaps by the immensity of recent history and the strong sense of social change. In France we saw the existential novel; in Britain an attempt to return to the line of eighteenth- and nineteenth-century fiction; in Germany the work of writers like Heinrich Böll who were attempting to give a more honest record of recent events; in America the moral realism of Jewish-American fiction.

In the 1960s, when the powerful impact of writers like Beckett, Borges and Nabokov, who had extended many of the experimental possibilities of Modernism, became clear, matters looked different. The movement now seemed to be away from realism and towards what came to be called 'metafiction' – a kind of novel that emphasised its own fictionality and its self-begetting character. There was the impact of the French *nouveau roman* as it had developed during the 1950s, emphasising the lexical nature of the text and foregrounding certain elements in it, states of mind, objects of description; there was the impact of the Nabokovian view of the fictional process as a parody of form, a game-like construct in which the very relationship of author to text, character to language, book to reader becomes volatile, so that the novel becomes an instrument whereby any one of its elements can be teased, given or not given significance, created or de-created. Reality, as Nabokov said, was now 'in quotes', and this applied to all forms of writing – even history-writing, journalism or biography.

By the 1970s there was a sophisticated reversion back to a concern with the onerous pressure of history and the real, and a reconciliation was found in 'magic realism', which had its chief origins in South American fiction and interwove the legendary and the historical in a way that began to appeal to writers generally. By the 1980s there was much talk of 'dirty realism', a self-conscious, hyper-detailed form of writing especially associated with American writers like Raymond Carver and Richard Ford.

This all suggests the continuing importance of that oscillation I mentioned at the beginning between two views of the novel, one as a report on history and the social and moral world, the other of it as a self-conscious and self-discovering fiction. As Iris Murdoch says in her important essay of 1961, 'Against Dryness', reprinted here, the novel has repeatedly been drawn between the 'journalistic' impulse, which tends to make it contingent and formless, and the 'crystalline', which tends to lead it toward the 'dry' consolations of form, and make it into a small, quasi-allegorical object. These terms do roughly equate with the spirit of nineteenth-century realism and the spirit of twentieth-century modernism, and Murdoch suggests that today writers lie in the shadow of both, attempting in a changed world, with a different imagination of the self, to do something new. It is a theme often referred to in these essays, for instance by David Lodge in his piece 'The Novelist at the Crossroads', where he considers the challenge to realism and the growing stress on the 'fictiveness' of fiction, and the relation between fictional structures and those we meet in journalism, autobiography and history-writing.

It is worth remarking that, of course, realism can be a form of radical experimentalism, as it was in the nineteenth century in the fiction of Flaubert and Dickens, George Eliot and the early Henry James. Similarly, experimental novels are concerned with exploring and discovering, if not directly depicting, a reality, even if it is Nabokov's reality 'in quotes'. 'I presume that the movement of fiction should always be in the direction of what we sense as real,' observes one 'postmodern' American writer, Ronald Sukenick, who calls one of his books, with appropriate paradox, *The Death of the Novel and Other Stories* (1969). 'Its forms are expendable. The novelist accommodates the ongoing flow of experience, smashing anything that impedes him in his sense of it, even if it happens to be the novel.'

In the previous edition of this book, I made much of the emphasis on 'fictionality'. The argument seemed particularly necessary then because, in Britain at least, there did seem to be a tradition of obstinate and often provincialised realism which limited the invention of the novel and discouraged British readers from taking fair account of major developments that were clearly taking place elsewhere. In fact the break was coming already, in the work of writers like Muriel Spark, Iris Murdoch, Anthony Burgess, Doris Lessing, Angus Wilson and John Fowles, many of them represented here. And by that time we were already seeing the emergence of a striking new generation of writers in Britain – as various as Angela Carter, Ian McEwan, Martin Amis, Julian Barnes, Bruce Chatwin, Graham Swift and Salman Rushdie – who had broken away from the provincialising spirit of much post-war British fiction. That general widening of horizons has led to a much more expansive and interesting discussion of the novel, and a much wider awareness of its general international character. Today many novelists seem impatient with the inherited codes both of realism and modernism. 'The characters in my novels are my own unrealised possibilities,' writes Milan Kundera in *The Unbearable Lightness of Being* (1984). 'That is why I am equally fond of them all and equally horrified by them. Each one has crossed a border that I myself have circumvented. It is that crossed border (the border beyond which my own "I" ends) which attracts me most. For beyond that border begins the secret the novel asks about. The novel is not the author's confession; it is an investigation of human life in the trap the world has become.'

Perhaps the common theme of the essays I have chosen for this book is that they are in their different ways about reaching for those unrealised possibilities of investigating human life in the trap the world has become. Kundera explains that his own novels are not born, like a child, out of life, but out of 'a situation, a sentence, a metaphor containing in a nutshell a basic human possibility that the author thinks no one else has discovered or said something essential about'. His books, then, are born out of experience and language, and they are endeavours to create a portrait of a reality that is human and has not been finalised, in a history that is not – as it might be for ideologues or politicians – a finished picture. They are both fictional and true, fantastic and realistic, and they relate to the many fictions that surround us, while becoming a discovering fiction of their own, perhaps more elusive and teasing, made, as he says, of laughter and forgetting. It is a creative, elusive view of the novel, and it perhaps explains why it seems no longer easy to fix on some distinctive contemporary movement or tendency, or treat contemporary writers with a firm critical finality. Perhaps that is why it is better not to seek a critical finality, but to listen to the writers themselves and hear what they have to say.

Malcolm Bradbury (1932–2000) was Professor of American Studies at UEA and co-founded the MA in Creative Writing. He was awarded both a CBE and a knighthood for his services to literature, across novel writing, criticism, screenwriting, journalism and education. The full range of his activities in these fields is described at www.malcolmbradbury.com.

The Fault Lines of Fiction

Lorna Sage

In 1993 Lorna Sage was asked by the Observer *to report on the state of fiction, 'following its fault lines and singing its praises'. She seems to have found mostly fault.* GF

More people in this country are writing fiction than ever before, an awful lot of them are getting published, and yet the literary pages this spring have been complaining more plangently than ever that there's a dreadful dearth of new British talent. Green shoots of recovery? Well, not in the novel, apparently, where we don't make anything any more, and imports dominate the (shrinking) market.

Literary editors look back with sad nostalgia to the days when Martin Amis was truly young and giving offence (remember *Dead Babies?*) and they knew where they were. On the other hand, it may just be that the seed is falling on stony ground and deaf ears in the review pages. One of the provocations to debate has been the *Granta*/Waterstone's promotion of the 'Best of Young British', but the disease has deeper roots. It's not just, as some think, that growing up with parents who wore flares mysteriously diminished your daemon.

The roots problem is one of several. The list goes something like this:

1. *The Tradition.* There isn't an ancestral 'tree' to climb, a tradition of what it means to be a British writer. That was lost (depending on your view) with Modernist internationalism, the generation of Lawrence, Joyce, Woolf, or petered out with Evelyn Waugh and Ivy Compton Burnett, or died with Amis, Wain, Brain, etc. (and Larkin, who was nearly a novelist, after all) in the post-war years, in self-parodying parochialism.

2. *Multiculturalism.* In the same post-war period Britain became 'a salad of racial genes' (to pinch a phrase from Nabokov, that grandest of literary refugees), and many British writers became citizens of elsewhere (Anthony Burgess, Muriel Spark, John Berger). One of the results of this is that some of the best descriptions of British life and the end of Empire came from writers like Kazuo Ishiguro, Timothy Mo, Salman Rushdie and Michael Ondaatje. Though there are aliens still 'at home' like J. G. Ballard, doing the job brilliantly, too.

3. *The Language.* The rows in schools about standard English are one sign of the fissile state of the language. And its 'world' Esperanto role has the odd effect of perpetuating grandiose expectations (a ghostly Word Empire) or, to put it more precisely, we're always tempted to see ourselves in the American context. The language is huge, the local culture diminished and divided.

4. *Europe v. America.* Where are our affiliations? Both places, seemingly another problem.

If we compare our fiction-economy with that of Italy or Germany or France we're doing pretty well. But we don't know that because we don't read enough fiction in translation, and because we're under the illusion that we are honorary Americans.

5. *Writing v. Reading.* We write too much, don't read enough. We encourage low-level 'creativity' at the expense of learning to pay attention, describe, criticise, etc. This seems to me true at all levels of education, but then it would, since I teach literature, and spend my life reading it and trying to write about it.

6. *The novel is anybody's.* The modern novel evolved along with the modern European nation state, the epic of nineteenth-century bourgeois life. So for a long time, unsurprisingly, it's been losing its definition, its sense of its own form, edges and identity. One sign of this is that writing a novel has become part of being a celebrity (cf. Stephen Fry, Clive James, Julie Burchill). This probably does more harm to perceptions of what a novel is than all the deconstructionist experiments of the avant garde put together.

7. *The Attention-Famine.* As a cumulative result of the above, and with dire effect among young reviewers and especially those who have novel-writing ambitions themselves (which sometimes seems to mean nearly everybody), new books and new writers have to battle for attention and often only get any through prizes and promotions, when they are required to represent all the others who didn't win, not to mention all those who (increasingly) don't write or read but express themselves otherwise. (Hanif Kureishi: 'You can't dance to fiction.')

Seven is a magic number, and that will do.

There seem to be two main ways for us to respond to this literary identity crisis. One is simply to cut out the whole distracting range of alien voices and other peoples' experience, real and imagined. The other is to take them on, and if writers do that or part of it then they're probably not going to do it very convincingly when they're still 'young'. Nor are readers, unless we start turning them out more precociously addicted than we do at the moment.

It would help if schools and universities promulgated some kind of post-war canon that would create common ground to argue over. The set texts. For instance: Angela Carter's *Wise Children* deals with most of these issues with brilliance, maturity, hilarity and inventiveness.

Another of our problems is that we still don't read women writers with attention, partly because they've seldom fitted in with the 'portrait of the artist' formula that makes, for instance, the *Guardian*'s James Wood so obsessed with the likes of American Harold Brodkey, who published his book of adolescent ambition (*Runaway Soul*) at sixty. The Oedipal pattern, the father-son relay race, still dominates all too many of the current hand-wringings about heirs and successors.

The real trick for any British writer is the one that Carter pulled off, to be local, an insider, and an inhabitant of the country of the past, and a mental traveller. Few manage so much. Nor did they in the good old days.

In 1960, when I was definitely young (seventeen) I made a vow not to read any more contemporary British fiction, which seemed to consist of 'angry young men' banging on the door of a club (with room at the top) I could anyway never join. (Amis, Braine, Wain, etc.) Instead I opted for the Irish, who knew what it was to be gratuitous and stylish and outside.

Nonetheless, I found myself, in the very last stages of pregnancy, being read to by my equally juvenile and equally delinquent husband. John Wain's *Hurry on Down* it was, I remember well, and I laughed so much I had to confess to labour pains, and go to hospital, though I'd meant to cheat the system and have my daughter under a laurel bush. The moral of this anecdote is that principles should always be compromised. And that the dissatisfaction with where you are is, at least now, and for several generations past, essential to being British. Our problem has to become our springboard.

Lorna Sage (1943–2001) was Professor of English Literature at the University of East Anglia. She wrote a classic of autobiography, *Bad Blood* (2000), and was a frequent contributor on literary topics to newspapers and journals, from *Marxism Today* to the *New York Times*. Her critical books include *Women in the House of Fiction* (1992), *The Cambridge Guide to Women's Writing in English* (1999) and *Moments of Truth: Twelve Twentieth-Century Women Writers* (2001).

Professional

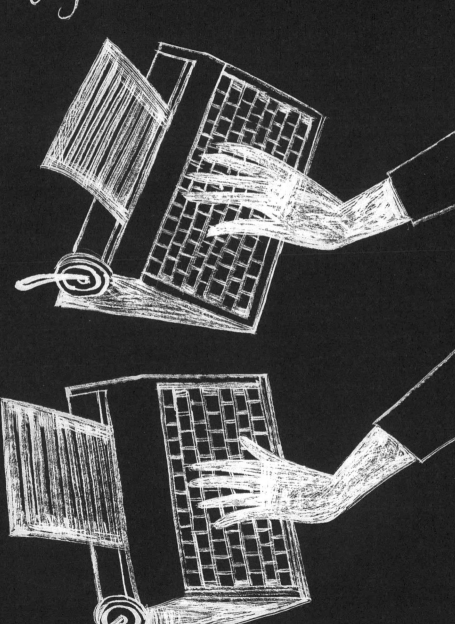

Trials of a Booker Judge (1983)

Angela Carter

What follows was first published in New Society *magazine on October 20, 1983. It was later republished in Carter's collection* Shaking a Leg: Journalism and Writings *(Chatto & Windus, 1997).* GF

Both *Private Eye* and *City Limits,* from their different corners, find the novels shortlisted for this year's Booker McConnell prize 'unsurprising' and 'uninspiring', respectively. This seems a bit unfair. At least two of the shortlist items – John Fuller's metaphysical jeu d'esprit about dissection and putrefaction, *Flying to Nowhere,* and that epic of anal penetration and heresy in the first century ad, *The illusionist* by Anita Mason, are as unlikely contenders for Britain's premier literary prize, going on that prize's past form, as may be.

Past form, of course; but not its present form. Indeed, this year's Booker shortlist might suggest the eccentric had become the norm in British publishing. It comprises, also, an epic, didactic fairytale, *Shame,* by Salman Rushdie, who won in 1981 and is eligible to enter again, and to win again, if necessary, because whoever drafted the rules in the first place did not have sufficient faith in Britain's literary capacity to entertain the notion that somebody might write two – or, dammit, more than two – good novels in the course of their lifetime. Or perhaps nobody remembered that giants such as Joseph Conrad, D. H. Lawrence and John Galsworthy – all potential prizewinners, especially the last-named – ever existed.

There is an exercise in imaginary linguistics, *Rates of Exchange* by Malcolm Bradbury; J. M. Coetzee's South African political allegory, *The Life and Times of Malcolm K;* and an epic, didactic novel about adolescent sexuality, the life cycle of the eel, and British social history, *Waterland* by Graham Swift. Unsurprising, uninspiring it might be, but the *Sunday Times* called it 'highbrow', as if with faint surprise.

But of course, the odd has *not* become the norm. It is simply that, over the last three or four years, the odd has become visible, even if those which were odd before the tip of the iceberg emerged are still, Booker-wise, in limbo. Two of the very oddest fiction writers eligible by nationality for the prize, Wilson Harris and J. G. Ballard, remain in the proud position of Most Eminent Figures never to have made it on to a Booker shortlist.

However, out of the hundred or so submissions this year – dear God! A *hundred!* – a significant number were not in the least odd in any way, because people neither levitated in them nor had *verismo* abortions on kitchen tables in them. (If magic realism is coming up, then social realism appears to have vanished virtually without trace.) There remained a sterling residue of novels of personal experience divorced from public context, the fiction of a middle class apparently reassessing experimental territory in which it feels newly secure.

The housing estate downwind may pong a bit, kids at university sometimes pick up the Wrong Type, a bogeyman or woman may lurch up from the lower orders now and then to give us all a nasty shock but, in this fiction, nobody ever needs to worry about the price of butter. These neo-middle-class novels bear no relation whatsoever to the 'adultery in NW3' novel. Writers of fiction would appear, on this showing, to have been mostly priced out of Hampstead, leaving it to Arabs and media personalities who often have better things to do with their time. In fact, there is no particular location for these scenarios. Events take place indifferently in the Home Counties and London suburbia. If the latter, the area is often newly gentrified, an interesting sociological touch.

The only way of characterising this kind of novel is to call it a typical *library book*. You read it to pass the time but you wouldn't dream of buying it; and what passes my understanding is how a halfway competent publisher's editor can say to him or herself about such a book: 'This is indeed worthy of winning ten tax-free grand in hand, plus publicity and prestige galore; everybody should read it and the world must have it whether it wants it or not!' And pack-a-bag it off, rejoicing in the richness of distilled experience the Booker judges will be about to relish. Because surely, if the prize is to mean anything, that is how anyone who submits a novel should feel.

Now what I've given you here is a vast, parodic generalisation. There was a lot more going on among the submissions than that, even novels about the civil war in Northern Ireland (one out of more than 100), about Zimbabwe's independence (one out of more than 100) and at least two dealt either directly or obliquely with the nuclear menace. There were novels about old folks and working-class childhoods and much more.

However, among a widely disparate spread of themes, the 'library book' novel – and some of them are very skilfully written indeed, almost worth keeping – asserted itself as a definite genre. It can usually, though not always, be identified by the presence of a charlady among the minor characters. Not a continental au-pair; she's disappeared from middle-class mythology. But an authentic throwback, your proper old-fashioned charlady.

All kinds of charladies. The traditional, comic charlady, no less amusing for nowadays taking her holidays in Spain. Charladies present but invisible, like the servants in Jane Austen, keeping the narrative going by ensuring the characters don't have to stop emoting every few minutes to wash up. Memorably, a mystic charlady given to visions of the Blessed Virgin Mary – the charlady as holy fool. These charladies are sometimes dignified with the title 'housekeeper', but they carry on behaving like chars from the good old days; and there was a notable absence of any novel done from the charlady's point of view, though it would seem an excellent method by which to approach in a fresh light the bitter-sweet tragic-comedy of middle-class life.

There is a fictional subtext underwriting the much-vaunted renaissance of British fiction and it is to do with as-you-were. The collective profile of the entrants remains predominantly WASP, in spite of Salman Rushdie.

As a Booker judge, I'd confidently expected all manner of good things to happen between the day the season opened in June and shortlist selection day in September. Fat lunches from publishers, perhaps; bottles of bubbly delivered in plain wrappers; flattery and sycophancy on all sides. Not on your life. This *is* Britain. The only unsolicited gift that arrived took the form of a package containing yet *more* books from a publisher who must remain nameless, lest that name become mud – books *in addition* to the ones this publisher had already submitted, sent, not for the competition, obviously, but to me, personally, as a freelance lover of literature. This package coincided with the peak period towards the end of August, when fiction was arriving at the house by the crateful. I leafed through the offerings it contained to check if there were any tenners slipped among the pages, but no such luck.

Then tales began to filter through to me of hysterical scenes in publishers' offices as writers begged and pleaded on their knees to be submitted for the Booker. A certain literary agent is said to have inserted a clause in a certain writer's contract to the effect that publication of the said writer's novel be contingent on Booker submission of that work.

I'm sure the hysteria surrounding the Goncourt is just as bad, if not worse. But the Goncourt has been around for a long time and, besides, hysteria characterises the daily life of the French intellectual at the best of times. Further, the French, or at least the Parisians are, as is well known, a booksy lot. The British, not.

Or – are the British turning into a booksy lot, under the influence of a literary prize promoted as if it were a sporting event?

Of course, the name 'Booker McConnell' helps. The 'Booker', for short. With the built-in word 'book' as a mnemonic as to what the prize is for and a suggestion, too, that one should visit Ladbroke's and place one's bet now. Nevertheless, the evidence, piling up over the years since 1969, when the first prize was awarded (no bullseye that; an unmemorable novel by P. H. Newby), suggests the existence in Britain of a market for fiction that only needs to be told what to buy in order to activate itself.

That sounds cynical. It isn't meant to be. The existence of this market implies the existence of an appetite. And so many novels are published these days it's hard to find your way among the maze of even those reviewed. It is also quite difficult to *buy* hardback fiction and the Booker business ensures that the shortlist at least achieves a very wide distribution.

After that false start, the then Booker judges struck gold in 1972 and 1973 with two of the best novels published here since the end of the war – John Berger's *G* and J. G. Farrell's *The Siege of Krishnapur*. Both were guaranteed to cause a degree of bewilderment, for different reasons. The attitudes of both these writers to the prize evidently caused offence. It seemed the prize was on its way.

But after that, for a long period, the judges seemed to take collective fright and award the prize for the Most Inoffensive Novel of the Year and no excitement accrued therefrom. The prize money went up from £5,000 to £10,000 – though this scarcely keeps pace with inflation; £5,000 in 1969 was worth a lot more than £10,000 is today. It is only since 1980, when William Golding won it, that the prize began to acquire a general audience and the Booker shortlist of five or six novels started to turn into an annual checklist for busy people of what is going on in the world o' books.

There remains the problem of what the Booker McConnell prize is actually given *for*. Is it for the Book of the Year, plus a handful of highly commendeds, like an Oscar? Or ought it to be the reward for a lifetime's contribution to culture – in which case, what then is the status of the shortlistees, poor things? If the judges increasingly opt for the former, they could easily oscillate to the latter view this year, next year…Iris Murdoch presumably won it for a body of work, since it can't have been *The Sea, The Sea*; Doris Lessing ought to. So should Anthony Burgess. (No surprises? No surprises. But that isn't the point of this sort of prize!)

The judges could do that, could change the entire nature of the prize and the direction in which it is taking the readers of Britain, because the judges change every year themselves. This year, Fay Weldon, chairperson; Peter Porter, Terence Kilmartin, Libby Purves, me. A certain bias towards booksiness, here – two novelists, a poet, a literary editor (and translator of Proust), a highly literate journalist.

Next year, it might be – who can tell?

But who the actual team of judges comprises isn't really the point. What matters, what affects the whole nature of the prize and the kind of writing it helps to promote, is the fact this team isn't stable.

If the team of judges, any team, were given a fair run of, say, three years, it would be possible for them to define the scope of the Booker prize, to continue to open up the crack it has willy-nilly inserted in the traditional philistinism of the British and help to start some kind of discussion as to what a novel is supposed to do in the general scheme of things. (Apart from making money, of course.)

The Booker is fun, already, a kind of football pools for publishers and writers. The hype and the hysteria and the vulgarity are all part of the process that has actually made the general public aware of it; so one can't knock them. But the prize could, and should, do rather more than it does now to help, not readers, but publishers, discriminate among their own wares.

Angela Carter (1940–92) taught on the Creative Writing course at UEA from 1980–1988. Her fiction included *The Infernal Desire Machines of Doctor Hoffman* (1972), *The Bloody Chamber* (1979), *Nights at the Circus* (1984) and *Wise Children* (1991). She also edited *Wayward Girls and Wicked Women: An Anthology of Subversive Stories* (1986) and a number of other books. In 2008 *The Times* named her as one of the fifty greatest British writers since 1945.

Turning to Crime

Henry Sutton

'Crime pays' has long been the adage within the publishing world. Check out the bestseller lists and you'll soon see why. Yet writing good crime fiction (and within that broad arena we can consider and incorporate all manner of sub-genres from the police procedural to the high-impact, high-action thriller, from the logistical to the psychological, even to the physiological) is really not very easy, and certainly not at all simply formulaic, despite an abundance of preconceptions.

What's more, crime fiction (broadly) can be as literary and certainly as urgent and relevant as so-called literary fiction. Labels, in a way, only serve to get in the way. And yet labels will persist, especially when it comes to crime and genre fiction, even though, arguably, literary fiction has become a genre all of its own. It's not just the publishers' and marketers' fault, or the teachers' and writers' fault, for that matter, but a greater need, I believe, when it comes to fictional narratives or 'fictions', if you like, for the reader and actually the writer to have some idea of not just positioning, but what to expect (and where to go) – down that mean street, as Raymond Chandler would have it (*The Simple Art of Murder*, 1950), or into, as E. M. Forster liked to think, some part-mystical realm where lies the heart of literary creation (*Aspects of the Novel*, 1927).

But busting boundaries and preconceptions and certainly genres is where the real business or art of real writing should, of course, actually lie, however bloody or dirty you get. My own writing (and my teaching) has become increasingly concerned with this (thorny/barded/spiked/loaded – you name it) issue. It began almost imperceptibly, though markedly: my long, slow shift from soft, provincial (albeit dysfunctional) countryside and manners, to harsh, unreliable, metropolitan neuroses (possibly psychopathy). Frankly, my fictional body count started to build well before I realised my work could possibly be described as crime fiction. Indeed, it wasn't until a review of one of my novels appeared in a crime and thriller round-up that I had any idea I might have actually slipped into a (Patricia) Highsmithian dark side.

What indeed this might mean, however, has become something like a cause, or at least a question, I find I'm continually addressing to not just my work, or the work of my students, but almost everything I read. Actually, and for what it's worth, I think I'm a (broadly) literary writer, interested in aspects (primarily psychological) of crime, though also and conceivably and in contradiction very much humour and satire, too, and so on. What really still turns me on as a writer, reader and teacher, is the sentence, how it's been constructed, where it falls, what it says. And then on and out from there – how a narrative, a world is created, and under what urgency and vitality, and dare I say uniqueness.

However, while labels and subgenres exist and indeed continue to be created, it's always helpful to cast about for like-minded souls, or commentary that might aid or at least abut my/your cause (which is really a question, the key question to me, and one that's wholly bound up with intent, though intent being subtly different from positioning). Of course this topic, the literary/genre divide, has been debated one way or another forever. What gives it any more currency right now is the fact that (so-labelled) crime and thriller fiction is so staggeringly popular, with sales in the UK alone up by 80 per cent over the last ten years, while general fiction has recently started to slide.

Lee Child, the UK's most successful crime and thriller writer, with worldwide sales of over forty million for his Jack Reacher novels, is particularly vocal on the great rift (as he sees it), perhaps exhibiting a certain amount of not bravado, but actually insecurity on his part. 'To have us judged by the literary establishment, is like a dog being judged by a flea,' he's said. 'We're doing our thing and they are doing their thing – ours is very big and theirs is very small. They [literary writers] know that we could write their books, but they can't write ours.' Is Child really suggesting that literary writers are stuck in a limbo of self-indulgent freedom, while genre/crime writers have other, more immediate and approachable concerns, not to mention acute literary talent? Maybe. Certainly he believes, as he's stated more than once, that literary writers don't get 'what it takes to create suspense and evolve a story, with a non-stop, seamless narration'.

And yet good crime writing, good genre writing, like all good writing, isn't just about non-stop, seamless narration. Shouldn't be. Can't be.

What seems to rankle both literary and genre writers most is the idea that neither can change their approach, their intent, and that they're somehow stuck with what they were born to do, and that one (usually, canonically the literary) form is more important than the other. As E. M. Forster famously said (in that book), 'There is no rule relating to the novel which a genius can't circumvent…The process of creation remains mysterious.' In other words there's this unquantifiable abstract governing ultimate literary endeavour, while genre narratives are more 'formulaic', relying on rules and givens.

Perhaps surprisingly (though not if you know him), from the literary corner, we have crime champion John Banville, who's not too taken with much literary fiction nowadays. He believes it to be weak, that the novel here and in Europe is in the 'doldrums'. 'The modernist experiment is over,' he's claimed. But what excites him is crime fiction – something he himself has turned to under the pen name Benjamin Black. While he argues that an important novel has to be about life, not just language, he also believes that the current popularity of the crime novel has a lot to do with the reassertion and enjoyment of the traditional literary values of plot, character and dialogue.

Perversely, crassly even, others might argue it's to do with a portrayal of ever more graphic violence coupled with a ravaged sensibility – that we actually get off on this stuff, as it's a little more extreme and thrilling than our daily lives. There's no doubt that many leading crime and thriller titles are extraordinarily violent. Do we really live in such violent times? Can these works at all be considered some sort of social barometer? Important even, beyond any literary context?

It has been said that a crime novel has to have a crime in it, but just because a novel has a crime in it doesn't mean it's a crime novel, and that what it comes down to is craftsmanship, and particularly now making the crimes life-like. In other words, there has to be an authenticity to the action, the place and the time. But, to me, this should be no less important for a non-crime orientated, realist 'literary' novel. Realism might be the ultimate point. For me, a loather of anything purporting to be magic realism, anyway.

Interestingly, and stretching the point of realism, there is a key difference between 'literary' true crime and 'literary' (or any other for that matter) crime fiction. Fiction, of whatever register, necessitates a moral stance and organisation, or if you like artistry. And that it, therefore, should somehow always aim to rise above the purely factual, purely graphic fray. As Martin Amis once memorably wrote (in *The Moronic Inferno*, 1986): 'Facts cannot be arranged to give them moral point. There can be no art without moral point. Otherwise, when the reading experience is over, you are left, simply, with murder – and with the human messiness and futility that attends all death.' He was specifically arguing against the literary merit of true-life crime stories, or narrative non-fiction, as produced so memorably by Truman Capote (*In Cold Blood*, 1965) and Norman Mailer (*The Executioner's Song*, 1980). In a not dissimilar vein, you could argue that the literary merit of any overly violent fiction is compromised by the shear tedious fact that it's simply there to remind us of mankind's infinite capacity for brutality and sadism, and our horrible appetite for lapping it up.

Good crime fiction and extreme violence most definitely need not go hand in hand, however you want to use a moral point or a moral compass (if you like) to drive the narrative, and wherever, indeed, you want to place some notion of redemption (an old ally of the 'genre'). For good crime fiction – and perhaps this is where a literary distinction or analogy might arise (though shouldn't in my realist mind) – to be ultimately effective, it simply has to ring true, with the authenticity of intent more important than any accuracy of procedure or description (it's fiction, after all). A good novel (in my mind), and here comes the literary vs genre question, is about life not just language, however the crime's positioned. A good novel, of any form and true intent, also requires exquisite craftsmanship.

Dorothy L. Sayers notoriously wrote in the introduction to her first *Omnibus of Crime* (1929), that the detective story 'does not and by hypothesis never can attain the loftiest level of literary achievement'. She went on to say that this was because it was a 'literature of escape' and not a 'literature of expression'. This outraged Raymond Chandler for one, who always championed the need to depict life in all its messiness. 'Everything written with vitality expresses that vitality – there are no dull subjects, only dull minds,' he wrote in 'The Simple Art of Murder'.

Interestingly, pertinently, agelessly he went on to talk about man's need to escape reality every so often: 'Everyone must escape at times from the deadly rhythm of their private thoughts. It is part of the process of life among thinking beings.' Chandler believed, not solely in the detective story by any means, but that all reading, for pleasure, is a form of escape.

What Chandler hated most about detective (or genre) fiction was how so many authors, Agatha Christie being a prime example, tried to impose such artificial patterns and wooden characters on the plot. For him realism (or life) starting with dialogue was key. He never forgot that most murders were unplanned, often random, and were indicative of a certain flavour of life (and death) found in a certain neighbourhood. He never forgot, too, the victim, and that murder is an act of infinite cruelty. And that solving it is no parlour game, conducted by a fop called Lord Peter Wimsey (Dorothy L. Sayers' long-serving sleuth). For Chandler (and me I began to realise, the more I looked into a genre I'd suddenly been associated with) the formal or classic mystery that poses a formal or exact problem around which neatly labelled clues are arranged, couldn't be more removed from reality and the beating heart of what makes a murder, a crime story really lift off the page.

What's more Chandler was quite categorical about one other thing: 'Brutality is not strength,' he proclaimed. He never once relied on cheap, graphic gore. He was interested primarily in investigating human conflict. The significance of his work and the significance of all decent crime fictions rely on the fact that, as he put it, quite possibly the tensions in a novel of murder are the simplest and yet most complete of the tensions on which we live in this generation – or, one could add, any generation.

Though for these crime stories to be believably escapist, to contain any true significance, and thus real power and depth (and we can incorporate literary worth in here if we want, and I do manifestly, believing that that ultimately comes from not just language but life and how you capture it), there has to be a brilliantly observed and understood sense of reality.

Well-conceived and well-executed and wrongly (in my mind) labelled escapist or for that matter genre fiction (like all serious fictional narratives) doesn't rely on raw, bloody fantasy, woefully contrived plotting, let alone a desensitised aesthetic, but acute perceptiveness and a willingness to explore the human mind in all its flux. Which, of course, is where the tension and any page-turning drive should really come from – the human mind, not the human heart, you could say. There's entertainment and then there's entertainment (not that Graham Greene, thankfully, really knew the difference). Escapism and escapism. Or if you want, realism and realism.

Nevertheless, all good writing should (in an ideally non-commercial, yet realistically believable world) both transcend any genre or label, yet be incorporated in something bigger called, for the moment anyway, literary. I'm happy with that (finally, perhaps); happy, too, to continue the journey, regardless of whether there is light or darkness at the end of the tunnel. Indeed, as if one could even determine such a thing (thinking of you, unavoidably, E. M. Forster).

Oh, and actually there is one other thing, that of course shouldn't really be important, but seems, as ever, unavoidable. I once asked Elmore Leonard (for me, the greatest crime writer on the planet) why he first went down those fictional mean streets, especially as he's always credited Hemingway as his greatest literary influence. 'Money,' he said. Like he had a choice, an artistic choice.

Henry Sutton (*b.* 1963) was UEA Writing Fellow in 2008 and continues to teach on the MA in Creative Writing. He is the author of six novels written in his own name, including *Gorleston* (1995), *Bank Holiday Monday* (1996), *The Househunter* (1998), *Flying* (2000), *Kid's Stuff* (2003) and *Get Me Out of Here* (2010), as well as a collection of short stories, *Thong Nation* (2005). As James Henry, he has co-written a DI Jack Frost crime novel in the tradition of the late R. D. Wingfield. He is Books Editor of the *Daily Mirror*.

Advice to a Young Writer

Rachel Hore

'I think I would have died if my first book hadn't been published. I was desperate to get started – I was possessed.' Maybe you're not quite as anxious as Jane Gardam was nearly thirty books ago (interviewed by Alex Clark in the *Guardian*, 8 January 2011), but what else do writers write for if not to disseminate their work, to communicate it, to be read? Many creative writers are pleased to begin honing their craft and building a readership by contributing to literary magazines, print or online; some to blogs or websites. For a few, so I gather, to be read in e-book form is a summit of ambition. Most, I dare imagine, still yearn for their words to become something of more permanent record, set into a physical object with the writer's name on the front, for the word to become flesh, immutable as a tablet of stone; in short, to become encased between the well-designed covers of a printed book. Shall we stop there? No, because the author is unlikely to be satisfied until the book is purchased in reasonable numbers, read, favourably commented upon and maybe even have won a small literary prize. And then, such being the nature of human ambition, there's the matter of the next book, and many will hope to turn writing into their life's work. But what is it like to be a published writer these days? How is it possible to make a career out of it and what effects do the demands of the marketplace have on one's writing?

Since the days when an author would dedicate his work to a wealthy patron, publishing has occupied those debatable lands where art meets economics. Publishing is a business and writers its suppliers. Even if the publisher in question is motivated primarily by a passion for literature, and not by the dirty business of making a profit, he or she will find themselves in the unenviable position of financier, and cash upfront to cover the costs of professionally editing, designing, printing (or digitalising) and publishing a book, and, not least, to pay the author a cut, has to come from somewhere, whether from the proceeds of previous successes, if such there be, from the public purse or private pockets. In addition, any publisher worth their logo will wish to do their absolute best by their author, and recoup their investment, by selling as many copies of the book as possible. This may mean considerable marketing and distribution costs. Even success has its drawbacks. Consider the position of the little publisher whose book is Man Booker Prize shortlisted: recourse to huge bridging loans might be the only way they can meet demand.

It is often said, rather bitterly by experimental writers who have found difficulty attracting a publishing contract, that publishers should take more risks with what they do, try a wider range of new authors, new kinds of writing. Maybe from a cultural point of view indeed they should, but the travails of the marketplace (book publishing has been constantly 'in crisis' since earliest days) can dictate otherwise. Remember that a publisher has to pay all his bills before publication and provide retailers with stock, often at a huge discount, on a sale-or-return basis and ninety days credit, and you'll see why they're usually conservative creatures. At the same time, even in firms more obviously run by accountants, editors who can scent a new trend or detect early signs of brilliance in a tyro writer are highly prized. Very few publishers' employees enter this business of low salaries and long hours if they are not passionate about books. What is admittedly less common these days is for the accountants in a commercial publishing house to allow authors to bed down if their books are not performing at a reasonable level of sales or if they honestly aren't ever likely to break through to the next level required.

We are moving further and further away from the old world of leisurely publishing lunches and over-optimistically printed quantities of stock towards a leaner and savvier one that is yet being born. To give some context, the 1980s was a period of huge centralisation and globalisation for transatlantic publishing. The tendency was towards huge multimedia companies: Murdoch's News International, Pearson, Bertelsmann, CBS. Big business assumed – and it was only partly wrong-headed – that intellectual property was the next golden goose. It thought that if a writer's work could be kept under the roof of one big company and exploited in all its forms by that company's many media outlets then big profits could be made. Soon many of the well-known old names: Bodley Head, Secker & Warburg, Hodder & Stoughton, Collins, found themselves subsumed, demoted to mere imprints in a few much bigger firms. On the plus side, this enabled economies of scale and more muscle in the marketplace. But as the new media juggernauts concentrated on fewer and bigger authors, so-called midlist writers found themselves in the minus column and having to look elsewhere. At the same time high-street bookselling was undergoing its own revolution. Tim Waterstone opened a network of big classy-looking shops staffed by educated employees who hand-sold a wide range of books in large quantities and made visiting a bookshop a pleasant pastime, when you could meet your friends for a cappuccino to discuss your purchases (Amazon hasn't solved the coffee shop bit yet). Chains like Dillons, Books Etc and Hammicks rose and fell; eventually, Ottakers and Borders followed. The dustier independents had to run to catch up and many didn't, but bookselling generally flourished, though publishers, busy bemoaning the demise of traditional markets such as exports and newsagent wholesaling, didn't sufficiently appreciate this at the time.

For a significant number of authors, it was a time of high advances. Rushdie, McEwan, Swift, Amis, Winterson and others of their generation were each paid hundreds of thousands of pounds for works of literary fiction, previously a Cinderella area. Even the world of London publishing gasped, though, when in 1994 HarperCollins famously paid Martin Amis half a million pounds for his novel *The Information* (and a book of short stories). That it was published in its paperback form deliberately without one of its main selling points, the title, on the cover, was simply the crowning calumny of this expensive affair.

Advances no longer flow so freely, nor does wine at publishing lunches. The multimedia bosses learned the hard way that making profit out of books is a much less exact science than they had believed, and that one single corporation is not necessarily the best home for all manifestations of a writer's oeuvre. But still, authors are often paid more than the predicted total royalties of a given book, a feature of the competitive market for good writers. Indeed, it is quoted that as many as 85 per cent of general publishing advances never earn out (see John B. Thompson's *Merchants of Culture*, 2010). As for company profits, it is common in a good year for net gains of a book publisher to be 4 or 5 per cent, rather than the 10 per cent that the tycoons hoped for.

Publishers did not help themselves by turning books into a commodity when they dispensed with the price-fixing Net Book Agreement in 1995, and supermarkets started selling paperbacks by price point, like tins of beans. The result is that the public now expects a book to cost £4.49, despite the years of work that might have gone into writing it, and never mind that people will pay £30 to see a football match with a more predictable narrative outcome and baser levels of articulacy on display. Lower shelf prices have to be funded by bigger discounts from publishers, which means that the principle of a lower royalty per discounted copy is now written into writers' contracts. Not too disappointing if you're a bestseller in Tesco, but alarming for middle-ranking writers. And there's a potentially disastrous knock-on effect for the authors of more elite publications not popular enough for inclusion in the 3 for 2 promotions which, anyway, their small, not-for-profit publisher cannot afford, and possibly denied shelf space altogether in favour of faster moving 'product'. In publishing and bookselling, just as in most other areas of modern life, we now have a premier division of huge sellers, a hungry second tier snapping away below, and then a long tail struggling not to fall into the abyss. It's for this long tail that the Internet actually now offers hope, opening new shop windows and channels of distribution for niche markets.

Let us be frank. A hardback novel by a first-time literary novelist, despite encouraging reviews, might sell as little as 200 copies. Ten years ago that figure might have been 500, ten years before that 1,000. That seemed a tiny enough figure then. An edition in paperback livery might now sell two to three thousand or even fewer. For comparison, Anthony Powell's first novel, *Afternoon Men* (1931), sold something less than 3,000 in all formats (*The Memoirs*, vol. 2, 1978). Of course, luck can strike: a major literary prize shortlisting, a television book show pick, but there's a lot of competition for these and sometimes you have to hang on and hope for them to happen, while apparently less deserving causes triumph. A poetry volume might only attract a couple of hundred purchasers, but then poets have not, in modern times, been encouraged to expect to make money from their verse.

There's a further caveat for the new writer. To get one book published does not a literary career make. Two-book deals are not uncommon from big publishers; they finance a little time for the author to write, offer a little stability for both sides and a sense of encouragement, but after that nothing is certain. Some publishers do keep the faith, recognising that most writers don't immediately produce their best work, but it's quite possible that the accountants will lose patience before book number three, which you haven't yet written anyway. This ruthlessness is not just the publisher's fault. The instant availability now of precise sales information about an author's books can cause retailers to reject the second one out of hand if the first has not performed well. Sometimes a different publisher with new ideas can be the only answer.

In the meantime, advances continue to float downwards, sometimes to well below five figures. It's not just literary fiction that suffers: serious biography is also an area that considers itself in crisis, with offers of ten or fifteen thousand pounds for commissioned work seen as realistic. It might be, when considering sales, but this level hardly serves to finance the self-employed writer's research. The message is clear: very few people can now survive as writers without other sources of income. This is taking some adjusting to in literary circles, but if one stands back philosophically, it's to see that in many ways the last twenty or thirty years have been a lucrative golden age in the history of writing and publishing. Go back further than that and writers have either had private means or they have had to take other jobs, or, God save us, like Thackeray and Dickens, they've written for the market. If none of these have applied, they've lived in attics and starved. Harsh but true. At least in the West today, even in a major recession, we are unlikely to die of starvation.

No one would argue with the fact that we are living through a period of huge change and that much of this is technology driven. Some, often newer, publishing ventures regard this with excitement: the Internet offers opportunities to disseminate new forms in new ways and to supply vast, previously untapped, readerships, and they have the skills and the flexibility to meet these. Others, and many of the well-known Transatlantic firms come into this category, are in a period of fear and uncertainty to which they're frantically trying to adjust. They see the old business models breaking down and are not sure precisely how new ones should form. It's well known that high-street retailing generally is losing ground against on-line sales, and this applies particularly to books. In addition, with the emergence of attractive, easily usable handheld e-book readers, and the exponential possibilities of the Internet opening up, a great deal of future publishing will be digital and move online. The exact nature of the outcome may depend on the battle that the likes of Apple, Google and Amazon are fighting high above publishers' heads. This is not to say that the printed book is now dead – though none of us can predict what the market will want in fifty years' time – but it will definitely become less important, and in some areas the demand for it will disappear altogether. Which of our schoolchildren, for instance, reaches first for a printed book when they want to look up a reference? All this, of course, has massive repercussions for the professional writer. But it could be a period of opportunity, too. You can e-publish your own books and cut out the middlemen.

So how does the professional writer make ends meet? First of all, he writes. He finds a small corner and a regular time to engage with his muse. When he's done that, he writes other things. Everybody needs good writers these days, people what can spell and do grammar and stuff, though it can be hard to find good payers. Think of other kinds of books you can write: there is a market; it needs books, or at least content. If Sebastian Faulks can write a James Bond sequel, well, so could you, of someone else. Probably – it can't be that hard. Or if you'd rather write at your usual lofty level, consider what kinds of non-fiction are required at the moment and see if you can fill the gap. Other ideas: introductions are always being required for new editions of classic works, ancient and modern. If you have the relevant expertise, this might be an area for you. If you don't have a specialism, develop one. The same might apply to literary journalism. It's not an easy world to break into, but if you're an expert on, say, translations from Portuguese or on crime fiction or contemporary gothic, you have an extra marketable value as a reviewer. Business and commercial writing might not sound glamorous, but it pays. Someone has to write all those company reports and brochures and in-house newspapers. There's editing and proofreading for publishers, too, if you can build up the contacts. A literary writer has to try very hard, it seems, if they want to avoid teaching Creative Writing these days. It can supply a modest regular income and 'regular' is a good word. Through it you encourage newer writers, and that's a warm feeling. Your personal circumstances might enable you to take jobs that allow you to travel or undergo new experiences that will feed your writing.

Let us pause for a moment for a little treat. Consider this: there is nothing to match the deliciousness of the moment when you hold a newly printed book of your work in your hands for the first time, a book that contains your words and maybe even has your name printed on the front. Inhale the scent of the paper, enjoy the almost visceral pleasure of viewing dark grey print in a well-chosen font on thick creamy paper. That's right. Mmm.

But let's go back a step here. What happens exactly between emailing your agent that script you've sweated over for two years, carefully typed in Bookman Old Style because you think the font says both 'modern' and 'gravitas', and that delightful moment I described a moment ago, that moment just before your girlfriend comes in and catches you sniffing the glued spine of a printed book?

Your literary agent – for you will try to find a literary agent, won't you? A good one will become your closest ally in this strange, fickle world of publishing – will have hammered out a deal with your editor that will cover every angle of your business relationship with them (for as much as you and your editor might come to like each other, it is a business relationship). Your responsibilities should be clear, and so should theirs. Though strangely enough, theirs do not contain a commitment to how many copies they'll sell of your book and whether they'll definitely renew the contract. Above all, if you've been commissioned, or if it's a two-book deal and your next book has been commissioned, you'll notice a delivery date. A big warning. Do not miss this date unless you've got permission to do so from your publisher in writing. A missed delivery date is the lychgate to the graveyard of many a literary career. It gives the power to a publisher to cancel the contract and sometimes they do. Secondly, you'll see that you've handed over control of a whole list of rights in your book. Get your literary agent to explain this at an early stage. If you have no literary agent, research what these rights are and consider whether granting them to the publisher is the most effective and profitable way of handling them. If you join the Society of Authors – the nearest thing there is to a writers' union – they'll advise you on these things and others.

Thirdly, there will in all likelihood be a section in your contract about editing. This is usually not as frightening as it sounds. If you've studied publishing history at all, you will realise that for many writers – whether Thomas Hardy, T. S. Eliot, F. Scott Fitzgerald, D. H. Lawrence, William Faulkner, Jung Chang…the list goes on and on – their published work has been at some level large or small a collaborative effort with an editor they trust, who has usually (but not always, witness Raymond Carver) helped the writer to bring out the best in the book. Long rambling passages, the bits you were always hazy about, the awkward phrase, the blatant inaccuracy, the potentially libellous part, all these are aspects that experienced editors leap on with a flourish of their (not often red) pencil. You are perfectly entitled to stand your ground on most of these except the libel, but you might well find that you don't want to, that the editor is, dammit, sometimes right. At least these days you won't have to cut out the fornication like Hardy, or the erotic stocking bits like Lawrence. Indeed, you might well be encouraged to put more of these in. What can be more annoying is often not anything to do with the big picture, but with the devilish detail: the copy editor who has a different view of the use of the comma to yourself or who tries to link up all your short paragraphs in order to save paper at the printer's. Politely, but doggedly changing everything back is the usual best way to respond. Polite is important, because a nasty show of artistic temperament will be remembered when it's time for the next contract…

You and your editor are likely to reach an entente cordiale over the script, but it's unusual for the author to be given ultimate say over a book's design, though most publishers take the trouble to consult. The author who tells her editor that 'my artist husband has come up with an idea for the jacket' is usually given a chilly reception, for these days book jacket (hardback) or cover (paperback) design and market knowledge about it are prime reasons why you used a proper publisher in the first place. The jacket is, above all, what sells the book. A really good jacket represents the contents of the book well, but it's also placing the book within the often very subtle confines of a genre or even a sub-genre, and if that's awry the whole process of getting an author's work into the hands of the perceived readership is put in jeopardy. This is not to say that publishers don't sometimes get the business wrong, but they are likely to be right a lot more often than authors are. Unless you are invited to do so, avoid offering thoughts of how you would visualise the cover of your darling work or even having them in the first place – you are likely to be surprised when it's something completely different that turns up. Talk to the editor if you're worried; discover the thinking behind a particular proposal. Having a literary agent to intervene on your behalf can be useful here. There remains, however, the possibility that the editor doesn't like the jacket either, and is hoping you will do her dirty work for her and turn it away.

Publishers are often more relaxed about the author's input with a book's internal design, but here, too, there will be areas for tough negotiation. Remember that extra photographic sections, illustrated end papers and high-quality paper are all expensive, sometimes prohibitively so for a short-run book. Oh, and did you agree at contract stage who would be responsible for sourcing those photos and paying any permission fees? Publishers who might be processing hundreds of books a year will often use a small selection of design templates for their text-based books, thus saving themselves time and money, and possibly paying service to a house style, so you might find your request for a particular font or specially designed title page politely side-stepped. You should expect at least legibility and readability, though, so if the proofs of your novel turn up in a tiny 8-point setting, you have reasonable grounds to protest. Despite all this, there are plenty of examples in existence of bespoke-designed books that have been created at every stage with the full involvement of editor and author.

Let's go back to attics for a moment. The solitary genius in their cold loft space is a mythical image that has long persisted in the popular imagination, but the point about myth is that it can express certain general truths. Creative writing – despite all its jolly, interactive new forms – largely remains a solitary pursuit, and it's a given that any regularly published writer will have to find the space, physical and mental, to shut themselves away for long periods and pursue their art. This, I'll mention again in a moment. But it's not just the grand, lonely nature of writing that the image implies. There's also the idea that the writer is somehow separate from the ordinary, chattering everyday world, an observer, set apart, possibly even psychologically unfit to be anything else. Some writers might wholeheartedly identify with this interpretation, others less so, preferring to be thought part of a literary community, a big conversation. More annoying, there's a certain implication that art doesn't – or maybe somehow shouldn't – pay: Art for Art's sake, but we won't dwell on that. Personally, I work in an attic because it's well away from the rest of the household and I can't hear the telephone.

Recently, something has changed and the genius has been dragged out of his attic. A published writer in the modern world is required not just to produce a wonderful piece of work in their chosen literary form, but to appear on stage to read it aloud and talk about it, to answer the public's queries about how it was researched, written and published, to woo hundreds of the book's 'friends' on Facebook, to blog every week about their thoughts on Life, to Tweet several times a day on matters of greater or lesser importance; in short, to project a public version of themselves, a persona. History, in the shape of Dickens and Betjeman reminds us that this idea is not entirely an innovation, but it certainly hasn't been widespread or technologically possible before. Indeed, many writers have disapproved of it or been terrified of the power of literary fame (Salinger and Harper Lee are the classic examples. It's more difficult to think of recent ones, perhaps they're going extinct?). For some writers, though, this is certainly hard labour for which they feel they're not suited, or, like Amis, that they get the wrong kind of attention, or worst, like Julie Myerson, that it's difficult to play at all without the whole thing blowing up in your face. But it is only fair to mention the many who would give their non-writing arms for the kind of attention that the likes of Stephen Fry, J. K. Rowling, Zadie Smith and Andrew Motion attract, but for whatever reason can't seem to make themselves heard above the clamour.

All this causes me to move on to the whole question of an author's readers and the changing nature of their relationship with them. Many authors would still say that they don't write with a readership in mind – Amis recently and notoriously in his rejection of the idea of writing books for children. Maybe if you're a genre writer of some kind you'll know your readers require certain expectations to be satisfied: a mystery solved or a love affair consummated and you'll do this, even if by some creative and intriguing route. Today, though they might try to ignore them, I'd defy any published writer to say they know nothing about their readers. Readers' comments appear on the pages of every on-line bookseller or review website. Readers contact writers via author websites or Facebook or meet them face to face on the literary festival trail. Whilst there's an enjoyable aspect to this for many writers, most also find they have to grow several extra layers of skin, for there's a certain species of common or garden reader that throws all tact to the wind at the touch of a computer mouse beneath their fingers. In the past, squeamish authors might declare that they 'never read reviews of their books in the newspapers', but things have got far more unpleasant than anything you'll find in the review section of the *Sunday Telegraph* or the *Guardian*. Newspaper reviewers are by and large a well read and temperate community who appreciate the amount of work that any author will have put into their book. Compare them to the average Amazon one-star reviewer who feels cheated of their £4.49 or has some indiscernible grudge to exercise, even being the friend of a rival author. If this kind of behaviour upsets you and affects your ability to write, then don't read it, it's as simple as that. Advice on your writing should only ever be sought from a very few trusted sources – you will soon learn who these are, and if your editor and literary agent aren't among them it might be time for something to change…

Are you still there with your backpack, in it for the long haul? Good. May the light of your creativity always shine brightly and illuminate the way for others as well as yourself. Many aspects of the professional writer's life are at best a delightful distraction (signing books) or at worst a necessary nuisance (tax planning). I would advise you to file royalty statements unopened behind the wardrobe, but that would be irresponsible. Absolutely central (as far as partners, family and friends will allow) is that you write: regularly and seriously, and that you read others' books critically. Sometimes there will be difficulties. If a publication is successful, the publisher might want the next work quickly. That's nice, but can put you in a panic, not least because you've lost time by having to do publicity. Coolly but firmly working out with them what is possible is the only solution. Sometimes the opposite happens and you're writing a work that as yet has no open arms to welcome it. That's very tough, and finding a community of writers for support might be a good answer.

Now in her eighties, Jane Gardam is still being published, and her penultimate novel *Old Filth* was shortlisted for the Orange Prize in 2005. Of writing fiction she says, 'It was just what I had to do. It seemed the only way to live to be me, to be happy.' Quite so.

Rachel Hore (*b.* 1960) teaches publishing on the MA in Creative Writing at UEA. She worked in London publishing for many years before moving with her family to Norwich, Norfolk. She is married to the writer D. J. Taylor. Her novels include *The Dream House* (2006), *The Memory Garden* (2007), *The Glass Painter's Daughter* (2009), *A Place of Secrets* (2010) and *A Gathering Storm* (2011).

The Career of the Playwright

Steve Waters

FUSTIAN: *A poet undergoes a great deal before he comes to his third night…first, the muses, who are humorous ladies and must be attended to; for if they take it into their head at any time to go abroad and leave you, you will pump your brain in vain; then, sir, with the master of the playhouse to get it acted whom you will generally follow a quarter of a year before you know whether he will receive it or not; and then, perhaps, he tells you it won't do and returns it again, reserving the subject, and perhaps the name which he brings out in his next pantomime; but if he should receive the play, then you must attend again to get it writ into parts, and rehearsed. Well, sir, at last the rehearsals begin; then, sir, begins another scene of troubles with the actors, some of whom don't like their parts and are all continually plaguing you with alterations; at length, after wading through these difficulties, his play appears on the stage, where one man hisses it out of resentment to the author; a second out of dislike of the house; a third out of dislike to the actor; a fourth out of dislike to the play; a fifth for joke's sake; a sixth to keep the rest in company. Enemies abuse him, friends give him up – the play is damned, the author goes to the devil. So ends the farce.*
SNEERWELL: *The tragedy, rather, I think, Mr Fustian.*

The past is not always another country. Henry Fielding's play *Pasquin* (1733) presciently clarifies the perennial forces and pressures that govern the life and career of the playwright. What's wonderful about Fielding's itemisation is it's no mere whinge; and his own incendiary ten-year career, which saw him hopping between official and unofficial stages, between genres and audiences, between author and producer, was brought to an end by the highest compliment the State could pay a playwright: the implementation of a law designed to specifically silence his work. Fielding's foreshortened and largely forgotten career as a playwright is suggestive of the degree to which all playwrights' careers are chequered ones, and that often will, tenacity and bloody-mindedness are as essential to survival as literary talent. To some extent the stage is and has always been a meritocratic institution – but even in Fielding's time supply was out-running demand. Now those twenty or so letterboxes across the land that might yield a production of a play are crammed with far more plays than can be accommodated; for the playwright is not only in competition with their peers, they are now in competition with a repertoire than could make them easily dispensable, a world of plays, the work of their successful seniors and, of course, the fearsome competition of a world of shiny new media for people who have little taste or time for the stage's limitations and pleasures.

This is a rather gloomy opening to a discussion of the career of the playwright – but Fielding implicitly celebrates the achievement of playwrights who manage to stay the course, despite the atrocious odds stacked against them. It might also compel us to examine more closely the suspiciously straightforward word 'career', which, on inspection, is rather more slippery than it seems. It has accreted a connotation of some sustained ascent through a rational profession, epitomised by the archetypal pyramidal structure of the civil service, which offered the original 'career open to talent'. To have such a career implies the steady ascent through levels: you enter with promise, you perform well, you are rewarded with responsibilities and you begin your steady climb up the ladder to the sunlit uplands of a knighthood and a pension. Yet merely to describe that model is to reveal its inadequacy as an image of the playwright's working life. Such graduated levels of rationality and stability are hardly evident in the theatre, and would be deadly in practice; images of senescent productions of *The Three Sisters* by the Moscow Art Theatre spring to mind, an embalmed notion of theatre with the writer as a state functionary ploughing on regardless of whether he grows and changes, churning it out.

But there's another, more hectic connotation conjured up by 'career': the sense of careering about, following a headlong, erratic pattern, less a game of chess, more snakes and ladders. This version of career is that of a life governed by fortune and seems more appropriate as a description of the playwright's fate – and, indeed, perhaps the careers of most people these days. As Richard Sennett notes, in the culture of the new capitalism most workers have been expelled from the graduated pyramid, instead lurching about between skills and milieus, experiencing lay-offs, set-backs and gear-shifts in a manner unknown to the generation before us.[1] To that extent, then, the almost random swerves and retreats that await any playwright don't necessarily mark her out from any other worker in the knowledge economy; we're all tossed around by 'impatient capital', with no fixed or constant workplace, with few opportunities for solidarity and precious little control over our destinies.

But the playwright's working life is governed by a further factor that makes their trajectory even more unpredictable, even more haphazard – they are both the maker and the artefact at once. This is true of all work in the creative arts; yet whereas the visual artist's career is often a deepening exploration of the field of possibilities they uncover (at worst akin to the tedious homogeneity of Gilbert and George, refining and elaborating their trite vision over thirty years), or whereas the novelist might open up a niche of loyalty which they can work the changes on (so I buy the next volume of Alice Munro for the world she's unleashed with steady care over thirty years, relishing the fact I am revisiting a known landscape, rather than craving novelty), the playwright is locked in a Faustian pact with the contemporary. Of course, we return to them for their voice or sensibility – but we also demand that their idiom be constantly refreshed, their social contents upgraded, that they keep abreast of the realities they describe; the premium on novelty is much higher. For whilst the word 'playwright' brings with it connotations of craft, of predictable skills that can be rustled up in response to fresh challenges, we are also all post-romantics and we trade in intuition, originality, inspiration – even a writer as instinctively crafty as Bertolt Brecht, put out to grass in LA during the Second World War, finding himself robbed of a context in which he could thrive, wrote that he could understand 'the hell of the untalented'. Playwrights must come up with the goods; yet they are not only operating in a shifting and fickle external landscape, they also are dependent on the whims and bidding of something more elusive – their vision. Linked to this is one of the most devastating aspects of being both a maker and a commodity, the impossibility of forming a clear image of one's own value; beyond crude determinants such as bums on seats and a fat royalty cheque, the playwright has to winnow from a giddy harvest of opinion their standing, whilst simultaneously remaining icily indifferent to it. As soon as they become hooked on Googling themselves, re-reading reviews or tracking the rise and fall of their peers, they are sunk.

This seems to be turning into a litany of woe; and perhaps I'm being disingenuous by not limiting my comments to my own experience – surely it's impossible to speak for all playwrights? Well, it's always perilous to generalise, but it's possible to discern a number of differently shaped careers which accord to the different personalities of playwrights; below, crudely drawn perhaps, is a rough typology derived from the small but intensively competitive model of the Renaissance stage, the very point when the market in plays and playwriting first resembled the world we are in now.

1. *The Christopher Marlowe.* The Marlowe is the sort of dramatist who expresses most purely and potently the trajectory of the romantic dramatist (obviously in Marlowe's own sense, *avant la lettre*), that of playwright as comet, as prodigy. The Marlowe is indifferent to career, caring only for the intensely inhabited moment; the Marlowe is the playwright as rock-and-roll star. The Marlowe shocks everyone into listening to them, blazes briefly, tears up the rule book and ends up in serious trouble. Around them, supporting and perhaps feeding off them, are more stable souls illuminated by their brilliant brevity. The Marlowe doesn't develop, doesn't do drafts, doesn't do painstaking, has no learning curve; nor do they serve their time on *EastEnders* or run Creative Writing MAs; their work, as a consequence, is not balanced, nor reasoned – as Rilke says of the statue of Apollo, it exists merely to challenge you to 'change your life'.

2. *The Ben Jonson.* The Jonsonian career is long and hard won, because it's defined against prevailing taste by someone who sees themselves on the stage in spite of their talent; it's driven by a more theoretical take on the process of writing, by being literate, by being cleverer than the rest. The Jonson is a survivor who'll oversee their own publications, who'll have the temerity to question those who judge them. The Jonson fashions communities of like-minded Jonsons, they get in with literary departments, they might even end up on the other side of the desk. The Jonson survives the drought of invention by knocking up versions of plays, situated at a sufficient distance from

their talent to define themselves in terms of craft and capacity. Finally, the Jonson's essentially conservative love for their form secures them a place in the repertoire and in the heart of the audience.

3. *The John Webster.* For the Webster their entire *oeuvre* is embodied in one or two entirely achieved plays in which they get it so right so completely that their energy and purpose is consumed in that achievement. The tragedy of the Webster is the perfection of their first plays preclude any further career, and they are doomed to watch the persistence of their work stubbornly lodged in the repertoire, killing off any advance. The Websters return, stunned, to their day jobs, baffled at what they once achieved, as if looking back on their stage life as an unrepeatable relationship or a great holiday.

4. *The Middleton/Rowley/Tourneur.* The Middleton/Rowley/Tourneurs have flashes of visibility, hit the target in their time, but remain firmly stuck there; the Middleton/Rowley/Tourneur is led by genre and form, rather than leading it; they collaborate as much as initiate. The Middleton/Rowley/Tourneur win audiences but leave little trace behind them – they survive by writing a lot of very substantial generic TV, they get very close to a breakthrough in film, and when they retire discover their early work has achieved a cult following.

5. *The William Shakespeare.* Ah, the Shakespeare! The writer who manages to marry intuition and craftiness, worldliness and vision. The Shakespeare is of the theatre, creating institutions that sustain their work. The Shakespeare moves effortlessly between writing media, dashing off a masque, a West-End farce and an elegant mini-series. The Shakespeare can endlessly reinvent themselves, deepening with age, whilst at the same time they are shrewd – they know how to work with the grain of the audience and remain in contact with it. Sadly, there are only a few of them – maybe, indeed, it's only the ur-Shakespeare who truly manages the balance. But what governs the flourishing of the Shakespeare within and beyond their time, is they're strangely open-ended and malleable souls, who remain open to experience yet defiantly themselves.

This glib summary might offer a map, but it dodges the crucial question: what is success to a playwright and will they know it when they get it? Is it *succès d'estime*, to be well reviewed, respected, to have monographs devoted to you? Is it the degree of cultural penetration – to shape the times, to be multiply performed, to define the age, to be endlessly reiterated? Or is it more crudely their stock-market rating, both current and futures price? After all, if a playwright is a commodity, their plays are even more so; in a sense the playwright is an inventor and their plays patents – can that idea infect the world market as much as the home one?

Having now had more than a decade during which time I've been able to call myself a playwright without blushing and too much explanation, I have sensed certain self-delusions and intractable myths which have haunted those years, which it may be useful to name and nail here; the life-lies that govern the career of this playwright, at least.

1. *The Breakthrough.* For a while people have dubbed you 'promising'; you've met with literary managers in small offices; you've had nice letters back on headed notepaper; you've detected a trace of interest in the voices of agents down telephones and now the much-craved first 'professional' production is in sight. Suddenly, the names of actors you should know more about have been run past you, directors are bobbing into view; the advance buzz is good and it seems to be coming your way, the breakthrough. After press night you'll be whisked from the world of signs and tokens, of ambivalence and uncertainty, the world of the day job and the ironic looks of colleagues, to another world where you can finally come out as a writer, defined by your unanswerable achievement. The phone will never stop ringing, the diary will burst with engagements and the bills will get paid and stay paid…

Yes, the breakthrough can come, but it's usually less of a Eureka moment than this toxic myth suggests. There are feeding frenzies around new writers; there's always excitement and loose talk and the possibility of being a lead writer on *Shameless*. But perhaps it's more useful to talk of breakthroughs, to think steady state rather than Big Bang. Certainly, the idea of today and tomorrow parting company is less than helpful for any writer. Certainly, craving the status of unassailable value, of being in a place beyond anxiety and judgement is unhealthy. Frenzies by their nature abate; the job is to keep breaking through, keep establishing your necessity. For some playwrights never recover from the pure hit of the breakthrough; they are crushed under it, never recovering from the weight of expectation.

2. *Everybody Loves You.* Theatres, (let alone theatre, film, TV and radio) are like neighbouring states refusing to enter into a currency union. From the outside there's an apparent transparency and rationality to their coinage. A writer surfaces at one theatre and their market rate is set; but in reality, in the kingdom of another theatre their currency is valueless. Yes Theatre One loves you, but Theatre Two thinks you stink, Theatre Three has never heard of you, Theatre Four thinks you're worthy, Theatre Five thinks you're opportunist. And when you try to translate your value into another medium, you don't even compute! You're not even legal tender! But then a year passes, the chairs are shuffled, the personnel move on and suddenly Theatre One finds you stale, Theatre Two believes you to be urgent and neglected, Theatre Three's gone bust, Theatre Four's gone dark and Theatre Five's devoted itself to new writing from Hungary. My career began in a pre-fabricated hut by Swiss Cottage Tube in 1998, namely Hampstead Theatre; nine years later I returned there and every single person bar one solitary finance officer had moved on. Indeed, the theatre building itself was now under a municipal fountain, transmigrated

into a glittering new space with a bar as long as a railway platform. Did my return, then, mean I'm a Hampstead Writer? That I'm only attuned to the tastes of folk in NW1?

One truth I think I can discern from this experience is the best strategy for a writer is to become more like yourself; to declare with Nietzsche that you love your fate! Become stubbornly and more effectively yourself.

3. *Hold the course.* There's (I think) a debate within Darwinian theory between the ideas of jumps and gradualism in evolution; between rupture and linear progress. Whether it's true or not I think that such an idea is useful for playwrights in contemplating their careers. Things accelerate and then decelerate. You're visible, you're invisible. It's back to careering, really – there will be no steady progress through to becoming Sir David Hare, not least because playwrights can be up-ended by history. Consider that great wave of socialist writing in this country from the 1970s – Churchill, Edgar, Brenton, Bond, Hare himself – beached in the 1980s, painfully reconstructing itself after the fall of the Berlin Wall, then, in the 1990s, the return of Howard Brenton, the reflorescence of David Edgar, the astonishing category-redefining career of Caryl Churchill. Or, in contrast, think of Pinter, dried up and critically reviled in the 1970s, suddenly finding his voice again with *One for the Road*, spawning a generation of new writers, now within the last years of his life and beyond, the most revived and staged playwright of our times. Of course, there's no doubt some playwrights go silent, too, not only because they die young, but because the theatre thinks it can do without them; and the silence their absent work makes is the saddest pause imaginable. But stick around, hold the course, keep writing – eventually you will probably become the repertoire. The evidence is abundant – Peter Nichols's sudden resurgence, Edward Bond's extra-territorial career; even, as I write, the return of Arnold Wesker to the Royal Court. For the final irony of the career of a playwright is that it simply isn't possible to resign, to retire, that there's no Hall of Fame to enter into, no refuge beyond judgement. Maybe there's a better word than 'career' we can use, maybe we should deploy the word 'calling'. It certainly helps to separate success from value, to remind all playwrights that this is a difficult, arrogant journey we've embarked on and we will need to invent our own rules and follow our own path to get to the end of it.

1   See Richard Sennett's *The Culture of the New Capitalism* (Yale University Press, 2006).

Steve Waters (*b.* 1965) is Lecturer in Scriptwriting at UEA and a former Director of the MPhil in Playwriting at the University of Birmingham. His work for the stage includes *English Journeys* (1998), *World Music* (2004), *Out of Your Knowledge* (2006) and *Little Platoons* (2011). His play *The Contingency Plan* (2009) is in development as a feature film. He is author of *The Secret Life of Plays* (2011).

My So-Called Career

Jane Harris

It took me many years to discover that what I really wanted to do was write fiction. Initially, I thought I might be destined to be an actress. While I was at Glasgow University in the 1980s I took part in a few student drama productions. Alas, I was never a particularly gifted performer and suffered from sphincter-clenching stage fright, but – ever-optimistic – these factors didn't deter me from going on to drama college in London, following graduation. I chose a method-acting school which turned out to have as many quirks and outlandish practices as one might expect. In mid-winter, as preparation for The Scottish Play, we endured a week-long improvisation in a dank and spooky Cornish farmhouse. My boyfriend was cast as Macbeth and I was his Lady, but after six days of foraged food and candlelight, our reign ended abruptly when 'rebel spies' (our fellow students: half-starved, partially insane and armed with real crossbows) seized power. One wild-eyed virago held a knife to my throat and might have used it had our director not tossed aside his liquorice Rizlas to intervene, with world-weary, honeyed tones: 'And there, let's bring it to a close.'

At the end of the course I re-entered the real world, vaguely traumatised, but possessing one invaluable piece of acting wisdom: to work, one needed membership of the actor's union, in the form of an Equity card. A catch-22 was involved: to get a card you needed to be in work, but to be in work you required a card. Luckily, there was one proven route. If you could style yourself as a performer on the nascent Alternative Comedy circuit and accumulate a few dozen contracts, then the Holy Grail of Equity would be within your grasp.

Two drama school friends and I hastily formed a female trio, The Gumdrops. We planned to storm the comedy circuit with our witty monologues and devastating a cappella skills (although I did strum the guitar, ineptly, on a few numbers). I was chief songwriter and my lyrics were meant to be humorous, with a vaguely feminist theme. One was about sex: 'Now here's the tragic story / of a girl like you and me / Oh how she longed for the glory / of orgasms multipl-ey.' In another, 'Superwoman', the first verse went something like this (what can I say? it was 1985):

> She wears Conran clothes and Shilling hats
> And she was one of the first with tickets to *Cats*
> Her best friend's bisexual, her hair by Sassoon
> And she goes to the Dordogne for a week in June
> She is Superwoman (doo-doo) Superwoman (doodle-de-doo)

Superwoman (doo-doo)
She's some bird, she's not plain
She's Superwoman and she drives me insane

My friends and I spent a month writing and rehearsing material, and then launched ourselves into stand-up comedy with an open-mike spot in Crouch End. Those King's Head punters might have been the nicest crowd for whom we ever performed. They clapped and cheered; some of them even hugged us, and I seem to remember that we were given roses. We left on a high and with the misapprehension that this was how life on the circuit would play out: being showered with adoration and flowers.

Nothing could have been further from the truth. Many of our contemporaries are now household names: Jeremy Hardy, Jo Brand, Lee Evans, Jenny Eclair, Mullarkey and Myers, and Julian Clary (when he still performed with Fanny the Wonderdog). By and large, we shared the bill with comedians who were vastly more talented and funny than we were, and our lack of experience soon began to show. Some of our solo spots went down better than others, but we hadn't the sense to cut or rewrite anything, with the result that each gig was more harrowing than the last as, increasingly, we lost faith in our material. Over a period of six months any confidence that we'd possessed seeped out of us. Towards the end we were pushing each other onstage, dreading the moment when we'd have to do our individual spiels, trying to force the others to perform more of theirs ('Do your bit!' 'No, you do yours!'). At tiny venues where it was impossible to sidle offstage between our awkward monologues, the two who were not performing would sit to one side, heads bowed, staring at the floor, awaiting the next cue. I can count those minutes as amongst the most desolate of my life.

Our worst gig was our last. It was at Greenwich, in the fondly remembered Malcolm Hardee's Tunnel Club, a place notorious for difficult audiences, and where, from the moment we walked onstage, hecklers started shouting: 'Get your tits out!' At the end of the evening, feeling sorry for us, Malcolm handed over two contracts instead of one, which allowed us to reach our Equity quota. He was encouraging, but that night was the last straw: The Gumdrops were too squashed to continue.

Thereafter, backed by talent spotters who had contacted me after one of our gigs, I tried my hand at jazz singing. I was teamed up with a talented pianist, and the plan was for us to gain experience by playing pubs and clubs, and then perhaps a cruise ship, before moving on to recording contracts and world domination in 5/4 time. However, pub singing was just as gruelling as the comedy circuit. Aside from my startling lack of charisma as a chanteuse, the venues we played were mostly in London's East End, and when it came to requests I had a language barrier: having grown up in Glasgow I often couldn't understand what audience members were asking me to sing. At one gig a plea for 'Blue Burial' had me stumped until hours later, when it finally clicked that the punter had been demanding 'Blueberry Hill'. Along with my accompanist – a very refined chap

– I soon grew weary of late nights, bad pay and inattentive audiences.

One evening, during a typically high-class gig at The Royal Duke in Shadwell, a drunken spectator ate my poor pianist's straw fedora, a hat of which he'd been most fond. Somehow, for me, this ridiculous event symbolised The End. I realised that I didn't relish performing enough to put in the hard grind required in order to succeed in Showbiz. There and then I decided to give up attempting to be an actor, a singer, a comedian, any kind of performer. I was done with it. That's all folks! I was going to get myself a real job.

And that's how I ended up working in Barking in a disused goods yard as a Training Officer on the Tory government's Community Programme – so, not a real job, after all: a placement in a scheme dreamed up to manipulate high unemployment figures. My role was to organise and facilitate training and send participants to college on day-release, where they studied everything from painting and decorating to business management. Having no clue what else I might do with my life, I threw myself into this job and took a part-time course in Training Management. My bosses were extremely supportive. I fell in love with them and they must have liked me, too, because I was promoted, several times, over the course of two years until I was in charge of a substantial budget. Ultimately, my immediate boss was given an executive post and I was discreetly asked if I'd like to apply for her job.

It was only at this point that I had a sudden revelation. What was I doing? This was not at all how I wanted to spend my life. I was an artist! What sort of artist I didn't know, but there was still some vague longing that had not been satisfied. I began to feel panicky and trapped, and out of this desperation grew an idea: I would travel around the world. My hope was that in doing so I'd discover my true vocation. Thus, I turned down the offer to apply for my boss's job and began to plot my escape. My hard-earned savings wouldn't be enough to allow me simply to travel for an extended period and I knew I'd have to find work en route but, in a way, that seemed an essential part of the plan. I wanted to get my hands dirty, to live life as it was lived in foreign lands, to learn new languages.

My great adventure began in the late summer of 1988, in France, where I picked grapes, initially in Beaujolais and then Sancerre. Our working day began at first light and from then until dusk we were outdoors, bent over the vines. The fresh air was like a tonic to me after years in a stuffy London office. Despite being physically exhausted most of the time, I had never felt so carefree.

As winter approached I headed for the Alps and found work, first at a ski resort in a huge hotel block that was run by an expat couple and then (after a few months, when I walked out of that job after the scandalous behaviour of my autocratic bosses became too much) at a French-run auberge in a mountain village. Apart from the owner's sister, I was the sole employee, a maid-of-all-work: dishwasher, kitchen porter, chambermaid and waitress. I had to be up at 6 a.m. to prepare breakfasts and often didn't finish until 10 p.m. We had only a few hours break in the afternoon between clearing up after lunch and preparations for dinner. Yvette, the owner, and her partner Michel were eccentric, temperamental, vicious and hilarious. They beat and kicked each other in the kitchen, they wept, they yelled. Michel, who acted as chef (although he had no formal catering experience or qualifications) began his day at 10 a.m. with several glasses of pastis, followed by wine with lunch, after which he'd sink a few tots of Green Chartreuse, take his nap, and then begin the cycle again at 5 p.m. with more pastis. Sometimes, Michel grew sentimental; more often, he was as aggressive as a little bull. One afternoon, in my first week, Yvette pointed out to him that he had a tiny hole in his sweatshirt. An argument ensued, the result of which was that he ripped off the shirt and rent it to shreds in front of our eyes, then threw it on the floor and jumped up and down on it for several minutes. I soon discovered that this sort of behaviour was habitual.

Almost every day, as we prepared lunches, Michel would turn to me and demand (in French, in a shocked tone): 'Did you see it this morning?' and I, always the sucker, would ask: 'What?' only to hear him reply: 'My arse!'

Then he'd laugh until he almost choked.

He hated me to leave anything of mine on 'his side' of the kitchen worktop. Once, when I forgot and left my tobacco there, he took an indelible pen and drew a black line down the wall, across the work surface and floor, in order to demarcate our separate spheres of operation. He liked to send me on rogue errands to the local shops, insisting that I ask the butcher for 'damp parsley', which, I soon began to suspect, was vaguely indecent in French. Michel's attitude to me was often salacious, but I managed to keep him at arm's length. His wife was forever glaring at me through narrowed, glittering eyes, but she kept me on, perhaps because I was what she called '*courageux*'.

Despite the moods and vicissitudes of my employers and the hard grind, I enjoyed my time at this hotel. For one thing, in my few free hours, I had begun to keep a travel journal. Michel and Yvette were fabulous characters, and always gave me something amusing to write about. I wasn't sure what my purpose was in keeping these notes and had no thoughts of turning them into fiction, but I enjoyed the act of composition.

At the end of the winter season Yvette gave me a huge bonus, confiding that no other employee had ever stayed with them for so long (believe me, this came as no surprise). With some cash in my pocket, I set off for Portugal, where I'd signed up for a course in Teaching English as a Foreign Language. This qualification was meant to be my passport for travel anywhere in the world. Indeed, I might still be an English teacher now had I not fallen ill with a virus soon after completing the course. I was living alone in a cheap apartment on the outskirts of Lisbon, waiting to begin work at a school that was due to open that autumn. I had no television, no radio, no books, no money. But I did have pen and paper and one day, out of sheer boredom, I started to write a story about Gavin, an ex-boyfriend. Gavin happened to be a transvestite and it had always intrigued me that he cried at his sister's wedding – not just because he was happy for her – but because he coveted her big white meringue of a frock. To my surprise, writing this story engrossed me more than anything else I'd ever done. I rewrote it about twenty times, obsessed by perfecting how the words looked on the page; how they sounded when I read them aloud. It was a revelation to me. Once the story was finished, I wrote another, and then another. Even when I began work at the language school I couldn't wait to get home in order to write more fiction.

At long last, I'd discovered what I wanted to do in life.

And so, I took a risk. I gave up teaching and returned to live in Glasgow, setting myself a target to publish a story within six months; if I failed, I'd give up the notion of becoming a writer altogether. Of course, this was completely unrealistic, but, as fate would have it, within a few months my story about Gavin was accepted for publication in a literary anthology. Upon reading the letter from the editors, I turned a celebratory somersault and almost smashed my parents' television, which would not have gone down well. I showed the letter to my father.

'Look!' I cried. 'My story's going to be in a book!'

'Some rat's ass publication, no doubt,' he replied. Then he peered at my face and added, for good measure: 'You've got spots.' (Here, in this short exchange, lies a clue that may hint at why I became a writer in the first place.)

Spurred on by this tiny measure of success, I took out a bank loan to buy a computer. Since my return to Glasgow, I had been working as an office administrator, an undemanding job which allowed me to write in my spare time. Every morning I got up at 5 a.m. to tinker with stories, and at weekends I sent them to magazines and anthologies. Several were accepted for publication, which encouraged me to keep going. But I still wasn't making a living out of fiction.

Hoping to take things to another level, I applied for the post of Writer-in-Residence at a Scottish University. I was aware that this was a precocious move, but they did invite me for interview. The panel consisted of half a dozen academics. Alas, as soon as I entered the room I was so overcome by nerves that my mind went blank. Asked to list my influences, I found that I couldn't even remember the name of a single author. When one tweed-clad gent asked me to talk about my plans for the future, I stammered out something about perhaps attempting an MA or PhD in Creative Writing at the University of East Anglia (at the time, UEA ran the only such postgraduate course in Britain). The academic gave a scornful laugh and, throwing down his pen, glanced at his esteemed colleagues before opining: 'I imagine that several of us around this table would give our eye teeth to study Creative Writing at UEA,' his inference being that any one of those assembled would have been a more appropriate scholar than me.

I suspect that it was this comment, and this comment alone, which made me determined to gain a place on Malcolm Bradbury's famous MA.

Needless to say, I wasn't offered the job of Writer-in-Residence. However, by some miracle I did get into UEA. With financial assistance from my father (credit where credit is due), I moved to Norwich in September 1991 and, at the age of 29, became a student once more.

When people ask me about Creative Writing at UEA, my sense is that, often, they only want to hear bad things: that the course was a waste of time, formulaic, over-priced, badly taught; most inquisitors are hoping for a tale of woe that will make them feel better, somehow, about themselves. However, in my experience, the MA was the most inspired learning experience of my life, brilliantly taught, not at all formulaic and the best way I could have begun my writing career. That year in Norwich allowed me to take myself seriously as a writer and I also learned how to accept constructive criticism of my work-in-progress. To my amazement, several of my fellow students had already written or were writing novels. Lacking the confidence to leap into a full-length piece of fiction, I continued to focus on short stories. However, our workshops made me think seriously, for the first time, about narrative and structure.

Admittedly, to begin with, I found the classes daunting, but I soon began to enjoy the process, the sheer novelty of sitting in the same room as Malcolm or Rose Tremain, listening to these wonderful writers deconstruct our work. I even enjoyed the academic components of the MA, which were inventive and absorbing. In addition, I took a Screenwriting option, taught by Rob Ritchie, whose inscrutable style was very different to what we had come to expect in prose workshops. Malcolm, in particular, couldn't hide his enthusiasm with the result that we were never under any illusions about which of us were his favourites.

I spent most of my year in Norwich in a state of heightened excitement. This was dampened only when several hotshots from a well-known literary agency came to speak to us. Afterwards, there was a drinks reception, during which the following conversation took place.

AGENT: What have you written?

ME: Just some short stories.

AGENT: You won't get far like that. You must write a novel.

ME: Actually, I was thinking of writing a screenplay.

AGENT: Screenplay? For that you must be a Pinter or a Mamet. And are you?

ME: Am I – what?

AGENT: A Pinter or a Mamet?

ME: Um…

I wasn't sure what I was, even by the time that the course ended in the summer of 1992. Perhaps I should have begun that screenplay or novel immediately, but, once my dissertation was finished, financial circumstances dictated that I find a job. At the time the Arts Council were hiring a few Writers-in-Residence for prisons and I applied for a post at HMP Durham. There were five other candidates. As part of the interview we were led through the prison to visit C-wing, a segregated area where the sex offenders were housed. An officer ushered us into a classroom; we had been forewarned that it was full of paedophiles and rapists. As we shuffled in, some of the inmates looked at us with undisguised curiosity. Others seemed irritated or just plain bored. I realised that this visit was a test: you either had the balls to make it through this part of the selection process or you didn't. Suspecting that the best way forward was to engage with the prisoners, if possible, I sat down next to one man and struck up a conversation. His name was George. He had no teeth and a lot of tattoos, most of them on his face. I soon discovered that he was almost as scared as I was, but we managed to sustain a conversation and I became so absorbed in listening to him that I've no idea what the other candidates were doing.

Some time later, we were escorted back to the education block. At this stage, unprompted, three of the writers took themselves out of the running, saying they had no desire to continue because they knew they wouldn't be able to deal with the stress of the job. This left three candidates. After another short delay, I was taken into a room and told that the job was mine, if I wanted it. In truth, I wasn't entirely sure that I did. However, I needed the money, so I accepted the offer.

On my first day, I signed various documents and was handed my own set of keys. I could go wherever I liked in the prison, although my base was to be in the Education Department, commonly known to the predominantly Geordie inmates as 'th'Education'. My remit was to help prisoners to write poems, fiction and memoirs, two and half days a week. Otherwise, I was free to do my own work.

HMP Durham is a grim Victorian gaol. At the time, slopping-out was still in practice. The main building housed male inmates, while the (supposedly) most dangerous women in Britain were kept in a high-security block known as H-wing. Working with groups of prisoners proved to be a challenge, since those who were really interested in writing were dotted around the various wings and it was impossible to gather them together in one place. As a result, my days evolved into a combination of one-to-one sessions with individuals throughout the prison, alongside weekly classes with the sex offenders on C-wing and, sometimes, small workshops for inmates from the remand wings who were allowed to attend classes in 'th'Education'.

Navigating the building was always an adventure. Worst of all was E-wing, which I had to pass through en route to other parts of the prison. E-wing was for men accused of burglary, assault and the like, non-sexual offences, yet I felt less at ease there than anywhere else. At slop-out time, men crept along the landings with covered plastic buckets or loitered in doorways. The air was always heavy with smells and there was often some joker who would simulate the sounds of approaching orgasm as I hurried on my way.

At times, the prison could be a darkly comic place. One day, as I was crossing the courtyard on my way to H-wing, a male voice rang out from the barred window of a lofty cell: 'Miss! Miss! Come up here and sit on me face!' At once, a second con yelled, crossly, from another cell window: 'You can't say that, man, that's Jane from th'Education.' After a pause, the first voice yelled again: 'Miss! Miss! Can I get on a class?'

One or two of the women prisoners were not only talented but highly motivated. Among the men, the most attentive group were the sex offenders, who were at the bottom of the pecking order and, therefore, grateful for any sort of attention. They included

Johnny, an educated, intelligent man who announced, grandly, on our first meeting: 'I'm a paedophile.' His memoir explored his preference for B.O.Y.S. (Bloom of Youth Syndrome). It made difficult reading, but was written with undeniable wit and perception. During our first session in Johnny's cell, a cheery screw popped his head round the door, calling out: 'Johnny Rotten?'

Johnny performed a pantomime leap from his bed.

'I deny everything!' he cried. 'I demand to see my solicitor.'

'Come and get your dinner, man,' said the screw, world-weary.

As we stepped out on to the wing, another paedophile, Jack – an earnest ex-miner with elastic features – shuffled up behind us, clutching a jotter.

'Watch him!' Johnny warned me, half in jest. 'He'll bite you!' adding sotto voce: 'If he's got his teeth in.'

Occasionally, I was called upon to 'babysit' men whose classes in 'th'Education' had been cancelled. One day I was asked to hold an impromptu session for some lads on remand who, for reasons I never got to the bottom of, couldn't attend their cookery lesson, in which they were allowed to eat the products of their labours. All were miffed, as on that day they were to have made spaghetti bolognese. They soon resigned themselves to a few hours in my care and demanded to know my opinion on everything, particularly the judiciary and feminism. Noting my Celtic features, Lenny asked: 'Have you got a bit of Irish in you, miss?'

'Please, call me Jane.'

'A-reet Jane,' he said, all a-twinkle. 'Would you like a bit of English in you?'

All attempts at getting these lads to do some serious writing having failed, I set them a tame exercise, a description of their idea of paradise. They responded to this with more enthusiasm, perhaps because it was familiar, a bit like school. For a while, there was much chewing of pens and scrubbings-out. I began to relax. Then Gary threw down his pencil.

'Miss, how d'you spell "cocaine"?'

'Way-ay, miss,' – all the pens went down – 'How d'you spell "horniest"?'

'"Geisha", miss?'

'"Erotic-est"?'

Meanwhile, in my time off, I attempted to do some writing of my own. I'd begun a Creative and Critical Writing PhD at UEA and I had also recently got married. My time in Durham was punctuated by trips to Norwich, where I attended PhD supervisions, and to Bristol, where my recently acquired husband was living. I seemed to spend most of my time in transit. I became intimate with the East Coast line and could only applaud the author of the train graffiti who, below the notice asking customers not to flush the toilet in stations, had inscribed the words 'except Peterborough'.

Eventually, my two-year stint at HMP Durham came to an end. My husband and I moved to Norwich and I began teaching Creative Writing to undergraduates at UEA, while continuing my PhD.

As part of my thesis I had intended to write a novel. However, I had no notion how to go about such a thing and no ideas that seemed worthy of novel length. And so, I had come up with a cunning plan: instead of attempting a conventional, full-length work of fiction, I decided to devise about sixteen linked stories, all on a Scottish theme, and (hopefully) pass them off as a novel. Some stories would be contemporary, some historical. A few were irreverent tales about Scottish icons, like Robert the Bruce. In my version, his catchphrase 'try, try again' evolves not because he's watching a spider, but because he's attempting, unsuccessfully, to pleasure himself.

One story I'd planned featured a Robert Burns-style poet-farmer. I'd done some research on Burns and was intrigued by the fact that he collected verse from ordinary people. I decided to write about a relationship between a nineteenth-century bard and a maid from whom he 'borrows' songs. I only ever intended this to be a short story. But, somehow, once I invented the character of Bessy, the maid, she took over. I wrote from her point of view, using a very particular voice which I could hear clearly in my head, a form of Irish/Scottish Victorian demotic, part-invented, part-inspired by my Irish family and friends, my Scottish upbringing and (eventually) by Victorian and Irish slang dictionaries.

This particular tale grew and grew. Eventually, I put aside the other themed stories to concentrate on Bessy, hoping that what I had in this material was a novel. On the first page Bessy had mentioned a mistress, before I even knew who this character might be. Increasingly, I lost interest in the poet-farmer and became intrigued by the main character's relationship with this woman. However, after about 20,000 words I ran out of steam, because I still didn't understand how to structure a full-length narrative. I lost faith in what I'd achieved and gave up, even abandoning the linked stories. All my research notes and fragments of writing were stuffed into a cardboard box and put away.

At about this time we moved to London where my husband had begun attending the National Film School. I began to write a completely different novel – *Home Rules* – a contemporary narrative which I completed over the next few years, after which – I suspect with more determination than erudition – I bashed out an accompanying critical component and thereby managed to be awarded a PhD.

Of course, I had every hope that *Home Rules* would be published. In fact, the (now-defunct) publishing house Flamingo showed interest in the novel for a while, but, ultimately, it failed at the last hurdle (marketing) and was rejected. After a brief depression, I returned to the drawing board and began another contemporary novel. However, London-living was proving to be so expensive in comparison to Norwich that I ended up having to take on several freelance jobs. As well as continuing to teach at UEA, I started work for film companies like Working Title and Miramax, assessing scripts and novels to see whether they were worth making into movies. In addition, I became a reader for The Literary Consultancy, (a company which provides a manuscript assessment service), reading novels and stories that had been submitted by clients and writing reports on how the manuscripts might be improved. All this was poorly paid, time-consuming work, but ultimately (I did it for seven years) it taught me a lot about the craft, particularly about how stories work.

Meanwhile, my own writing became squashed into a few hours at the end of each day. My husband was looking for short scripts to direct, and so in 1998 – temporarily disenchanted with prose and my latest attempts at a novel – I started writing short films. Four of these were made and they did reasonably well, in short film terms: they won several prizes and two were BAFTA-nominated. Following this I was offered a commission to write a full-length feature script. I had an idea for a dark comedy about bitter, middle-aged divorced men in Norwich. Unfortunately, the production company wanted something more commercial – a romantic comedy about trendy young people in Brighton. Desperate to please, I compromised my ideas. The first draft of the resulting script was a mess. Before I had embarked on the rewrites, the production company folded, and so did my development deal.

By this stage I was nearly forty and – ten years after I'd published my first story – I was still struggling to make any money from writing. In despair, I decided to dig out my old manuscripts, to see if there was anything worth salvaging. I brought some boxes down from the attic and rummaged through them. As soon as I unearthed the files of material on Bessy I knew that I'd found something to get excited about. I still loved her character and voice, and now that I was more confident about plot, I felt sure that I could develop a page-turning narrative.

Thereafter, I spent three months working on a detailed plan of the story. Only when I was really fed up, did I begin writing the novel itself. I called it *The Observations*. Although the new plot was very different, I re-used much of the original material. For instance, page one of the novel is exactly as I wrote it in 1993. Many other fragments remain, but they've been woven into a different, more complex structure. It was rather like making up a patchwork quilt from squares of material. Initially, I only had about 25 per cent of what I needed. In order to finish, I had to create the other 75 per cent of the squares, then stitch the whole thing together in a way that made sense.

The first draft took eight months, and then, because I was desperate for money, I worked hard at rewriting the first 100 pages, in the hope that I might get an advance based on a partial manuscript. An agent sent the extract to a number of publishing houses and – to my enormous relief – three editors were interested. There was a modest bidding war and, in the end, I decided to go with Faber and Faber, because they publish many of my favourite authors.

After that, it all got a bit crazy, with foreign sales headed up by a pre-emptive bid from Penguin in America, which meant that they made a substantial offer (to me, an astonishing amount of money, given my years of privation) hoping that I wouldn't consider any other publisher. In the UK *The Observations* was published in April 2006 and was kindly received by reviewers. Translation rights sold first to Italy and Holland and, to date, the novel is published in more than twenty different territories, with translation rights still selling, most recently to Russia. In Italy, where my Italian publishers mounted a publicity campaign across radio and television, *Le Osservazioni* became a bestseller. Here in the UK, television rights sold, the novel was dramatised on Radio Four, and W. F. Howes have produced an audiobook version. *The Observations* went on to win the USA Book of the Month Club's First Fiction Prize and was shortlisted for a number of other prizes, including The Orange Prize for Fiction, the Prix du Premier Roman in France, and the Saltire Society First Book of the Year. The income from foreign sales was enough for me to give up my part-time jobs and – so far, with the help of royalties – I'm still able to support myself exclusively by writing (although never say never!).

Such good fortune seems unbelievable to me, even now. It was a long, messy journey to the publication of my first novel, with many disappointments, setbacks and frustrations. However, in the end, it all seems worthwhile. I was a late starter, but I'm so glad that I never gave up. Rediscovering that fragment of *The Observations* in a cardboard box was one of the most fortuitous things that ever happened to me. My advice to any fledgling writer would be: never give up; never throw anything away.

In fact, the germ of an idea that I'd stored in that same box was the inspiration behind my second novel, *Gillespie and I*. All I had were a few words on a piece of card: 'Artist, Glasgow, 19th Century' – but from those vague beginnings the entire novel grew. Again, it took me a while to write: five years this time, as opposed to twelve or thirteen. I see that as great progress! *Gillespie and I* was recently published in the UK (in May 2011) and has been widely and kindly reviewed. The novel made the bestseller lists soon after publication and both the *Sunday Times* and the *Independent* included it as one of their top reads of the year. It's early days yet but, at the time of writing, Harper Collins USA are due to publish *Gillespie and I* in January 2012 and translation rights have already been bought by Italy and Holland.

All this is good news. And yet, perhaps because of the years I spent struggling to make a living, I still worry about long-term financial security: about how much less I'll be making from e-books than I've done from hardbacks and paperbacks, about the fact that I have no pension, about the fact that you're only ever as good as your last book. I can't do anything else but write. Perseverance is everything. These days, I tend to think of writing as a journey, but one in which – I suspect – I may never reach my destination.

Jane Harris (*b.* 1961) received her MA in Creative Writing from UEA in 1992 and was awarded a PhD in Creative and Critical Writing by the university in 1995. Her first novel *The Observations* (2006) was shortlisted for many prizes, including the Waterstone's Newcomer of the Year Best Novel, the Orange Broadband Prize for Fiction Best Novel, the Glen Dimplex Award, the British Book Awards Newcomer of the Year, and the South Bank Show/*Times* Breakthrough Award. Her most recent novel is *Gillespie and I* (2011).

Between Drafts

Keith Tutt

I'm moving home at the moment and seem to spend a good part of my working life walking the long aisles of B&Q looking for obscure plumbing parts, unorthodox light fittings and particular packs of bathroom tiles (that turn out to be broken on arrival home) to fix the various things that are wrong with the new place. Yesterday there was a blockage in the drains; time to buy some rods (from B&Q) and roll up my sleeves.

I'm between drafts, you see. A few weeks ago I completed the first 'vomit draft' of a new version of a script about a London taxi driver with a dark secret that was previously a novel and before that was an earlier version of the screenplay. To say that this one's had a difficult birth would be true. Nevertheless, I am not taking that to be 'a bad sign'. Finding the right form for a project or a story is not always as direct a process as I'd like and things can move from idea through a poem to a novel, from a painting to a poem, from an animation to a graphic novel and from a single thought image to a screenplay. Sometimes, also, from something to nothing. Nevertheless, I'm pretty happy with the vomit draft, which, in the end and after a slowish start, took about thirty writing days. I should explain that the vomit draft is generally completed as quickly as possible in order to (1) make you feel better that it's no longer inside you, and (2) reveal aspects of the story that might not arise if you wrote more slowly and with too much intellectual (rather than instinctive) thinking. Not all vomit drafts are conceived equal and in this case it was based on a pretty clear treatment of about six pages (plus all the knowledge of the other novel and screenplay versions that have gone before it). In the past I've done a quick first draft from a detailed twenty-page treatment and still had new ideas along the way. The enemy at this stage is 'staleness'. It has to be a live birth with characters and story elements that want to be alive and in the world.

But now I'm between drafts and moving home. This is not getting my current film script written, nor indeed the one after that or the ones even further out in deep space awaiting their discovery and translation into form. It has to be done, however, for I am attempting to create an environment that will function like the deck of the Starship *Enterprise* and allow me to boldly traverse my inner universe in the search for cosmic nuggety stuff to employ in scripts and books. But even the Starship *Enterprise* must have had toilets and drains and, though it had the luxury of ejecting its waste into space (we presume), there may have been times when they got blocked. And what I have are blocked drains. Or, to be more accurate, one giant distraction from work.

For most of the scripts I've written for films and TV since my first in 1982, I've been quite aware of the different models and craft techniques that different writers and writing teachers employ and offer (respectively). To put it another way, I'm not a stranger to the work of Robert McKee, Syd Field, Christopher Vogler, Paul Gulino, Ronald R. Tobias and John Truby. (Americans, all of them). I'm not sure whether I'm carrying some American gene that tends to make me like these models, but I am aware that there is, for many English writers who write scripts, an aversion to anyone and anything that smacks of telling the writer how to 'do it'. And, perhaps if we were talking about novels, poetry, short stories, I might agree. But scripts for films and TV seem to be something different. For one thing they do not have an identity in themselves; they are also, quite firmly, not works of literature. They are, if anything, instruction manuals. They are also implicit requests for certain people to spend money; usually a lot of money. There are some interesting questions related to this, such as: 'Would I spend x million dollars/pounds/yen turning this script into a long stream of images and sounds?'; 'Will this film generate three times (generally enough for it to at least break even) its production budget at the box office?'; 'Will this film be seen by, entrance, make cry, make laugh, make sick, make scared, y million people?'; 'Will the success of this film make it more possible for me to sell more scripts for more money and have more of the best pieces of my writing work transformed into films?'

Another question: 'What will make it more likely to get my scripts turned into films?' At this point it's worth remembering (before, hopefully, instantly forgetting) that only a very tiny proportion of film scripts get made into films. One might think that this applies only to the waitresses and car-parking flunkies and taxi drivers and gas-station operatives and gardeners and sharecroppers who all have a script that they expect to get made. It's also true, however, for really great writers. David Mamet, perhaps one of America's greatest living playwrights and screenwriters (*Speed-the-Plow, Oleanna, Glengarry Glen Ross*) has admitted that only a small percentage of the scripts he writes for the screen (either under his own name or others) get made into films.

Let's return to the question: 'What will make it more likely to get my scripts turned into films?' We may be able to increase our chances by working on things strategically. So, we can narrow the task down to three areas: ideas, execution, business. (Some like to call it the three *C*s: Creative, Craft, Commercial). So for ideas we can ask some pretty specific questions: 'How many ideas do I have?' By which I mean: 'How many ideas do I have that are in some readable form that look, feel and sound like a real, producible film project? Although I also mean: 'How many ideas do you have or expect to have in your lifetime that at least you can consider 'great ideas', ideas good enough to change your life and the lives of others who experience the idea?'

We can come back to ideas and what form they need to be in, but now we need to turn to the second aspect of screenwriting: Execution or Craft. Of all the written forms it's my belief that screenwriting is the most technical. Hence all the technical gurus who are willing to tell you about three-act structure, advanced versions of three-act structure, the hero's journey, the 22-step-story model, the sequence approach, and so on and so on. These models are all designed to improve the storytelling structure of the script to fit the internal subconscious diet of what satisfies our own inner story beast. Not only do scripts have to hit various important story points at various intervals in the script, they also have to do a hundred other things really well. Like create unforgettable, motivated characters, provide interesting, twisty dialogue that works on at least two levels at once, and give an entertaining visual experience for the reader. The list goes on: use props in interesting ways that integrate the law of three; take advantage of the Karpman drama triangle and the ever-changing roles that characters take up between victim, persecutor and rescuer; create a convincing story world; foreshadow events in cunning ways that make the audience feel clever; and on and on…

The process of turning a great idea for a film into a great film script is one that encompasses a variety of storytelling skills, as well as a large number of decisions. It was Martin Amis who said that writing is making a thousand decisions a page and, while he was talking about prose fiction, the same is roughly true for scripts. Before the actual script can be initiated there are usually a number of important stages to go through before an actual script is written. These involve: the premise, the synopsis, the outline treatment, a step treatment, a full treatment, a scriptment and finally (but not really finally at all) a script draft.

Many writers spend a long time (days, weeks, months) working on a one- or two-sentence premise that functions as a cohering idea for both the project and the writing process as well as a device to use when pitching the idea or even when publicising the film. At this stage it also gets known as the 'logline'.

Premises are wondrous devices that can, when right, bring together everything that you need to know about the story. They answer the question 'What's your film about?' in a professional, intriguing and appealing way. Let's try to make one up; I was watching that documentary series on TV last night about Scottish trawlermen caught somewhere between a trough and a wave in the North Sea. It always scares the wits out of me. If, though, it were a film it might have a premise like: 'A washed-up trawlerman, offered one last chance to put together a crew to track down and capture a monstrous giant squid, finds that his inner demons are at least as dangerous as the creature he finally confronts.'

Now this might not be the best film in the world and seems to owe something to *Jaws*, which is more of an ensemble piece and a kind of road movie at sea. It's an overcoming-the-monster story, an action-adventure film with some mythic elements. Our film could contain some horror elements, but overall it sounds like it could be a bit dated, unless it were either updated or maybe set historically. Feels a bit derivative. There's certainly a more naturalistic film to be made about the death of the fishing industry that focuses on an ensemble of increasingly out of work trawlermen (no, they don't go into stripping) or desperate trawlermen pushed to the brink to preserve their livelihood. It would include a boat that didn't come back (killing someone close to our main character) and, perhaps, a triumphant ending which involved the main character making a permanent difference to his community in some way. The discovery of something on the seabed (a ship, a plane), the raising of which seems to remove some metaphoric curse over the community. It seems to offer a mythic adventure structure, an odyssey-based story that is, nevertheless, based in reality. So we might have a premise that runs: 'A desperate trawlerman, driven to despair through falling catches, has to work increasingly dangerous fishing grounds. But in the darkest, remotest part of the sea he discovers the wreck of an aeroplane that will change his life and the life of his community for ever.' For the moment, though, just don't ask me how…

Let's think of another: maybe something a bit Woody Allenish. 'A nebbish theatre director falls in love with his leading lady, only to discover that she is having an affair with his wife.' A bit basic perhaps, but could be taken in a more interesting direction if it turns out that the leading lady is also two-timing Woody's wife with Woody's best friend. An 'oh, the complexities of love' kind of story…although we may need to decide whether it's a full-blown rom-com (in which case it might need to be more 'high-concept' and that this might need to be reflected in the title) or a comedy drama that's a bit more subtle and nuanced in the relationships and allows for scenes that don't have a comic pay-off. It will also have clear themes about the nature of relationships and the ways that we screw up our intimate lives. Nevertheless, I'm pretty sure that both these examples won't pass the time test: are they still attractive a week later? Worth reserving my energies for the ideas that won't let me go, rather than the ones that I can't let go.

P.S. The premise for the current script? A widowed taxi driver, determined to commit suicide, is faced with a search for the truth about his wife's death. In the process he discovers both reasons to live and reasons to die, and has to face a dilemma that only he can resolve.

It's important to be writing in one's own territory; not to be straying into worlds where we know nothing but are pretending to be expert guides. Climbing through the branches of the genre tree, we might decide that we're better at writing thrillers, horror, sci-fi, fantasy, action adventure and any of their sub-genres. We've studied all the films in these areas and we know what's currently in vogue and we're looking for the next kink in the curve that will offer an original treatment that will appeal to a contemporary audience. If we're business savvy we will study the journals and mags that tell us what Hollywood (or London or Mumbai or Berlin) is buying at the moment. If we're well connected we'll be talking with directors and producers and asking them what they're looking for at the moment. (They may tell us that they'll know it when they see it…) If we're passionate we may be looking to take one of our brilliant ideas and re-working it to fit a specific genre or a particular production method or format. Or we may just feel that our long-term genius project is just plain brilliant for any age or audience and let others decide about how it gets sold…

Understanding genre is an aspect of the business side of films which is intimately tied up with the notion that the primary function of a film script is as a set of instructions for a group of 'other' people (often a very large group) to carry out. Prior to that stage in the script's life of actualisation, it also has to do a great job in selling itself, its storytelling, its dramatic sense to various people who hold various pots of money and have the responsibility to spend it in the way that's most likely to bring them more money, more kudos, better career prospects, and so on.

Anyway, I got the drain rods home and went outside the back door to look at the manhole cover that's been winking at me for a couple of days now. And as I lifted it off I was greeted by a swarm of ants, which had made one of those beautiful ant houses – filled with tiny tunnels – around the inside of the lid. I felt bad as I hosed them down into the ceramic drains that led inevitably to the septic tank. All that work. All that life. Now, though, it was time to get to work with the rods. And soon I had dislodged a McDonald's scale stream of fat that was blocking up the pipework from the kitchen wastes into the drains. And after the fat came some strange, mushroom-like blobs that bobbed up and down in the ebbing water of the drains. And after a few times of not being able to get hold of them, I finally brought them to the surface on the spiky metal end of the rodding tool. They were not large white mushrooms at all. They were, in fact, either baby, or foetal, rats with tiny white feet and tiny white heads with tiny pointed faces and those buck-teethed mouths. I gagged on the spot. If those were the babies, where, I wondered, was the mother? Or, indeed (although I know nothing of rats' breeding habits) the father? And as I turned around quickly I saw, out of the corner of my eye, the largest, fattest, hairiest, scariest…stop, please!

I've now read the draft of my taxi-driver story that I finished five weeks ago before I started moving. It's hard getting back into it after such a break. I know it still needs work in a number of departments. It's an unorthodox, multi-stranded plot and there's some reorganising to be done. It's ambitious in a way that I haven't been ambitious before. But I think it needs to try to do something interesting and different if it is to work in the market place. We're all now in a post-*Inception* world. So I have to make some decisions about the way the story gets told that will, almost certainly, dictate the extent to which the film that the script becomes is a success. There is so much to get right, so much to improve, so much to bring together. I hope that, following this next draft and together with my director, we can make the script the best script that we've both been involved with. That we can make a piece of work that moves and stimulates a significantly sized audience. I hope that I can bring together all my learning and experience from the years I've spent doing this and apply all this accumulated 'stuff' to next week's writing. In other words 'fix it!' And I will fix it, just as soon as I've found that rat.

Keith Tutt (*b.* 1959) was Royal Literary Fund fellow at UEA from 2009 to 2010. His screenplays include an adaptation of Martin Amis's novel *Other People: A Mystery Story*, and his documentaries include *Killing Us Softly?* (BBC, 1993), about the safety system of the Sizewell 'B' power station. In 2000 he won a BAFTA for his work on the BBC children's animation series *Pablo*. Keith has also published six non-fiction books.

The Two-Typewriter Trick

Erica Wagner

If I say that my year at UEA (1990–91) taught me that inspiration is over-rated, perhaps you'll think it a backhanded compliment. I can assure you that it's not.

In the years before I came to Norwich, O best beloved, I never allowed myself to start a second piece of writing before I'd finished the first. This meant that I spent a great deal of time completely stalled, waiting for the Muse to descend – because she usually declined to do so, this was an approach both frustrating and unproductive. I'd get halfway through a story, hit a roadblock and, more often than not, that would be that. Not a roadblock, really – more the end of the road, full stop. And then Malcolm Bradbury taught me – all of us – the two-typewriter trick.

He'd hit upon it when, decades before he'd started the Creative Writing MA (at the behest, as we all know, of his first student, the young Ian McEwan). He was trying to break into the then-thriving market for short fiction: women's magazines at the time (let's say that this was the late 1950s, the very early 1960s) always ran stories.

So he and a friend, a fellow writer, bought themselves ten second-hand typewriters. They set them up in a room: there was paper on every platen. He and his friend each started writing, and when one reached a creative impasse he'd shout 'Stuck!' – and both had to switch machines. Each picked up the other's thread; each built on the other's ideas. In no time they had ten stories to send out – all under feminine pseudonyms, of course.

This seemingly slight, amusing tale changed my life. I abandoned preciousness; I gave up on the Muse; I took to hard work and variety. If something doesn't work, try something else. Keep going. Just write, and write all the time. I'm happiest now if I have two or even three things on the go – not counting journalism, which goes in an entirely separate mental box. It's not that there is any real cross-pollination, or at least none that I am consciously aware of: it's more that I have a sense of being light on my feet, dancing between ideas and forms, able to shift into another register at will.

Over time, too, I came to appreciate constraint, a side-benefit of either making myself write when I thought I wasn't inclined to, or starting another piece when I was sure I didn't have any ideas. When I first wrote stories for the radio, I asked myself how I could possibly ensure that a piece would come in at 2,200 words. Turns out I could. More recently, I've been collaborating on a show with the French storyteller Abbi Patrix and his partner, Swedish musician Linda Edsjö. It's a sequence of stories, performed by Abbi and Linda, some of them taken from traditional material, some of them invented, mostly by me. But those inventions occur with specific performers (and hence, specific voices) in mind; if we decide that a little humour is called for, well, I'd better write something funny.

It is an entirely different process from writing a novel or a piece of short fiction on my own; but when I've gone back to my solo work, I'm enriched and emboldened. Would I have had the courage to take on something like this without Malcolm and the two-typewriter trick? I'm not so sure. It's worth recalling, at this juncture, what a great influence Malcolm's vision has had in this country. When the course at UEA began, 'Creative Writing' as a discipline was a thing regarded, here, with not a little suspicion: great writers were born, not made, and only those uncouth Americans thought otherwise.

Even as little as a decade ago I was astonished by a piece that appeared in another newspaper at the time of Malcolm's death, deploring the pernicious spread of such courses: ridiculous to think that writing could be taught. (I wrote to the paper in question to ask whether the journalist would leave a concert in disgust should he discover that the musicians had had lessons – alas, my letter was never printed.) Now, of course, Creative Writing courses – run not only by universities but by publishers, agents and newspapers too – are thick on the ground. By now, I've taught a couple of them myself. No: attending a Creative Writing course isn't going to transform someone without talent, or even workmanlike skill, into a Dickens or Tolstoy – or an Ian McEwan.

And yet: to return to the analogy of the music lesson, not everyone who learns to the play the piano hopes to become a concert pianist. There is pleasure to be had in the act itself, from learning from your fellow musicians, your fellow writers, the tips and tricks that will allow you to take greater satisfaction in your craft. We are storytelling animals: some argue that our species prospered because of our gift for story, a notion I find easy to credit. Stories help us remember what's happened to us; they help us make sense of our lives. Why shouldn't anyone who wishes to improve their storytelling skills?

Since I left UEA twenty years ago, however, the publishing business has undergone radical change: it's impossible to foresee how that change will continue. Certainly, however, the dominance of the bestseller skews the market – and skews, sometimes, the expectations of the people who attend Creative Writing courses. The few courses I've taught have always focussed on the craft of writing – sure, there are 'How to Get Published' courses, but frankly I'm not sure what they can offer beyond the obvious (be really careful of punctuation; make sure to spell an agent's/editor's name right).

It is in the craft, for me, that the pleasure lies: and where I return, again and again, to the two-typewriter trick. The act of writing is like solving a puzzle – except that I have to make the pieces as well as fit them together. Over the years I've tried to gather and hone the strategies which enable to me to shape my work to my own satisfaction. There's never an end to this process: every day I sit down at my desk is an education. But on that desk there are always – if only in my imagination – two typewriters.

Erica Wagner (*b.* 1967) received her MA in Creative Writing from UEA in 1991. She has published a volume of short stories, *Gravity* (1998), a novel, *Seizure* (2007), and a non-fiction book, *Ariel's Gift: Ted Hughes, Sylvia Plath and the Story of* Birthday Letters (2001). In 2007 she was a judge of the Man Booker Prize. She is literary editor of *The Times*.

Endings

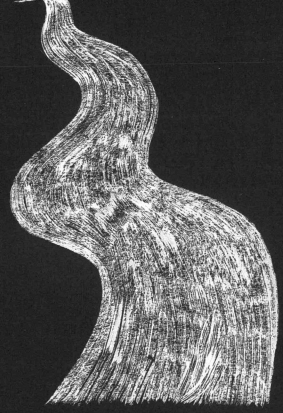

Tensions in a Wild Garden

Rose Tremain

In Memory of Angus Wilson (1913–91)

The novelists Angus Wilson most admired were Dickens and Dostoevsky. For him, the greatness of these two writers lay in 'their extraordinary mixture of black and comic vision, which allowed them to see how profound absurdity can be and how utterly ridiculous most of the profound things are'. He felt that, above all their other qualities, it was this understanding of the tragi-comic that enabled them to look without flinching at a world 'in which human beings become disjointed, so that one part of them cannot really be responsible for the other'. He often admitted that their work exercised a profound influence on his own. What he could not have predicted was that an absurd and bleak disjunction would blight his own life in his last years. The illness from which he died separated him almost totally from his former self. Here was a man who had used words fast and furiously, a one-time public orator, a fabled raconteur – and he was left with almost no speech at all. Tragic though his death is, it has at least liberated him from a half-life which any one of his central characters would have found hilariously intolerable.

Angus entered my life in 1964. I was a student at the then new University of East Anglia and I had chosen this university because I knew that he was teaching there. I knew he was there because I had read an article in a magazine about his Suffolk garden, and in the three years that followed, these were the two sides to him that I came to know best: the superlatively gifted teacher of literature who refused to treat literature as a thing set apart from life, and the creator of a wild garden, of an artefact which simulates the disorder of nature in an orderly way and which was, by his own admission, the place 'at the very heart of my symbolic view of life'.

Later, through his work, through his friendship and through the routines that he favoured, I came to understand in some measure the tensions and contradictions that drove him on and which the image of the wild garden comes near to encompassing. He loved the order and tranquillity of his Suffolk cottage, yet he travelled to every continent in the world and hated to be trapped in English self-absorption for long periods of time. He described himself as an agnostic liberal humanist and yet he understood the complex inadequacies of this moral position in the presence of what he termed 'transcendent evil'. At parties, lectures and social gatherings of all kinds, he presented a gregarious, witty and effortlessly generous persona, but his bonhomie masked a deep private pessimism which led, from time to time, to bouts of depression, from which only his writing seemed to be able to liberate him.

His novels take on these internal conflicts and contradictions and grapple with them in absorbingly different ways.

He could make totally believable two characters as far apart in world and time as Sylvia Calvert in *Late Call* and Hamo Langmuir in *As if by Magic*. Sylvia's restoration of purpose at the end of her journey is as deeply and as truthfully felt as Hamo's consciousness of 'perpetual, desperate woe' at the end of his. Yet neither is an Angus Wilson type. There is really no such character. For Angus never revisited old fictional territory.

He was a very acute observer. I sometimes felt that his writer's vigilance was so constant that it must have tired him. And yet it was this vigilance, allied to a profound curiosity about the world that gave his fiction its zest and its social accuracy.

He wanted his novels to encompass life, not merely be about life. He was more concerned to move his readers than to dazzle them. Though at times – and particularly with his extraordinarily successful portraits of female characters – he does both. He admired Joyce's *Ulysses* 'less for the intellectual pyrotechnics than for the character of Bloom, the most entirely moving figure of twentieth-century fiction'. He criticised Henry James for his refusal to enter life's unsavoury arena and loved Dickens so passionately for his refusal ever to leave it.

Angus Wilson was a great novelist and a profoundly lovable man. I will encounter no one like him again in my lifetime.

Rose Tremain (*b.* 1943) did her BA in English at UEA and taught on the MA in Creative Writing from 1988 to 1995. Her novel *Music and Silence* won the best novel prize in the 1999 Whitbread Awards, building on the recognition she received in the award of the 1989 *Sunday Express* Book of the Year for her novel *Restoration*, and the 1992 James Tait Black Memorial Prize for *Sacred Country*, which also won the Prix Femina Étranger. In June 2008 she won the Orange Prize for *The Road Home*.

The Soaring Imagination

Lorna Sage

In Memory of Angela Carter (1940–92)

Angela Carter died yesterday aged fifty-one and at the height of her powers as a novelist. The boldness of her writing, her powers of enchantment and hilarity, her generous inventiveness, all make this premature and tragic death harder to take. We needed her around.

She interpreted the times for us with unrivalled penetration: her branching and many-layered narratives mirrored our shifting world of identities lost and found, insiders versus outsiders, alternative histories and utopias postponed. In her stories there's a magical democracy – no class distinction between probable people and improbable (even impossible) ones, or between humans and animals and allegories. All of her writing was at odds with conventional realism, yet she mapped with great precision the history and topography of our fantasies. She was miraculously 'at home' in this epoch, where people and their 'images', facts and their shadows, co-exist so closely and menacingly.

Like the twin heroines of her last novel *Wise Children* (1991) she began and ended in south London, though her parents were migrants from the north: her journalist father Hugh Stalker, a Scot; Olive a Yorkshirewoman. She had a brief spell as a junior reporter, then married in 1960 and went to Bristol University in 1962, where she contrived to specialise in medieval literature and read a lot of anthropology, sociology and psychology, more or less on the side. She stayed on in Bristol, and three of her first four novels are set in the provincial Bohemia she both inhabited and analysed with fascination.

She wrote brilliantly about the way styles were being recycled, and her own style had, appropriately enough, a patina of second-hand charm, all quotation and parody. The best known of these books, *The Magic Toyshop* (1967), won the Somerset Maugham Award, and has been filmed and – something unimaginable even ten years ago – has become a set text in schools. *Love*, written in 1969–70, but not published until 1971, was a lethally accurate and extremely beautiful elegy on the decade of her first youth.

By now she had become a vagrant and an adventurer. Her first marriage was over and she went off to Japan, first on a visit and from 1970 lived there for two years. Although this experience is seldom directly reflected in the fiction (except for *Fireworks*, 1974), her habit of seeing yourself and your culture from the outside is everywhere evident in her later work. (Similarly with more theoretical material on displacement – structuralist stuff from Levi-Strauss, Barthes, Foucault). She'd already found a new fictional formula in *Heroes and Villains* (1969), a picaresque structure that enabled her to write open-endedly about change, and in the novels that followed – *The Infernal Desire Machines of Dr Hoffman* (1972), *The Passion of New Eve* (1977) – she produced some of the most suggestive speculative fictions of our time.

Angela somehow understood, not just theoretically but sensuously and imaginatively, that we were living with constructs of ourselves, neither false nor true but mythical and alterable. It was, of course, a founding femininist perception. As well as writing fiction she was, after her return to England in 1972, writing pieces for the *Guardian* and *New Society*, and associating with the women behind Virago Press, particularly Carmen Callil.

For the moment, however, this didn't help her sales: it wasn't until the Eighties that readers caught up with her, though *The Bloody Chamber* (1979) won golden opinions for its brilliant and erotic rewritings of fairy tales, and her exercise in cultural history, *The Sadeian Woman*, in the same year, shocked some people into the realisation that she knew exactly what she was doing.

During recent years she has come into her own. Though her work has always been alive and dangerous enough to deny her the major literary prizes, she has become part of the contemporary canon, whether you construct it under the aegis of 'postmodernism' or 'feminism'. *Nights at the Circus* (1984) and *Wise Children* are no less complex but more ribald and relaxed. Since the later Seventies she has settled in London again, with Mark Pearce. Their son was born in 1982, when she was forty-two, and set her thinking in new ways about time and parenthood. In the last novel, Nora and Dora Chance grow old most ungracefully and there's clearly personal feeling in Angela's enjoyment of their indecorous old age.

She will never have the chance herself to shock us at seventy, but the books will retain their power to do it. She is a splendid example of the woman writer who made it from the margins, but also, just as important, a writer who always demonstrates how vital counter-cultural impulses are to the very existence of any worthwhile tradition. It's a wise child that knows its own mother, as she'd have said.

Perhaps the saddest thought at this moment is that she was so good at making room for hope. There wasn't any for her, however, in these last short months, before lung cancer killed her, and it's no use pretending that she wouldn't have produced new work just as wonderful, given the chance.

Lorna Sage (1943–2001) was Professor of English Literature at the University of East Anglia. See page 275.

Pipe-smoker of the Year

Clive Sinclair

In Memory of Malcolm Bradbury (1932-2000)

When I first set eyes on Malcolm Bradbury he looked like a man on the youthful side of middle age. He wore a tweedy jacket and smoked a pipe, a dead ringer for Inspector Morse. Except for the giggle. No, Malcolm was anything but morose. It was 1966 and he was in his second year on the faculty of the University of East Anglia. I was a freshman. The campus was still under construction, and the departments were still in a state of flux. So when Malcolm said, 'Let there be American Studies,' and stepped westward, I followed in his footsteps. I've been doing much the same ever since.

Anyway, he still looked on the youthful side of middle age when I last saw him (at the Savoy, rather than UEA), not so long ago. By then he was no average pipe-smoker but Pipe-smoker of the Year. He accepted the accolade with his typical mix of diffidence and enthusiasm. The diffidence was no pose. It was his birthright as an Englishman. It was the source of his comedy. Its natural expression was the giggle.

The enthusiasm was more problematic, more American. It had to be kept in check, lest it become greed. When he did let it off the leash, Jekyll certainly became Hyde, instead of humane but bumbling Dr Petworth, there emerged fierce and screw-it-all Howard Kirk, the Genghis Khan of academia. *The History Man* was his most famous, his most American and his greatest book.

I happened to be visiting my son in America when his knighthood was announced, so didn't pick up the news until the middle of this year. I immediately sent him a note of congratulation. He was delighted by the honour, but this time his enthusiasm was offset by something darker than diffidence: his life had been blighted by ill-health. Even after it became apparent that the illness was serious, I couldn't envision anyone other than a youthful Bradbury on the verge of middle age. Still can't, even though I know he's dead. Indeed the photographs accompanying his obituaries all confirm my impression.

In the 1950s, when he published his first novel, America was viewed in Manichean terms: it was either the fountainhead of vulgarity or it was the laboratory of the future. Kingsley Amis took one view, Malcolm another.

When one of the former's alter egos comes across a copy of Saul Bellow's *Herzog*, he picks it up in disgust and flings it across the room (seeing it as the source of his son's lunacy). Unlike Malcolm, who was eager to expose his charges to Bellow's books. On a memorable occasion we got more than the books. Getting wind that Bellow was in London, Malcolm somehow got us all invited to a seminar led by the great man himself at the

American Embassy in Grosvenor Square (then a war zone).

As if the internal conflict between Englishness and Americanisation wasn't enough, Malcolm also had to juggle the opposing demands of teaching and writing. Was it possible to be both an academic and an artist? Would not the professor be rendered too self-conscious to perform in a more spontaneous way? Bellow offers some relevant advice in the aforementioned *Herzog*: 'On the knees of your soul? Might as well scrub the floor.'

And so, together with his colleague and friend Angus Wilson, he started the MA in Creative Writing. At first it was dismissed as essentially un-English, an American fad, in fact. But success changed the carpers into harpists.

I was never a fully paid-up member of the course, but I was a regular visitor for a number of years. In the late 1970s (when I returned to UEA to complete my doctorate) the Creative Writing programme was in the doldrums (despite its brilliant beginning). There was but one student, and he was no Ian McEwan.

Ever the kindly diplomat (more Petworth than Kirk), Malcolm was finding it harder and harder to say positive things about his student's prose. Then he hit upon the wheeze of inviting all the indigenous writers (both the manqués and published) to join him.

It was worth it; the following year's intake included none other than Kazuo Ishiguro, Andrew Jefford (then a tenebrous prose-poet, now a sommelier with a pen) and James Sorel-Cameron (whose blazing debut *Mag* has proved a hard act to follow).

Of course, none entered as unlettered caterpillars and emerged as silver-tongued butterflies, but all were assisted immeasurably by the course (I include myself). You cannot teach anyone without talent to be a writer, but you can educate the skilled in the art of reading others with greater sensitivity, and themselves with the ruthless eye of a perceptive editor.

To decide to be a writer is an act of will, an existential act even. To be seen as such in another's eyes makes the clothes fit better, almost convinces you that you're not a fool or a charlatan. Malcolm's great gift was to enable you to believe in yourself. I believed in him. I hope he did too.

Clive Sinclair (*b.* 1948) received a BA from UEA in 1969 and a PhD in 1983. His many books include *Hearts of Gold* (1980), winner of the Somerset Maugham award, *Cosmetic Effects* (1989), *The Lady with the Laptop* (1996) and *Meet the Wife* (2002), winner of both the PEN Silver pen and the Jewish Quarterly Prize for Fiction.

After Nature and So On

Andrew Motion

In Memory of W. G. Sebald (1944–2001)

Dear Max,
it would be so like you still to be here

twinkling behind your sad specs,
smoothing your sleek walrus down

to bring a *diminution of disorder*
after a whole morning of listening

to questions no one on earth can answer.
But then you were always a past-

master at taking the weight,
and later, knowing the best response

must be *to arm ourselves with patience*,
sliding away to worry it through and over.

I see you now just as you are for ever –
out of the wreckage and off once more,

footing the stop-start quick white line
which holds two halves of the road apart

and joins them together, until such time
as you turn again and abide my questions.

Andrew Motion (*b.* 1952) was Professor of Creative Writing at UEA from 1995 to 2003. Poet Laureate between 1999 and 2009, he has published more than fifteen volumes of poetry, most recently *The Cinder Path* (2009), as well as four novels and many other books, including *Philip Larkin: A Writer's Life* (1997), *Keats: A Biography* (1997) and *In the Blood: A Memoir of my Childhood* (2006).

Difficulties of the Do-It-Yourself Epitaph

Lorna Sage

A review of Last Words: Variations On a Theme in Cultural History *by Karl S. Guthke, published in the* Observer *on 3 January 1993.* GF

People used to rehearse for dying. Now we muff our lines and drift and stumble into oblivion.

Nonetheless, we remain fascinated by stylish exits, perhaps, as Karl Guthke suggests in this genial, sceptical and gently pedantic study of the cult of Last Words, precisely because dying is now at once so privatised and so mass-produced that to wring any articulate meaning out of the moment is indeed heroic.

In the early Christian centuries you knew how to die, the script was written, you did it by formula ('Father, into Thy hands I commend my spirit') with priestly prompters and an audience. Then in the Renaissance the nature of the drama shifted.

Shakespeare's dying heroes and heroines have forgotten the old lines, and are given much grander ones. Montaigne expresses the opinion that to die without notice would be best, a view the eras of piety would have recoiled from in terror. In short, the dying started simply not to know what to say any longer.

The eighteenth century seems to have been the turning point. Early on (1718) a *Collection of Dying Speeches*, very probably put together by Daniel Defoe, unpicked a good deal of the mystique of (even) secular credos by pointing out that patriots and traitors seemed to die with similar strength of conviction, and similar sentiments. 'We are come to an Age in which the Dying Words of Men are little more to be credited than their Living Words…'

And towards the end of the same century Madame Guillotine was responsible for a profusion of bloody eloquence that fed the habit, but in the long run fed cynicism, too.

What we're left with is our need for the sense of an ending, a last-ditch attachment to the value of the individual life; the same sort of motive, probably, that's behind the appetite for biography. As Professor Guthke says, it doesn't matter as much as you might think whether recorded last words are apocryphal or not, since they're really addressed to our desire for this wistful, world-without-end meaning. Goethe's famous last words, 'More light,' the archetypal Enlightenment farewell, have at least four variants, including, in his valet's account, a humble request for the *pot de chambre*, but none of them is without interest. Like the others here, like Oscar Wilde or Socrates or Lady Mary Wortley Montague, he is standing in for the rest of us. Lady Mary's last words, by the way, were 'All very interesting.' And so it is.

Lorna Sage (1943–2001) was Professor of English Literature at the University of East Anglia. See page 275.

Head

Derek Mahon

What I hold, life size, is the near-final
revelation of form, a moulded head inclined
to an absorbing task, some job in hand.
Running my fingers round from the spinal
bump of the skull to the shut lip and eye
I wait for it to give tongue, to avail
of language; and it does, but silently,
its thought enclosed in that intent oval.

Words come to a head and fail, but faces win –
artful inflections of the giving skin
stretched over the tense wiring of desire.
She lies there at an angle, the work done,
inert but wide awake, the watchful brain
at rest, once more preparing to inspire.

Derek Mahon (*b.* 1941) was Henfield Writing Fellow at UEA in 1975. He studied at Trinity College, Dublin, and the Sorbonne, and has held journalistic and academic appointments in London and New York. His collections of poetry include *Harbour Lights* (2005), *Life on Earth* (2008) and *An Autumn Wind* (2010). His version of Rostand's *Cyrano de Bergerac* was produced at London's National Theatre in 2004. He has received numerous awards, including Lannan and Guggenheim Fellowships and, in 2007, the David Cohen Prize for recognition of a lifetime's achievement in literature.

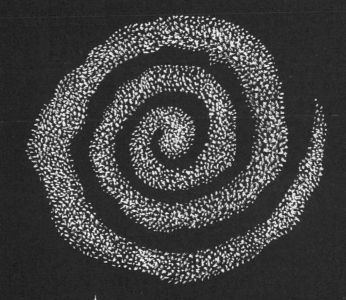

Appendix

UEA Creative Writing Alumni Bibliography *1971–2011*
Andrew Cowan

A

Adams, Liz (MA 2007)
Green Dobermans (2011)

Alderman, Naomi (MA 2003)
David Higham Award winner (2002)
Disobedience (2006) – *Sunday Times*
Young Writer of the Year Award
winner (2007); Waterstone's 25
Authors for the Future (2007);
Orange Broadband Prize for New
Writers winner (2006); Glen
Dimplex Award shortlist (2006)
The Lesson (2010)

Allan, Clare (MA 2000)
Poppy Shakespeare (2006) – Orange
Broadband Award for New Writers
shortlist (2007); Arts Foundation
Fellowship shortlist (2007), *Guardian*
Book Prize Shortlist (2007)

Allan, Nicholas (MA 1981)
Numerous award-winning picture
books for children, including:
The Hefty Fairy (1989)
The Magic Lavatory (1992)
The Queen's Knickers (2000)
Where Willy Went (2006)
Father Christmas Needs a Wee (2009)
Picasso's Trousers (2011)
and a novel:
The First Time (1995)

Allen, Mary (MA 2002)
A House Divided (1998)

Almond, David (BA 1973)
Sleepless Nights (1985)
A Kind of Heaven (1997)
Skellig (1998) – Carnegie Medal
winner (1998); Whitbread Children's
Book Award winner (1998);
Carnegie of Carnegies shortlist (2007)
Kit's Wilderness (1999) – Nestle
Smarties Book Prize (Silver Award)
winner (1999); Michael L. Printz
Award winner (USA 2001);
Guardian Children's Fiction Prize
shortlist (1999); Carnegie Medal

shortlist (2000)
Counting Stars (2000)
Heaven Eyes (2000) –
Whitbread Children's Book Award
shortlist (2000); Carnegie Medal
shortlist (2000)
Secret Heart (2001)
Skellig: A Play (2002)
Where Your Wings Were (2002)
Wild Girl, Wild Boy: A Play (2002)
The Fire-Eaters (2003) – Nestle
Smarties Book Prize (Gold Award)
winner (2003); Whitbread Children's
Book Award winner (2003); *Boston
Globe*-Horn Book Award (USA 2004);
Carnegie Medal shortlist (2003);
Guardian Children's Fiction Prize
shortlist (2003)
Kate, the Cat and the Moon (2004)
Clay (2005) – Carnegie Medal
shortlist (2006); Costa Children's
Book Award shortlist (2006)
My Dad's a Birdman (2007)
Jackdaw Summer (2008)
The Savage (2008)
The Boy Who Climbed Into the Moon
(2010)
My name is Mina (2010) – *Guardian*
Children's Fiction Prize longlist (2011)
The True Tale of the Monster Billy Dean
(2011)

De'Ath, Amy (BA 2008)
Erec & Enide (2010)

Atkinson, Diane (MA 2004)
Votes for Women (1988)
The Suffragettes in Pictures (1996)
Funny Girls: Cartooning For Equality
(1997)
*Love and Dirt: The Marriage of Arthur
Munby and Hannah Cullwick* (2003)
*Elsie and Mairi Go To War: Two
Extraordinary Women on the Western
Front* (2009)

Aw, Tash (MA 2003)
The Harmony Silk Factory (2005) –
Whitbread Prize First Novel winner
(2005); Commonwealth Writers'
Prize for Best First Novel winner
(2005); Booker Prize shortlist
(2005); International Impac Dublin
Award longlist (2007)
Map of the Invisible World (2009)

Azzopardi, Trezza (MA 1998)
The Hiding Place (2000) – Geoffrey
Faber Memorial Prize winner (2001);
James Tait Black Memorial Prize for
Fiction Best Novel shortlist (2000);
Booker Prize shortlist (2000);
Remember Me (2004) – Arts Council
Wales Book of the Year
shortlist (2005)
Winterton Blue (2007)
The Song House (2010)

B

Batchelor, Paul (MA 2000)
Fighting In the Captain's Tower (with J.
P. Nosbaum, 2002)
To Photograph a Snow Crystal (2006)
The Sinking Road (2008) – Glen
Dimplex New Writers Award for
Poetry shortlist (2008); Jerwood
Aldeburgh First Collection Prize
shortlist (2008)
Winner: *The Times* Stephen Spender
Prize for Poetry Translation (2009)
Winner: Edwin Morgan
International Poetry Competition
(2009)

Baylis, Nick (MA 1993)
The Science of Well-being (2006)
Learning From Wonderful Lives (2006)
The Rough Guide to Happiness (2009)

Beard, Richard (MA 1995)
20: A Novel of (Not) Smoking (1996)
Damascus (1998)
The Cartoonist (2000)
*Muddied Oafs: The Last Days of
Rugger* (2003)

Dry Bones (2004)
Manly Pursuits: Beating the Australians (2006)
Becoming Drucilla: One Life, Two Friends, Three Genders (2008)
Lazarus is Dead (2011)

Bedford, Martyn (MA 1994)
Acts of Revision (1996) – *Yorkshire Post* Best First Work winner (1996)
Exit, Orange and Red (1997)
The Houdini Girl (1999)
Black Cat (2000)
The Island of Lost Souls (2006)
Flip (2011)

Bell, Julia (MA 1996)
The Creative Writing Coursebook (ed., with Paul Magrs, 2001)
Massive (2003)
Dirty Work (2007)

Benn, Tom (MA 2010)
The Doll Princess (2012)

Bidwell, Tom Dalton (BA 2005)
Credits include:
Risky and Fluke (National Student Drama Festival, 2006) – *Sunday Times* NSDF Award winner (2006)
Rumour and the Rope Trick (Stephen Joseph Theatre, 2007)
Things To Do Before You Die (BBC Radio 4, 2008)
BBC Writers Academy (2008/09)
Company Along the Mile (West Yorkshire Playhouse 2009)
Scripts for EastEnders, Casualty, Dr Who (BBC)
Screen International 'Star of Tomorrow' (2010)
Coming Up (Channel 4, 2010)
Wish 143 – Academy Awards nomination (2011)

Birch, Druin (MA 2004)
Digging Up the Dead: Uncovering the Life and Times of an Extraordinary Surgeon (2008)
Taking The Medicine (2009)

Birne, Eleanor (MA 2002)
When Will I sleep Through The Night (2011)

Blank, Jane (BA 1986)
Naked Playing the Cello (2003)
The Geometry of Love (2008)

Block, Brett Ellen (MA 1998)
Destination Known (2001) – Drue Heinz Literature Prize winner (2001)
The Grave of God's Daughter (2004)
The Lightning Rule (2006)
The Definition of Wind (2010)

Blomer, Yvonne (MA 2004)
A Broken Mirror, Fallen Leaf (2006) – Gerald Lampert Memorial Award for Poetry shortlist
Landscapes and Home (2011)
The Book of Places (2011)

Borek, Ben (MA 2004)
Donjong Heights (2007)

Bower, Sarah (MA 2002)
The Needle in the Blood (2007)
The Book of Love (2008)

Bowker, Peter (MA 1991)
TV and film credits include:
Casualty (BBC1, 1992–7)
Peak Practice (ITV, 1995)
The Uninvited (ITV, 1997)
Where The Heart Is (ITV, 1998)
A Christmas Carol (2000)
The Canterbury Tales: The Miller's Tale (BBC1, 2003)
Blackpool (BBC1, 2004) – BAFTA shortlist (2005); Golden Globe Awards shortlist (2006)
Viva Blackpool (BBC1, 2006)
Occupation (BBC1, 2009)
Desperate Romantics (BBC2, 2009)
Wuthering Heights (ITV, 2009)

Bowler, Tim (BA 1972)
Midget (1994)
Dragon's Rock (1995)
River Boy (1997) – Carnegie Medal Best Novel winner (1998)
Shadows (1999)
Storm Catchers (2001)
Starseeker (2002)
Firmament (2004)
Apocalypse (2004)
Blood on the Snow (2004)
Walking with the Dead (2005)
Frozen Fire (2006)
Bloodchild (2008)
Playing Dead (2008)
Closing In (2008)
Breaking Free (2009)
Running Scared (2009)

Boyne, John (MA 1995)
The Thief of Time (2000)
The Congress of Rough Riders (2001)
Crippen (2004)
Next of Kin (2006)
The Boy In the Striped Pyjamas (2006) – CBI Bisto Book of the Year winner (2007); Irish Book Award: People's Choice Award Book of the Year winner (2007); Irish Book Award: Children's Book of the Year winner (2007); WH Smith Children's Book of the Year shortlist (2007); the Ottakar's Children's Book Prize shortlist (2007); the Prix Farmiente shortlist (Belgium, 2007); the Paolo Ungari Award (Italy, 2006); Borders Originial Voices (Young Adult) shortlist (USA, 2006)
Mutiny on the Bounty (2008)
The House of Special Purpose (2009)
Noah Barleywater Runs Away (2010) – Shortlisted for the Irish Book Award (2010), Sheffield Children's Book Award (2011), Children's Book of the Year – winner (Slovakia, 2011)
The Absolutist (2011)

Bradby, Lawrence (MA 2003)
Breathe In, Conk Out (2001)
Best Bloody Job in the World (2002)
Bookmark Book (2003)
Sweep and Veer (2005)
Mechanical Operations in Cambourne (with Helen Stratford, 2009)

Brar, Amman (Paul) (MA 2004)
Credits include:
Short play, Radio 4
Writer in residence, Tamasha Theatre Company

Braun, Harriet (MA 1993)
Credits include:
Mistresses (BBC1)
Hotel Babylon (BBC1)
Lip Service (BBC3, 2010)

Brennan, Catherine M (MA 2008)
Beneath the Deluge (2008)

Bridgeman, Laura (MA 2003)
Credits include:
Maison Splendide (London New Play's Festival, 1996)
Junk (Gay Sweatshop, 1997) *Medicine Girl* (Guinness Ingenuity Award winner, 1997)

Etiquette (BBC Radio4, 2000)
ID 1000 (The National Youth
Theatre, 2007)

Bryan, Lynne (MA 1985)
Envy at the Cheese Handout (1995)
Gorgeous (1999)
Like Rabbits (2002)

Bueno, Bernardo (current PhD)
Minimundo (2006) – South, National
and Books Literary Award Best New
Author Prize winner (2007);
Acorianos Award for Best Short Story
Collection shortlist (2007)

Bullock, Emily (MA 2004)
The Separate Principle (2008)

Burch, Druin (MA 2004)
Digging Up the Dead (2007)
Taking the Medicine (2009)

Butcher, Pat (BA 1973)
The Perfect Distance (2005)

Butler, Jenna (MA 2004)
Forcing Bloom (2007)
Weather (2008)
Winter Ballast (2008)
Aphelion (2010)

Butler, Sue (MA 1999)
Vanishing Trick (2004)

Byers, Sam (MA 2003; current PhD)
Idiopathy (2012)

C
Campbell, Aifric (MA 2003, PhD
2007)
The Semantics of Murder (2008) – Glen
Dimplex New Writers Award for
Fiction shortlist (2008)
The Loss Adjustor (2010)
On The Floor (2012)

Candy, Edward (pseudonym of
Alison Neville, MA 1975)
Which Doctor (1954)
Bones of Contention (1954)
The Graver Tribe (1958)
Strokes of Havoc (1966)
Parents' Day (1967)
Dr Amadeus (1969)
Words for Murder Perhaps (1971)
Scene Changing (1977)
Voices of Children (1980)

Cartright, Anthony (BA, 1996)
The Afterglow (2004) – Betty Trask
Award winner (2004); James Tait
Black Memorial Prize shortlist
(2004)
Heartland (2009)

Castalia, Drew (MA 2009)
Credits include:
Tempting Fates (2008)
Lions (with Will Simpson and Jacob
Marcet, 2009)
The Adventures of Young Sherlock Homes
(2009)

Chaundy, Fabian (BA 2011)
Credits include:
'Are You Smarter than a Fifth
Grader?' (MEGA TV, Chile, 2008)
BKN (MEGA TV, Chile, 2008–11)

Chevalier, Tracy (MA 1994)
The Virgin Blue (1996)
Girl with a Pearl Earring (1999)
Falling Angels (2001)
The Lady and the Unicorn (2003)
Burning Bright (2007)
Remarkable Creatures (2009) – IMPAC
Dublin Literary Award longlist
(2010)

Clare, Tim (MA 2004)
We Can't All Be Astronauts (2009) –
East Anglian Book Awards shortlist
(2009)

Clark, Cassandra (MA 1991)
Hangman Blind (2008)
The Red Velvet Turnshoe (2009)
The Law of Angels (2011)

Cleminshaw, Suzanne (PhD 1991)
The Great Ideas (1999) – Whitbread
First Novel Award shortlist (1999)

Clifford, Graham (MA 2001)
Welcome Back to the Country (2010)

Close, Kristina (MA 2001)
Small Infidelities (1997)

Corbalis, Judy (MA 1990)
The Wrestling Princess and Other Stories
(1986)
The Cuckoo Bird (1988)
Oskar and the Ice-pick (1988)
Porcellus, the Flying Pig (1988)
The Ice-Cream Heroes (1989)
Your Dad's a Monkey (1989)

Flying Pig to the Rescue (1991)
Put a Sock in it, Percy (1994)
Tapu (1996)
Mortmain (2007)

Corbett, Sarah (MA 1998)
The Red Wardrobe (1998) –
Eric Gregory Award winner (1998);
Forward Prize shortlist (1998); T. S.
Eliot Prize shortlist (1998)
The Witch Bag (2002)
Other Beasts (2008)

Corcoran, Josephine (MA 1997)
Credits include:
Jocasta (Chelsea Centre Theatre,
1997)
Algebra (first prize in the Ian St
James' Awards, broadcast on BBC
Radio 4, 1998)
The Songs That Houses Sing (BBC
Radio 4, 2000)

Corrick, Martin (MA 2000)
The Navigation Log (2002)
After Berlin (2005)
By Chance (2008)

Cowan, Andrew (MA 1985)
Pig (1994) – Betty Trask Award
winner (1993); Authors' Club First
Novel Award winner (1994); Ruth
Hadden Memorial Award winner
(1994); *Sunday Times* Young Writer of
the Year Award winner (1994);
Scottish Arts Council Book Award
winner (1995); The Saltire Society
First Book Award shortlist (1994);
The *Yorkshire Post* Best First Novel
shortlist (1994); The David Higham
Prize for Fiction shortlist (1994); The
Hawthornden Prize shortlist (1995);
The Steinbeck Award shortlist
(1995)
Common Ground (1996)
Crustaceans (2000)
What I Know (2005) – Arts Council
Writers' Award (2004)
The Art of Writing Fiction (2011)

Cowie, Douglas (MA 2000, PhD
2007)
Owen Noone and the Maurauder (2005)

Craib, Ben (MA 2009)
Winner Menagerie Theatre
Company New Writing Competition
(2009)

Writer in Development, Half Moon Young People's Theatre (2010) Founding director, Alleycat Theatre Company (2010)

Cremins, Robert (MA 1991)
A Sort of Homecoming (1998)
Send in the Devils (2001)

Cross, Helen (MA 1997)
My Summer of Love (2001) – Betty Trask Award winner (2002)
The Secrets She Keeps (2005)
Split Milk, Black Coffee (2009)

Crowe, Emma (MA 2005)
Credits include:
Finalist in *The Play's the Thing* (Channel 4, 2006)
Hooked (Hampstead Theatre, 2008)
Civil (Soho Theatre)
One Runs, The Other Doesn't (Royal Court Theatre, 2010)
Charged (Soho Theatre, 2010)
Kin (Royal Court Theatre Upstairs, 2010)

Curran, Fiona (MA 2003)
The Hail Mary Pass (2005)

D

Dafydd, Fflur (MA 2000)
Y Gwir Am Gelwydd (1998)
Lliwiau Liw Nos (2005)
Atyniad (2006) – Prose Medal, National Eisteddfod of Wales winner (2006)
Twenty Thousand Saints (2008) – Oxfam Hay Prize for Emerging Writers winner (2009)
Ffordd o Fyw (2009)
Y Llyfrgell (2010) – Daniel Owen Memorial Prize winner (2009)

Dafydd, Sian Melangell (MA 2006)
Y Trydydd Peth (2009) – Prose Medal, National Eisteddfod of Wales winner (2009)

Daley-Clarke, Donna (MA 2001)
A Lazy Eye (2005) – Commonwealth Writers' Prize Best First Book winner (2006)

Darby, Katy (MA 2006)
David Higham Award Winner (2005)
Open Secrets (2004)
Half-Life (2005)
Whores' Asylum (2012)

Davis, Deborah (MA 2001)
Credits include:
Dickens Confidential (BBC Radio 4 Afternoon Play)
Letters to Fan-Fan (BBC Radio 4 Afternoon Play)
Court Pastoral (International Play Festival 2003)
Balance of Power (BBC Radio 4 10-part drama series)

De Abaitua, Matthew (MA 1994)
The Red Men (2007) – Arthur C. Clarke Award shortlist (2007)
The Art of Camping: The History and Practice of Sleeping Under the Stars (2011)

Debney, Patricia (MA 1992)
How to be a Dragonfly (2005)
Losing You (2007)

Dhingra, Leena (MA 1991)
Amritvela (1988)

Doughty, Louise (MA 1987)
Crazy Paving (1995)
Dance with Me (1996)
Honey-Dew (1998)
Fires in the Dark (2003)
Stone Cradle (2006)
A Novel in a Year (2007)
Whatever You Love (2010) – Costa Novel Award shortlist (2010); Orange Prize for Fiction longlist (2011)

Dunn, Suzannah (MA 1989)
Darker Days Than Usual (1990)
Quite Contrary (1991)
Blood Sugar (1994)
Past Caring (1995)
Venus Flaring (1996)
Tenterhooks (1998)
Commencing Our Descent (1999)
The Queen of Subtleties: A Novel of Anne Boleyn (2004)
The Sixth Wife (2007)
The Queen's Sorrow (2008)
The Confession of Katherine Howard (2010)

Dunthorne, Joe (MA 2005)
Curtis Brown Prize winner (2005)
Submarine (2008) – Desmond Elliot Prize shortlist (2008); Wodehouse Bolinger Prize shortlist (2008); Commonwealth Writers' Prize Best First Book shortlist (2009); Dylan

Thomas Prize longlist (2008); Wales Book of the Year longlist (2009)
Faber New Poets 5 (2010)
Wild Abandon (2011)

E

Edwards, Richard (MA 2003)
Credits include:
Soho Theatre Young Writer's Programme (2004)
A Year of Your Love (London Independent Film Festival, 2009)

Elderkin, Susan (MA 1994)
Granta Best of Young British Novelists (2003)
Sunset Over Chocolate Mountains (2000)
The Voices (2003)

Emanuel, Oliver (MA 2002)
Credits include:
Magpie Park (West Yorkshire Playhouse)
Flit (National Theatre of Scotland)
By The Light of the Moon (BBC Radio7)
Joseph and Joseph (BBC Radio4)
The Sacrifice (Silver Tongue Theatre)
Iz (Silver Tongue Theatre)

Enright, Anne (MA 1987)
The Portable Virgin (1991) – Rooney Prize winner
The Wig My Father Wore (1995)
What Are You Like? (2000) – Encore Award winner (2001); Whitbread Prize Best Novel shortlist (2000)
The Pleasure of Eliza Lynch (2002)
Making Babies: Stumbling Into Motherhood (2004)
The Gathering (2007) – Man Booker Prize winner (2007); Orange Broadband Prize for Fiction shortlist (2008)
Talking Pictures (2008)
Yesterday's Weather (2009)
The Granta Book of the Irish Short Story (editor, 2010)
The Forgotten Waltz (2011)

Evans, Diana (MA 2003)
26a (2005) – Betty Trask Award winner (2005); Orange Broadband Prize for New Writers winner (2005); Arts Council Decibel Writer of the Year Award winner (2006);

Whitbread Prize First Novel shortlist (2005); *Guardian* First Book Award shortlist; Arts Foundation Fellowship shortlist (2007)
The Wonder (2009)

Evans, Richard (MA 2003)
The Zoo Keeper (2008)

F
Falconer, Alison (MA 2008)
Credits include:
Theatrescience commission (2010)
Man in Black (BBC Radio 7, 2010)

Faqir, Fadia (PhD, 1990)
Nisanit (1990)
Pillars of Salt (1996); ALOA Literary Award shortlist (Denmark, 2001)
My Name is Salma (2007)

Farnell, Chris (BA 2005)
Mark II (2006)

Farrell, Paul (MA 2001)
Credits include:
The Fete (2004, short film)
Crossroads (2005)
Doctors (2006)
Silent Witness (2006)
Waking the Dead
Primeval (ITV 2009)
Murphy's Law (SKY 2009)

Finucan, Stephen (MA 1996)
Happy Pilgrims (2000)
Foreigners (2003)
The Fallen (2009)

Fish, Laura (MA 2002, PhD 2007)
Flight of Black Swans (1995)
Strange Music (2008) – Orange Prize for Fiction longlist (2009)

Fisher, Max (MA 2003)
Credits include:
A Better Direction (Screen East Digital Shorts, 2004) – Best Regional or Network Drama, Creative Norfolk Awards shortlist (2005)
The Great British Citizenship Test (Screen East New Voices 2003)

Fletcher, Susan (MA 2002)
Eve Green (2004) – Whitbread First Novel Award winner (2004); Betty Trask Award winner (2005)
Oystercatchers (2007) – Romatic Novel of the Year Award shortlist (2008); Dylan Thomas Prize longlist (2008)

Corrag (2010) – John Llewellyn Rhys Prize shortlist (2010); Writers' Guild Best Fiction Book Award shortlist (2010)

Flusfeder, David (MA 1988)
Man Kills Woman (1993)
Like Plastic (1996) – Encore Award winner (1997)
Morocco (2000)
The Gift (2003)
The Pagan House (2007)
A Film by Spencer Ludwig (2010)

Forbes, Caroline (MA 1989)
The Needles on Full (1985)

Foster, Stephen (MA 1998)
It Cracks Like Breaking Skin (1999) – MacMillan PEN Award shortlist (1999)
Strides (2001)
She Stood There Laughing (2004)
The Book of Lists, Football (2006)
Walking Ollie (2006)
Are You With Me? (2007)
Along Came Dylan (2008)
From Working Class Hero to Absolute Disgrace (2009)

Foulds, Adam (MA 2000)
The Truth About These Strange Times (2007) – Betty Trask Award winner (2007); *Sunday Times* Young Writer of the Year Award winner (2008); Desmond Elliott Prize shortlist (2008)
The Broken Word (2008) – Costa Poetry Award winner (2008); Jerwood Aldeburgh Prize winner (2008); Somerset Maugham Award winner (2009); John Llewellyn Rhys Prize shortlist (2008); *Sunday Times* Young Writer of the Year Award shortlist (2009)
The Quickening Maze (2009) – Encore Award winner (2011); Man Booker Prize shortlist (2009); *South Bank Show* Literature Prize winner (2010); Walter Scott Prize shortlist (2010); IMPAC Dublin Literary Award longlist (2010)

Fowler, Bo (MA 1995)
Scepticism Inc. (1998)
The Astrological Diary of God (1999)

Frank, Sophie (MA 2000)
The Mattress Actress (2000)

G
Gabriel, Sarah (MA 1996)
Eating Pomegranates: A Memoir of Mothers, Daughters and Genes (2009)

Garland, Charles (pseudonym of Charles Hamel-Cooke, MA 2006)
Credits include:
The Biz! (Thameside Theatre, Essex 2003)
On the Same Side (rehearsed reading, London, 2007)

Gattis, Ryan *(MA 2002)*
Roo Kickkick and the Big Bad Blimp (2004)
Kung Fu High School (2005)

George, Clare (MA 2000)
Cloud Chamber (2003)
The Evangelist (2005)

Gilbert, Francis (MA 1991)
I'm a Teacher, Get Me Out of Here (2004)
Teacher on the Run (2005)
Yob Nation (2006)
The New School Rules (2007)
Parent Power (2008)

Gilligan, Ruth (MA 2011)
Forget (2006)
Somewhere in Between (2008)
Can You See Me? (2009)

Goldman, Jordan (MA 2005)
Credits include:
Deadwood (US, 2006)

Goar, Jim (current PhD)
Whole Milk (2006)
Seoul Bus Poems (2010)

Gray, Nigel (MA 1984)
Numerous books for children include:
I'll Take You to Mrs Cole (1985) – Federation of Children's Book Groups Best Book of the Year Award winner; Limburg Children's Book Prize winner (Holland); German Young People's Literature Prize winner; Smarties Prize shortlist
Shots (1986) – Children's Book Foundation Book of the Year Award winner; The Other Award shortlist; *Observer* Teenage Fiction Prize shortlist; *Guardian* Children's Fiction Award shortlist
The One and Only Robin Hood (1987)

A Country Far Away (1988) –
Children's Book Foundation Book of
the Year Award winner; Christian
Media Children's Book Prize winner
(France); *Parents Magazine* Best
Books of the Year Award winner
(USA)
A Balloon for Grandad (1988) –
Children's Book Foundation Book of
the Year Award winner; Mother
Goose Award runner-up
Little Pig's Tale (1990) – WA Premier's
Award shortlist (Australia)
Anna's Ghost (1991) – WA Premier's
Award shortlist (Australia)
Running Away from Home (1995) –
APA Award shortlist (Australia)
The Frog Prince (1996) – WA Premier's
Award shortlist (Australia)
Fun House (1998)
Little Bear's Grandad (2000) – Prix
Chronos winner (France);
Federation of Children's Book
Groups Best Books of the Year
Oliver Twist Finds A Home (2002)
Pip and the Convict (2005)
Robin Hood's New Clothes (2006)
My Dog, My Cat, Mum and Me (2007)
Saving Jasper (2008)
Books for adults include:
The Silent Majority (1973)
Come Close (1978)
The Rebels and the Hostage (1978) –
North West Arts Award winner
Phoenix Country (ed. 1980)
Life Sentence (1984) – Steele Rudd
Award shortlist (Australia)
Happy Families (1985)
The Worst of Times (1986)
Writers Talking (1989)
Skeleton in the Cupboard (2000) – WA
Premier's Award shortlist (Australia)
Strangers (2000)

Greenawalt, Anne (MA 2007)
Growing Up Girl (2008)

Greenwood, Bel (MA 2005)
Community theatre commission
(2007)
Escalator Award winner 2009

Guest, Tim (MA 1999)
My Life in Orange (2004)
Second Lives (2007)

H
Habila, Helon (current PhD)
Waiting for an Angel (2002) –
Commonwealth Writers Prize Best
First Book award winner
Measuring Time (2007)
Oil on the Water (2010) –
Commonwealth Writers' Prize, Africa
Best Book shortlist (2011)

Hale, Stephanie J (MA 1993)
Firebug (1999)
Millionaire Women, Millionaire You
(2010)

Hamel-Cooke, Charles (MA 2006)
see entry for Garland, Charles

Hanif, Mohammed (MA 2005)
A Case of Exploding Mangoes (2008) –
Commonwealth Writers' Prize Best
First Book winner (2009); Corine
International Book Award winner
(2009); James Tait Black Prize
shortlist (2009); *Guardian* First Book
Award shortlist (2008); Man Booker
Prize longlist (2008)
Our Lady of Alice Bhatti (2011)

Hannah, Lucy (MA 2002)
*Nancy Wake: The Gestapo's Most Wanted
Woman* (2006)

Hare, Bruno (BA 1996)
The Lost Kings (2010)

Hargrave, Stephen (MA 1986)
London, London (1989)

Harper, Graeme (aka Brooke Biaz,
PhD 1997)
Black Cat, Green Field (1998) –
National Book Council Award for
New Fiction (Australia, 1998); NSW
Premier's Award winner (Australia,
1998)
Swallowing Film: Short Film Fiction
(2000)
Colonial and Postcolonial Incarceration
(2000)
Comedy, Fantasy and Colonialism
(2001)
Dancing on the Moon (2004)
Signs of Life: Cinema and Medicine
(with A. Moor and K. C. Calman,
2005)
Teaching Creative Writing (2006)
Small Maps of the World (2006)

*The Unsilvered Screen: Cinema and
Surrealism* (with R. Stone, 2007)
*Creative Writing Studies: Practice,
Research, Pedagogy* (with J. Kroll,
2007)
Moon Dance (2007)
On Creative Writing (2010)
Research Methods in Creative Writing
(with J. Kroll, 2011)

Harris, Jane (MA 1992, PhD 1995)
The Observations (2006) –
Waterstone's Newcomer of the Year
Best Novel shortlist; Waterstone's 25
Authors for the Future (2007);
Orange Broadband Prize for Fiction
Best Novel shortlist; Glen Dimplex
Award shortlist (2006); Saltire
Society First Book of the Year Award
shortlist; British Book Awards
Newcomer of the Year shortlist
(2007); *South Bank Show/ Times*
Breakthrough Award shortlist (2007)
Gillespie and I (2011)

Harris, Oliver (MA 2004)
The Hollow Man (2011)

Harrop, Nick (MA 2002)
Credits include:
Etiquette (BBC7)
The School Run (BBC3)
The Milk Run (Radio 1)
The Consultants (Radio 4)

Herdman, Ramona (MA 2001)
Come What You Wished For (2008)

Hesketh, Sarah (MA 2007)
Napoleon's Travelling Bookshelf (2009)

Higson, Charlie (BA 1977)
King of Ants (1992)
Happy Now (1993)
Full Whack (1995)
The Fast Show Book (1996)
Getting Rid of Mr Kitchen (1996)
Silver Fin (2005)
Blood Fever (2006)
Double or Die (2007)
Hurricane Gold (2007)
By Royal Command (2008)
The Enemy (2009)
The Dead (2010)
Monstroso (2010)
The Fear (2011)

Hirson, Denis (PhD 2004)
The House Next Door to Africa (1987)
We Walk Straight So You Better Get Out of the Way (2005)
I Remember King Kong (2005)
White Scars (2006) – *SA Sunday Times* Alan Paton Non-Fiction Prize runner-up (2007)

Hodgkinson, Amanda (MA 2001)
22 Britannia Road (2011)

Hogan, Edward (MA 2004)
David Higham Award winner (2003)
Blackmoor (2008) – Desmond Elliott Prize shortlist (2009); Dylan Thomas Prize shortlist (2008); *Sunday Times* Young Writer of the Year Award shortlist (2009)
The Hunger Trace (2011)

Holland, Jonathan (MA 1984)
The Escape Artist (1994)

Houghton, Paul (MA 1987)
Harry's Last Wedding (unpublished) – Betty Trask Award winner (1989)

House, Richard (PhD 2008)
Bruiser (1997)
The Uninvited (2002)

Howell, Brian (MA 1996)
The Dance of Geometry (2002)
The Sound of White Ants: Stories of Modern Japan (2004)
The Study of Sleep (2007)

Hubbard, Sue (MA 1995)
Everything Begins with the Skin (1994)
Depth of Field (2000)
Ghost Station (2004)
Rothko's Red and Other Stories (2008)
Adventures in Art (2010)
The Idea of Islands (2010)
A Girl in White (2012)

Hughes, Kathryn (MA 1986)
The Victorian Governess (1993)
George Eliot: The Last Victorian (1999) – James Tait Black Memorial Prize for Biography winner (2000)
The Short Life and Long Times of Mrs Beeton (2005)

I
Illis, Mark (MA 1987)
A Chinese Summer (1988)
The Alchemist (1990),
The Feather Report (1992)
Tender (2009)

TV Credits include:
EastEnders
The Bill
Peak Practice
Emmerdale (2000–present)

Ingrams, Elizabeth (MA 2005)
Japan through Writers' Eyes (2009)

Ishiguro, Kazuo (MA 1980)
Granta Best of Young British Novelists (1983 and 1993)
A Pale View of the Hills (1982)
An Artist of the Floating World (1986) – Whitbread Prize Best Novel winner (1986); The Booker Prize shortlist (1986)
The Remains of the Day (1989) – The Booker Prize winner (1989)
The Unconsoled (1995) – Whitbread Prize Best Novel shortlist (1995)
When We Were Orphans (2000) – Whitbread Prize Best Novel shortlist (2000); The Booker Prize shortlist (2000)
Never Let Me Go (2005) – James Tait Black Memorial Prize for Fiction Best Novel shortlist (2005); Booker Prize shortlist (2005); Arthur C. Clarke Award Best Novel shortlist (2006)
Noctures: Five Stories of Music and Nightfall (2009)

Ivory, Helen (current PhD)
Eric Gregory Award (1999)
The Double Life of Clocks (2002)
The Dog in the Sky (2006)
The Breakfast Machine (2010)

J
Jackson, Mick (MA 1992)
The Underground Man (1997) – Society of Authors First Novel Award winner (1997); Booker Prize shortlist (1997); Whitbread First Novel Award shortlist (1997)
Five Boys (2001)
Ten Sorry Tales (2005)
Bears of England (2009)
The Widow's Tale (2010) – East Anglian Book Awards Book of the Year winner (2010)

James, Christopher (MA 2000)
Eric Gregory Award 2002
National Poetry Award winner 2008
The Invention of Butterfly (2006)

Jarrett, Clare (MA 2006)
Catherine and the Lion (1996) – Mother Goose Award winner (1996)
Dancing Maddy (1999)
Jamie (2001)
Jamie and the Lost Bird (2002)
The Best Picnic Ever (2004)
Arabella Miller's Tiny Caterpillar (2008)

Jenkins, Janette (MA 1995)
Columbus Day (1999)
Another Elvis Love Child (2002) – Amazon Second Novel Award shortlist (2002)
Angel of Brooklyn (2008)

Jensen, Marie-Louise (BA 1986)
Between Two Seas (2008) – Waterstone's Children's Book Prize shortlist (2008)
The Lady In The Tower (2009) – Waterstone's Children's Book Prize shortlist (2009)

Johnson, Margaret (MA 2003)
Titles include:
All I Want (2000)
Next Door to Love (2005)
Murder Maker (2006)
Wild Country (2007)
Running Wild (2009)
Big Hair Day (2010)

Jones, Joshua (BA 2011)
Thought Disorder (2010)

Jones, Wendy (MA 2001)
Portrait of an Artist as a Young Girl (2006)
The Thoughts and Happenings of Mr Wilfred Price, Purveyor of Superior Funerals (2012)

Jordan, Meirion (MA 2008)
Moonrise (2008) – Forward Prize Best First Collection (2009)
Stranger's Hall (2009) – East Anglian Book Awards shortlist (2009)

Joseph, Anjali (MA 2008, current PhD)
Saraswati Park (2010) – Betty Trask Award winner (2011); Desmond Elliott Prize winner (2011); The Hindu Best Fiction Award shortlist (2010); Commonwealth Writers' Prize, South Asia and Europe Best First Book shortlist (2011); Royal Society of Literature Ondaatje Prize shortlist (2011)

Joy, Avril (BA 1972)
The Sweet Track (2007)

K

Karnezis, Panos (MA 2000)
Little Infamies (2002)
The Maze (2004) – Whitbread Prize
First Novel shortlist (2004)
The Birthday Party (2007)
The Convent (2010)

Kapur, Vikram (PhD 2009)
There Is A Fire (2002)
The Wages of Life (2004)

Kilalea, Katharine (MA 2006)
One Eye'd Leigh – Dylan Thomas Prize
longlist (2010)

Kinsman, Rob (MA 2003)
Credits include:
Doctors, (BBC1)
Dickens Confidential (BBC Radio 4)
High Hopes (BBC Radio 4, 2010)

Kissick, Gary (PhD 2007)
Winter in Volcano (2000)
Another Kissing Couple Has Exploded
(2007)

Klavans, J. K. (MA 1979)
It's a Little Too Late for a Love Song
(1984)
God, He Was Good (1985)

Klein, Leonora (MA 2004)
A Very English Hangman (2006)

Kobak, Annette (MA 1997)
Isabelle: Life of Isabelle Eberhardt (1988)
Joe's War: My Father Decoded (2004)
Madame De Stael (2010)

L

Lai, Larissa (MA 2001)
When Fox is a Thousand (1995) –
Astraea Foundation Emerging
Writers Award winner
(1995); Chapters/Books in Canada
First Novel Award shortlist
Salt Fish Girl: A Novel (2002) –
Sunburst Award Tiptree Award
shortlist; City of Calgary W. O.
Mitchell Award shortlist
Sybil Unrest (with Rita Wong, 2008)

Lal, Judith (MA 2001)
Eric Gregory Award (2002)
Flageolets at the Bazaar (2007)

Lambert, Charles (MA 1996, PhD)
Credits include:
The Wolves of Kromer (2001)

Lambert, Richard (MA 2010)
The Magnolia (2008)

Lambert, Sonia (MA 2000)
Three Mothers (2007)

Lambert, Zoe (MA 2002)
Ellipsis 2 (with Jane Rogers and Polly
Clark, 2007)

Lapadula, Marc (MA 1984)
Numerous plays and screenplays
produced, including:
Not by Name
Last Order
The Rains Change
Night Bloom (1998)
In Uniform Thanksgiving (1999)
Dancer (2001)
Two Shakes (2005)
Mentor (2006)

Laurens, Joanna (MA 2003)
Credits include:
The Three Birds (Gate Theatre,
London, 2000) – *Time Out* Most
Outstanding New Talent award
winner (2000); Critics' Circle
Theatre Award for Most Promising
Playwright winner (2001)
Five Gold Rings (Almeida Theatre,
London, 2003) – Pearson Award
winner (2003)
Poor Beck (RCS Other Place, 2004)

Lawes, Jane (BA 2008)
Summertime and Somersaults (2012)
Friendships and Back Flips (2012)
Surprises and Superstars (2012)

Leal, Stephanie (MA 2007)
Metrophobia (2009)

Lee, Tom (BA 1993)
Greenfly (2009)

Lehoczky, Agnes (MA 2006; PhD
2010)
ikszedik stacio (Hungary, 2000)
Medalion (Hungary, 2002)
Budapest to Babel (2008)
*Poetry, the Geometry of the Living
Substance: Four Essays on Agnes Nemes
Nagy* (2011)

Liardet, Frances (1998)
The Game (1994) – Betty Trask Award
winner (1994)

Litt, Toby (MA 1995)
Granta Best of Young British
Novelists (2003)
Adventures in Capitalism (1996)
Beatniks: An English Road Movie
(1997)
Corpsing (2000)
Deadkidsongs (2001)
Exhibitionism (2001)
Finding Myself (2003)
Ghost Story (2004)
Hospital (2007)
I Play the Drums in a Band Called Okay
(2008)
Journey into Space (2009)
King Death (2010)
I'm with the Bears (2011)

Lofthouse, Jacqui (MA 1993)
The Temple of Hymen (1995)
A Bluethroat Morning (2000)
Boundaries Road (available only in
Dutch: Een Stille Verwijining, 2004)

Loudon, Andrew (MA 2002)
Credits include:
The Tralier (2003)
The Red Gloves (2004)
When Raymond Met Julia (2005, Snap
Theatre Company)

Lowe, Gill (MA 2002)
Hyde Park Gate News (2005)

M

MacCann, Philip (MA 1990)
The Miracle Shed (1990)

Madden, Deirdre (MA 1985)
Hidden Symptoms (1986)
The Birds of the Innocent Wood (1988) –
Somerset Maugham Prize
Remembering Light and Stone (1993)
Nothing is Black (1994)
One by One in the Darkness (1996) –
Orange Broadband Prize for Fiction
Best Novel shortlist (1997)
Authenticity (2002)
Snake's Elbows (2005)
Thanks for Telling Me, Emily (2007)
Molly Fox's Birthday (2008) – Orange
Prize for Fiction shortlist (2009)
Jasper and the Green Marvel (2012)

Manlow, James (MA 2001)
Attraction (2004)

Manthorpe, Victoria (MA 2003)
Children of the Empire (1996)

Marriott, Suzannah (BA 1985)
Titles include:
Beads of Faith (2002)
The Art of Motherhood (2004)
Your Non-toxic Pregnancy (2005)
Natural Pregnancy (2006)
Green Babycare (2008)

Martin, John (MA 2005)
Beyond Belief (2006)

Martins, Susanna Wade (MA 2005)
Norfolk: A Changing Countryside
(1988)
Historic Farm Buildings (1991)
History of Norfolk (1997)
Farmers, Landlords and Landscapes:
Rural Britain 1720–1870 (2004)
A Great Estate at Work: The Holkham
Estate and its Inhabitants in the 19th
Century (2008)
The Countryside of East Anglia:
Changing Landscapes 1870–1950 (with
Tom Williamson, 2009)
Coke of Norfolk (1754 – 1842): A
Biography (2009)

McEwan, Ian (MA 1971)
Granta Best of Young British
Novelists (1983)
First Love, Last Rites (1975)
In Between the Sheets (1978)
The Cement Garden (1978)
The Comfort of Strangers (1981) – The
Booker Prize shortlist (1981)
The Child in Time (1987) – Whitbread
Prize Best Novel winner (1987)
The Innocent (1989)
Black Dogs (1992) – The Booker
Prize shortlist (1992)
The Daydreamer (1994)
Enduring Love (1997) – James Tait
Black Memorial Prize for Fiction Best
Novel shortlist (1997); Whitbread
Prize Best Novel shortlist (1997)
Amsterdam (1998) – The Booker Prize
winner (1998)
Atonement (2001) – James Tait Black
Memorial Prize for Fiction Best
Novel shortlist (2001); Whitbread
Prize Best Novel shortlist (2001); The
Booker Prize shortlist (2001);

WH Smith Literary Prize; National
Book Critics Circle Award winner;
Los Angeles Times Prize for Fiction;
Santiago Prize for the European
Novel
Saturday (2005) – James Tait Black
Memorial Prize for Fiction Best
Novel winner (2005); The Booker
Prize shortlist (2005)
On Chesil Beach (2007) – *Reader's*
Digest Author of the Year Award
(2008); Galaxy Book of the Year
(2008); Man Booker Prize shortlist
(2007)
Solar – Bollinger Everyman
Wodehouse Prize for Comic Writing
winner (2010)
Peggy V. Helmerich Distinguished
Author Award (2010)
Jerusalem Prize (2011)

McGill, Robert (MA 2002)
The Mysteries (2004)

McHugh, Ian (MA 2002)
Credits include:
The Uncanny (Old Vic, London 2002)
Behind Closed Doors (Old Vic, London,
2003)
Believe What You Will (RSC, Stratford,
2005)
How to Curse (Bush Theatre, London,
2007)
A Cloven Pine (Bush Theatre,
London, 2007)
Heather and Denny (Bush Theatre,
London, 2007)
Come to Where I'm From (New Wolsey
Theatre, Ipswich, 2010)
Women Who Start Fires and the Men Who
Stalk Them (Arcola Theatre, London,
2010)
Publications:
Behind Closed Doors (2003)
How to Curse (2007)

McNay, Mark (MA 2004)
Fresh (2007) – Arts Foundation Prize
for New Fiction winner (2007); Glen
Dimplex New Writer of the Year
Award shortlist (2007); Saltire
Society First Book of the Year Award
shortlist (2007); McKitterick Prize
shortlist (2007)
Under Control (2008)
Aye Write! Bank of Scotland Prize for
Scottish Fiction shortlist (2009)

Miano, Sarah Emily (MA 2002, PhD
2007)
Encyclopedia of Snow (2004)
Van Rijn (2006)

Miller, Andrew (MA 1990)
Ingenious Pain (1997) – James Tait
Black Memorial Prize for Fiction Best
Novel winner (1997); Italian
Grinzane Cavour Prize (1997);
International IMPAC Dublin Literary
Award (1999)
Casanova (1998)
Oxygen (2001) – Whitbread Prize Best
Novel shortlist (2001); The Booker
Prize shortlist (2001)
The Optimists (2005)
One Morning Like A Bird (2008)
Pure (2011)

Monson, Jane (MA 2000)
Speaking without Tongues (2010)

Moorhead, K. R. (MA 2007)
The First Law of Motion (2009)

Morgan, Clare (MA 1991)
Touch of the Other (1984)
An Affair of the Heart (1996)
What Poetry Brings to Business (2010)
A Book for All and None (2011)

Morgan, Esther (MA 1998)
Beyond Calling Distance (2001) – Eric
Gregory Award (1998); Aldeburgh
Poetry Festival Best First Collection
Award (2002); John Llewellyn Rhys
Memorial Prize (2002); East England
Arts' Six of the Best Award (2002)
The Silence Living in Houses (2005)
Winner Bridport Poetry Prize (2010)

Morton-Smith, Tom (BA 2002)
Credits include:
Black Boxes & Amber Rooms (Minotaur
Theatre Company 2001)
Appendix (Pleasance Theatre,
London 2004)
Blood on the 3 for 2 Display (Gardner
Arts Centre, Brighton 2006)
Rodeo (Royal Court Theatre, Latitude
Festival 2006)
The Hygiene Hypothesis (Latitude
Festival 2007)
Origins (Hampstead Theatre 2007)
12 Metres from the Seabed (350 from the
Shore) (Shakespeare's Globe 2007)
Salt Meets Wound (2007)

Moses, Antoinette (MA 2004, PhD 2009)
Numerous books of language-learner literature for children and young adults, including:
John Doe (1999)
Dolphin Music (1999)
Jojo's Story (2000) – winner of Extensive Reading Award (2005)
Frozen Pizza and Other Slices of Life (2002)
Let Me Out (2006) – winner of Extensive Reading Award (2007)
Book Boy (2010)
Scriptwriting credits include:
Autumn (Norwich Castle Museum, 2001) – winner Playwrights East competition (2001)
The Colours In Between (Hotbed Festival of New Writing, 2002)
Break Out (2007) – Wolsey Theatre's 'Summer Shorts' winner (2007)
Cuts (2008) – Samuel Beckett Theatre Trust award longlist (2008)
Credits include:
Rehearsed readings, Cambridge (Menagerie Theatre Company) and Norwich

Mukherjee, Neel (MA 2001)
A Life Apart (2010; previously published in India as Past Continuous) – co-winner Vodafone-Crossword Award (2009); winner Writers' Guild Best Fiction Book Award (2010); shortlisted for the DSC Prize for South Asian Literature (2011)

Mulholland, James (MA 1994)
Special and Odd (2007)

Murray, Paul (MA 2001)
An Evening of Long Goodbyes (2003) – Whitbread Prize First Novel shortlist (2003)
Kerry Irish Fiction Award shortlist (2003)
Skippy Dies (2009) – Bollinger Everyman Wodenhouse Prize for Comic Writing Best Novel shortlist (2010); Man Booker Prize longlist (2010); Costa Novel Award shortlist (2010); National Book Critics Circle Award shortlist (USA, 2011)

Murray, Tiffany (MA 1999, PhD 2006)
Happy Accidents (2004) – Bollinger Everyman Wodehouse Prize for Comic Writing Best Novel shortlist (2005)
Diamond Star Halo (2010) – Bollinger Everyman Wodenhouse Prize for Comic Writing Best Novel shortlist (2010)

N
Naylor, Molly (MA 2008)
Credits include:
There Will Be Glamour (Latitude, 2009)
Whenever I Get Blown Up I Think Of You (Cambridge Junction, 2011)

Neale, Derek (MA 1993, PhD 1997)
A Creative Writing Handbook: Developing Dramatic Technique, Individual Style and Voice (2009)
Writing Fiction (with Linda Anderson, 2009)
Life Writing (with Sara Haslam, 2009)

Neuhaus, Denise (MA 1989)
The Love of Women (1993)
The Christening (1995)

Neville, Alison (MA 1975)
see entry for Candy, Edward

Newman, Sandra (MA 2002)
The Only Good Thing Anyone Has Ever Done (2002) – *Guardian* First Book Award shortlist (2002)
Cake (2007)
How Not to Write a Novel: 200 Classic Mistakes and How to Avoid Them (with Howard Mittelmark, 2010)
Changeling: a Memoir (2010)
Read This Next… (with Howard Mittelmark, 2010)
The Country of the Ice-Cream War (2012)

Niechcial, Judith (MA 2004)
A Particle of Clay: The Biography of Alec Skempton, Civil Engineer (2002)
Lucy Faithful: Mother to Hundreds (2010)

Nosbaum, J. P. (MA 2000)
Fighting in the Captain's Tower (with Paul Batchelor, 2002)

O
O'Donaghue, John (BA 1991)
Letter to Lord Rochester (2004)
The Beach Generation (2007)
Brunch Poems (2009)
Sectioned: A Life Interrupted (2009)

O'Mahoney, Nessa (MA 2003)
Bar Talk (1999)
Trapping a Ghost (2005)

Ockrent, Ben (MA 2006)
Credits include:
The Pleasure Principle (for Tristan Bates Theatre, 2007)
Short films for *Newsnight*, BBC2 (2007)
Khoa San, comedy drama series for World Productions / BBC (commission 2008)
Joe Mistry, comedy series for Hartswood Film & TV / BBC (commission 2008)
Kidnapped, drama series for Company Pictures / BBC (commission 2008)
Honey for Tricycle Theatre (2009)
Playsong (with Greg Thompson, Alex Baranowski, Holly Reiss, Adam Venus, Joanna Woodward and Rebecca Trehearn: Tristran Bates Theatre, 2010)

Okoh, Janice (MA 2008)
Credits include:
SE8 (BBC Radio 4, 2010)

Ormerod, Jane (MA 1997)
Nashville Invades Manhattan (spoken word CD, 2007)
11 Films (2008)
Recreational Vehicles on Fire (2009)

Osborne, John (BA 2000)
Radio Head: Up and Down the Dial of British Radio (2009)
What if Men Burst in Wearing Balaclavas? (2010)
The Newsagent's Window (2010)
The New Blur Album (2011)

P

Page, Jeremy (MA 1994)
Salt (2007) – Jelf First Novel Award
shortlist (2007); Commonwealth
Writers' Prize for Best First Book
shortlist (2007)
The Wake (2009) – Winner of the
fiction and poetry prize at the East
Anglian Book Awards (2009. Also
shortlisted for the New Angle Prize
(2011)

Page, Kathy (MA 1988)
Back in the First Person (1986)
The Unborn Dreams of Clara Riley
(1987)
Island Paradise (1989)
As in Music and Other Stories (1990)
Frankie Styne and the Silver Man (1992)
The Story of My Face (2002) – The
Orange Prize for Fiction shortlist
(2002),
Alphabet (2004) – Governor General's
Award shortlist (Canada, 2005)
The Find (2010)

Parkes, Linda Rose (MA 1975)
The Usher's Torch (2005)
Night Horses (2010)

Patterson, Glenn (MA 1986)
Burning Your Own (1988) – Betty
Trask Award winner (1988); Rooney
Prize for Irish Literature winner
(1989)
Fat Lad (1992)
Black Night at Big Thunder Mountain
(1995)
The International (1999)
Number 5 (2003)
That Which Was (2004)
Lapsed Protestant (2006)
Luxus (with Victor Sloan, 2006)
The Third Party (2007)
*Once Upon a Hill: Love in Troubled
Times* (2008)

Patton, Kevin (MA 2001)
Kayos and Old Knight (1995)
Ankhst (2006)
Yeah, Like that's Gonna Happen (2010)

Peak, David (MA 1983)
No.4 Pickle Street (1988)
The Cotoneaster Factor (1990)
Go Gentle (1991)

Pheby, Alex (PhD 2010)
Grace (2009)

Phelps, Stephen (MA 2003)
Credits include:
Wordsmith (BBC Radio 4 Afternoon
Play)
Once a Friend (BBC Radio 4
Afternoon Play)
Clear Water (BBC Radio 4 Afternoon
Play)
Walking the Line (BBC Radio 4 Friday
Play)
Piper Alpha (BBC Radio 3 Drama on
Three)
The World in a Briefcase (BBC Radio 4
documentary)

Pinner, Richard (MA 1985)
Credits include:
Penny Dreadful (1991)
Rosie Blitz (1995)
The Bowery (2000)
and more than twenty other plays.

Pountney, Christine (MA 1997)
Last Chance Texaco (2000)
Best Way You Know How (2005)

R

Rabinovitch, Dina (MA 2000)
Take Off Your Party Dress (2007)

Radcliffe, Mark A. (MA 1994)
Gabriel's Angel (2010)

Rees, Eleanor (MA 2002)
Feeding Fire (2001) – Eric Gregory
Award winner (2002)
Andraste's Hair (2007) – Forward
Prize Best First Collection shortlist
(2007); Glen Dimplex New Writers
Award for Poetry shortlist (2008)
Eliza and the Bear (2010)

Reeves, Emma (MA 2001)
Credits include:
Little Women (Duchess Theatre,
London, 2004)
Clinging to Lord Nelson (BBC Radio 4,
2004)
The Story of Tracy Beaker (BBC, 2004)
Anne of Green Gables (Lilian Baylis
Theatre, Sadlers Wells, 2004)
Doctors (BBC1, 2005)
Secret Sis (BBC, 2005)
The Story of Tracy Beaker (BBC, 2005)
On the Cusp (BBC Radio 4, 2006)
Young Dracula (BBC, 2007)
Belonging (BBC, 2007)
Half Moon Investigations (BBC, 2008)
Spirit Warriors (CBBC, 2008)

My Almost Famous Family (BBC, 2009)
Carrie's War (West End production,
2009)
Sadie Jones (BBC, 2010)
Tracy Beaker Returns (BBC, 2010)

Rice, Ben (MA 2000)
Granta Best of Young British
Novelists (2003)
Pobby and Dingan (2000) – Somerset
Maugham Award winner (2000);
Mail on Sunday/ John Llewellyn Rhys
Prize shortlist (2001)
Etiquette (2009)

Ridley, Elizabeth (MA 1996)
Throwing Roses (1993)
*The Remarkable Journey of Miss Tranby
Quirke* (1997)
Rainey's Lament (1999)
Dear Mr Carson (2006)

Riviere, Sam (current Phd)
Eric Gregory Award 2009
Faber New Poets 7 (2010)

S

Saadat, Rhian (MA 2000)
Window Dressing for Hermes (2004)

Sattin, Anthony (MA 1984)
An Englishwoman in India (1986)
Lifting the Veil: British Society in Egypt
(1988)
Shooting the Breeze (1989)
The Pharaoh's Shadow (2000)
The Gates of Africa (2004)
A Winter on the Nile (2010)

Saunders, Tom (MA 1987)
Brother, What Strange Place is This?
(2004)
Roof Whirl Away (2008)
Inappropriate Happiness (2009)

Scarrow, Simon (MA 1992)
Under the Eagle (2000),
The Eagle's Conquest (2001)
When the Eagle Hunts (2002)
The Eagle and the Wolves (2003)
The Eagle's Prey (2004)
The Eagle's Prophecy (2005)
The Eagle in the Sand (2006)
Young Bloods (2006)
The Generals (2007)
Fire and Sword (2008)
Centurion (2008)
The Gladiator (2009)
Fire and Sword (2009)

The Legion (2010)
The Fields of Death (2010)
Gladiator: Fight for Freedom (2011)

Schabas, Martha (MA 2007)
David Higham Award winner (2006)
Various Positions (2011)

Schiller, Daphne (MA 1986)
In My Element (1981)
Cargo of Emeralds (1986)
Soundings (1989)
Saying Goodbye to the Sea (1993)
The Scarlett Fish (2002)

Scudamore, James (MA 2004)
The Amnesia Clinic (2006) – Somerset
Maugham Award winner (2007);
The Costa First Novel Award shortlist
(2006); The EDS Dylan Thomas
Prize shortlist (2006); The Glen
Dimplex New Writers Award shortlist
(2006); The Commonwealth Writers'
Prize shortlist (2007)
Heliopolis (2009) – Man Booker Prize
longlist (2009)

Selvidge, Lisa (MA 1996)
The Trials of Tricia Blake (2006)
Writing Fiction Workbook (2006)
A Divine War (2007)
Summer Times in the Argarve (ed.2008)
Beyond The Sea: Stories from the Algarve
(2009)
The Last Dance Over the Berlin Wall
(2009)
The Strange Tale of Comrad Rublov
(2010)

Sheal, Alex (MA 2006)
David Higham Award winner (2004)
The New Writer International Prize
for Contemporary Fiction winner
(2008)

Sheers, Owen (MA 1998)
The Blue Book (2000) – Forward
Poetry Prize (Best First Collection)
shortlist (2000); Arts Council of
Wales Book of the Year shortlist
(2001)
The Dust Diaries (2004) – Arts Council
of Wales Book of the Year Award
winner (2005); Ondaatje Prize
shortlist (2005)
Skirrid Hill (2005) – Somerset
Maugham Award winner (2006)
The Water Diviner's Tale (2007,BBC
Proms)

Resistance (2007) – Hospital Club
Creative Award winner (2008);
Writers' Guild Best Book award
shortlist (2008)
Unicorns, almost (2009, Old Vic)
White Ravens (2009)
A Poet's Guide to Britain (2010)

Sheldon, Jeremy (MA 1996)
The Comfort Zone (2002)
The Smiling Affair (2005)

Sheppard, Robert (MA 1979)
Daylight Robbery (1990),
The Flashlight Sonata (1993)
Empty Diaries (1998)
Far Language (1999)
The Lores (2003)
Tin Pan Arcadia (2005)
Complete Twentieth Century Blues
(2008)
Warrant Error (2009)
Berlin Bursts (2011)
When Bad Times Made for Good Poetry
(2011)
The Given (2011)

Sherwood, Barrie (PhD 2008)
The Pillow Book of Lady Kasa (2000)
Escape from Amsterdam (2007)

Simmonds, Kathryn (MA 2002)
Snug (2004)
Sunday at the Skin Launderette (2008) –
Forward Prize Best First
Collection winner (2008); Felix
Dennis Prize for Best First Collection
winner (2008); Glen Dimplex New
Writers Award for Poetry shortlist
(2008); Costa Poetry Award shortlist
(2008); *Guardian* First Book Award
longlist (2008)

Simons, Jake Wallis (PhD, 2009)
The Exiled Times of a Tibetan Jew
(2005)
The English German Girl (2011)

Sinclair, Clive (BA 1969, PhD 1983)
Granta Best of Young British
Novelists (1983)
Bibliosexuality (1973)
Hearts of Gold (1980) – Somerset
Maugham Award winner (1981)
Bed Bugs (1982)
The Brothers Singer (1983)
Blood Libels (1985)
Diaspora Blues: View of Israel (1987)
Cosmetic Effects (1989)

For Good or Evil (1991)
Augustus Rex (1992)
Ivor Abrahams (1994)
The Lady with the Laptop (1996) –
Winner Pen Silver Pen Prize (1997);
Winner Jewish Quarterly Prize
(1997)
Kidneys in the Mind: A Lecture (1996)
*A Soap Opera from Hell: The Facts of Life
and the Facts of Death* (1998)
Meet the Wife (2002)
*Clive Sinclair's True Tales of the Wild
West* (2008)

Skinner, Richard (MA 1996)
The Red Dancer (2002)
The Velvet Gentleman (currently
available only in French, Italian and
Japanese, 2008)

Smerin, Jessica (2001)
Babel Junction (with Akkas Al-Alli,
Stacy Makishi, Samina Baig and
Michael Mcmillan, 2005)

Smith, Alexander Gordon (BA 2003)
Titles include:
Inspired Creative Writing (2004)
Inspiring Young Readers (2007)
The Inventors (2007)
The Inventors and the City of Stolen Souls
(2008)
Furnace: Lockdown (2009)
Furnace: Solitary (2009)
Furnace: Death Sentence (2009)
Furnace: Fugitives (2010)
Furnace: Execution (2011)
The Fury (2011)

Smith, Arthur (BA 1976)
My Name is Daphne Fairfax (2009)

Smyth, Amanda (MA 2001)
Black Rock (2009)

Smith, Rob Magnuson (MA 2010)
David Higham Award winner (2009)
The Gravedigger (2010) – Pirate's Alley
William Faulkner Award winner
(2004)

Smyth, Cherry (MA 2000)
When the Lights go up (2001)
A Strong Voice in a Small Place (2002,
ed.)
The Future of Something Delicate (2006)
One Wanted Thing (2007)

Sorel-Cameron, James (MA 1980)
Mag (1990)
A Generation of the Dark Heart (1991)
Storm Blind (1993)

Stannard, Julian (PhD)
Rina's War (2001)
The Red Zones (2007)
The Parrots of Villa Gruber Discover Lapis Lazuli (2011)

Stewart, Paul (MA 1979)
More than fifty titles for children, many with illustrator Chris Riddell, including:
The Thought Domain (1988)
The Weather Witch (1989)
Adam's Ark (1990)
Castle of Intrigue (1994)
Stage Fright (1995)
Clock of Doom (1996)
The Wakening (1996)
The Midnight Hand (1997)
The Hanging Tree (1998)
Stormchaser (1999)
Midnight over Sanctphrax (2000)
Fright Train (2001)
The Last of the Sky Pirates (2002)
Vox (2003)
Freeglader (2004)
Winter Knights (2005)
Clash of the Sky Galleons (2006)
The Curse of the Nightwolf (2007)
Return of the Emerald Skull (2008)
Legion of the Dead (2008)
Phantom of Blood Alley (2009)
Returner's Wealth: Wyrmeweald (2010)
Bloodhoney (2012)

Stickley, Joel (BA, 2003)
Who Writes This Crap? (with Luke Wright, 2007)

Stokes, Ashley (MA 1998)
Touching the Starfish (2010)

Stone, Jon (BA 2004)
I'll Show You Tyrants (2005)
Scarecrows (2010)

Studzinska, Agnieszka (MA 2003)
Snow Calling (2010)

Swift, Todd (MA 2004)
Budavox (1999)
Elegy for Anthony Perkins (2001)
Cafe Alibi (2002)
Rue de Regard (2004)
Winter Tennis (2007)

T
Tan, Hwee Hwee (BA 1995)
Foreign Bodies (1997)
Mammon Inc. (2001)

Teasdale, Ben (MA 1997)
Credits include:
The Adventures of William Shakespeare (Company Pictures)
100 Head Eddy (Cartoon Network)
Oddmoor (CBBC)
Sleeper (Box Productions / Channel 4)
The Magister (BBC3)
At Home with the Lucifers (BBC3)
The Irredeemable Brain of Dr Heinrich Hunsecker (BBC3)
The Baader-Meinhof Gang Show (Channel 4)
Strange Times (BBC 3)

Thorpe, Lorna (MA 2000)
Dancing to Motown (2005) – Poetry Book Society Pamphlet Choice
A Ghost in My House (2008)
This is Your Life (2011)

Thurston, Scott (MA 1991)
Poems 1994–2004 (2004)
Hold (2006)
Momentum (2008)
Internal Rhyme (2010)

Tilton, Mark (MA 1997)
Film credits include:
Hell For Leather (1998) – Prix Action Light award winner (1999)
The Truth – (2006, FilmFour)
Beheading of a Silent Dog (2008)
Sins of London (2009, incl. *Infidel*, winner of Best UK Short, Raindance Festival 2009)

Tissington, Sally (MA 2006)
Crocodile on the Carousel (2012)

Tondeur, Louise (MA 2002)
The Water's Edge (2003)
The Haven Home for Delinquent Girls (2004)

Topolski, Carol (MA 2004)
Monster Love (2008) – Orange Broadband Prize for Fiction shortlist (2008); Guildford Book Festival First Novel Award shortlist (2008)
Do No Harm (2010)

Tremain, Rose (BA 1967)
Granta Best of Young British Novelists (1983)
Sadler's Birthday (1976)
Letter to Sister Benedicta (1978)
The Cupboard (1981)
The Colonel's Daughter and Other Stories (1984) – Dylan Thomas Award winner (1984)
Journey to the Volcano (1985)
The Swimming Pool Season (1985) – Angel Literary Award winner (1985)
The Garden of the Villa Mollini and Other Stories (1987)
Restoration (1989) – Angel Literary Award winner (1989); *Sunday Express* Book of the Year Award winner (1989); Booker Prize shortlist (1990)
Sacred Country (1992) – James Tait Black Memorial Prize winner (1992); Prix Fémina Etranger winner (France 1993)
Evangelista's Fan and Other Stories (1994)
Collected Short Stories (1996)
The Way I Found Her (1997)
Music and Silence (1999) – Whitbread Novel Award winner (1999)
The Colour (2003) – Orange Prize for Fiction shortlist (2004)
The Darkness of Wallis Simpson (2005) – Frank O'Connor International Short Story Award shortlist (2006)
The Road Home (2007) – Orange Broadband Prize winner (2008)
Trespass (2010) – Man Booker Prize longlist (2010)

Tuckett, Jennifer (MA 2004)
Credits include:
Ron's Pig Palace on Wheels (Premio Candino Arta Terma, Italy, 2005; International Play Festival, UK, 2004)
I Am a Superhero (Sprite Productions, 2009/10)

U
Upton, Kim (MA 2003)
Credits include:
Stanley and Me (2005, Anglia TV)

V
Vandermerwe, Meg (MA 2001)
This Place I Call Home (2010)

W

Wagner, Erica (MA 1991)
Gravity (1998)
Seizure (2007)

Wakeman, John (MA 1990)
Room for Doubt (1985)
A Sea Family: New and Selected Poems
(2005)

Walls, Martin (BA 1989)
*Small Human Detail in Care of National
Trust* (2000)
Commonwealth (2005)

Warner, Tom (MA 2001)
Eric Gregory Award 2001
Faber New Poets 8 (2010)

Watson, Christie (MA 2008)
Tiny Sunbirds, Far Away (2011)

Whatley, Ryan (BA 2005)
Horizon Therapy (2011)

Whitaker, Phil (MA 1996)
Eclipse of the Sun (1997) – John
Llewellyn Rhys Prize winner
Triangulation (1999) – Encore Award
winner
The Face (2003)
Freak of Nature (2007)

Whitfield, Kit (MA 2000)
Smooches (2003)
Where Cats Meditate (2003)
Where Dogs Dream (2003)
Little Angles (2004)
Girlfriends (2004)
Bareback (2006, published in USA as
Benighted) – Author's Club Best First
Novel Award shortlist (2006)
In Great Waters (2009)

Whyman, Matt (MA 1992)
Man or Mouse (2000)
Columbia Road (2002)
Superhuman (2003)
Boy Kills Man (2004) – Booktrust
Teenage Prize shortlist (2004); de
Jong Jury Prize shortlist (Holland,
2006)
The Wild (2005) – Renfrewshire
Teenage Book Award shortlist (2006)
Inside the Cage (2007)
Unzipped: A Toolkit for Life (2007)
Street Runners (2008)
Goldstrike (2009)
Icecore: A Thriller (2009)
Oink: My Life with Minipigs (2011)

Wigfall, Clare (MA 2000)
The Loudest Sound and Nothing (2007)
BBC National Short Story Award
winner (2008)

Wilkes, James (MA 2004)
A DeTour (2006)
Ex Chaos (2006)

Williams, Luke (MA 2002)
The Echo Chamber (2011)

Williams, Lynda (MA 2006)
Credits include:
Solid (screenplay under
consideration at 20th Century Fox/
Fox Searchlight, & with Samuel L.
Jackson Screen East Digital Shorts
commission, 2009)

Wilson, D. W. (MA 2010, current
PhD)
Man Booker Scholarship 2009
Once You Break a Knuckle (2011)

Wilson, Snoo (BA 1969)
Plays include:
*Boswell and Johnson on the Shores of the
Eternal Sea* (1972)
Preston Lackey (1973)
The Rickmeister (1975)
Blowjobbers (1976)
The Glad Hand (1978)
Flaming Bodies (1979)
The Josh Machine of All Beasts (1982)
Our Lord of Lynchville, Loving Reno
(1983),
More Light (1987)
HRH (1994)
Sabina (1998)
Moonshine (1999)
Love Song of the Electric Bear (2003)
Novels:
Glad Hand (1979)
Greenish Man (1979)
Grass Window (1984)
Spaceache (1984)
Inside Babel (1985)
Moonshine (2000)

Wilson, Timothy (MA 1986)
Master of Morholm (1986)
The Ravished Earth (1989)
Treading on Shadows (1990)
The Straw Tower (1991)
Hester Verney (1993)
Roses in December (1993)
A Green Hill Far Away (1994)
Purgatory (1994)

John Twopenny (1995)
Heartsease (1996)
The Strawberry Sky (1996)
The Poppy Path (1997)
I Spy (1997)
Cruel To Be Kind (1998)
A Singing Grave (1999)
Close to You (2002)

Wright, Luke (BA, 2003)
Who Writes This Crap? (with Joel
Stickley, 2007)

Wong, Jennifer (MA 2009)
Summer Cicadas (2006)

Woods, Gregory (PhD 1983)
We Have the Melon (1992)
May I Say Nothing (1998)
The District Commissioner's Dreams
(2002)
Quidnunc (2007)

Wood, Naomi (MA 2008)
The Godless Boys (2011)

Worral, Carrie (1996)
Grace (1998)

Z

Zavala, Hernan Lara (MA 1981)
De Zitilchen (1981)
El Mismo Cielo (1987)
Contra el Angel (1992)
Odilon Tuch (1992)
Despues del amor (1994)
Charras (1996)
Cuentos Escogidos (1997)
*Peninsula, peninsula / Peninsula,
peninsula* (2008)

Acknowledgements

With thanks to all writers and copyright holders for their kind permission, and apologies if ownership of any of the rights in the following list has been wrongly attributed. GF

'Literature as a Living Art' © Giles Foden was published in draft on www.malcombradbury.com in autumn 2010; 'Toe' © Tom Warner; 'Thank You, Brother Martin' © Mick Jackson first appeared in the *Observer* magazine (15 August 2010); 'Discovering Books' © Mohammed Hanif first appeared in *The Sunday Telegraph* (20 July 2008); 'Interlude: Beginning Writing' © Amit Chaudhuri; 'Choosing English' © Patricia Duncker; '1970' © Ian McEwan combines three previously published pieces: the foreword to the 1991 UEA creative writing anthology, *Exposure* (published by CCPA-UEA) , the introduction to the 1995 UEA creative writing anthology, *Class Work* (published by Sceptre), and 'The Great Listener', a memorial article for Malcolm Bradbury published in the *Guardian* (9 November 2000); 'This is the Gig' © Anne Enright was first published as introduction to the 2008 anthology of UEA creative writing and also in the *Guardian* (22 November 2008); 'The Dusty Piano' © Tracy Chevalier; 'A Traumatic Process' © Louise Doughty; 'The Five Per Cent That Matters' © Glenn Patterson was originally published in the Swedish magazine *.doc* and (in a shorter version) in the *Irish Times*; 'A Norwich Butterfly' © John Boyne; 'On the Ghan' © Susan Elderkin was first published in the *Observer* (24 July 2005); 'Losing My Voice' © Andrew Cowan; 'The Dogged Imagination' © James Scudamore; 'My Failed Novel' © Nam Le was first published in the Melbourne newspaper *The Age*; 'My Japan' © Kazuo Ishiguro was first published in *Early Japanese Stories* (Belmont Press, 2000); 'The Scientific Anglian' © Jeremy Noel-Tod;

'Dust, Like Pollen' © Rebecca Stott; 'Questions I Never Asked My Creative Writing Tutors' © Lynne Bryan; 'My Brush with Radical Chic' © John Spurling was published in draft on www.johnspurling.com.; 'Afterword' © David Lodge was first published in *Liar's Landscape: Collected Writing from a Storyteller's Life*, by Malcolm Bradbury (Picador, 2006); 'Influence' © Anne Enright is the text of the Graham Storey Lecture given at Cambridge University on 1 March 2010; a shorter version was printed in the *London Review of Books* (17 February 2011) under the title 'Lessons from Angela Carter'; 'Open Questions' © Marina Warner was first published as the introduction to *Moments of Truth: Twelve Twentieth-Century Women Writers* by Lorna Sage (Fourth Estate, 2001); 'Angus Wilson's Lost Legacy' © D. J. Taylor; 'A Watch on Each Wrist: Twelve Seminars with W. G. Sebald' © Luke Williams; 'Saffron' © Paul Muldoon; 'Faking it' © Martyn Bedford is a revised version of an article first published in the *Guardian* (21 April 1998); 'Why Shouldn't We?' © Adam Mars-Jones was first published as the introduction to the 1993 UEA Creative Writing anthology *Mafia!* (published by CCPA-UEA); 'Killer Fiction' © Joe Dunthorne is a revision of a piece first published in the *Independent on Sunday* (1 June 2008); 'Writing My Life' © Francis Gilbert reproduces material from his ongoing PhD in Creative Writing and Education at Goldsmiths' College, University of London, with some added reflection on his time at UEA; 'Listening in Restaurants' © Antoinette Moses; 'The Translators' © George Szirtes was first published in his book *The Burning of the Books and Other Poems* (Bloodaxe, 2009); 'The Short Story' © Jean McNeil was first published as the foreword to *The Mechanics Institute Review*, no. 6, published by Birkbeck College in 2009;

'Temple of Truth' © Richard Holmes is a revised version of two pieces, 'Time's Golden Handshake', published in the *Guardian* (1 December 1990) and 'It's a Real Life Opportunity for Everyone', published in the *Sunday Times* (13 May 2001); 'Revisiting *The Novel Today*' © the Estate of Malcolm Bradbury is Malcolm Bradbury's introduction to the second edition of his anthology *The Novel Today: Contemporary Writers on Modern Fiction* (Fontana, 1990); 'The Fault Lines of Fiction' © Lorna Sage was first published in the *Observer* (2 May 1993); 'Trials of a Booker Judge' © Angela Carter was first published *New Society* (1983) and reprinted in *Shaking a Leg: Collected Journalism and Writing* (Chatto & Windus, 1997); 'Turning to Crime' © Henry Sutton; 'Advice to a Young Writer' © Rachel Hore; 'The Career of the Playwright' © Steve Waters; 'My So-Called Career' © Jane Harris revises and combines articles previously published in the *Observer* (8 May 2011), *The Times Higher Educational Supplement* during December 1992 and *Mslexia* magazine (Autumn 2006); 'Between Drafts' © Keith Tutt; 'The Two-Typewriter Trick' © Erica Wagner; 'Tensions in a Wild Garden' (Angus Wilson) © Rose Tremain was first published in the *Guardian* (3 June 1991); 'The Soaring Imagination' (Angela Carter) © the Estate of Lorna Sage; 'Pipe-smoker of the Year' (Malcolm Bradbury) © Clive Sinclair was first published in the *Independent* (29 November 2000); 'After Nature and So On' (W. G. Sebald) © Andrew Motion was first published in the 2002 UEA Creative Writing anthology *Paper, Scissors, Stone* (published by CCPA-UEA); 'Difficulties of the Do-It-Yourself Epitaph' © Lorna Sage was first published in the *Observer* (3 January 1993); 'Head' © Derek Mahon is reprinted from his *New Collected Poems* (2011) by kind permission of the author and The Gallery Press.

First published in 2011 by Full Circle Editions

This compilation copyright © University of East Anglia 2011

Text copyright © The individual authors and rights-holders:
see acknowledgements and permissions on page 351

Illustrations copyright © Jeff Fisher 2011

The moral right of the authors and artist has been asserted

Design and Layout copyright © Full Circle Editions 2011
Parham House Barn, Brick Lane, Framlingham, Woodbridge, Suffolk IP13 9LQ
www.fullcircle–editions.co.uk

Set in New Baskerville & Gill Sans
Paper: Munken Pure 120gsm from FSC Mixed Sources

Book design: Jonathan Christie

Printed and bound in Suffolk by Healeys Print Group, Ipswich

ISBN 978-0-9561869-8-0

Note on the typeface:
Baskerville is a transitional serif typeface designed in 1757 by John Baskerville
(1706–75) and was an attempt to improve upon the types of William Caslon.
Baskerville increased the contrast between thick and thin strokes, making the
serifs sharper and more tapered, and shifted the axis of rounded letters to a more
vertical position. The curved strokes are more circular in shape, and the characters
became more regular. These changes created a greater consistency in size and form,
although the perfection of his work seems to have unsettled his contemporaries,
and some claimed the stark contrasts in his printing damaged the eyes. Abroad,
however, he was much admired, notably by Fournier & Bodoni. *Baskerville* was revived
in 1917 by Bruce Rogers for the Harvard University Press and in 1923 in England
by Stanley Morison for the British Monotype Company. *New Baskerville* was designed by
Matthew Carter and John Quaranda in 1978.

LOTTERY FUNDED

University of East Anglia